HIGHER
EDUCATION
IN
AMERICAN
SOCIETY

Revised Edition

Frontiers of Education

A Series Dedicated to Educational
Organization, Policy, and Institutions

In Cooperation With the University of Rochester

Series Editors: G. Dennis O'Brien
Guilbert C. Hentschke

Other titles in the series:

Former Series Editor: Philip G. Altbach

The American University:
Problems, Prospects, and Trends
edited by Jan H. Blits

The Courts and American Education Law
Tyll van Geel

Excellence in Education:
Perspectives on Policy and Practice
edited by Philip G. Altbach, Gail P. Kelly, and Lois Weis

Higher Education in American Society (first edition)
edited by Philip G. Altbach and Robert O. Berdahl

Paradigms and Promises:
New Approaches to Educational Administration
William Foster

HIGHER EDUCATION

IN

AMERICAN SOCIETY

Revised Edition

Edited by Philip G. Altbach
and Robert O. Berdahl

PROMETHEUS BOOKS
Buffalo, New York

Published by Prometheus Books
700 East Amherst Street, Buffalo, New York 14215

Library of Congress Cataloging-in-Publication Data

Higher education in American society.

(Frontiers of education)
Bibliography: p.
Includes index.
1. Education, Higher—United States. 2. Educational sociology—United States. I. Altbach, Philip G. II. Berdahl, Robert Oliver. III. Series.
LA228.H5   1987   378.73   87-25790
ISBN 0-87975-420-6 (pbk.)

Printed in the United States of America

Contents

1

Higher Education in American Society: An Introduction

Robert O. Berdahl and Philip G. Altbach

For a time in the 1960s, when student activists received daily television coverage and a book a week seemed to be published concerning the "academic crisis," higher education was, according to public opinion polls, the key concern of the American people. Now, a much less dramatic crisis engulfs higher education. While few headlines are generated, America's colleges and universities face an unprecedented situation. Stimulated by demographic changes, fiscal stringency, and a major intrusion of government involvement in all aspects of higher education, the late 1980s will be a period of considerable stress. In this book, we are concerned largely with the relationship of this crisis to higher education, particularly to how colleges and universities relate to their external environments. We are especially concerned with the key questions of autonomy, accountability, and academic freedom in this context. Our contributors, all experts in their respective fields, have brought their expertise to aspects of these complex relationships.

Basic and time-honored concepts in higher education have undergone substantial transformation. Histories of academic freedom, for example, have considered the evolution of the concept.[1] But Walter Metzger has argued that the 1915 definition of academic freedom, propounded by the American Association of University Professors, is no longer adequate to cover the complexity of external relations now confronting the contemporary college and university.[2] Arguing that academic institutions have become "delocalized"— removed from their traditions of being relatively small, isolated, inexpensive, and fairly self-governing—they have been transformed into today's large and costly academic systems, interacting extensively with society and much influenced and/or controlled by some of these social forces. We need to think carefully about the cumulative impact of these changes. This volume tries to understand the complex relationship of higher education to society. This Introduction provides some basic definitions and some possible conceptual frameworks for the following chapters.

SOME GENERAL CAUTIONS

First, we should confirm what our title implies: this book is essentially about *higher* education, rather than the broader term, postsecondary education, and it is mostly about *American* colleges and universities, although the historical chapter and the Clark essay in the conclusion make reference to comparative material. Our focus on traditional colleges and universities does not mean that we ignore the importance of emerging nontraditional institutions, but we felt a prior obligation to help clarify the substantial changes already taking place in long-standing units.

Second, in dealing with a university's or college's (hereafter we will use the generic term "college" for short) relations with society, it is easy to err in one of two directions: on the one hand, it is possible to exaggerate the golden glow of the past when colleges supposedly operated without social intrusions; on the other, one may overreact to grim pressures of the present and assume that all is now lost for higher education.

In fact, neither response seems fully warranted. In describing Metzger's "localized" college, we purposefully qualified the description of its size, isolation, cost, and self-governance with the term "relatively" because, as Duryea's following chapter on historical perspectives indicates, colleges were never totally isolated or self-governing. From their start, colleges have had an ambivalent relationship with their surrounding communities: involved and withdrawn; needing and being needed; serving and criticizing. Yet, and this is important to keep in mind, American higher education has never strayed too far from the mainstream of American society—criticism has been within the acceptable standards of the day. Throughout most of its history American higher education has been more a transmitter of culture than a creator of divergent cultural or ideological norms. The links between higher education and the state, church, and in general the Establishment have traditionally been strong.

Academic institutions have nevertheless pursued their own goals and have often jealously guarded their internal independence and their commitment to autonomy and academic freedom. In a way, this sense of mission and commitment that allowed colleges to survive and prosper in early adversity may well see them through even the admittedly difficult conditions of the present and near future. Yet, it would seem that the contemporary academic institution, the "delocalized" college in Metzger's terms, is faced with several potentially threatening external factors: among them, enrollment decline, fiscal austerity, and increased governmental pressure for accountability. These challenges add up to new relationships between higher education and society that may constitute changes *in kind* rather than *in degree*. In particular, increased interest by some state governments in assessment of institutional learning outcomes may raise difficult new issues. Nevertheless, in observing the reactions of the main internal constituencies—the faculty, students, and administrators/trustees—we see promising signs of continued vitality and adjustability.

A FEW DEFINITIONS

Although our authors will offer their own working definitions of key terms, we think it wise to pause here briefly and outline the *general* usage of some concepts that play a fundamental role in this volume.

Academic freedom will mean the freedom of the scholar in his/her teaching and research to pursue a scholarly interest wherever it seems to lead and without fear of termination of employment for having offended some political, religious, or social orthodoxy.

Professional autonomy will mean the extent to which the control over immediate working conditions of the faculty member (whether or not some of the conditions also pertain to academic freedom issues) has been decentralized to the working level professionals.

College autonomy of a *substantive nature* will apply to the power of a college to determine its own goals and programs—the *what* of Academe.

College autonomy of a *procedural nature* will apply to the power of a college to determine the means by which its goals and program will be pursued—the *how* of Academe.

Although all four concepts are inevitably blurred in real academic life, we suggest that it will be helpful in analyzing a college's relations with its environment to keep the four terms conceptually distinct. Academic freedom, as here defined, is an *individual* protection; professional autonomy applies to a *collegial* process; and substantive and procedural autonomy constitutes *corporate* concepts relating to the legal entity, whether it be a single campus or a multi-campus system.

Thus, intrasystem decisions could deny autonomy to a local campus but such actions would not qualify for this volume's focus on relations between the corporate structure of colleges and their *external* constituencies. As another example, there might be a "professional autonomy" decision by a dean, college president, or board of trustees concerning an internal curriculum issue, or a "substantive autonomy" decision by an external, statewide board of higher education concerning a disapproved field of study—and neither of these would necessarily involve an "academic freedom" issue unless the grounds for the decision had to do with orthodoxy of the curriculum in question. Or, along another dimension, one could envisage a set of external *procedural* controls so severe (e.g., pre-audits of budgets for propriety as well as legality of expenditures) that they have serious impact on a college's ability to achieve its self-chosen *substantive* goals.

Some of these terms are further explored in Baldridge, et al.,[3] Berdahl,[4] and Dressel,[5] but we raise them briefly here so that readers may consider how they evaluate the proper balance between each of these dimensions and their opposite concept: accountability.[6]

A POSSIBLE CONCEPTUAL FRAMEWORK

Assuming the rough validity of these definitions, the chapters of this book may yield more significant insights if viewed across the categories of analysis used by Martin Trow to understand the interrelationships of the various aspects of college life as higher education expanded in the postwar period. Although current problems point toward possible contraction, it is still highly instructive to consider Trow's analysis of the impact of change of size on purposes, structures, access, curriculum, teaching styles, degree standards, research patterns, modes of financing, and internal and external governance systems as American higher education moved across the spectrum from "elite" to "mass" higher education and poised on the brink of "universal access." Though "universal access" may not be fully realized in the near future, Trow shows how the three "ideal" categories may be used to understand the linkages between and among the specific consequences as higher education systems grew.

For example, Trow deals with the varying nature of the "locus of power and decision-making" as follows:

> With respect to ultimate power and effective decisions, elite institutions are dominated by relatively small elite groups: leaders in significant institutions—political, economic, and academic—who know one another, share basic values and assumptions, and make decisions through informal face-to-face contact. An example of this would be the small number of leading civil servants, government ministers, university vice-chancellors, and members of the University Grants Commission who shaped the face of the British university system for many years in small committee rooms or around tables at the Athenaeum Club.
>
> Mass higher education continues to be influenced by these elite groups, but is increasingly shaped by more "democratic" political processes and influenced by "attentive audiences." These are parts of the general public who have special interests and qualifications, and develop a common view about higher education in general or some special aspect, such as the forms and content of technical education. Higher education policies increasingly become subject to the ordinary political processes of interest groups and party programs. One kind of attentive audience is the employers of the products of mass higher education, who are interested in the nature of their skills and qualifications. Another attentive audience is the body of "old graduates" who retain an interest in the character and fortunes of their old university. These groups often develop political instrumentalities of their own, such as associations with an elected leadership, and develop lines of communication to the smaller groups in government, legislatures, and the universities themselves who make the actual decisions, both day to day and over the long range.

When the system moves toward universal access, increasingly large portions of the population begin to be affected by it, either through their own past or present attendance, or that of some friend or relative. In addition the universities and colleges—what is taught there, and the activities of their staff and students—come to be of general interest, leave the pages of the serious press and magazines, and are reported in the popular journals and on television. They thus attract the interest of mass publics that increasingly come to see themselves as having a legitimate interest in what goes on in the institutions of higher education, if for no other reason than their enormous cost and obvious impact on society. And these mass publics begin to make their sentiments known, either through letters to public officials or through their votes in special or general elections. The change in the size and character of the publics who have an interest in higher education and exert an influence on higher educational policy greatly influences the nature and content of the discussions about higher education, who takes part in them, and the decisions that flow out of them. The claims of academic men to a special expertise, and of their institutions to special privileges and immunities, are increasingly questioned; much of what academic men understand by academic freedom, and the significance of the security of academic tenure for the protection of their pursuit of truth regardless of political interests of popular sentiment, all are challenged by the growing intervention of popular sentiments into these formerly elite arenas. [Paragraphing added.]

Growth itself stimulates prescriptive planning: the more higher education grows, the more money is needed for it, the more interest there is in it among larger parts of the population, the greater demand there is for tight control over its shape and costs. The growing demand for "accountability" of higher education, for its ability to demonstrate its efficiency in the achievement of mandated and budgeted goals, inevitably translates itself into tighter controls and prescriptive planning. . . . The growth of higher education, given a prescriptive control system, places ever greater demands on that system to maintain and increase its control over numbers and costs, structures and standards.

The pressures for uniformity or convergence associated with central governmental control over higher education, are several:

- The uniform application of administrative forms and principles, as in formulas linking support to enrollments; formulas, governing building standards and the provision and allocation of space; formulas governing research support, etc.;

- Broad norms of equity, which prescribe equal treatment for "equivalent" units under a single governing body;

- Increasingly strong egalitarian values, which define all differences among public institutions—in their functions, standards, and support—as inequitable.

There are counter forces that help to sustain and even increase diversity in higher education. In some places there is a multiplicity of governmental bodies involved in higher education: the United States is an extreme case in this respect. More generally, there are variations in the degree of diversity of sources of support, both of public and private funds. The growth of institution and systems toward mass higher education puts a strain on administrative structures designed for a smaller, simpler, elite system, and activities begin to elude the controls of an overburdened and understaffed administration. The near monopoly within the academic world of specialized knowledge about the nature of the academic fields and their needs and requirements is the ultimate basis of academic autonomy, and slows (though it may not prevent) rationalization and the application of standardized formulas governing admissions, academic standards, support, workloads, etc. (This is, of course, the more true where the knowledge base is greater and the intellectual authority of the academics concerned is higher—which is why academic autonomy is defined more successfully in elite institutions.)[7]

ANOTHER CONCEPTUAL FRAMEWORK

Although some of Martin Trow's discussion of college expansion now sounds a bit dated, his analysis of the linkage of consequences across his different categories continues to furnish valuable insights into current conditions, since we are living with the implications of the past several decades of growth.

Howard Adelman, a Canadian philosopher, provides us with another perspective from which to analyze developments in higher education. His analysis is not directly related to the growth syndrome, but it is complementary to Martin Trow's views and useful to help in understanding the nexus of relationships between higher education and society.[8]

Adelman argues that North American higher education has gone through a number of different phases in the past two centuries, and that these phases shape a whole series of relationships. Such factors as curriculum, finance, and governance are all altered by the different phases. He posits four models of academic development:

1. *The Sanctuary of Truth*, in which absolute moral truths are taught to certain special students with the aim of turning out high moral character;

2. *The Sanctuary of Method*, in which professional education inculcates high professional skills in the search for infinite knowledge;

3. *The Social Service Station*, in which the college agrees to "serve" the community with products and services recognized to be appropriate to the collegiate tradition; and

4. *The Culture Mart*, in which the boundaries between the college and the community are progressively blurred, and all "educational activities," whether on campus or off, whether by formal colleges or other institutions performing educational services, get validated and legitimized by colleges acting as educational brokers.

Adelman identifies Jose Ortega y Gasset as the philosopher of the first model,[9] Abraham Flexner as that of the second,[10] Clark Kerr as that of the third,[11] and the Wright Commission Report on Postsecondary Education in Ontario as the articulation of the fourth.[12] According to Adelman's analysis, we in North America are deep into the dominance of the Social Service Station model, now, with elements of the first two still existing here and there, and with governmental planning systems trying to assess the values and costs of moving on more fully toward the last model.

These analytical models are by no means the only ones which might be called into play to explain the postwar development of higher education in the United States. For example, Samuel Bowles and Herbert Gintis argue that education, including higher education, has responded to the changing needs of the labor market and that colleges have increasingly been brought into the capitalist sphere.[13] In this framework, it is not surprising that government authorities have moved increasingly to control higher education— hence, the growth of accountability. They argue that the links between government, industry, and higher education have grown stronger as the need for highly trained manpower in a technological society has grown in the postwar period.

This volume does not posit any uniform framework of analysis. As editors, we asked only that our contributors deal with specific topics that related to the higher education and society nexus. Each author provides an analysis of his or her specific subject. Each, naturally, comes to the topic with a range of assumptions. What has been provided in this volume, then, is a range of perspectives concerning the key elements of the relationship between higher education and society.

THE ORGANIZATION OF THE BOOK

We have tried to select topics that focus most directly on the important issues relating to higher education-society questions and that are relevant as we come to the late 1980s. We have not been able to deal with all topics. But we feel that this volume provides the basis for an analysis of contemporary American higher education.

The first part of the book elaborates on the fundamental concepts by including a chapter on the historical background to the current scene, one on the evolution of academic freedom in the United States and its relationship to autonomy, one on more recent developments concerning academic freedom, and an essay on the broad concepts of accountability and autonomy. Then, we conclude this part with a treatment of the emerging issues for the late 1980s and an analysis of the economic factors concerned with higher education.

Part Two then treats the major *external* constituencies of universities and colleges: state and federal governments, the courts (treated as a separate dimension of external power), and so-called "private" constituencies (meaning those without a governmental base, such as foundations, associations, consortia, regional groupings).

The third part then presents analyses of the reactions of the major *internal* constituencies to the increased roles of the external forces. Chapters cover the faculty, students, and presidents, and another examines the reactions of the campus constituency to recent major reports on curriculum reform.

A final chapter offers our concluding perspectives along with some comparative material drawn from other higher education systems; for we all need to be reminded that problems facing American higher education are not necessarily unique to this country, and that we could profit much from increased knowledge of foreign systems. But this is a subject for another volume!

NOTES

1. Richard Hofstader and Walter P. Metzger, *The Development of Academic Freedom in the United States* (New York: Columbia University Press, 1955).

2. Walter P. Metzger, Sanford H. Kadish, Arthur De Bardeleben, and Edward J. Bloustein, *Dimensions of Academic Freedom* (Urbana, Ill.: University of Illinois Press, 1969).

3. J. Victor Baldridge, David V. Curtis, George Ecker, and Gary L. Riley, "Diversity in Higher Education: Professional Autonomy," *Journal of Higher Education,* 48 (July/August, 1977), pp. 367-388.

4. Robert O. Berdahl, *Statewide Coordination of Higher Education* (Washington, D.C.: American Council on Education, 1971). See also Carnegie Commission on Higher Education, *Governance of Higher Education* (New York: McGraw Hill, 1973).

5. Paul L. Dressel, *The Autonomy of Public Colleges* (San Francisco: Jossey-Bass, 1980).

6. Kenneth P. Mortimer, *Accountability in Higher Education* (Washington, D.C.: American Association for Higher Education, 1972).

7. Martin Trow, "Problems in the Transition from Elite to Mass Higher Education," *Policies for Higher Education: the General Report on the Conference on Future Structures of Post-secondary Education* (Paris: Organization for Economic Co-operation and Development, 1974).

8. Howard Adelman, *The Holiversity: A Perspective on the Wright Report* (Toronto: New Press, 1973).

9. Jose Ortega y Gasset, *The Mission of the University* (New York: Norton, 1944).

10. Abraham Flexner, *Universities: American, English, German* (New York: Oxford University Press, 1968). Originally published in 1930.

11. Clark Kerr, *The Uses of the University* (New York: Harper Torchbooks, 1963).

12. *The Learning Society: Report of the Commission on Post Secondary Education in Ontario* (Toronto: Ministry of Government Services, 1972).

13. Samuel Bowles and Herbert Gintis, *Schooling in Capitalist America* (New York: Basic Books, 1976).

Part 1

The Setting

2

The University and the State:
A Historical Overview

E. D. Duryea

Looking back on the relations between universities and society in Western culture, one can discern a similarity between the institutions of the current century and their ancestors in the twelfth and thirteenth centuries. Both have reflected what Marjorie Reeves highlights as "a tension between two impulses: one, the drive towards a search for 'pure' knowledge, and the other, the acquisition of knowledge and skills for specific social ends."[1] Both have evidenced a combination of legal and *de facto* obligations to an external sovereignty and a measure, at times extensive and at times limited, of internal autonomy.[2] The commitment to extending human learning inherently and inevitably brings to the fore the critical importance of what we know today as academic freedom. The service to society implemented by educational programs directed toward socially significant knowledge and skills—historically, the combination of a common learning and preparation for one of the "higher" vocations or professions—and the exportation to the external society of a professional expertise responds to the broader implications of accountability.

A further observation suggests that in this perception the modern and the medieval draw together in form and function after an intellectual hiatus of about four centuries, during which the medieval era waned and the universities in Western culture were converted to handmaidens of state and church, both Catholic and Protestant. To my thinking, it is most important to understand this historical evolution in order to understand contemporary tensions between academic freedom and institutional autonomy, on the one hand, and accountability to the state, on the other. To convey such an understanding, at least in its more manifest aspects, constitutes the purpose of this brief historical essay.

At the same time, wisdom requires a sense of perspective in reading an interpretive essay such as this, which constructs a historical montage covering several centuries of complex developments. Relationships associated with academic freedom and the nature of the autonomy-accountability dualism are relative. One would look hard to find a perfect condition of freedom, obviously, and similarly, one would be hard put to identify either complete autonomy or full accountability. The most accountable institutions of recent times, the nineteenth-century German universities, allowed professors a high degree of autonomy to handle internal affairs and press their academic interests within a system that assured the final authority to the state through its educational ministry. Also, while this paper rests on the thesis of an intellectual decadence and subservience to church and state during the fifteenth through eighteenth centuries, it does not mean to imply that what we call the eras of the Renaissance and Enlightenment left the universities to lie fallow. They remained, in fact, significant establishments to which, especially in England, an expanding middle class, deriving a livelihood from commerce and industry, turned as vehicles for social and political mobility. Sons of the new gentry of Renaissance England learned their classics and manners at Oxford and Cambridge; those of the burghers of the German states found in the universities there a curricular response to their needs. But the balance suffered and the scales dipped sharply in the direction of an accountability of service performed in accord with theological and political postulates held by the religious-political governing authorities.

To develop this historical analysis, therefore, requires an initial, brief survey of the medieval era that sets a general pattern for the development of the university in Western culture. Then, it serves to review, succinctly at least, the transition from medieval to modern associated with the Renaissance and, particularly, the shift to a secular orientation associated with classical humanism and with the origins of modern knowledge in the "Enlightenment" of the seventeenth and eighteenth centuries. Finally, one must come to grips with the drastic changes in higher education that led, during the nineteenth century in this country, to what Laurence Veysey describes as "the emergence of the American university."

From this perspective, the concept of the university as an autonomous institution within a society evolved early in the middle ages, in close company with the use of the corporate form as the basis for the government of universities. However, one must recognize that the medieval universities could not escape from their societal context, either in terms of accommodation to the prevailing values and medieval power structure (primarily in terms of religious beliefs and the authority first of the Roman Catholic Church and then of secular kings and emperors) or of the performance of an educational function relevant to their times. Conflicts over scholarly independence and restraints upon it do not lack medieval precedents. Likewise, while the idea and form of institutions of higher learning draw from experiences in the twelfth and thirteenth centuries, both underwent thorough change during the progression of secular knowledge. Contemporary conceptions of academic freedom and autonomy derive from the professionalization of the professoriate accompanying a swing toward specialization and investigation during the late nineteenth and early twentieth centuries.

MEDIEVAL BACKGROUND

The medieval centers for higher learning gained their institutional structure in the course of the twelfth century in conjunction with the intellectual fluorescence of that era, stoked by the penetration into Western Europe of the learning of an earlier era, especially that of ancient Greece. By the beginning of the thirteenth century they had evolved into formal institutions, of which that at Paris created the prototype for the universities in northern Europe and set a pattern for institutions in this country. Paris stood out among these medieval centers as a consequence "of the particular intellectual achievements of the galaxy of outstanding scholars who raised it to the forefront of academic life in northern Europe,"[3] and as a universally recognized source for interpretation of ecclesiastical doctrine within the Catholic Church.

The formation of the University of Paris following the turn of the thirteenth century created that dual relationship, now expressed as autonomy and accountability, that has remained throughout the centuries a particular tradition of universities. Paris, as a formal institution, congealed from the informal associations of scholars—masters and students—who gathered around the cathedral school of that city. Its development "was determined by, and reveals to us, the whole bent and spiritual character of the age to whose life it became organic."[4] The success of the Paris center, confirmed through the influx of teachers and students, inevitably led to conflicts with the local church officialdom and Parisian citizenry. As head of the cathedral school around which the university was taking its particular form, the Bishop of Paris and his representative, the Chancellor, sought to maintain their control of the burgeoning educational center. The expanding mass of scholars inevitably proved an abrasive element at times disruptive of town life and led to retaliatory efforts by secular officers to maintain their law over a turbulent mass of strangers. The scholars did not lack their own aspirations for separate jurisdiction. For protection and authority, they turned to an external but superior power, that of the Papacy. Without elaborating the course of events, the university achieved a local autonomy for the price of submission to a more distant sovereignty, that of the Church. The form of this autonomy came as papal bulls or charters that granted to the university power over its internal affairs as a Church corporation that owed its legal existence to the Pope. This arrangement adhered to medieval practice, which supported corporate associations holding an inherent right of existence separate from that of members, and served a wide range of activities, ranging from religious orders to mercantile and craft enterprises.

In the centuries that followed, as national kings pushed aside the popes and grasped power as a divine right, the University of Paris (and European universities in general) lost not only its preeminence but its independence, as it ineffectually sought to maintain medieval religious prerogatives within "a state already modern, national and territorial."[5] In effect, what the king gave by charter the king could withdraw; the university had become an institution authorized by and obligated to the state. Yet, there had been established and still remained a general acceptance, "of the principle that the essence and core of a university was its autonomy,"[6] leading to a dualism between political reality and academic tradition carried on in an uncertain equilibrium.

Similarly, the origins of the ideal of scholarly freedom can be viewed in association with the medieval universities. One can perceive a parallel between the twelfth century and the nineteenth in the sense that both stand out as critical for Western thought. The former presents us with an era during which scholars in the West "became aware of the vast corpus of classical material which hitherto had been but dimly glimpsed."[7] A new learning reached Europe from the pens of adventuresome clerks (for only in the monasteries and other Church agencies were there literacy and some pretense to knowledge) who found in Arabian manuscripts the writings of the Greeks, especially of Aristotle. Supported by a social stability consequential to the unifying force of Christianity, these medieval scholars undertook the task of understanding and communicating this past learning and did so in the lecture halls of the nascent university centers. Among them, creative thinkers such as Peter Abelard, Roger Bacon, Thomas Aquinas, and William of Ockham grappled with the implications of this new knowledge for the revealed truth of the Christian faith. In the process they began to apply human reason to ecclesiastical doctrine.

This latter tendency, the application of reason to faith, raised the hackles of the orthodox Churchmen; it led to a response from them that sought to eliminate what they viewed as heretical thought and to what well may be the first great case of academic freedom. The famous case in point involved Abelard, who was brought to trial by the Church. In the words of his accuser, Saint Bernard, he was guilty of "trying to make void the merit of Christian faith, when he deems himself able by human reason to comprehend God altogether."[8] It was the controversy of realism vs. nominalism that stood behind the trial; whether there was a source for understanding (or truth) independent of human thought or whether reality constitutes what the senses perceive and the mind interprets, a controversy that gave to Western culture a gleam of intellectual light so tantalizing that it could not be ignored. While it moved outside the vision of medieval scholars and their successors in the universities in the following centuries, the application of reason to comprehend reality reentered Western thought as the basis for secular, and especially scientific, knowledge. In time, it returned also to the universities, and therein lies the modern concept of academic freedom and its association with nineteenth- and twentieth-century specialized knowledge.

Finally, while the fame of the medieval universities may well have rested upon the excitement of its speculative theology and heady exposure to new philosophical ideas, their sustenance derived from a more mundane function. According to A. B. Cobban, "their roots were extricably bound up with utilitarian values. They evolved as institutional responses to the pressures to harness educational forces to the professional, ecclesiastical, and governmental requirements of society."[9] They provided educational opportunity and appropriate training for students who looked to careers within the administrative hierarchy of the Church or civil government or as legal or medical practitioners. For the majority of students, the universities served as an entree to rewarding careers, no matter how attendance might be cloaked in the guise of their clerical status. More than one contemporary master complained about the worldliness of students and their commitment to a quick passage through the lower arts courses so that they might enter the advanced faculties into a chosen career. Learning was pursued in an active relationship to the social order, as an essential service to its society.[10]

In summary, the Paris model formed an institutional pattern antecedent to that of the twentieth-century system of higher education in its major components. It drew to its halls creative intellectuals who pressed hard on the borders of the then existing conceptions of reality, which, while speculative rather than empirical, constituted a commitment to the extension of knowledge. Their efforts inevitably led to major conflicts over the intellectual or academic freedom of creative scholars. It set clearly the condition of the institution as a corporate body owing its existence to an external sovereign, but possessing a degree of autonomy to manage its internal affairs, including the nature of its educational program. It served as a passage to "higher" or professional careers. The English universities evolved in the Parisian pattern and set a general pattern for the early colleges of this country, along with the Protestant institutions of the continent and Scotland. The essential point, of course, is that the pattern of government, in terms of its relationship with church and state, remained in the English-United States tradition: that these institutions maintained a corporate form, that scholars of these universities retained a tradition of internal autonomy, and that the higher learning continued to serve as the gateway to significant roles in society.

TRANSITION FROM MEDIEVAL TO MODERN

If the nature of the medieval university carried over to the higher education of this country in the twentieth century, what about developments during the intervening centuries? In responding to this query, it is important to note two cultural or intellectual streams that flowed into higher education in this country. One led to the eighteenth-century and early nineteenth-century colleges through influences associated with the Protestant Reformation and the humanistic ideals and studies of the Renaissance. The other lay with the development of secular knowledge attendant with the growth of science and related philosophies, which motivated European intellectuals during the Enlightenment of the seventeenth and, especially, the eighteenth centuries. It becomes important, therefore, to give some attention, albeit briefly, to the forces at work in connection with the university and higher learning during this intervening era.

Western culture passed from the medieval era into the Renaissance and the Enlightenment as the Roman Catholic Church suffered a loss of its hegemony over European affairs. At the turn of the fifteenth century the Great Schism had left the papacy dominated by secular power; it was barely recovering its ecclesiastical authority when, a century later, Luther inaugurated the Reformation that broke northern from southern Europe. However, one senses that the problems of Christian orthodoxy accompanied and participated with other forces at work that set a new social context for the universities. Their essence was a secular turn in the interests and values of Europeans, away from what has been called that "principle of a single and uniform but articulate whole . . . based upon the conviction of a solidarity of mankind as the beloved children of God, united through God's infinite charity."[11]

It is important to remember that the Renaissance is a historical conception and not a specific historical epoch. It designates a number of related and interacting changes that entered European life as the authority of the Roman Church declined during the fourteenth and fifteenth centuries. Its origins intermingled with the intellectual movements of the middle ages; its spokesmen never broke with the essential tenets of Christianity. Historically, one probably associates the Renaissance primarily with the flowering of culture expressed through the rebirth of the classical literature from Greek and Roman sources and inspiring artistic and literary achievements. It does not serve, therefore, "to speak of the Renaissance as though it were a single age or single force. . ." but rather the name serves to identify that flowering of intellect and culture that accompanied "the great fundamental economic growth of European society and its rising middle class."[12]

One has to recognize also that probably the most fundamental aspect of this cultural change lay in the secularization of Europe. Without casting aside Christian beliefs and doctrine, the people of Europe were accepting and acting upon values more closely associated with the affairs of this world and reacting less to the consequences of their actions for the life hereafter. The Renaissance emerged in part as a consequence of the growth of trade and commerce that established new, commercial sinews across Europe, replacing the theological ties of the Church and breaking down the locally oriented economies of the previous era. The commerce and, to a degree, industrialization in such trades as weaving and metallurgy intermingled with the formation of national states. Temporal power shifted into the hands of national kings who grasped control from the pope and Holy Roman Emperor to carve up Europe geographically; papal sovereignty gave way to divine right; filial loyalty for the Father in Rome to national patriotism. Finally, the Protestant Reformation culminated these inroads upon European homogeneity. It represented, in the words of historian Preserved Smith, "the natural, though unconscious, adaptation of religion to the needs of a new social situation." "The individualism, the nationalism, the commercialism of the new age were all reflected in the Protestant church."[13]

In the evolution from medieval to modern, it is important also to recognize that, in company with the breakup of theological unity and the secularization of thought and culture, one finds the gestation of contemporary knowledge and relationships between education and society. The former emanated as a major aspect of modern civilization with the gradual development of science and the emergence of a whole system of new knowledge, knowledge that looked to the future rather than the past, knowledge completely secular and permeated with the idea of progress. Pending the fluorescence of knowledge, however, a mercantile nationalism, accompanied by the ready acceptance and thus dispersion of Protestant theology, impacted upon European universities and created conditions that strongly influenced the role of the early American colleges in our society. A humanistic tradition in education based strongly on the Greek and Roman classics framed the ideal of an educated man, which in turn served as the criteria for service in the courts of kings and the establishments of the Renaissance elite. Concurrently in the Protestant realms, political and religious leadership formed an alliance that set out to combine the church, state, and education into one coordinated effort built around the propagation of the faith and preservation of theological orthodoxy.

For education, and especially the universities, the social and political restructuring of Europe introduced a new constituency and new studies that strengthened accountability to society but undermined commitment to creative thought and new knowledge. What we view today as the great minds and pioneering thinkers[14]—the counterparts of the provocative medieval intellects who pressed beyond orthodoxy—found their destinies outside the halls of the universities with few exceptions. Conditions of the times supported submission to royal and religious authority. In the first part of the seventeenth century, for example, English philosopher Thomas Hobbes stressed the obligation of the universities to the good of the king, and the great German mathematician Leibniz rejected the very idea of academic freedom.[15] Within the broader parameters of the Renaissance, a segment of educators known as humanists promoted educational reforms that stressed Greek and Roman antiquity and the ideal of Cicero, which conceived of an education for the man who would serve as the humane and just leader. Education stressed "in the spirit of classical antiquity and of Christianity" to the end of "training in virtue and good letters" and "of the learned, responsible gentleman who devotes himself to the tasks of government."[16] Histories of the English universities confirm that the inroads of the humanistic, classical studies achieved a position alongside of the remnants of medieval scholasticism. Whatever our view of such learning today, it responded and thus was accountable to the power structure of a social order; and, as such, it carried over into the curriculums of the early colleges in this country.

Protestantism imposed obligation to church and state. To achieve doctrinal hegemony within their domain, Protestant leaders allotted a primary role to the schools and universities. In contrast to Catholicism, in the reformed churches "the external and institutional side was subordinated to the heart and conscience of the individual."[17] Whatever their sectarian differences—at times critical for the individual's relations to God—both Luther and Calvin concurred on the supreme authority of the Bible and on the access of individuals to the scriptures. As a consequence, their creed required the translation of God's word into the vernacular, the literacy to enable its reading, and an educated and informed clergy to lead their flocks. Protestant reform in the German universities, to illustrate, "meant a broad attack on the autonomy of academic corporations by demanding the subordination of academic affairs to the needs of the territorial-confessional state for trained administrators, ministers, and teachers."[18] It led to a system of educated cleric and lay officials. As the German historian Freidrich Paulsen observed, "about the middle of the seventeenth century there was hardly a single village in Germany without a clergyman who had received his education at a university."[19]

Similarly, the maintenance of the English church, of which the crown was head, required an educated and conforming clergy. With their corporate existence dependent upon royal authorization, the universities proffered the available and essential means to this end. One finds that during the reigns of the Tudors and Stuarts of the sixteenth and seventeenth centuries the pressures for religious conformity mounted within the universities in support of an educated ministry. Therefore, it was not surprising in the controversy over tithes upon local communities to support an appointed clergy to find the rhetoric, "no universities, no ministry . . . no learning, no confutation of heresy."[20]

The age of the Renaissance, therefore, marked a shift toward the latter in the balance between autonomy and accountability. As one thinks about this period, however, it was not so much that political and theological leaders viewed education as a bastion of orthodoxy. This same view held in the medieval period as well. Rather, the shift inhered in the authority of secular state administrations, committed to one church or another, designed to achieve conformity and support through direct control. This contrasted with the ideal and reality of the university as a place apart, an autonomous institution in which the acceptance of sovereignty from the more distant papacy buffered it from the immediate force of local and national powers. Whatever the occasional deviation, as in the case of the Puritans in their resistance to the national church of England, the church-state-education triad translated into a conformity that accentuated responsibility over any pretensions of autonomy.

FORMATION OF CONTEMPORARY HIGHER EDUCATION

This discussion has proposed that the present system of higher education evidences in many important ways a regeneration of its medieval antecedents. Obviously, our current scene presents a far greater diversity of institutions and certainly displays an accretion of services carried out across the spectrum, from community colleges to research universities, and from vocational, training courses to advanced graduate study and research. Yet, the essential functions of extending knowledge, of instruction, and of service through professional preparation and professorial expertise do parallel medieval centers of learning in dimensions not present during the Renaissance. The governing trinity of the Reformation weakened during the nineteenth century, a consequence of the secularization of society. Accompanying this was a renewal of the medieval conception of the university as a center for learning and of the belief, at least among its intellectual leaders, that "the essence and core of a university was its autonomy."[21] That dualism referred to before in this commentary between academic tradition and political reality once again began to characterize relationships between academe and the society. The nineteenth century, therefore, proved to be a metamorphic period as the Reformation college was transmuted into the modern university.

The first colleges of this country were formed in the spirit of the Reformation, as the colonists carried over into the new world their old world experiences and beliefs. Consequently, in the words of Jurgen Herbst, it was to be expected that the "traditional theme of the trinity of church, state, and college found expression in the New World."[22] The leaders of the churches held parallel roles in church and government and as overseers of the colleges in a kind of interlocking directory. They could and did insist upon religious orthodoxy and educational conformity despite the fact that the corporate basis for the colleges was separate from the agencies of government and committed to secular, humanistic studies.

For the trustees and presidents of the early colleges—and indeed for those who taught with them—questions of academic or intellectual freedom simply did not surface. A prescribed curriculum in the Renaissance tradition accompanied a sectarian commitment to Christian morality, within which the teachers had limited freedom for the pursuit of personal intellectual interests in instruction or scholarly interests. In the main, the colleges responded to a public need for an educated clergy and proffered an accepted entree into mercantile, political, and professional careers. Governors, legislators, and the general public as well—to the extent that they thought about the colleges—viewed them as performing a public function; and, although chartered with private, self-perpetuating boards of control, they remained subject to legislative will. As late as 1812, for example, the Overseers of Harvard College accepted without judicial protest changes in their charter made by the Massachusetts legislature. Thus, while this conformity was by no means perfect in either curricular or organizational dimensions, there the issue of accountability versus autonomy in either intellectual or organizational dimensions did not exist.

In the course of the nineteenth century, the Renaissance triad disintegrated, as both the nature of the society and advanced learning changed. By the turn of the twentieth century higher education had achieved a position of broader significance for the development of a culture becoming dependent upon science and technology and committed to educational opportunity. Professors were gaining status as specialists and experts and were beginning to view themselves as professionals worthy of special professional freedom in their research and instruction and a voice in the decisions affecting the conditions that impacted upon their employment. The secularization of higher education, the specialization of faculty members in their academic endeavors, and the new premium placed upon research afforded a basis for relations with society, one attested to in 1915 with the formation of the American Association of University Professors. The consequence was a renewed vigor in the perception of the university as a place apart, a center for learning holding a right to a special and autonomous role within the society.

Thus, by the twentieth century there reappeared the discord inherent in the two pressures for an autonomous role and the necessity for society to control an enterprise increasingly essential to its welfare. To grasp the essence of this issue, it becomes important to give attention to two developments. The first extends from medieval origins but arose more directly from what is known as the Enlightenment of the seventeenth and eighteenth centuries in the form of the growth of knowledge based upon secular interpretations of reality, especially those of a scientific nature. The second inheres in the organizational structure of higher education associated with the establishment of colleges and universities under the control of corporate governing boards manned by private individuals separate from the direct agencies of government. Each will be discussed briefly.

Knowledge and Its Social Importance

The inception of scientific thought as we know it today probably lies with the *New Atlantis* of Francis Bacon; if so, its gestation goes back through Copernicus certainly to William of Ockham.[23] But, after Bacon, if not entirely as a consequence of him, scientific thought does take off on the road to the twentieth century in company with a stress upon human reason via the seventeenth and eighteenth century Enlightenment of the intellectuals who constituted a kind of international association, a "loose, informal wholly unorganized coalition of culture critics, religious skeptics, and political reformers from Edinburgh to Naples, Paris to Berlin, Boston to Philadelphia."[24] "Inheriting from their ancestors the belief in absolute truth and in a reasonable and comprehensive universe, these philosophers of the Enlightenment found a new standard of truth in science, and a new scheme of the universe in the astronomy of the seventeenth century."[25]

For American higher education the passage of reason bifurcated during the Enlightenment. One stream flowed directly to the early colleges. The intercourse between Adams, Jefferson, Franklin, and their associates and counterparts in Europe is well enough documented. Enlightenment ideas came to this country through France and England and, probably most influentially, Scotland. The new studies of the sciences had begun to enter the colleges before the Revolution and achieved a general acceptance, although one tertiary to Christian ethics and mental discipline, in large part because they did not appear to challenge established religion but were viewed as a further elaboration of the great work of God. In general, scientists may have agreed upon the importance of analysis based upon observation but remained committed to the view of John Locke that reason and experience fitted with divine revelation.[26]

The other Enlightenment stream moved through the German universities as in the early nineteenth century they solidified and expanded scientific and philosophical studies that originated in the new conceptions of "the world and man" accompanying the eighteenth-century awakening to the powers of observation and reason. In the years before the Civil War when the colleges of this country joined in support of the Yale Report's commitment to piety and humanistic, classical learning, the Germans were fashioning new disciplines and were gaining prestige for their scholarship. Until about the 1870s, German universities were virtually the only institutions in the world in which a student could obtain training in how to do scientific or scholarly research. German academicians had achieved the prospect and in large part the reality of "a full-time occupation role, that of the university professor whose professional duties explicitly included research."[27] They received appointments on the basis of formal qualifications and achievements. "The right to lecture at the university was the right of the recognized scientist."[28] In the course of the century, they offered a lodestar to adherents of educational reform in the country, discontent with the constraints of their college regimes and desirous of changes that would place their own institutions in line with advances in the intellectual realm. In the four decades following 1870, they succeeded in this endeavor and fashioned an academic reorganization spearheaded by a university model of specialized disciplines grounded upon advanced, graduate study in tandem with research and scholarship. In this country, as previously in Germany, the professor began to achieve status associated with a new role. Less and less a teacher and disciplinarian, he became, at least in the first-rate institutions, a person of professional substance in terms of a role as an academic specialist regarded as an expert and consulted in the mundane world. The engineer, agriculturalist, purveyor of veterinary medicine, economist, psychologist, and political scientist had something to contribute that gained by the First World War respectful, if at times tenuous, recognition amplified in the decades that followed.

This new role also carried with it a pressure for autonomy. Professional expertise set a scholar aside from the more direct intrusions of the uninitiated and allowed at least a partial monopoly on those admitted to profession. Specialization accompanying expertise gained organizational structure in the form of disciplinary and professional departments that had unto themselves the knowledge necessary for not only the recruitment of new staff but the formation of courses of study and determination of research priorities and extended, through constellations of related departments in the forms of schools, to the curriculum itself. Whatever the influence of the donor, the legal authority of the state, or the formal power of trustees and regents, it became less and less possible for them to extend this external influence into the basic academic substance of the higher learning. Harvard President A. Lawrence Lowell was to write in 1921 of the faculty as a "society or guild of scholars,"[29] and a 1924 report of a committee of the American Association of University Professors was to complain that professors had come to look upon the university "as a place where their own departmental specialties can be practiced without let or hindrance."[30]

The intellectual transformation of Western culture identified with the extension of knowledge had a correlate in the industrial revolution and the prominence in the American society of an egalitarian ideology. For the nineteenth century, this meant an alteration of political, economic, religious, and moral components of life and the passing of the mercantile economic and political systems of the republican era that had been attuned to the European-oriented culture of the eastern seaboard and headed by an educated elite who had led the nation to its independence and set it upon its course in history. In this context, advocates of accommodation to the new knowledge had counterparts who promoted an applied orientation in tandem with expansion in opportunity. As the industrial system matured in this country (in agriculture as well as in the factory and commerce), higher education took on a responsibility for preparing students for roles that covered a spectrum from applied engineering and agriculture to psychologically-based personnel services. "The industrial system," as economist John Galbraith has observed, "by making trained and educated manpower the decisive factor of production, requires a highly developed education system. . . . Modern higher education is extensively accommodated to the needs of the industrial system. . . .The great prestige of pure and applied science and mathematics in modern times, and the support accorded to them, reflect the needs of the technostructure."[31] In effect, the nineteenth-century reforms combined commitment to the extension of knowledge with service of direct usefulness to society.

The growing recognition of the value of a college or university education and the egalitarian sentiment for opening up opportunity for all to move toward economic success in life stimulated the growth of public higher education. The initiative for a system of public colleges and universities came largely after the Morrill Act of 1862 provided for the land-grant colleges. The act reaffirmed a national commitment to support education by assigning the proceeds from the sale of lands to support in each state a college designed to promote programs in engineering and agriculture along with the more traditional studies. The importance of the Morrill Act lies with the impetus it gave to increased state assistance to higher education. Public support necessitated greater responsiveness to public needs and desires expressed through legislative appropriations that accentuated a curriculum geared to "useful" programs in engineering, agriculture, home economics, veterinary medicine, business administration, and other more applied areas. Perhaps as significantly, it made going to college an accepted part of the American middle-class tradition.

However, the popularization of public colleges and universities inevitably meant an enlargement in their supervision on the part of public authorities. One finds this clearly etched in founding statutes. Nearly two-thirds specified educational programs of one type or another. Those for the University of Oregon, for example, required "instruction and complete education in all departments of science, literature, professional pursuits, and general education" and those for Kentucky, for programs in law, medicine, and surgery. Commonly, statutes prohibited political and sectarian tests for admission and "sectarian affiliations or beliefs" as criteria for faculty positions. It was a common practice to include requirements for annual reports to the governor and/or legislature covering financial affairs and internal management. Legislative restrictions upon educational programs, admission policy, and financial affairs were uniformly upheld by courts.

For private institutions, philanthropic support intruded its own type of control, perhaps more subtlely through personal rather than legal pressures, not without parallel to federal funding for students, research, and plant that brought with it policy constraints as effective as legal ones. By the turn of the century, however, courts did impose some limitations upon institutional control over students—for both public and private colleges—on the basis of reasonableness in rules and regulations and due process and proper hearings in suits brought in response to perceived injustices related to admissions and the award of degrees. Although reluctant to intrude judicial judgment in place of that by college faculties and administrators, courts did accede to a limited supervision. However, it does not appear that such appeals to the courts set precedents for the plethora of cases in more recent decades; rather, courts recognized that boards as corporate bodies held ultimate authority for the management of their institutions in the context of what delegations were made to faculties for educational affairs and to administrators.[32]

Thus, by the turn of the twentieth century the concept of higher learning had acquired a broadened context of its role within the general society and an institutional basis for its application to an increasingly wide swath of social activity. That central impulse of the transition from medieval to modern—the progression and extraordinary elaboration of knowledge—had fueled a commitment to greater access to formal education. For relations between higher education and society, it brought with it a combination of increased autonomy within the academic structures at the level of the professoriate in departments and schools and an increase in the basis for governmental control that accompanied the amplification of public support. With reference to the first condition, Walter Metzger has written: "There can be no doubt that secularization, specializaton, and the new premium placed upon research improved the status of the profession, both in domestic ranking and on the competitive world exchange."[33] For the second condition, although an active turn toward centralized systems of state colleges and universities did not come into being until more recent decades, precedents had appeared in a half-dozen states prior to our entry into World War I and, certainly, legislators and governors did not hesitate to intrude their desires upon institutions when an occasion arose.

Corporate Basis for Government

The corporate form in the medieval university created an autonomy from local authority within the sovereignty of the papacy that established its right to existence by means of papal bulls or charters. This conception of a corporate association separate from government yet obliged to it for its establishment carried over to the early colleges through precedents associated with the English universities and with English legal custom in general. By the eighteenth century in England the corporation had become an accepted legal conception, a distinctive social unit holding designated rights in law similar to those held by individuals. In this regard, English common law set a pattern for similar arrangements in the colonies and served as a starting point for the development of a more indigenous conceptualization in this country. Colonial leaders used the English tradition of the corporation as a mechanism for conducting certain public services, such as the colleges (and toll roads and bridges, public wharves, canals, parish organizations, towns, etc.), separate from agencies of government. As corporations, the early colleges owed organizational existence to the sovereignty of the state but functioned as relatively autonomous societal agencies. Apparently as a consequence of precedents in Holland and Scotland, although clearly concomitant with the Reformation trinity, corporate authorization went to a board composed of nonacademic members. This arrangement assured control to the religious-political leadership of the early Protestant church-state and, in the course of the nineteenth century, to the succeeding power elites more secular in nature.[34]

The point here is not that the establishment of the nine colonial colleges as chartered corporations provided them with the same kind of institutional autonomy we have known in the present century. Quite the contrary, until the Dartmouth College Case decision of 1819, they were viewed as public institutions subject to direction and even control as appeared necessary from the colonial and state governments. Yet, the corporate form of organization in time did carry with it a degree of autonomy, clearly greater for private institutions, inherent in the delegated control of internal affairs. In the Dartmouth College Case decision the Supreme Court under Chief Justice Marshall defined the college as a private, eleemosynary institution and interpreted its charter as a contract as binding upon the State of New Hampshire as on the trustees, "a contract, the obligation of which cannot be impaired without violating the constitution of the United States." As a consequence the autonomy of private colleges gained a legal barrier to intrusions from governmental sources. It also led to a reexamination of the state-college relationship and to the establishment of public colleges during the expansion of higher education following the Civil War, rather than to the provision of state funding for existing private ones. By the Civil War the practice of establishing colleges through boards of trustees or regents holding corporate powers, although by no means a legal necessity, had fixed a generally observed practice "of delegating immediate responsibility to a special corporation."[35] The state university derived its form of control from precedent in the early colleges through what can be viewed as a public corporation. Thus, even though clearly regarded in the legislatures and courts as agencies of state government, public colleges and universities retained, in most of their features, the corporate structure; their boards controlled internal affairs.

Nevertheless, it must be recognized that during the later decades of the nineteenth century limits upon the authority of public boards, limits that founded precedents for the expansion of supervision and control by state governments in the latter half of this century, did exist. Courts in general, for example, recognized the legal sovereignty of legislatures and governors in ways that deprived boards in the public sector of managerial freedoms enjoyed by their private counterparts. As noted above, this included directions in founding statutes over who was to be admitted and what educational programs were to be offered. Even more significantly, an existence based upon statute could terminate by legislative action, a condition that carried important implications for intrusions into internal affairs by state agencies. The exceptions to this were the eight or nine constitutionally-based universities whose mandate lay with popular referendum, which placed the institution beyond direct legislatural control.[36] Notwithstanding legal limitations occasionally enforced in practice, as Alexander Brody points out in his 1935 survey of the legal basis for public higher education, "even after the universities came to be regarded as agencies of the central government, they were permitted to retain, in most of its features, the corporate structure that they had acquired during their development."[37]

In summary, the reorganization of the colleges into a system of higher education at the close of the nineteenth century brought together two mutually supportive conditions. The ascension of specialized knowledge drew the professoriate back to a commitment of the advancement of learning and, in turn, to a segmentation of institutional organization into separate and frequently inner-directed departments. Expertise and the professional status of academic service placed a premium on self-direction in teaching and, especially, research. The corporate form carried with it the medieval tradition of the university as a place apart, a bastion of learning protected by a delegation of limited sovereignty to carry out a mission for learning. It provided for an institutional autonomy respected in general, if violated from time to time in the specific. By the First World War, higher education had achieved a reasonable, if at times uncertain, balance between intellectual freedom and institutional autonomy *and* accountability for an educational service and accompanying public control. An examination of the elements of this balance provides the focus for a brief concluding discussion.

TWENTIETH CENTURY

By the first decades of the present century, therefore, the medieval conception of the university as a place apart, a sanctuary for scholars, had a renaissance. Through the corporate form of government derived from its medieval creation, higher institutions secured legal status separate from agencies of state government. Through their acceptance of the extension of secular knowledge and its use in the service of society, the universities, and in turn other institutions, had achieved a status that afforded to the professoriate a professional status that supported their intellectual freedom and control of academic affairs.

   As in the case of their medieval precursors, the universities and colleges of this country in the twentieth century did not enjoy total autonomy but functioned within a myriad of societal constraints that accompanied the various forms of support essential to their maintenance. Regents and trustees intruded into internal affairs their own values and priorities, frequently reflective of conservative forces at work within the society. Administrative officers and, indeed, many professors as well adjusted their academic preconceptions to the desires and needs of the marketplace. Although undergirded by traditions associated with private institutions, those in the public sector could hardly ignore the financial and legal sinews that tied them to legislatures and state executives. Freedom and autonomy by their vary nature signify relative conditions, and the point here is that, relatively, higher education in this country had acquired an independence in many ways parallel to that of its medieval progenitor as a consequence of parallel functions.

   Yet, whether illustrative of some pervasive historical pattern or simply idiosyncratic to the times, social forces have entered into the educational arena in the course of this century to shift the balance away from professorial freedom and institutional autonomy toward accountability to and control by public governments. As the century progresses, one senses that in many ways higher education begins to find itself enmeshed in the Reformation trinity of church, state, and education without the church, an enterprise subject to the determinations of governmental instrumentalities as to what its proper functions should be. In concluding this historical overview, therefore, it makes sense to very briefly identify the forces at work that give weight to both sides of the balance.

On the side of freedom and autonomy, several conditions had continued to weigh the scales and may prove ultimately of sufficient heft to keep higher education as at least a distinctive enterprise worthy of special status. Overall, they associate with the linking during the last century of the colleges with the extension of specialized knowledge and its applications. The higher educational system that ensued served as the institutional instrument to this end, and the graduate school emerged as a fountainhead from which the values associated with specialized knowledge and its extension were dispersed throughout the enterprise. More importantly, the extension of knowledge and derivative applications complemented the requirements of an expanding industrial economic system dependent upon a science-based technology. The resulting professionalization of the professoriate and their segmentation into departments and professional programs brought within their purview, and control, the critical academic decisions having to do with selection and promotion of members and the organization of and criteria for instruction and research. This specialization combined with increasing institutional size and complexity to construct an effective barrier against direct supervision from administrative and external sources. Initially, this concentration fitted with perceptions of board members about their role and limitations upon their supervision. It was bolstered by an influential system of accrediting agencies, both regional and specialized, through which the professoriate has assured the primacy of its judgments regarding the quality of departments and programs, libraries, and instructional and research facilities. Finally, the American Association of University Professors gained strength as an influential advocate for the cause of academic freedom and professorial role in institutional decision making.

However, the professional strength of faculty members during the course of the century came up against contravening forces that have augmented the role of state and federal governments in affairs of higher education. These counterforces rest upon two conditions: the legal bases for the existence of colleges and universities and for an increasing supervision of the society in general; and the power of financial support that flowed increasingly from governmental sources, first through the expansion of state colleges and universities and secondly through federal and, to some extent, state funding of higher education (to students, institutions, and research activities).

There are many specific reasons for intrusions by the public polities into the internal affairs of academe. However, viewed as a whole, they demonstrate that the success of colleges and universities in achieving a significant role in the society has made increasingly clear that they cannot stand apart from the main currents of the society. American higher education during the course of this century has steadily become a critical resource for an increasingly sophisticated and complex culture. It mans the portals to careers in a wide variety of occupations and professions, provides expertise to government and industry as well as other societal entities, and generates knowledge essential for a wide swath of affairs, ranging from personal and social health to the maintenance of the economic system to space exploration. Through the expansion in size and number of its institutions, it has itself become a significant sector in the local, state, and national economy. In an era—most clearly demonstrated in the post-World War II years—during which government has extended its supervision and direction across the entire economic and social spectrum, it could hardly be otherwise than that colleges and universities would find themselves similarly treated.

For the colleges and universities, having no prospect of the security of isolation from the activities of the society—except perhaps for the small church-related colleges—because of the very nature of the services they provide, efforts to maintain a balance between autonomy and control come hard against influences that simply outweigh them. Institutions in their need for research support, physical plan development, and students cannot remain aloof from the federal financial trough. And financial support does not come unencumbered but rather brings with it rules, reports, and sanctions. Although percentages of total state expenditures may not have risen dramatically, the amount of money involved has; and state governments simply have to create budgetary and control systems that provide a proper accounting for the use of public funds. A variety of social improvement programs, primarily at the federal level, have led not only to an aggravation of controls by administrative agencies but have opened the way to referrals to the judiciary in increasing numbers and led to a pattern of decisions that subject institutions to a great deal more legal accountability than possible previously. This latter condition has its affirmation in the emergence in recent years of a new professional area, that of legal counsels for colleges and universities, a professional group with its own national association.

Perhaps the most salient aspect of the changing nature of relations between academe and society is characterized by the title of a paper by Gellhorn and Boyer, "Government and Education: The University as a Regulated Industry." "As the influence of regulatory procedures, programs and techniques spreads throughout higher education," they comment in summary, "there will be fundamental changes not only in the way the university interacts with the outside world but also in the way it governs itself internally."[38] A parallel assertion can be made in respect to financial support. In effect, the balance between autonomy and control, which indeed rested in large part upon the pivot provided by the corporate status of governing boards, tips steadily toward the latter. The prospects of a restoration of the balance are no more promising in the late twentieth century than were those for regaining the independence of the great medieval universities in the sixteenth century as the Reformation swept over northern Europe. Rather, higher education will have to come to terms with government and devise the arrangements and develop the attitudes that at least facilitate a constructive interaction. At best, one suspects that the remaining strength of academic freedom and professional autonomy may shift to disciplinary and professional departments, not unlike the nineteenth-century German universities in which the professors exercised control over academic affairs within the domination of the education ministries.

NOTES

1. Marjorie Reeves, "The European University from Medieval Times," in *Higher Education: Demand and Response,* W. R. Niblett, ed. (San Francisco: Jossey-Bass, 1970), p. 61.
2. E. D. Duryea, "The Corporate Basis of University and College Government: A Historical Analysis," unpublished, 1973.
3. A. B. Cobban, *The Medieval Universities* (London: Methuen, 1975), p. 78. The universities of northern Europe of that era, of which that at Paris was preeminent, contrast in many distinctive ways to those that originated in Italy and in general appeared in southern France and in Spain. The former derived from associations of masters, while the latter initially sprang from gatherings of students seeking instruction in civil law and other medieval studies and in time came under the control of the local principalities. Those in Spain were founded by the kings. The influence of the southern university centers seems to have flowed into Spain and Latin America. Certainly, they exercised minimal influence upon the northern nations, such as England, Holland, and Germany, which served as precedents for the college foundings in this country.
4. Hastings Rashdall, *The Universities of Europe in the Middle Ages,* ed. F. M. Powicke and A. B. Emden, 3 vols. (London: Oxford University Press, 1936), 1:3.
5. Jacques Verger, "The University of Paris at the End of the Hundred Years War," in *Universities in Politics,* ed. J. W. Baldwin and R. A. Goldthwaite, (Baltimore, Md.: Johns Hopkins University Press, 1972), p. 48.
6. A. B. Cobban, *The Medieval Universities,* p. 75.
7. Ibid., p. 7.
8. Quoted in John H. Randall, *The Making of the Modern Mind* (New York: Columbia University Press, 1976), p. 94.
9. A. B. Cobban, *Medieval Universities,* p. 8. The decline of the medieval university intertwined intimately with the decline of the Roman Church that interfaced with the emergence of industry and commerce and of the rise to importance of economic interests. Even in the thirteenth century secular rulers—the Holy Roman Emperor and the kings—also participated in the founding of universities by secular decrees and acts. But throughout the thirteenth and fourteenth centuries secular or national kings slowly gained preeminence and power as the Church floundered increasingly in the problems associated with its loss of temporal power and with internal corruption. The Great Schism of 1378 to 1447, during which two popes competed for

control, marked the end of the Church's domination of Europe and the shift of European power to national kings. An interesting footnote to this era was the influential role played by the doctors of the University of Paris in the final solution to the papal conflict. But this also marked the end of the university's preeminence in European affairs.

10. It should be noted that in addition to the value for vocational ends, the arts or lower faculty of the study of the medieval university did require a learning common to all students that contained "certain forms of knowledge which . . . all educated people ought to have, together with the basic skills necessary to the arts of communication." In doing so, the medieval institutions established the concept of an educated person that has persisted in Anglo-United States cultures. Marjorie Reeves, "European University from Medieval Times," p. 64.

11. Anton-Hermann Chroust, "The Corporate Idea and the Body Politic in the Middle Ages," *The Review of Politics* (1947), p. 423.

12. John H. Randall, *Making of the Modern Mind,* pp. 111, 143.

13. Preserved Smith, *A History of Modern Culture,* 2 vols. (Gloucester, Mass.: Peter Smith, 1957), I:357.

14. Francis Bacon and his concept of the inductive method, deriving axioms from observations; Kepler and Galileo in astronomy; Descartes' rational philosophy; Pascal's studies of the atmosphere; the investigations of Boyle into combustion and the atmosphere, leading to the mathematically-based synthesis of Newton; and Newton himself, as the creator of a system of physics that lasted as the conception of reality until the end of the nineteenth century—examples of the pioneering scientists who set the foundation for modern thought.

15. Preserved Smith, *History of Modern Culture,* I:343.

16. Fritz Caspari, *Humanism and the Social Order of Tudor England* (New York: Teachers College Press, 1968), pp. 256, 279.

17. John H. Randall, *Making of the Modern Mind,* p. 52.

18. Jurgen Herbst, "The First Three American Colleges: Schools of the Reformation," *Perspectives in American History* 8 (1972), p. 19.

19. Freidrich Paulsen, *German Education Past and Present* (London: T. Fisher Unwin, 1908), p. 90.

20. Christopher Hill, "The Radical Critics of Oxford and Cambridge in the 1650s," in *Universities in Politics,* p. 112.

21. Frederick Rudolph, *The American College and University* (New York: Alfred A. Knopf, 1962), p. 26.

22. Jurgen Herbst, "First Three American Colleges," pp. 14-17.

23. Richard M. Weaver, *Ideas Have Consequences* (Chicago: University of Chicago Press, 1948), p. 3.

24. Peter Gay, *The Enlightenment* (New York: Vintage Books, 1966), p. 3.

25. Preserved Smith, *History of Modern Culture,* 2:20.

26. Merle Curti, "The Great Mr. Locke: America's Philosopher, 1783-1861," *Huntington Library Bulletin* 11 (April 1937), p. 114.

27. Joseph Ben-David, "The Profession of Science and its Power," *Minerva* 10 (July 1972) p. 369.

28. Ibid., p. 370.

29. A. Lawrence Lowell, "Faculty and Governing Boards," *School and Society* 13 (February 19, 1921), pp. 236-7.

30. Committee T, "Place and Function of Faculties in University Government," *AAUP Bulletin* 10 (May 1924), pp. 27-8.

31. John K. Galbraith, *The New Industrial State* (Boston: New American Library, 1967) p. 377-8.

32. This discussion of statutes and the courts derives from a study under way by the author examining the corporate authority of governing boards from 1870 to 1910.

33. Walter P. Metzger, "Origins of the Association," *AAUP Bulletin 55* (Summer 1965), p. 230.

34. The English pattern of awarding corporate authority to academics did influence the original arrangements at Harvard and William and Mary, however. But neither college set the precedent for those that followed: that fell to Yale, which was formed with a single board of nonacademic members. Both Harvard and William and Mary subsequently shifted control to nonacademic boards.

35. Alexander Brody, *The American State and Higher Education* (Washington, D.C.: American Council on Education, 1935), p. 112.

36. Other exceptions to this situation existed for normal schools and state teachers' colleges established by or under departments of education. The idea of constitutional authorization for a college or university appeared first in Michigan in 1850 when the university was placed under a Board of Regents elected on the basis of judicial circuits. In all, "twenty-seven of the states make explicit reference to higher education in their constitutions. The remainder of the states, through exercise of policy powers have legislative provision for higher education" (Kern Alexander and E. S. Soloman, *College and University Law* [Charlottesville, Va.: The Michie Company, 1972] p. 26). Of the states with constitutional provisions, according to Alexander and Soloman, at least nine guarantee constitutional autonomy for universities: Michigan, Minnesota, California, Colorado, Georgia, Idaho, Oklahoma, Nevada, and Arizona.

37. Alexander Brody, *American State and Higher Education,* p. 115.

38. Ernest Gellhorn and Barry B. Boyer, "Government and Education: The University as a Regulated Industry," *Arizona State Law Journal* (1977), p. 593.

3

Autonomy and Accountability: Some Fundamental Issues

T. R. McConnell

In characterizing their so-called binary system of higher education, the British have ordinarily referred to the universities as the "autonomous" sector and the polytechnics, together with certain other institutions of advanced further education, as the "public" sector. It is true that the British universities have had a long and distinctive history of relative independence. Yet, as they have become more and more dependent on government funds—now reaching something like 90 percent of their financial support—they have become increasingly subject to external guidance from the University Grants Committee, and through the UGC from the government itself. The public sector is more directly controlled and financed by the Department of Education and Science at the top and locally by the education authorities, and has recently become subject to guidance by the newly established National Advisory Board.

AUTONOMY AND ACADEMIC FREEDOM

Autonomy Not Absolute

The British universities have come to recognize that autonomy cannot be complete or absolute. A scholar and administrator in British higher education, who served as vice chancellor of one of the newer technological universities, put the issue as follows:

> Absolute autonomy is of course impossible: a network of relationships with both national and local Government to determine how the needs of society and individual citizens should be met is inescapable. There can be no formal set of answers, only an ever-changing balance of interests within which the maximum degrees of freedom must be strenuously maintained.[1]

If a college or university is effectively to define its goals and select or invent the means of attaining them, it must have a high degree of independence. Bowen has observed that the "production process" in higher education is far more intricate and complicated than that in any industrial enterprise.[2] Turning resources into human values defies standardization. Students vary enormously in academic aptitude, in interests, in intellectual dispositions, in social and cultural characteristics, in educational and vocational objectives, and in many other ways. Furthermore, the disciplines and professions with which institutions of higher learning are concerned require different methods of investigation, diverse intellectual structures, different means of relating methods of inquiry and ideas to personal and social values, and variable processes of relating knowledge to human experience. Learning, consequently, is a subtle process, the nature of which may vary from student to student, from institution to institution, from discipline to discipline, from one scholar and/or teacher to another, and from one level of student development to another. The intricacy and unpredictability of both learning and investigation are factors that require a high degree of freedom from intellectually limiting external intervention and control if an institution of higher education is to perform effectively.

On first thought one might identify academic freedom with autonomy. Certainly a high degree of intellectual independence is necessary for faculty and students in choosing the subjects of study and investigation, searching for the truth without unreasonable or arbitrary restrictions, and expressing their scholarly conclusions without censorship. Some forms of external control or even some kinds of subtle efforts to influence teaching, learning, or research may endanger intellectual freedom. However, Berdahl has pointed out that "academic freedom and university autonomy, though related, are not synonymous . . . academic freedom as a concept is universal and absolute, whereas autonomy is of necessity parochial and relative."[3] Berdahl was writing about the statewide coordination of higher education through such agencies as state coordinating boards and consolidated or systemwide (such as the University of California Board of Regents) governing boards. Presumably designating the missions of sectors or particular institutions after appropriate studies and consultation would not be an unwarranted invasion of autonomy by such boards. Specifying the academic programs, academic organization, curriculum, and methods of teaching for the attainment of designated missions is likely to be considered an unjustified form of intervention. A coordinating or governing board might phase out a doctoral program at a particular campus (after appropriate study and consultation) without unwarranted invasion of institutional autonomy or violation of academic freedom. The federal government might impose antidiscrimination procedures in admitting students, or appointing and promoting faculty members, without interfering unjustifiably in academic affairs provided the means do not make unreasonable demands on the institutions or violate necessary confidentiality of records. If appropriate safeguards are followed, no invasion of academic freedom need be suffered.

Requirements for accountability may impose onerous procedures on an institution, e.g., accounting for the use of research grants (as noted later in this chapter), but even these restraints may not endanger academic freedom. Whether restrictions on DNA research, referred to below, put an undesirable limit on choice of problems for investigation remains to be seen. In this case public protection may justify what seems to be an infringement on academic freedom.

In any event, Dressel, in a recent analysis of the autonomy of public institutions, came to the following conclusion: "Academic freedom is not ensured by institutional autonomy, and recent restrictions of institutional autonomy have had relatively little effect on academic freedom."[4]

One may agree that the absence of external controls does not guarantee academic freedom, and that certain elements of external control do not endanger intellectual independence. But an institution's right to mobilize its intellectual resources—and, within reasonable limits, even its financial resources—toward the attainment of its agreed-upon purposes is at least strongly fortified by a relatively high degree of autonomy.

NATURE OF ACCOUNTABILITY

As this is being written, intellectual freedom in colleges and universities is not under special threat, but autonomy is being steadily eroded. Financial austerity causes legislatures, statewide coordinating boards, and even consolidated governing boards to look more critically at institutional roles, at the availability and distribution of functions and programs, at effectiveness, and at educational and operational costs. As the federal government extends support for higher education it prohibits discrimination in the admission of students and in the appointment and promotion of faculty members. This is an example of the fact that the public at large is becoming more conscious of its institutions of higher education. States and localities are more demanding of education and service, more critical of what they perceive institutions to be doing, more vocal in expressing their criticisms and desires. Public institutions, always answerable to the general interest, will no longer be excused from defending what they do or don't do. No longer can a university shunt public criticism aside as a mere expression of intellectual shallowness. It will increasingly have to explain itself, defend its essential character, and demonstrate that its service is worth the cost. It will become increasingly answerable, i.e., accountable, to its numerous constituencies for the range of its services and the effectiveness of its performance. "The extension of substantive autonomy to an individual, organization, or group implies responsibility and accountability," Dressel wrote recently.[5] He went on to outline the elements of accountability as follows:

Responsible performance, then, involves using allocated resources legally and wisely to attain those purposes for which they were made available. Responsible performance requires continuing accumulation of evidence of the extent to which purposes are achieved; reviewing the evaluation evidence to clarify the avowed goals and their interpretation; consideration of the relevance, effectiveness, and costs of the processes used to achieve the goals; and continuing effort directed at improving the educational processes used or finding more effective processes.[6]

Relationships between the federal government and research universities have recently become strained as the former has attempted to impose techniques of accountability for federal research grants that the institutions have considered unreasonable, onerous, and unnecessarily expensive. In 1978 the National Commission on Research was organized for the purpose of proposing means of resolving the differences between the two parties. The commission recognized three forms of accountability: financial and administrative, involving evidence of financial propriety and compliance with administrative regulations; scientific, concerned with achievement of results and progress toward scientific objectives; and social, referring to the extent to which specific social goals have been fulfilled. The commission concluded that "When well designed, the system of accountability involves an appropriate balance between independence and control, between incentives and constraints, and between the costs and benefits of the various procedures and requirements used."[7]

Accountability and Intervention

Accountability is not confined to an institution's external relationships. Internally, a college or university is a complex of mutual responsibilities and reciprocal pressures for accountability. Important as these bases of accountability are, this chapter will be devoted to a discussion of accountability to external agencies. External accountability often emanates from external intervention, but intervention often goes well beyond reasonable requirements for accountability. In any event, intervention and accountability should be discussed together. The first subject is higher education's accountability to the public interest.

Accountability to the Public

Ultimately, public institutions of higher education are broadly answerable to the people who support them. Recently, after California voters had failed to approve a state bond issued providing large sums for the construction of medical school facilities and had given other evidences of disaffection, the president of the University of California recognized the ultimate accountability of the university when he said to the Assembly of the Academic Senate:

Make no mistake, the university is a public institution, supported by the people through the actions of their elected representatives and executives. They will not allow it to be operated in ways which are excessively at variance with the general public will. By various pressures and devices the university will be forced to yield and to conform if it gets too far away from what the public expects and wants.[8]

At one time the people were relatively remote from their public institutions, but citizens now find their future economic, social, and cultural life increasingly influenced, in some cases virtually determined, by their colleges and universities. Consequently, the public university has had to become responsive to a wider range of economic interests and to a more diverse pattern of ethnic and cultural backgrounds and aspirations. Minority groups are pressing for financial assistance, for remedial programs when necessary for admission or attainment of academic standards, and for academic programs that will meet their interests and perceived needs. As special interest groups have pressed the university to provide the services they believe they need, students have organized to promote their interests. To avoid declining enrollments, many colleges and universities have responded to the student market by establishing new vocational and professional programs of study, and most institutions are struggling to redistribute faculty, equipment, and professional curricula. This trend has been especially observable in the community colleges, and the effect will change the pattern of enrollment in four-year institutions to which community college graduates have transferred in large numbers in the past.

Serving the public interest has become a complicated process; not all institutions will undertake the same missions or serve common purposes. Accountability is still further complicated by a question of what special interests should be served and what should be put aside. Only when an institution's goals are defined, the groups to be served are identified, and the relevant programs of teaching, research, and public service are determined can an institution's effectiveness be estimated. Thus, accountability is both general—to the broad public interest—and particular—to more limited constituencies.

Accountability to the public is mediated by operation of several layers of representation between it and the institutions in question. Colleges and universities are answerable immediately to their governing boards. Most boards have statutory status. They were created by legislatures and are in nearly all respects under legislative control. Seven or eight states have given constitutional status to their public universities. This unusual situation has been characterized as follows:

The idea was to remove questions of management, control, and the supervision of the universities from the reach of politicians in state legislatures and governors' offices. The universities were to be a fourth branch of government, functioning co-authoritatively with the legislature, the judiciary, and the executive.[9]

The purpose in creating their constitutional position was to give the universities a much greater degree of autonomy and self-direction than statutory status would provide. Their autonomy, however, has been materially eroded over the years. A study of statutory and constitutional boards showed that the supposedly constitutionally autonomous university "is losing a good deal of its ability to exercise final judgment on the use not only of its state funds but also of those derived from other sources. It now undergoes intensive reviews of budgets and programs by several different state agencies, by special commissions, and by legislative committees, all of which look for ways to control."[10]

GOVERNMENT INTERFERENCE

State Government Intervention

Whether an institution has statutory or constitutional status, or even whether it is public or private, it is moving into the governmental orbit. As Clark put it: "In the changing relation between higher education and government, higher education . . . moves inside government, becomes a constituent part of government, a bureau within public administration.[11]

Most students of university governance believe that government officials should not serve on governing boards, since this identifies the institution too closely with political and governmental agencies. In California the governor, the lieutenant governor, the superintendent of public instruction, the president of the state board of agriculture, and the speaker of the legislative assembly are among the ex officio voting members of the Board of Regents of the University of California. A governor may also use his appointive power in attempting to influence governing boards. For example, it was charged that in appointing four new Regents, former Governor Jerry Brown of California chose persons who would follow his opposition to the university's connection with the Livermore (California) and Los Alamos (New Mexico) atomic weapons laboratories. Whether that was true or not, the Regents voted to renew management contracts with the Department of Energy. Former Governor Brown's outspoken and blunt opposition to the weapons laboratories evoked critical comment, an example of which is the following excerpt from the editorial page of the San Francisco Chronicle:

> Throughout his time in office, the Governor has shown contempt for the University and for what it represents . . . . As a veteran observer of the Regents says, "He's there on his own issues, investment in South Africa, farm mechanization or nuclear politics, the topics he feels appeal to his followers."[12]

The new members of the Board of Regents appointed by the Governor may have proved to be open-minded and judicious in their attitudes and votes on most university matters. In any event, it would seem more appropriate for a governor to appoint to a university governing board persons who investigate issues thoroughly, consider the interests of the institution and the public open-mindedly and objectively, and vote independently of political figures and political biases. It may be noted that the California Regents have adopted a plan for divestiture of its investments, (for example, in endorsement funds) in South Africa.

Although he may influence institutions via their governing boards, it is ". . . through the executive budget process that the governor makes his impact and gives significant leadership on major issues of higher education policy."[13] The state finance or budget officer, who is ordinarily responsible to the governor, may also exercise an important element of authority by controlling shifts or changes in line-item budgets. Some state finance departments conduct pre-audits of expenditures that not only pass on the legality of the use of itemized funds, but give the state officer the opportunity to rule on the substance or purpose of the expenditures. In recent times the long arms of state finance officers have reached into academic affairs by conducting program audits or even program evaluations.[14] The question of external program audits will be discussed at a later point.

Important as the understanding and support of executive officers of state government may be, public colleges and universities are even more directly answerable to the legislature. The institutions are dependent on legislative understanding of their broad missions and programs, the legislature's financial support, and the lawmakers' judgment of the institutions' educational effectiveness.

As noted above, even a constitutionally autonomous public university is ultimately accountable to the legislature for the ways in which it uses its state-appropriated funds and for the effectiveness of its educational services. For some years certain leaders in the state legislature have criticized the University of California for neglecting undergraduate education. One of the persistent critics has been the chairman of the powerful Assembly post-secondary education committee. The university's legislative critics were recently given more ammunition by studies that revealed that Berkeley campus faculty members were devoting less time to teaching and other contacts with students. A new chancellor who took office in 1980 at Berkeley responded to legislative criticism by appointing a vice chancellor for undergraduate education. The president of the university called on the faculties of all the campuses to increase their teaching loads and to spend more time with students. The actions of the president and the Berkeley chancellor were open recognition that the university is accountable to the legislature and the people of the state.

Program Auditing

State agencies, including legislatures, have begun to move into program evaluation. Dressel has outlined what is involved in program auditing:

> Issues raised in program evaluation include the consistency of the program with
> the assigned institutional role and function; the adequacy of planning in regard
> to the objectives, program structure, processes, implementation, and evaluation
> of outcomes; the adherence of program operation to the objectives, structural
> features, processes, sequence, and outcome appraisal originally specified or the
> presentation of a sound rationale for any deviations from the original prescrip-
> tion, an evaluation of planning and operation and use of feedback for alteration
> and improvement, and provision for cost benefit analyses.[15]

After he had investigated legislatively-mandated program evaluations in
Wisconsin and Virginia, Berdahl declared that "Academic programs, quality
considerations, course content, faculty evaluation—these had always been
considered too close to the heart of academe to be subjected to normal state
accountability measures."[16] Berdahl warned that if institutions, systems, or
statewide coordinating boards, in company with colleges and universities
under their surveillance, do not keep their academic programs under periodic
appraisal, external agencies will take over this function.[17]

Federal Intervention

With increasing federal financial support and numerous federal laws and
regulations governing use of the funds, both public and private educational
institutions find themselves increasingly accountable to agencies of the federal
government. Total federal support recently reached about 15 billion dollars
awarded and controlled by a variety of governmental bureaus. As this was
written, the two houses of Congress agreed on a bill authorizing 10.2 billion
dollars in authorizations for higher education programs. It was inevitable—
and appropriate—that higher institutions should be held accountable for the
way in which they expend these funds. However, tension between universities
and federal granting agencies has steadily increased as the institutions have
been subjected to regulations and accounting procedures they consider unnecessarily extensive, expensive, and often inappropriate.

One of the major causes of strain between the federal government and
the universities is the failure of government agencies to recognize, in the
words of the report of the National Commission on Research, that "Universities carry out teaching, research, and service as an integrated whole, not as
separate functions." The commission went on to say that since teaching,
research, and perhaps public service are closely related, accurate costs cannot
be assessed to each of the related outcomes.[18] Nevertheless, the commission

recognized the necessity for accountability. What is needed, said the commission, is a joint effort between research universities and government bureaus to devise methods of accountability that recognize the peculiar characteristics of the academic enterprise.

A clash of interests between the federal government and higher education characterizes a dispute over federal investigators' right, not only to inspect, but also to remove confidential personnel files from the Berkeley campus of the University of California in determining the university's compliance with federal antidiscrimination laws. The university was afraid that if the files were permanently maintained in federal offices they might be subject to access by other parties for other purposes under the public information provision and so lose their confidentiality. Nevertheless, a Labor Department official threatened that if the university did not comply with the department's insistence on removing the files, the Secretary of Labor would cancel immediately about 25 million dollars in contract funds and ultimately cut off a total of 75 million dollars that the Berkeley campus received in federal aid.

Just before the deadline the university and the Department of Labor came to an agreement that although files might be removed, they would be returned to the university upon the conclusion of the federal government's investigation for compliance review.[19]

One of the most recent examples of the federal government's demand for accountability was its regulation of DNA research. After an international group of 150 scientists met to discuss how DNA research should be conducted, the National Institutes of Health appointed a committee that promulgated regulations governing the safety of recombinant DNA research done with NIH funds. It was not long until a university faculty member experienced first hand the new strictures on DNA investigation. A bio-safety committee of the University of California at San Diego forbade a faculty member in biology to conduct any more cloning experiments after it was charged that he copied genetic material from a virus then banned from use in such investigations. The university's bio-safety committee reported its action to the National Institutes of Health and the NIH said that it would form a committee to study the university's report and consider what action it might take against the university or the professor.[20]*

It would be an exaggeration to say that research universities have become departments of federal and state government, but it is not too much to say that they have become more directly accountable to government agencies in manifold ways and that it has become difficult to distinguish governmental intervention in university affairs from *reasonable* governmental requirements for accountability. It is clear, however, that recent issues and events have

---

*The NIH Committee found the faculty member guilty of violating the federal guidelines. *(Daily Californian,* March 26, 1981.)

accelerated invasions of university autonomy. Senator Moynihan has gone so far as to say that "universities must now expect a long, for practical purposes permanent, regimen of pressure from the federal government to pursue this or that national purpose, purposes often at variance with the interests or inclinations of the universities themselves."[21]

Governmental Accountability of Private Institutions

Although governmental intervention, regulation, and incipient control of certain activities may threaten public more than private institutions of higher education, the latter are increasingly held accountable by governmental agencies. Private research universities, as are publicly supported ones, are accountable for the way in which they use federal grants. Furthermore, private institutions are required to comply with other federal regulations, such as those prohibiting discrimination in employment.[22] The Carnegie Council on Policy Studies in Higher Education recommended that "Financial aid to students should be the primary (though not necessarily the exclusive) vehicle for the channeling of state funds to private institutions."[23] Some state governments, however, do make direct grants to private colleges and universities. An Illinois commission recommended that as a means of avoiding government intervention in private higher institutions, direct state grants should be channeled to them in the form of contracts administered by the statewide coordinating board.[24]

JUDICIAL INTERVENTION

Recourse to the Courts

Increasingly intimate relationships between government and higher education mean that colleges and universities are in and of the world, not removed and protected from it. Toward the end of the period of student disruption on college campuses this writer observed:

> Judicial decisions and the presence on campus of the community police, the highway patrol, and the National Guard symbolize the fact that colleges and universities have increasingly lost the privilege of self-regulation to the external authority of the police and the courts. . . . it is apparent that colleges and universities have become increasingly accountable to the judicial systems of the community, the state, and the national government.[25]

A recent book on higher education and the law summarized legal conditions bearing on higher institutions and gave numerous examples of court decisions involving trustees, administrators, faculty members, and students, as well as cases involving relationships between institutions and both state and federal governments. Recourse to the courts to settle disputes has increased greatly during the past decade. Faculty members may sue over dismissal, appointment, tenure, and accessibility to personnel records. Students may sue to secure access to their records, over discrimination in admissions (e.g., the DeFunis case at the University of Washington and the Bakke case at the University of California in Davis), and over failure by an institution to deliver what it promised from the classroom and other academic resources. Institutions may take governments to court for the purpose of protecting their constitutional status and, as we have illustrated above, in contention over the enforcement of federal regulations.

The traditional aloofness of the campus has been shattered. Kaplin has pointed out the "Higher Education was often viewed as a unique enterprise which could regulate itself through reliance on tradition and consensual agreement. It operated best by operating autonomously, and it thrived on the privacy which autonomy afforded."[26] The college or university sanctuary was once considered to be a necessary means of protecting the institution and its constituencies from repressive external control and from invasions of intellectual freedom. Now other means must be devised to protect an institution's essential spirit while it bows to the world of law and tribunal.

ACCOUNTABILITY TO OTHER AGENCIES

Accountability to Coordinating Boards

Financial austerity, the need to diversify opportunities for higher education, governmental demands for accountability, and other influences have pushed decision making upward in the authority structure both internally and externally. In the course of this development, statewide governing and coordinating boards have come to play an influential, often critical, role in the evolution of higher education.

Three broad kinds of agencies have been organized for statewide or systemwide planning and coordination. These are (1) the advisory coordinating board, (2) the regulatory coordinating board, and (3) the consolidated governing board. In 1979 there were ten advisory boards, eighteen regulatory boards, and twenty consolidated governing boards.[27] Consolidated governing boards are powerful bodies. Regulatory coordinating boards, with which we are mainly concerned here, have also become influential agencies. Where does the coordinating board fall between institutions or systems and the state government? Millett, who once served as chancellor of the Ohio Board of Regents, a statewide coordinating board, believes that such an agency is a part of state government and as such "will inevitably be identified primarily with state government officials and processes," while the consolidated governing board is identified with state institutions of higher education.[28]

Another view of the status and function of statewide coordinating boards is that they should not be "identified primarily with state government officials and processes," as Millet asserts,[29] but that they should be "suspended at a strategic—and extremely sensitive—point between the institutions and sectors, on the one hand, and the public and its political representatives, on the other." The function of coordinating boards as intermediaries has been expressed as follows:

> Coordinating agencies have the responsibility of helping protect institutions (and sectors) from ill-advised influences and incursions by the legislative and executive branches of government and from unwise public pressures, and the responsibility of leading the system of higher education to serve demonstrable and appropriate public needs—all the while retaining the confidence of both sides.[30]

This view brings the nature of the coordinating board more nearly to that of the consolidated governing board, although the latter will in most cases be more intimately identified with the institutions. The primary function of coordinating boards is to plan the development of higher education in their states in cooperation with institutions of postsecondary education and their basic constituencies. Then, according to Glenny, the board should provide a thorough analysis and evaluation of systemwide or statewide academic programs in relation to long-range strategy. Proposed budgets should be appraised in relation to educational priorities, differential institutional functions, and relevant allocation of financial resources.[31] Thus the boards may exert their influence and authority by holding institutions or systems accountable for the effective performance of the functions for which they have accepted responsibility. Dressel has declared that coordination is here to stay and that it will continue to confront institutions of higher education with issues of autonomy and sometimes debatable requirements for accountability.[32]

Accountability to Accrediting Agencies

Accreditation is a process for holding postsecondary institutions accountable to voluntary agencies for meeting certain minimum educational standards. Recently, however, both federal and state governments have entered this arena too.

Institutional and program accreditation are the two types usually noted. Six regional agencies are responsible for accrediting entire institutions with their schools, departments, academic programs, and related activities. Program accreditation, extended by professional societies or other groups of specialists or vocational associations, is extended to a specific school, department, or academic program in such fields as medicine, law, social work, chemistry, engineering, or business administration. A variation is an agency for accrediting single-purpose institutions, such as trade and technical schools. These kinds of accrediting bodies are independent, voluntary agencies. A recent list includes nearly seventy such accrediting bodies.[33]

Two of the principal factors that have brought accreditation to the fore in discussions of accountability are the consumer movement and the allocation of state and federal aid to postsecondary education. Certain federal laws require the secretary of education to publish a list of nationally recognized agencies considered to be "reliable" evaluators of academic quality as a basis for distributing federal aid. An account of the federal government's attitude toward voluntary accrediting bodies recently noted that the head of the Division of Eligibility and Agency Evaluation of the U.S. Department of Education had urged that federal oversight of accreditation should be strengthened. "Stressing the need for greater public accountability," said the report, "he and his supporters say it is more important than ever for the government to know how its money is being spent, especially in light of some institutions' widely reported abuses in handling student-aid funds."[34] Representatives of higher education, on the other hand, have urged that instead of using its own criteria for identifying acceptable accrediting agencies, the federal bureau should use those proposed by the Council on Postsecondary Accreditation, an organization of voluntary accrediting agencies.

In the meantime, state governments have become parties to the debate as they determine eligibility for state aid to both public and private postsecondary institutions. Most states charter and license degree-granting institutions, but some observers believe that in most instances the standards specified are insufficient to assure quality. At its annual meeting in 1979 the Education Commission of the States declared that the states should establish minimum standards for all postsecondary institutions.

ACCOUNTABILITY FOR STUDENT DEVELOPMENT

A Complicated Process

It is apparent that educational institutions are increasingly to be held answerable for the attainment of their professed goals in the form of demonstrable changes in students. Bowen had declared that "The idea of accountability in higher education is quite simple. It means that colleges and universities are responsible for conducting their affairs so that the outcomes are worth the cost."[35] This view may be simple in conception, but it is also extremely difficult in implementation. First of all, it is difficult but essential to translate goals into relevant outcomes. An even more complicated task is to devise means of determining the extent to which students have attained these outcomes. The first question to be asked is, how has the student changed at a given point in relation to his characteristics at entrance? This requires information on how students vary at the starting point, not only in previous academic achievement, but in general and special academic aptitude; intellectual dispositions, such as a theoretical or pragmatic orientation; and interests, attitudes, values, and motivations, to mention only some of the dimensions of personality that are relevant to the educational process. These attributes not only establish base lines for estimating the amount of change over stated periods, but some of them are indicative of students' educability.

Studies of the influence of institutions on student development also require means of measuring or describing college characteristics, "the prevailing atmosphere, the social and intellectual climate, the style of a campus," as well as "educational treatments."[36] One of the complications involved in describing college environments is that student characteristics and institutional qualities are by no means unrelated. Student attributes are significant determinations of institutional character. Furthermore, most institutions are not all of a piece and the "total environment" may have less influence on particular students than the suborganizations or subcultures of which they are members.

It is even more difficult to determine the impact of the environment on students. I have mentioned some of the difficulties elsewhere:

> First, environmental variables probably do not act singly, but in combination. Second, changes which occur in students may not be attributable to the effect of the college environment itself. Developmental processes established early in the individual's experience may continue through the college years; some of these processes take place normally within a wide range of environmental conditions, and in order to alter the course and extent of development, it would be necessary to introduce fairly great changes in environmental stimulation. Third, changes which occur during the college years may be less the effect of college experience as such than of the general social environment in which the college exists and the students live.[37]

For these and many other reasons it is extremely difficult to relate changes in behavior to specific characteristics of the college or to particular patterns of educational activity.

Studies of change in students' characteristics have revealed wide differences from person to person and detectable differences from institution to institution. One example, an investigation of changes in intellectual orientation, has been summarized as follows:

> An index of intellectual disposition was constructed from the following tests of the Omnibus Personality Inventory: thinking introversion, theoretical orientation, estheticism, complexity, autonomy, and religious liberalism. Students' scores on the index were distributed among eight categories. At one extreme (categories 1-3) were students with broad intellectual and esthetic interests, openness to new ideas, intellectual independence, and sufficient freedom from traditional patterns

of thought to permit imaginative and creative responses. Students at the opposite extreme (categories 6-8) had little interest in ideas, were more concerned with the concrete and practical than the general and abstract, were relatively more conventional and less flexible in their thinking, and had few if any artistic interests. We studied differential change in intellectual disposition in eight institutions that embraced a wide range of both student and institutional characteristics. Three colleges—Antioch, Reed, and Swarthmore—were highly selective, small, residential, elite institutions. Three church-related institutions—St. Olaf, the University of the Pacific, and the University of Portland—were in the sample. . . . St. Olaf and the University of Portland had relatively close connections with their sponsoring denominations. The sample was rounded out by two large public institutions, San Francisco State and the University of California at Berkeley.

With the exceptions of Reed (where the proportion of freshmen in the three top categories was so large that little change was possible) and the University of Portland, there were higher proportions of seniors than freshmen in the highest three categories at all institutions. Thus, one could conclude that the world of ideas was more appealing to seniors than to freshmen. . . . Twenty-four percent of Swarthmore students (the largest proportion among the eight institutions) shifted from categories 6-8 to categories 1-3. The colleges with the next largest proportions were Antioch and St. Olaf (8 percent). The percentage change at Reed was zero, but there were only nine students in the three bottom categories as freshmen. Of the seventy-six students who could have changed at the University of Portland, only 1 percent did so.[38]

Bowen has summarized the evidence on changes in students in both cognitive and noncognitive outcomes, and also differences in the effects of different institutions. "On the whole," he wrote, "the evidence supports the hypothesis that the differences in impact are relatively small—when impact is defined as value added in the form of change in students during the college years."[39] Nevertheless, institutions are accountable for stimulating the development of students in ways which give evidence that colleges and universities have attained their professed goals in reasonable measure.

To date, the research on changes in students has been done mainly in undergraduate education. Fundamental studies on the attainment of outcomes also need to be made in professional and graduate education, as well as in research and public service. Bowen has discussed at some length the social benefits that flow from professional training and the social outcomes from research and public service. He also has emphasized the interaction of liberal and professional studies, and the contribution of research and public service to education of various kinds and levels. Learning is an integrated process which may involve scholarship, investigation, and the relationship of knowledge to personal enrichment and social welfare.[40] Although the definition and measurement of outcomes are especially difficult at higher educational levels and the environmental forces involved are hard to determine, studies of student development in such fields as professional training, graduate education, and research should be pursued.

Educational Costs

After summarizing the available evidence on the outcomes of higher education, Bowen observed that "a tidy dollar comparison of costs and benefits is
conspicuously absent." However, he summarized the financial value of higher
education as follows:

> First, the monetary returns from higher education alone are probably sufficient
> to offset all the costs. Second, the nonmonetary returns are several times as
> valuable as the monetary returns. And third, the total returns from higher edu-
> cation in all its aspects exceed the cost by several times.[41]

It is usually said that institutions should be accountable for both effectiveness and efficiency, the latter having to do with the cost of the outcomes
attained. But costs are extremely difficult to compute in analyzing differences
in student change both within and among institutions. And, as pointed out
above, it is extremely difficult to relate changes to significant features of
educational environments. Nevertheless, as enrollments in postsecondary education level off or decline, institutions will be increasingly held accountable
for the attainment of goals inherent in their assigned or professed missions.
"Accountability accentuates results," wrote Mortimer, "it aims squarely at
what comes out of an educational system rather than what goes into it."[42]
Perhaps it would be more telling to say that accountability aims squarely at
what comes out of an educational system *in relation to what goes into it.* The
outcomes to be attained must be more explicitly defined and the means of
determining accomplishment must be more expertly devised. Then resources
must be distributed among institutions and among academic services in ac-
cordance with chosen educational values and defensible costs of their attainment. Bowen has made a significant contribution to the analysis of institutional costs including expenditures per student, cost differences among institutions, and the implications of cost data for administrative policies and decisions.[43] But we have a long way to go before sound means of determining
cost-effectiveness are developed.

SUMMARY

Although autonomy cannot be absolute, only a high degree of independence
will permit colleges and universities to devise and choose effective academic
means of realizing their professed goals. First of all, institutions must assure
academic freedom to faculty and students. Autonomy does not guarantee
intellectual independence, but some forms of external intervention, overt or
covert, may undermine such freedom.

While intellectual fetters must be decisively opposed, institutions may legitimately be expected to be held accountable to their constituencies for the integrity, and so far as possible, for the efficiency of their operations. Colleges and universities are answerable to the general public, which supports them and needs their services. Responding to the public interest, federal and state governments are increasingly intervening in institutional affairs. At times government pressure may induce an institution to offer appropriate services; at other times government agencies may attempt to turn an institution, or even a system, in inappropriate directions. Only constructive consultation, and requirements for accountability that recognize the fundamental characteristics of academe will effectively serve the public interest and give vitality to the educational enterprise.

Most institutions, including those supported by legislatures, are not immediately controlled by the general public. Public accountability is mediated by several layers of representation. Institutions are directly answerable to their governing boards. They may be responsible to a consolidated governing board. They may be first responsible to institutional or systemwide governing boards, and these in turn may be in certain regards under surveillance of statewide coordinating boards. Institutions thus may be controlled by a hierarchy of agencies, an arrangement that may complicate their procedures for accountability, but provide a measure of protection from unwise or unnecessary external intervention.

Colleges and universities are moving into a period when they will be expected to provide, not only data on the attainment of defined outcomes, including changes in students during undergraduate, graduate, and professional education, but evidence that results have been gained at "reasonable" cost. Institutions of higher education will have to specify their aims, stand ready to justify activities by demonstrating their contribution to objectives, and defend the cost of the enterprise.

NOTES

1. Peter Venables, *Higher Education Developments: The Technological Universities 1956-1976* (London: Faber and Faber, 1978), 305.

2. Howard R. Bowen, *Investment in Learning* (San Francisco: Jossey-Bass, 1977), 12.

3. Robert O. Berdahl, *Statewide Coordination of Higher Education* (Washington, D.C.: American Council on Education, 1971), 5.

4. Paul L. Dressel, ed., *The Autonomy of Public Colleges* (San Francisco: Jossey-Bass, 1980), 13.

5. Ibid., 5.

6. Ibid., 96.

7. National Commission on Research, *Accountability: Restoring the Quality of the Partnership* (Washington, D.C., 1980), 17.

8. C. J. Hitch, "Remarks of the President" (Address delivered to the Assembly of the California Academic Senate, Berkeley, Calif., June 15, 1970).

9. Lyman A. Glenny and Thomas K. Dalglish, *Public Universities, State Agencies, and the Law: Constitutional Autonomy in Decline* (Berkeley, Calif.: University of California, Center for Research and Development in Higher Education, 1973), 42.

10. Ibid., 143.

11. Burton R. Clark, "The Insulated Americans: Five Lessons from Abroad," *Change* 10 (November 1978), 30.

12. *San Francisco Chronicle,* 23 September 1980.

13. John W. Lederle, "Governors and Higher Education," in *State Politics and Higher Education,* ed. Leonard E. Goodall (Dearborn, Mich.: University of Michigan, 1976), 43-50.

14. Paul L. Dressel, *Autonomy of Public Colleges,* 40.

15. Ibid., 43.

16. Robert O. Berdahl, "Legislative Program Evaluation," in *Increasing the Public Accountability of Higher Education,* ed. John K. Folger (San Francisco: Jossey-Bass, 1977), 35-65.

17. Ibid.

18. National Commission on Research, *Accountability,* 3.

19. Letter from Chancellor Ira Michael Heyman to the members of the Berkeley faculty, 2 October 1980.

20. *Chronicle of Higher Education,* 21, September 8, 1980.

21. Daniel Patrick Moynihan, "State vs. Academe," *Harpers* 261 (December 1980), 31-40.

22. Robert O. Berdahl, "The Politics of State Aid," in *Public Money and Private Higher Education,* ed. David W. Breneman and Chester E. Finn, Jr. (Washington, D.C.: Brookings Institution, 1978), 321-352.

23. Carnegie Council on Policy Studies in Higher Education, *The States and Private Higher Education* (San Francisco: Jossey-Bass, 1977), 63.

24. Commission to Study Nonpublic Higher Education in Illinois, *Strengthening Private Higher Education in Illinois: A Report on the State's Role* (Springfield, Ill.: Board of Higher Education, 1969).

25. T. R. McConnell, "Accountability and Autonomy" *Journal of Higher Education* 42 (June 1971), 446-463.

26. William A. Kaplin, *The Law of Higher Education* (San Francisco: Jossey-Bass, 1978), 4.

27. Elizabeth French and Robert Berdahl, *Who Guards the Guardians?* Occasional Papers Series, Department of Higher Education, State University of New York at Buffalo, 1980, 3.

28. John D. Millett, "Statewide Coordinating Boards and Statewide Governing Boards," in *Evaluating Statewide Boards,* ed. Robert O. Berdahl (San Francisco: Jossey-Bass, 1975), 61-70.

29. Ibid., 70.

30. Kenneth P. Mortimer and T. R. McConnell, *Sharing Authority Effectively* (San Francisco: Jossey-Bass, 1978), 225.

31. Lyman A. Glenny, *State Budgeting for Higher Education: Interagency Conflict and Consensus* (Berkeley: Center for Research and Development in Higher Education, University of California, 1976), 148-150.

32. Paul L. Dressel, *Autonomy of Public Colleges,* 99-100.

33. *Chronicle of Higher Education* 20 (June 16, 1980).

34. Ibid.

35. Howard R. Bowen, "The Products of Higher Education," in *Evaluating Institutions for Accountability,* ed. Howard R. Bowen (San Francisco: Jossey-Bass, 1974), 1-26.

36. C. R. Pace, "When Students Judge Their College," *College Board Review* 58 (Spring 1960), 26-28.

37. T. R. McConnell, "Accountability and Autonomy."

38. Ibid.

39. Howard R. Bowen, *Investment in Learning,* 257. Other evidence on changes in students over the college years is presented in Alexander W. Astin, *Four Critical Years* (San Francisco: Jossey-Bass, 1977).

40. Howard R. Bowen, *Investment in Learning.*

41. Ibid., 447-448.

42. Kenneth P. Mortimer, *Accountability in Higher Education* (Washington, D.C.: American Association for Higher Education, 1972), 6.

43. Howard R. Bowen, *The Costs of Higher Education* (San Francisco: Jossey-Bass, 1980).

4

Academic Freedom in Delocalized Academic Institutions

Walter P. Metzger

EDITOR'S NOTE: This essay, written in 1969, provides a relevant historical perspective to many of the issues discussed in this volume. We reprint it because the issues it raises are so relevant to contemporary debates and because it considers how American higher education developed at a crucial historical period.

The gist of the argument that follows is that the theory of academic freedom as it has been articulated in this country has become, in critical respects, outmoded. By this I do not mean to imply that the value of academic freedom has diminished; it is not only relevant to the modern university, but essential to it—the one grace that institution may not lose without losing everything. A theory of academic freedom, however, goes beyond an affirmation of its value to a description of the forces and conditions that place this desired thing in peril, and a prescription of the norms and strategies that may offset those specific threats. It is in this latter sense, as a mode of analysis and advice concerning the realities of social power, that I believe the inherited canon has, to a large degree, outlived its day.

One should not suppose that the American theory of academic freedom owes its staleness to senescence. Though it draws on an ancient legacy of assumptions, it did not become crystalized in this country until as late as 1915, when Arthur O. Lovejoy of The Johns Hopkins University, E. R. A. Seligman and John Dewey of Columbia University, and a number of other academic luminaries wrote the *General Report on Academic Freedom and Academic Tenure* for the newly founded American Association of University Professors. To call this report a classic is to comment on its quality, not its venerableness—a document only two generations old hardly qualifies as an-

Reprinted with permission from Walter P. Metzger, et al., *Dimensions of Academic Freedom* (Urbana, Ill.: University of Illinois Press, 1969), pp. 1-33.

tique. But a short period in the life span of ideas may constitute a millennium in the time scale of institutions, especially American institutions, which have been known to change at breakneck speeds. What has happened in the half-century since 1915 is that American universities have been remodeled while the ideas once consonant with them have not. The result has been a growing discrepancy between milieu and theory—an ever widening culture lag.

By the lights of 1915, a violation of academic freedom was a crime designed and executed within the confines of the university. Dissident professors were the victims, trustees and administrators were the culprits, the power of dismissal was the weapon, the loss of employment was the wound. Concentrating on this stage and scenario, the authors of the 1915 statement concluded that the key to crime prevention lay in the adoption of regulations that would heighten the security of the office-holder and temper the arbitrariness of the "boss." So persuaded, they persuaded others, and in time these institutional regulations, known as academic tenure and due process, came to be widely adopted if not always faultlessly applied. It should be noted, however, that by defining a violation of academic freedom as something that happens *in* a university, rather than as something that happens *to* a university, these writers ignored a set of issues that had caused their foreign counterparts much concern. Nothing was said in this document about the relations of the academy to state authority. Except for brief allusions to the class obsessions of wealthy donors and the populistic foibles of local legislators, nothing was said about the external enemies of the university, though history made available such impressive candidates as the meddlesome minister of education, the inquisitorial church official, the postal guardian of public morals, the intruding policeman, and the biased judge. Finally, nothing was said about threats to the autonomy of the university that were not, at one and the same time, threats to the livelihood of its members; indeed, it was not even clearly acknowledged that a corporate academic interest, as distinct from an individual academic's interest, existed and had also to be preserved. In short, 1915's criminology (and the criminology operative today—cf. the policing efforts of Committee A of the AAUP) was wise to the ways of the harsh employer, but it lacked a theory and vocabulary for dealing with the outside offender and the nonoccupational offense.

Along with this definition of the crime went a recommended rule of good behavior: a university, the report declared, should never speak as an official body on matters of doctrine or public policy. In the lengthy history of universities this gospel of institutional restraint had not had many preachers or practitioners. Indeed, there were many more examples of commitment: e.g., the adherence of the continental universities after the Reformation to the confessional preferences of the local rulers, the involvement of Oxford and Cambridge in the dynastic struggles of Tudor England, the proselytizing efforts of the church-built colleges in America prior to the Civil War. The authors of the 1915 statement took aim at this tradition by attacking some of its basic premises: that truth is something to be possessed rather than end-lessly discovered; that truth-questions yield to the edicts of institutions rather than to the competitive play of minds. Intellectual inquiry, they insisted, had to be ongoing and individual; organizational fiats defeat it because organiza-tions are mightier than individuals and fiats are inevitably premature. In support of their brief for neutrality they likened the true university to an "intellectual experiment station" where new ideas might safely germinate, to an "inviolable refuge" where men of ideas might safely congregate, and—most simply—to a "home for research." By no stretch of analogy was the modern university to be considered a missionary society, a propaganda agency, an arm of a political party: it was a residence, a hothouse, a sanctuary—the figures of speech were adoring, but they left the university with nothing of substance to proclaim.

How was this no-substance rule to be effectuated; what were the means to this lack of ends? Here our near-yet-distant academic forefathers made another enduring contribution. Conceivably they could have argued, taking a cue from the independent newspaper with its balanced display of editorials, that an academic institution achieves neutrality by appointing men of varying opinions to its faculty. Or they could have argued, with an eye on the renunciative code of conduct common in the military and civil service, that an academic institution achieves neutrality by prohibiting its members from speaking out on public issues, especially on those foreign to their specialties. Significantly, the authors of the AAUP report did not accept either of these possibilities, but instead set forth a formula possibly suggested by the eco-nomic market: let the university disown responsibility for everything its mem-bers say or publish and then let it permit its members to say and publish what they please. This formula, which was to be made more explicit in later decretals, had obvious advantages over the others. Neutrality by disownment was easier to administer than neutrality by selection, harder to abuse than neutrality by proscription. But it also created a peculiar asymmetry: it as-serted, in effect, that professors had the right to express opinions but that their colleges and universities did not.

By including the concept of personal freedom under the rubric of aca-demic freedom, these writers made their doctrine even more asymmetrical. Traditionally, academic freedom had merely offered on-the-job protection: freedom of teaching and research. These, it had been supposed, were the main arenas where professors exhibited special competence and where they deserved a special latitude; beyond lay a terrain of utterance which professors, like any other citizens, were presumed to enter at their own risk. The authors of the 1915 report would not accept such zonal ordinances. Academic free-dom, they asserted, protects professors in all of their identities—as teachers, scholars, scientists, citizens, experts, consultants—and on every sort of plat-form. It applies not to a category of speech but to a category of persons.

The first and most important thing to be said about the college or university of 1915 was that it possessed and exercised impressive powers within a demarcated area. This attribute, which I shall call its "localness," derived in part from the clarity of that demarcation. The lands of the college of that period usually made up a contiguous property and were often marked off by fences that kept the students in corral and warned the outsider of the line of trespass. Usually they were located in sequestered regions either on the outskirts of major cities or in the bucolic settings of college towns. Spatially these institutions lived apart, and this apartness contributed to their autonomy.

In addition to acreage and location, style and organization fostered localness. Administratively, with the exception of a shrinking number of ecclesiastically controlled institutions, each unit was entirely discrete, with its own board of regents or trustees, its own executive figure, its own sublieutenancy of deans, its own budget, its own rules and regulations. Legally each was endowed by charter or statute with a vast amount of discretionary authority. Extensive in the management of property, that authority was virtually without limit when it came to the regulation of persons. In 1915 neither outside law nor internal dissonances restrained the exercise of student discipline. It was common in those days for students to live under rules they did not fashion and to be expelled for infractions without a trial. When students asked the courts to intervene they usually were disappointed, the courts generally taking the position that students had, by implied or explicit contract, consigned themselves to the mercies—quasi-parental and therefore tender—of those who had initially let them in. It should not be supposed that students submitted gladly to this regimen. The annals of these institutions disclose too many revels in the springtime, too many rebellions in the fall and winter, to support the view that, uniquely in America, 18 to 22 were the docile years. Yet it is also clear that few in this febrile population challenged the legitimacy of that regimen. Students sought to outfox, not unseat, their elders; they made a game of the rules, but accepted the rules of the game. This kind of popular acquiescence, together with the virtual absence of serious judicial review, gave the academy the appearance of a foreign enclave, ruling indigenous peoples with laws of its own devising, enjoying a kind of extraterritoriality within the larger state.

Of course institutions calling themselves academic came in many different shapes and sizes. The grandest institutions of the period—those that had gathered into their custody the tools of modern scholarship and research—were much more involved with the world around them than colleges that were little more than *écoles*. But the worldliness of the Harvards and Wisconsins did not yet undercut their localness. For one thing, research tools were on the Edison scale of cost: Brookhaven magnitudes were not yet imagined. By means of the usual fund drives and appropriations, these institutions could sustain the cost internally and thus keep control of what their members did and spent. For another thing, the scholars and scientists they assembled were still burdened with heavy academic duties. At this point in time, while there were many teachers who did no research, there were practically no researchers who did not teach—and teach assiduously and regularly. In a much more than *pro forma* sense, men who worked *in* the university also worked *for* the university and were responsive to its interests and requirements.

Even in their transactions with their patrons the colleges and universities of 1915 had a great deal of decisional independence. It is a convention of academic history to deny this, to conclude from their chronic neediness, their perennial courting of the legislatures, their incessant wooing of potential donors, that they were the most obsequious of creatures. But I suspect that those who assert this take as their implicit model of comparison the English university of the nineteenth century, an institution that owed its aplomb and self-reliance to ancient clerical endowments, enormous property holdings, and the privileges of the class it served. Without that invidious comparison, the American college would seem to have been made of sterner stuff. For one thing, the bulk of collegiate instruction was still going on in private institutions which, despite many resemblances to the public ones, had a narrower constituency to account to, and far more discretion in defining that constituency. Some were dependent on very rich patrons, and not the braver for it; still, very often, behind the captains of industry who invested fortunes in universities, there would be a charismatic president who told them how their money should be spent. In the public sector, the whims of the men who held the purse strings had to be catered to more consistently, and presidents of state institutions were often chosen for that capacity. Yet even here the processes of negotiation that took place between legislators and administrators left considerable discretion in local hands. Members of appropriations committees seldom developed the educational expertise needed to initiate novel policies. Far from being sources of innovation, these committees were political arenas where administrators would bargain with their counterparts for public monies and where the essential educational decisions would concern the division of the take. Nor was there much regulation of the system, either in the public or the private areas. Large-scale private philanthropy, though it had worked important reforms in such limited fields as medical education, was not yet a ubiquitous improver; agencies for self-regulation, like the regional accrediting associations, tended to be self-protective bodies, shielding the run-of-the-mill establishment against its fly-by-night competitor. Far less than in railroads or in banking were the firms in academe made to conform to specific standards. And the reason for this is not hard to find. Serving a small segment of the population, not yet central to the economy, taken more seriously for its fun and frolics than for its earnest devotions, the college or university of 1915 was regarded as a public ornament and curiosity, not yet as a public utility.

Above all—and this is what makes the period seem an age of innocence, our own academic *belle epoque*—the organs of the central state were not intrusive. For years the federal government had given land to universities without conditions, or had laid down conditions (e.g., the furtherance of agriculture and technology) without imposing very strict controls. In 1915 Washington did not even have an apparatus for dealing systematically with academe. The federal interest in education, which was at that time almost negligible, could be contained in a lowly Bureau of Education whose primary task was to get statistics; the federal interest in (nonagricultural) science, which was even at that time quite considerable, could be met by governmental agencies like the Geological Survey and the Naval Observatory, and did not impinge on the universities. Americans tended to attribute this phenomenon—substantial federal assistance without a significant federal presence—to the genius of their Constitution and their history. Doubtless a literal reading of the Tenth Amendment, plus the hold of Jeffersonian prejudices, did erect barriers to state intrusion. Where such barriers did not exist, as in Great Britain in the nineteenth century, universities felt much more statist pressure. Thus, for all their vaunted independence, Oxford and Cambridge were compelled to submit to extensive changes suggested by royal commissions in the 1850s and 1870s and enforced by parliamentary decrees. But there was still another explanation, albeit one less visible to contemporaries, for the special state of American affairs. In large part our federal government was undemanding simply because it had no urgent demands to make. A nation that had just entered world politics but had not yet become a world power, that lived in the Edenic security of a miniscule army and a safe frontier, lacked one of the principal motives for intermeddling—the motive of martial necessity. Let that motive be supplied, as it would in a future far more imminent than most Americans in 1915 could foresee, and the central state would not scruple to lay a levy on the spirit of the university, as well as on its faculties and young men. Full recognition of this came in 1918 when, on behalf of a country mobilized and gladiatorial, the Congress transformed every college male into a soldier, every college dormitory into a barracks, every college lawn into a training ground under the aegis of the Secretary of War. The Student Army Training Corps, like the agencies of propaganda filled with scholars, was decried as a folly and an aberration as soon as World War I closed. But at the outbreak of World War II the academic system was once more militarized, and this time the marriage of Mars and Minerva would not only be solemnized but preserved.

It is not very difficult to see why the authors of the 1915 statement on academic freedom ignored the macrocosm of society and concentrated on the smaller campus world. It was there that significant things could happen. A college or university was then no mere appendage of government, no mere component in a great machine. It was a unit of considerable completeness, an agency possessed of powers that were almost governmental in kind. It suggested a checkerboard view of power and a concept of academic freedom that was equally sectioned and discrete.

So much for the general bias of the theory. To account for its specific arguments one has to note another feature of the system: its capacity to generate within each unit an inordinate amount of status strain. This was the period when the academic profession came of age: when it came to think of itself as specialized, competent, and scientific; when it sought to act as mentor to society on a wide range of social issues; when it demanded the deference and the courtesy that befitted these pretensions and that role. It happened, however, that this was also the period when many academic trustees and administrators adopted a style of management that conceded little to these demands. Derived from the views and manners of prerogative-minded business managers, falling between an older authoritarianism with its familial emphasis and a yet-to-come bureaucratism with its codes and forms, the style struck many professors as both overweening and capricious, and in any case hostile to their status claims.

An example of the irritating potential of this new managerial psychology can be found in one of the earliest academic freedom cases investigated by the AAUP. In 1915 the Board of Trustees of the University of Pennsylvania dismissed the economist Scott Nearing on grounds they refused to disclose. (The evidence is all but conclusive that they took exception to his opinions, which were radical then, but not yet Marxist.) In explaining why he did not have to explain, George Wharton Pepper, a prominent trustee of the university, said: "If I am dissatisfied with my secretary, I suppose I would be within my rights in terminating his employment." Was, then, a professor simply a clerk? an amanuensis? The chancellor of Syracuse was willing to concede that he was more than that, that he dealt in some fashion with ideas. Still, this administrator did not believe that the creative function of the professor gave him leave to oppose the man who signed his check. The dismissal of Nearing, Chancellor Day believed, was entirely proper. "That is what would happen to an editorial writer of *The Tribune* if he were to disregard the things for which the paper stands. . . ." Were, then, the trustees of a university, like the publishers of a newspaper, the formal proprietors of the property? The editors of the New York *Times,* in choosing not to go so far, offered their own enlightening treatise on academic relationships in America. As they saw it, the university belonged to the donors, who were its fount of wisdom and ideology *in saecula saeculorum;* the trustees were the agents of the donors, charged with the execution of that immortal claim. Professors? They were simply spoilsports, ever ready, under the academic freedom cover, to ask for privileges they never bought:

> Men who through toil and ability have got together enough money to endow universities or professors' chairs do not generally have it in mind that their money should be spent for the dissemination of the dogmas of Socialism or in the teaching of ingenuous youth how to live without work. Yet when Trustees conscientiously endeavor to carry out the purposes of the founder by taking

proper measures to prevent misuse of the endowment, we always hear a loud howl about academic freedom.

We see no reason why the upholders of academic freedom in this sense should not establish a university of their own. Let them provide the funds, erect the buildings, lay out the campus, and then make a requisition on the padded cells of Bedlam for their teaching staff. Nobody would interfere with the full freedom of professors; they could teach Socialism and shiftlessness until Doomsday without restraint.

Among the changes wrought by time has been the departure of this kind of liveliness from the editorial pages of the New York *Times*.

Cast in general terms, the report of the AAUP professors did not seem to stoop to rebuttal. Yet these Gothic business doctrines shaped the contours of its major themes. The norm of institutional neutrality was not just an ethicist's abstraction: it was a denial of the proprietary claims of trustees, donors, and their spokesmen. The widening of the zone of academic freedom was not simply a reflex of libertarianism: it was an effort to reduce the sphere in which philistine administrators could take action. And the notion that men were in conflict with their organizations—and that this conflict drew the battle lines of freedom—stemmed only in part from an individualistic ethos: it also expressed the viewpoint of a profession whose institutional existence offered too meager status gains. For all its transcendent qualities, the 1915 report was a tract developed for its times.

The times, I submit, have changed. Not everywhere, not in all respects. A small denominational college may still look as it looked in 1915. A major university may still be living off the precedents set long ago. Here and there a donor may still wish to establish an ideology in the course of establishing a schoolroom, or a trustee may still be tempted to utter the platitude of possession. But at the height where one loses particulars and gains synopsis one can see enormous transformations. Of these, one of the most important has been the flow of decisional power from authorities on the campus to those resident outside. Richer, larger, more complex than ever before, the typical modern institution of higher learning is less self-directive than ever before. It has become, to coin a word, "delocalized," with consequences we are just beginning to perceive.

Delocalization has not been a single process but a congeries of processes, all working in the same direction and achieving a common end. The engulfing of many universities by the central city, with the result that everything that they do in the way of land use becomes imbued with political implications and ensnarled in municipal law, is one delocalizing process. The growth of bureaucratized philanthropy as a principle source of academic innovation, the subordination of the judgment of admissions officers to legislative judgments concerning civil rights, the involvement of universities in social welfare and thus with clients it can serve but not control, may be considered others. And so too may the integration of public higher education, the assault on the principle of extraterritoriality, and the enlargement of federal influence due to federal sponsorship of research. These latter processes are so important, both in affecting the character of academic institutions and the viability of the academic freedom theory, that I should like to examine each in some detail.

In 1915 only two states attempted to coordinate the activities of their tax-supported institutions of higher learning. By 1965 only nine states let their state university, land-grant colleges, technical institutes, and teachers' colleges go their separate ways. The trend, moreover, has not only been toward greater coordination but also toward higher degrees of integration. By 1965 as many as fifteen states had given superordinate public bodies the power to alter and create new schools by plan. SUNY, the gigantic State University of New York, was established in 1949 to take charge of forty-six existing public institutions and to set up as many new ones as its over-all blueprint would prescribe. By current reckoning the California Master Plan brings seventy-six junior colleges, eighteen state colleges, and a nine-campus university under the sway of dovetailing central bodies. In the coordinated systems the power of central bodies may be limited to reviewing budgets and programs initiated by the institutions themselves. In the more integrated systems the off-campus boards of control may make decisions on capital investment and tuition levels, architectural design and new site locations, entrance requirements and degree capacities, while the on-campus boards and administrations may make decisions on how those decisions will be carried out. These vertical and horizontal combinations of plants in similar and diverse lines, these unequal allocations of power between the central office and the local branch, this division of territorial markets state by state, make the integrated academic organization and the modern business corporation seem very much alike, if not of kin. And these resemblances are not lost on the faculties they appoint. If we are employed by the educational duplicate of General Motors or United States Steel, some of them seem to be saying, let us be responsive to that reality: let us elect a single bargaining agent to match the collective strength of management; let us fight for our economic interests without the constraints of a service ethos; let us, if need be, strike. Localized institutions tended to generate professional resentment, but delocalized institutions seem to eviscerate professional élan.

The rationalization of public higher education proceeds from three demands that are made upon it: (1) that it accommodate vast enrollments; (2) that it stimulate economic enterprise; (3) that it accomplish both objectives at something less than crushing public cost. These very demands speak eloquently of the new importance that has come to be attached to this activity. So high is the putative correlation between income earned and degree awarded that a college education has become compulsory, not by the edict of law but by the mandate of ambition. So close is the symbiosis of productive industry on the knowledge industry, so glaring is the cheek-by-jowl abutment of technological parks and college greens, that the advertised presence of a campus has become, next to tax abatements, a primary lure to new investment. Private higher education has grown as a consequence of these connections, but public higher education has grown much faster, so that today it enrolls almost two-thirds of all academic students, and is much more heavily subsidized, receiving one hundred dollars in tax money for every thirty-five dollars its private competitors receive in gifts. With the change in the public-private balance, the old popular affection for the small-scale venturer has given way to a quest for tax economies, and the alleged efficiencies of central planning is urged successfully even in staid legislative halls. What had once been regarded as a mere propaedeutic enterprise has thus become, in the course of time, a key to the life chances of everyone, an object of urgent public policy, and a stimulant to the GNP. New layers of relevance have been added; but in the process the old attribute of localness has been stripped away.

The assault on extraterritoriality—the second delocalizing process—engages another set of forces, at work both in the private and public sectors, both on the campuses and beyond. On the campuses the assault is being mounted by a new generation of student radicals: white revolutionaries and Negro militants, advocates of more effective student power, persons lonely in their alienations or drawn into dissentient subcultures—the varied student cadres that distinguish the convulsive present from the prankish and catatonic past. Each group has its own visions and motivations, as can be seen from the instability of their alliances; and none is yet numerically dominant in any student body in the land. But they are increasingly becoming a powerful, pace-setting minority and they share, amid all their differences, a common animus against the discipline which their predecessors did not oppose. Different groups issue different challenges to that discipline. Advocates of student power dispute the validity of rules that are made for but not by the student client; theirs is a constitutional challenge aimed, as are all the challenges of emergent classes, at the habit and principle of exclusion. Partisans of the New Left break the rules to change the policies these rules facilitate; theirs is a tactical challenge aimed, as are all radical challenges, at the going morality of ends and means. At times these challenges overreach their mark. The breaking of certain rules may mean the disruption of the operations of the university, which may require the intercession of police forces and the use of violence on a massive scale. The end of this chain of consequences is a greater loss of internal authority than any may have anticipated or approved. The surrender of the administration to the harsh protectorship of policemen is often more costly to its authority than the precipitating student offense. On the other hand, only the most Sorelian of student radicals could delight in all aspects of this denouement: the substitution of military for civilian options, the traumatization of students by police attack, the devolution of a community based on shared assumptions into a community nakedly based on force. Of late, the politics of confrontation has found another way to exceed its immediate object. Students engaged in coercive protest have come to insist that amnesty be granted before they will agree to relent. For those who reject the legitimacy of the guardians and who wish to stay to do battle yet another day, this demand serves practical and symbolic purposes. But amnesty wrested from the institution may not always bring total forgiveness: violations involving trespass or vandalism may result in criminal arrests. Where the institution is the sole complainant, it may influence the disposition of these cases; but it may find it hard to convince the courts to dismiss the charges when it has surrendered the means to protect itself. The natural effect of amnesty, granted under duress, is thus to displace the disciplinary power from the universities to the civil courts. Whether courts or universities act more justly is a question one need not resolve. It is clear, however, that they do act differently, the one being more interested in behaviors, the other in underlying intentions; the one just beginning to grant academic freedom legal status, the other having long made this the value it cherishes above all. But the thrust of modern student politics is to give the temporal rather than the spiritual authority a legitimate judicial role.

Meanwhile, forces outside the university have been working to constrain academic discipline when it *is* applied. Starting in 1961, the federal courts have been deciding that the disciplinary actions of officials in publicly supported colleges and universities must adhere to the due process standards of the Fourteenth Amendment of the Constitution. Whether the officials of private institutions must adjust their conduct to these standards is not, at the moment, certain; but it is highly probable that they will one day be made to do so or suffer reversal in the courts. One may note that the cases setting the legal precedent involved the interests of Negro students who had been punished for participating in sit-ins by administrators of Negro colleges yielding to the pressures of Southern whites. Clearly the judicial concern for student rights was inspired by a judicial concern for civil rights and not by purely academic considerations. Here again, the college, in acquiring new social significance, has lost a measure of its old autonomy. But here one may be permitted the conclusion that, on balance, justice gained.

I come finally to the last delocalizing tendency: the growing involvement of the federal government with the affairs and fortunes of academe. This is perhaps not the order or the language that the most passionate critics of that involvement would prefer. But the virtue in saving it till last is that we may then perceive it not as something *sui generis* but as part of a broader development; and the virtue in using the word "delocalizing" when a more accusative vocabulary is at hand is that we can avoid the dubious imputation of Pentagon plotting, power elitism, establishment cooption, and the like. Nevertheless, after this dispassionate preface, I hasten to admit that I believe the issue now before us is of burning importance. The advent of a formidable central state—harnessed almost without limit for a world struggle apparently without end, richer than any other benefactor by virtue of the federal income tax resource, able to seek solutions to any social problem, if need be, by purchasing compliance with the cure—is a momentous event in the life of our universities. Such a behemoth, as it draws close, cannot help but siphon authority from other agencies. In part, but only in part, the speed and volume of the drain from the universities can be measured by the increase in its assistance. In 1964 federal contributions to higher learning totaled $1.5 billion. Though this came to only one-tenth of the total funds received, it constituted, because of its distribution, a large percentage of the incomes of the major places—83 percent of Cal Tech's, 81 percent of MIT's, 75 percent of Princeton's. For home reference, it may be noted that Columbia, third among recipients, got $51,000,000, an intake that amounted to almost half of that year's operating budget, while the University of Illinois, then sixth in order, got $44,000,000, a smaller part of its total budget but a not inconsiderable sum. By 1966 the federal contribution had doubled and the federal share of total contributions had risen to approximately one-fifth. In that year the largesse was a little more evenly distributed, but the major institutions were even more glaringly beholden to the generosity of the central state.

It is in the "how" as well as in the "how much" that we locate the delocalizing pressure. During and after World War II, academic scientists high in government and governmental and military officials high on science hit on two devices for channeling federal funds to universities. One was the project grant or contract, which a faculty member negotiates with the granting agency with minimal involvement by his university; the other was the specialized research center, which the university operates for the agency, sometimes without the participation of any faculty member. These devices are supposed to confer a variety of social and scientific benefits. It is claimed that the distant granting agency, with its advisory panels of distinguished scientists, is more likely to rate applicants on their merits than are members of a department when they judge their own. It is claimed that the separation of federal subsidy from federal employment helps preserve individual research initiative, since an academic scientist is free, as a governmental scientist is not, to pursue the project of his own desire. And it is claimed that the funds allocated under these formulas make possible the purchase of scientific apparatus which would otherwise be lost to the academy in the expensive space and atomic age. It is tempting to investigate these claims, to ask whether personal, institutional, or regional loyalties never tincture the judgments of reviewing panels, whether certain kinds of extravagantly priced equipment—like accelerators with ever increasing BEVs—deserve the national priority they have been given, whether freedom of choice is not subtly constrained by the workings of the well-known principle that a man need not marry for money, he may simply seek out the company of wealthy women and marry one of them for love. But these are not the questions before us: what is pertinent is that these devices rob the university of autonomy, the one by making it a bystander in the fostering and reward of its members' talents, the other by making it a kind of subcontractor, dispensing someone else's cash to attain someone else's objectives. Here one might add a quantitative footnote: today, from two-thirds to three-quarters of all money expended on academic research comes from the federal giver through these circumventive routes.

"Washington," notes Clark Kerr, in his study of the "multiversity," the delocalized institution unsurpassed, "did not waste its money on the second-rate." Did it make what was first-rate even better? Looking at the institutional breeding places of the greatest scientific advances of the last two decades, Kerr concludes that the federal research effort did give existing excellences an added gloss. But on the evidence he himself musters, a more pessimistic conclusion might be formed. Taking what is given without question and doing what is asked for by the gift, the front-rank university tends to find itself rich but troubled, powerful in its impact on the nation but weak in the control of its own affairs. It falls prey to what Kerr refers to as "imbalances": the dominance of science over the humanities, the dominance of research over teaching, the dominance of graduate interests over undergraduate concerns. It takes on an ever increasing number of those whom Kerr refers to as "unfaculty": scholars who are added to the staff to assist externally aided projects. Set to the sponsored task but performing no other service to the institution, never eligible for tenure no matter how often contracts are renewed, this new academic breed lives at the periphery of the profession. Fifty years ago only a relatively small group of graduate students, serving as assistants to their senior faculty, was in as marginal a position. Since then, the ranks of this subaltern force have grown, to take care of the burden of instruction that the increased number of students has created and that a research-minded faculty will not assume. In the leading universities these two anomalous groups—the teacher who is still a student and the researcher who is not a teacher—make up a very large part of the total academic work force. With enrichment, then, has come a new diminishment: an increase in the number of appointees who are in but not of the university, sharing in its tasks but not its perquisites, existing under the predestinarian doctrine (so alien to professional doctrine) that good works can never assure election.

A full estimate of the losses incident to gains must include the acceptance of secrecy and deceit, not as adventitious vices but as part of the academic way of life. Federal support for military research must bear a part of the responsibility for the institutionalizing of shady tactics. The aim of military research is to secure time advantages against the enemy; often, to secure these time advantages, it is necessary to prevent premature disclosures; frequently, to prevent disclosures, it is necessary to test the loyalty of participants, limit access to facilities, guard the research records, or control what appears in print. With the Pentagon no less interested in quality than the National Science Foundation or the National Institutes of Health, it was inevitable that funds for the necrophilic sciences, as well as funds for the healing and heuristic arts, would flow to the better universities. But federal support for military research does not account for all the slyness and covertness that afflict modern academic life. Only a small part of federal support is avowedly military (in 1966, of the total sum applied by the granting agencies, only 10 percent went to academia from the Department of Defense). If the secretiveness of warrior organizations accounts for something, the enfeeblement of academic organizations accounts for more. A high susceptiveness to deception was built into the very flabbiness of the grant arrangement. Almost any agency out to promote an unpleasant mission can find a pretext for lodging it in the university, to acquire gilt by association. Federal undercover agents find it easier to carry on their impostures amid the para-academic members of a research project than amid the faculties at large. Above all, universities involved in the project system developed a trained incapacity to look suspiciously at their gift horses, if indeed they looked at all. Thus it happened at Michigan State University that a program for training policemen for Vietnam, set up by a mission-minded agency without close monitorship by the university, was infiltrated by agents of the CIA. The structure, if it did not require hugger-muggery, was certainly not well made to prevent it. And thus it happened that the same surreptitious body gave secret subsidies to a variety of academic enterprises, ranging from area study institutes to international conferences; once inserted, trickery by government became routine.

This is not to say that trickery by government does not exist on the campus in other forms. Modes of underhandedness have long been associated with law enforcement: viz., the policeman posing as a student, the student doubling as a policeman, the government employer asking teachers to snitch on their students and peers. Especially prominent in "Red scare" periods, these forms of deception are not uncommon in the current period, when drugs take precedence over dogmas as items on the list of search. But these tricks have the capacity to outrage professors in almost all institutions where they are practiced. The secret subsidies of the CIA, by contrast, seem to be a good deal less inflaming. For a decade or so they went undetected, though not without the collaboration of a good many professors and administrators in the know. When some of these were uncovered (largely by left-wing student muckrakers), they did cause a stir in certain faculties. Still, it is almost certain that the taint has not been removed from certain projects and that administrative and professional winking goes on. As late as 1964 Clark Kerr could maintain that the federal grant procedure was "fully within academic traditions." Since the CIA revelations, the academic mood has probably not been so complaisant. Yet it is doubtful that many members of the profession would think it wise to change the title of their book from *The Uses of the University* to *How the University Has Been Used*.

How to account for the differences in responses? Simply to say that one form of police penetration serves to enrich professors while the other may serve to chastise them puts the matter of self-interest much too crudely. It would be, I think, both more subtle and more accurate to say that no process of delocalization, unless it threatens the well-being of professors, is presumed to violate academic freedom; and that without a violation of academic freedom, no insult to the university causes broad alarm. In fact, by the tests which the inherited creed imposes, some of the trends I have spoken of seem to have strengthened academic freedom. Ideological dismissals have become rare to the point of being oddities in the larger delocalized institutions. This is all the more impressive because outspoken opposition to war in wartime, which had always been subject to academic penalties, has been allowed to flourish in these places. Furthermore, with very few verified exceptions, the governmental granting agencies have not discriminated against opponents of governmental policies. Not only in crimes, but also in crime prevention, the current period seems to improve upon the past. Tenure (for those eligible to receive it) is at least as safe in integrated public systems as in any other. Academic due process has, if anything, become more rigorous and more codified as the scattered *gemeinschafts* of before merge into centralized *gesellschafts*. Federal-grant universities, with their congeries of projects, are less likely to get domineering presidents (they are lucky to get presidents able and alert enough to keep track of all that is going on). Less privileged colleges and universities, hoping for federal assistance, are less likely to prescribe religious or other doctrines (this is one reason why certain Catholic institutions are moving toward lay boards of control and even toward the norm of neutrality). For renowned professors the new order is particularly comfortable and protective. If they have greater leverage in bargaining with their institutions, they may thank the federal grantor for adding to their other marketable assets the value of a movable money prize. The flow of perquisites from Washington dissolves their reliance on the local paymaster, while the tenure granted by alma mater prevents their subservience to the outside source. Status satisfactions only dreamed of may now in actuality be possessed. The autonomy and integrity of universities? These heavenly things on earth are not contained in this philosophy.

This is hardly the place to write an academic freedom theory that would meet this day's demands. All I can do is sketch out certain areas where changes in the reigning wisdom would do us good. I ask you to take this as a prolegomenon; a theoretical and practical formulation of the academic ethics we require must await another Lovejoy or Dewey, distilling salient ideas from new institutional experiences.

At the top of the list of credos ripe for change I would put the view that a crime against academic freedom is a crime against an academic person's rights. In relevant doctrine it may still be that; but it may also be an attack on academic integrity, sustained by the university as a whole. It should be the name we give to the intrusion of lock-and-key research into an ostensibly open enterprise.

Next I would part with the notion that curbs on administrative power answer all of academic freedom's needs. They answer only part of its needs; the other and equally essential instrument is effective academic government. It was well understood by the makers of our Constitution that freedom could be jeopardized by the weakness, as well as the tyranny, of officials.

In the quest for relevant doctrine, I would also take issue with the notion that the only respectable university is a politically neutral university. It may not be easy to reconceive this notion. The norm of institutional neutrality has rolled through our synapses so often we hardly ever challenge it with thought. Therein lies the problem: applied unthinkingly to every issue, it loses its value as a norm and becomes a recipe for paralysis. One illustration may make this clear. The Selective Service Administration recently decreed that college students would be deferred if they achieved a certain grade-ranking or passed a certain standardized test. In other words, instead of classifying by status (all college students), it classified by status and performance (only *good* college students), and fixed the criterion of judgment. To grasp the implications of this procedure one need only ask what the consequences would have been if the draft authorities had decided to defer not all women but only *good* women, not all husbands but only *good* husbands, not all workers in essential industries but only *good* workers in essential industries. In academic no less than in conjugal and economic matters, privacy and autonomy are threatened when virtue is not its own but the state's reward. The academy, however, took little corporate action to defend its corporate rights. Proposals for institutional reliance (say by not ranking students or sending in the grades) were usually defeated by the argument that such acts would be politically unneutral, signifying institutional opposition to the draft or the war in Vietnam. This ritualistic application of the neutrality principle resulted from a failure to distinguish between essentially political questions and essentially educational questions having political implications. A theory adequate for our times would have to emphasize that distinction. It would have to serve the norm of institutional neutrality for questions of the former sort and for them alone. For questions of the latter sort, and I believe the class-rank issue falls squarely within this category, it would formulate a different norm—a norm of institutional regulation, under which things central to the academy could be dealt with by the academy and not passed to other powers by default. Some questions would fall on or near the borderlines and raise jurisdictional dilemmas. But many more would fall to one side or another once the theoretical line was drawn. Thus, whether the state should built an arsenal of secret weapons would plainly be a political question; on this, for reasons that were given long ago and have never lost their validity, the university should be mute. But whether classified research, under state support, should be permitted on the campus would plainly be an academic question; on this, for different reasons, the university should be heard. To assert a normative choice is to reject the radical view that the university must always be political or consent to the evils of society, and the traditionalist view that the university must always be neutral or succumb to the divisiveness of society. Neither argues potently that the university must be independent, and act or not act as its needs demand.

Even if theories were remade, many pressures to delocalize would continue. To ask that the academy come to grips with these is to ask it to formulate counter-policies in apparent conflict with its needs. Delocalization is in part a product of the growing importance of the university: no one could realistically suggest that it retreat to its older insignificance. Delocalization is in part an answer to the financial exigencies of the university: it would be difficult to demand an autonomy that required enormous dollar sacrifices. Moreover, certain delocalizing forces serve as a counter to the overreach of others: large universities in consolidated public systems may squeeze a measure of autonomy from the fact that they can draw on federal subsidies as well as on state appropriations. Nevertheless, some measure of localness can be restored in ways neither retreatist nor impoverishing. The breaking up of large public configurations into smaller subregional complexes might be a step in this direction. The use of collaborative techniques like the sharing of faculties among independent colleges might be another. The diversion of federal aid into student loans, on a scale large enough to let client fees bear the major burden of client costs; the increase in federal aid in the form of institutional lump-sum payments; the decrease in federal aid for big science under academic auspices (other auspices might handle it as well)—all might reinvigorate local power. The localist need not be contemptuous of the rationalizer or believe that he is living in a cost-free system. He need only insist that rationalizations be really rational and that, in the building and rebuilding of systems, costs of every kind be assayed.

5

Academic Freedom in the Modern American University[1]

Sheila Slaughter

This chapter attempts to put academic freedom in historical context, to examine a series of recent academic freedom cases, and to consider new problems that the academy is currently facing with regard to academic freedom. The history of academic freedom in the United States is seen as developing along with the modern American university; thus, the record to which close attention is paid is that of the last century. The series of academic freedom cases reviewed are those presented by the American Association of University Professors (AAUP) during the decade 1970-1980. The new problems considered are those that arise from changing conditions in the academy: continued retrenchment, closer control of faculty work load, emerging partnerships between industry, university and government, a resurgence of close relationships between the university and the military.

ACADEMIC FREEDOM IN HISTORICAL CONTEXT

Academic freedom has its roots in the universities of medieval Europe. Universities were able to take advantage of the conflict between church and state to claim a modicum of freedom. Professors had a voice in maintaining an established curriculum, were able to set academic standards, and elect their leaders. Their prerogatives were managerial rather than intellectual. Both church and state had more authority in determining the shape of acceptable belief than did academics. While the freedom of faculty was tightly circumscribed, the medieval university was the site where the notion of a professional occupational class was established, one with privileges beyond those accorded to the ordinary person, privileges rooted in the higher learning professors had acquired.[2]

The next major contribution to modern definitions of academic freedom took place in German universities during the eighteenth and nineteenth centuries. Although professors in German universities were civil servants who had to take an oath of allegiance to the state, they possessed a limited degree of academic freedom with regard to the internal operation of the university. *Lernfreiheit* guaranteed freedom from administrative intervention in learning, and applied particularly to students' freedom to shape a course of study: to attend various universities, to choose professors with whom to study, to attend or cut classes. *Lehrfreiheit* affirmed the German professors' right to conduct their classrooms as they would, and follow their research where it led. This freedom was generally confined to the academic community, and did not include speech or writing external to the university.[3]

The many American academics who received Ph.D.s in German universities in the late nineteenth century brought notions of academic freedom back to the developing U.S. graduate schools. However, their effort to transfer these freedoms was highly selective. *Lernfreiheit*, which pertained largely to students, was not imported. *Lehrfreiheit* was expanded until it became very like a First Amendment freedom, protecting external utterances of professors as well as internal freedom to teach and research.[4]

While American academics made broad claims in the name of academic freedom, they had great difficulty in enforcing them. The U.S. system of academic governance was very different from that of European universities. The United States was characterized by a peculiar institution: lay control. Trustees and their administrative agents, not the faculty, had and have formal legal authority over the university. The laissez-faire economic doctrine that informed the legal system in the last quarter of the nineteenth century exacerbated the professors' difficulties. When questions concerning a professor's right to tenure of office occurred, the courts took the position that governing boards and faculty were equal parties to a contract. If a faculty member could leave at his pleasure, so the board could fire at its pleasure. As with the laborer who needed the factory for his livelihood, the weaker position of the institutionally dependent professor vis-a-vis the board was ignored. What tenure existed depended on the good will of trustees and could be abrogated at any instant with unqualified judicial approval.[5]

Professors in the 1880s and 1890s, fresh from German universities and full of their own expertise, came regularly into conflict with administrators and trustees. In the main, they were social scientists trying to use their new knowledge to mitigate the harsh social conditions of industrial America. They sought substantive reforms, advocating changes that in many instances would have slighty curbed the power that accrued to property owners. When their advocacy was at odds with lay authorities, they were often fired, their claims to academic freedom disregarded. The famous academic freedom cases of the 1880s and 1890s stemmed from this sort of conflict between professor and lay boards, or presidents representing lay boards: Carter Adams at Cornell, Bemis at Chicago, Commons at Syracuse, Andrews at Brown, Ely at Wisconsin, Ross at Stanford. Only one of these professors was reinstated.

After recanting the views which had provoked the Regents ire, Ely was retained.[6]

Although the dismissals of the 1880s and 1890s exposed professors' precarious position, they also precipitated a still continuing public debate on academic freedom. Professors started to proselytize for it and presidents of major graduate universities also began to offer limited support. Key to professors' and sympathetic university managers' claims was the centrality of knowledge in a technological age. Professors saw themselves as experts providing necessary technical information for the smooth functioning of a complex society and argued that academic freedom was necessary to create new social knowledge and make scientific discoveries. Enlightened university managers saw it as creating working conditions that would assure the generation of new knowledge critical to an industrial era. As Yale's President Arthur T. Hadley put it, the problem was to secure "the advantages of freedom without exposing ourselves to the worse dangers. . . . [to] combine. . . . the maximum of progress with the minimum of revolution."[7]

In the Progressive era faculty began to demonstrate that they could contribute to the solution of technical and social problems. Ever growing numbers of Ph.D.s began to serve government and the private sector as experts, revealing the utility of knowledge and thus building support for academic freedom.[8] However, in the second decade of the new century, economic recession and resurgence of violence between capital and labor revealed the limits of Progressivism. In response to widespread agitation over social and economic issues, a wave of repression swept over the country. Faculty as well as labor suffered. In 1913, violations of academic freedom made national headlines for the first time since 1900.[9]

Reluctant to lose the prestige they had gained through consulting outside the university and the increased occupational autonomy they had achieved within it, senior faculty at elite institutions in 1915 used the newly formed American Association of University Professors (AAUP) to present a "Declaration of Principles on Academic Freedom and Tenure." The Association made explicit the agreement senior faculty and enlightened trustees had tacitly worked under since the turn of the century: faculty would undertake the management of knowledge in return for academic freedom. In effect, faculty gained some occupational autonomy by assuming trustees' responsibilities for monitoring the social content of knowledge to ensure that its revolutionary potential was dampened by a code of scholarship emphasizing deliberation, "long views into the future," and "a reasonable regard for the teaching experience."[10] The rights that came with this responsibility were limited: freedom to follow research where it led, to pursue advanced and controversial ideas with graduate students, to speak freely outside the university in areas of professional competence and with the decorum befitting a professor on general social and political issues. These rights were extended only to professors with long years of service.[11]

The 1915 Declaration of Principles was issued to guide employment relations between faculty and university managers and trustees. University officers at a handful of graduate centers engaged in research and recognized its importance. However, most trustees did not, and the AAUP was forced to undertake their education. It began to publish didactic instances of infringements of professorial rights in the *Bulletin* and the 1915 Declaration became the first rather than the definitive document in a long series of policy statements. Taken together, these published investigations and policy statements were the beginning of an extralegal body of occupational case law focused on internal university due process. It would shape academic personnel policy and definitions of academic freedom into the 1980s.

The First World War, however, revealed the problems of protecting academic freedom when this was entrusted to senior faculty supported by sympathetic university managers. While most professors wholeheartedly embraced the war, some stood forth against it, exercising their rights as citizens. The AAUP did nothing to protect these dissidents, many of whom were fired.[12]

Although the AAUP failed to protect the academic freedom of antimilitarist professors, it worked closely on the war effort with associations of college and university managers: the Association of American Colleges, American Association of State Universities, American Association of Agricultural and Experimental Stations, and others. This cooperation with officials representing a wide spectrum of institutions prepared the way for a detailed accord with college and university managers after the war.[13] In 1924, working under the auspices of the American Council of Education, the AAUP gained managerial approval of a shortened form of the 1915 Declaration as well as a more explicit definition of due process mechanisms. Although the rights defined were no more extensive than in 1915, the AAUP hoped to make academic freedom more secure by reaching a formal agreement with officials from a variety of managerial associations.[14]

This hope was not fulfilled since the 1925 Conference Statement did not deal with the perplexing issue of civil liberties. Economic depression and social strife in the 1930s involved increasing numbers of professors in left politics and academic freedom cases that turned on ideological issues. A fair number of trustees and administrators at universities of all types supported academic freedom so long as controversy was confined to the classroom and academic journals but proved unwilling to allow professors to speak freely in the political arena, whether within their field of specialization or not. Civil liberties were at issue, not technical competence. The professors fired in political cases were rarely terminated for giving scientific advice to mainstream public or private agencies. Instead, they were fired when publicly championing unpopular or controversial social causes.[15]

The 1940 Statement of Principles, drawn up conjointly with the Association of American Colleges, was in large part an attempt to clarify professors' civil liberties. With regard to "extra-mural utterances" made in the course of exercising the political rights of a citizen, the professor no longer has the same latitude as other men and women. "His special position in the community imposes special obligations." While the professor should be "free from institutional censorship or discipline," he should nonetheless always keep in mind "that the public may judge his profession and his institution by his utterances. Hence, he should at all times be accurate, should exercise appropriate constraint, should show respect for the opinions of others, and should make every effort to indicate that he is not an institutional spokesman." Finally, professors are expected to lead exemplary lives since "moral turpitude" also constitutes grounds for dismissal.

In return, precise definition was given for the first time to the tenure process. After a probationary period of a maximum of seven years, professors, after peer review, should have permanent or continuous tenure of office that can be terminated only for "adequate cause." What adequate cause might be is not addressed, but the interpretation appended to the 1940 document specifically states that the exercise of a professor's political rights as a citizen might legitimately be considered sufficient.[16]

In essence, the 1940 Statement relieved the AAUP of any obligation to insist that professors be accorded the same rights as citizens in comparable positions in times of widespread social unrest. Civil liberties were exchanged for tenure. As a past president of the AAUP and law professor, William Van Alstyne, has pointed out:

> The trade-off that the AAUP appeared to have accepted with the Association of American Colleges in 1940 (namely, to cultivate public confidence in the profession by laying down a professionally taxing standard of institutional accountability for all utterances of a public character made by a member of the profession) is substantially more inhibiting of a faculty member's civil freedom of speech than any standard that government is constitutionally privileged to impose in respect to the personal politics or social utterances of other kinds of public employees.[17]

The 1940 Statement is of critical importance since it still stands as the AAUP's basic formulation of academic freedom and tenure.[18]

Recent scholarship, however, reveals that neither the AAUP nor tenure were institutions sufficient to protect professors accused of Communism during the Cold War. Ellen W. Schrecker, in *No Ivory Tower: McCarthyism and the Universities,* provides a compelling account of violations of academic freedom during the height of the Cold War.[19] Preliminary skirmishes between professors in the American Communist Party (CP) and state investigating bodies began on the eve of World War II. There was a truce of sorts during the war, but afterwards hostilities began in earnest. In 1947, Truman's Executive Order 9835 instituted a new loyalty-security program. The efforts of the executive branch were augmented by House and Senate investigating committees, the most famous of which belonged to Senator Joseph McCarthy, as well as state investigating committees. It is estimated that approximately twenty percent of all the witnesses called before congressional and state investigatory committees were college professors or graduate students. If they were not able to clear themselves, they very often lost their jobs. At the height of the witch-hunts, in 1953, attention centered on education. In that year alone, more than 100 academics were called before committees, of whom 30 lost their jobs.

Professors who cooperated with the committees by revealing the names of persons with whom they had shared radical political activities in the 1930s were usually spared the ignomy of a public hearing. They were able to "name names" in closed session and continue their professional duties. Professors who would not cooperate posed great difficulties for the committees because the government officials who manned them had no power to impose sanctions: CP membership, in and of itself, was not a crime. However, universities solved the external committees' problem by creating internal committees that re-examined and sometimes fired professors identified by state or Congressional investigating committees. According to Schrecker:

> Professors who refused to cooperate with the committees but did cooperate with their colleagues—and this seems to have been the largest group—sometimes kept their jobs, if they had tenure and taught at private colleges or universities, and sometimes lost them, especially if they were at public institutions. Professors who refused to cooperate with both the congressional and academic investigations were almost always fired.[20]

Professors who did not cooperate were labeled as "unfriendly witnesses." They very often had been in the CP in the 1930s, but had drifted out of their own accord after the war. The activities for which they were being called to task by legislative committees in the 1950s had occurred a decade or more before and were at that time not illegal. Following guidelines developed by the Association of American Universities, an organization of the presidents of prestigious universities, administrators urged faculty to cooperate with external committees. If the professors did not, and instead invoked the Fifth Amendment, a constitutionally guaranteed freedom, universities very often called them before internal investigating committees. Suspect professors did not necessarily have to "name names" before the university committees, but they were asked by their colleagues to recant their ideological sins.

Many professors who had been in the CP refused to "name names" before state investigating committees, and thus were embroiled in university hearings. Often they did not regard their sojourn in the party as heinous, and therefore found it impossible to convince their colleagues of their ideological purity. In retrospect, they saw the CP, especially in the United Front period, as a political organization that had been extremely active in promoting social justice and fighting against fascism. Contrary to the view expressed in investigatory tribunals, they did not experience the American CP as a monolithic entity demanding unqualified obedience and unconditional devotion to the cause of violent revolution. Indeed, some remember their CP meetings as lively forums for wide ranging intellectual debate. However, the adherence of Party leadership to the Soviet line, especially at the time of the Hitler-Stalin pact, as well as information about the Soviet purge trials, disillusioned many professors. Although some did not leave the Party immediately, most had drifted away by the end of World War II. While they were no longer CP members, many continued to be committed to radical causes, especially the emerging peace and civil rights movements. Because they refused to recant their ideas, or curtail their political activity, they were often fired by their universities.

If professors were fired, they often had great difficulty in getting another academic job. An academic "blacklist" seemed to be in place. Some blacklisted professors, especially physical scientists, were able to find jobs in industry, if these did not involve defense work which entailed security clearances. Others went overseas and taught in England, Israel, India, if they were able to get passports. If blacklisted professors could not get passports, which was often the case after refusal to participate with an investigating committee, they frequently went to Canada, where they were usually able to obtain university positions. Sometimes blacklisted professors were never able to work in academe again.

Although appearance before investigating committees was what most often drew university attention to professors who questioned the Cold War or capitalism, this was not the only activity which identified professors as ideologically deviant. As Lionel Lewis has discovered in his study of violations of academic freedom during the McCarthy era, left-liberal political activism also raised questions. After those who appeared before investigating committees, the largest number of professors who were involved in academic freedom cases in the late 1940s and early 1950s were those who worked for Henry Wallace. Wallace was a third party candidate who ran for President in 1948 on a platform that stood for continuing the social and economic reforms of the New Deal.[21] He was not a "Cold Warrior" and did not take a hard line against the Soviet Union. His foreign policy caused conservatives to raise questions about his patriotism, which were intensified by CP support for his candidacy. Although Wallace himself was not a Communist, CP support and conservative criticism created a climate in which universities found it necessary to dismiss some professors who worked openly for him.

It is hard to measure the impact of these dismissals on the rest of the academic profession. The only information that bears on this question is a study performed in 1955 to discover how social scientists were responding to McCarthyism.

Many of the respondents, especially those Lazarsfeld and Thielens categorized as liberals, confessed that they were scared. Over 25 percent of them revealed that they had indulged in some form of political self-censorship, either in their professional activities or in their private lives. Significantly, the survey exposed a considerable discrepancy between the respondents' unquestionably liberal opinions and their willingness to act upon them.[22]

There was very little organized activity against the congressional and state investigating committees. The AAUP, which was the association most likely to take a stand against McCarthyism, did little to oppose it. Internal disorganization kept the AAUP from actively investigating cases. Indeed, the AAUP made no strong stand against McCarthyism until 1957. At that point a Special Committee reiterated the 1947 position which said professors did not have to cooperate with outside investigating committees, and could avail themselves of the Fifth Amendment, but urged cooperation with internal investigations.

Professors continued to be fired as late as 1959; two went to jail for contempt of Congress that year. But recognition of excesses of McCarthyism began to curb the scope of investigating committees' powers. Social and economic changes also rendered them less powerful. The "due process revolution" began, the economy flourished, and the Cold War thawed.

In the 1960s, the growth of the university presented professors with an opportunity to recoup some of the occupational autonomy lost during the McCarthy period. The rapid expansion of postsecondary education resulted in a shortage of Ph.D.s, giving faculty some leverage with regard to civil liberties. This advantage was reinforced by strong social reform movements—civil rights crusades and the war on poverty—in the wider society. The narrow construction of academic freedom as protecting faculty only in a professional capacity began to be expanded through defense of civil liberties on First Amendment grounds. Frequently the AAUP worked with professors engaged in litigation, and an interpretation of academic freedom that conferred civil as well as professional liberties became fairly well established.

However, successful defense of academic freedom cases continues to depend on discovery of procedural violations rather than on enforcing a widely agreed upon, substantive definition of academic freedom, and the point at which liberty becomes license still remains elusive. Academic freedom is an evolving concept, depending on the strength of social movements external to the academy, the degree of professorial organization, judicial decisions, institutional procedure, administrative discretion and the collective consciousness of senior faculty at any given institution. Since the degree of academic freedom varies with historical circumstance, it can best be understood in terms of specific cases in a particular time period.

ACADEMIC FREEDOM CASES: 1970-1980

Since the AAUP is the only national organization that consistently reports academic freedom cases in rich detail and fairly standard format, the data presented are based on investigations made by Committee A and publicly reported in the association's journal, supplemented by interviews with AAUP staff members.[23] There are, however, numerous problems in using AAUP data to assess the state of academic freedom. First, examination of complaints and cases handled in a five-year period (1975-1979) indicates that only a small percentage of cases ever become available for public scrutiny. A complaint is the registration by a professor of a suspected violation of academic freedom; a complaint becomes a case when the AAUP staff finds it merits further investigation. Forty-three percent of the 2,135 complaints received were handled by the AAUP staff without ever achieving "case" status. Although 1,312 (57 percent) became cases calling for further probing, only 23 cases (2 percent) were subject to full-dress investigation and public report by Committee A. Even if the 366 cases (27 percent) said to be successfully closed are omitted on the grounds that positive resolution does not result in publication, approximately 70 percent of the cases are unaccounted for. Thus, the nature of complaints as well as the vast majority of cases, all indicators of the climate of academic freedom, remain unknown.

Second, the cases reported by Committee A reflect the AAUP's selection process. They are chosen for their importance in illuminating a pressing problem through setting precedent.[25] Although clarifying issues and procedures critical to the profession is laudable and central to the AAUP's self-definition, many unremarkable cases go unrecorded. Third, while the AAUP will investigate complaints lodged regardless of whether or not faculty belong to the association, it rarely takes action unless aid is requested. Presumably, persons seeking such intervention must have some degree of conviction as to the justice of their case, the responsiveness of the academic system, and the effectiveness of the AAUP. The timorous, the deviant, and the cynical may never call attention to perceived violations of their academic freedom.[26] Fourth, as in the past, many faculty may turn to organizations and institutions other than the AAUP—associations of learned disciplines; caucuses, conferences, and support groups in their field; unions; the ACLU; the courts; political parties.

In sum, the AAUP is the only consistent, central, national data source for academic freedom cases, but it tells us little about the possible universe. There is no way of estimating the percent of complaints and cases handled by the association compared to actual violations. However, the AAUP does serve clearing-house and consultant functions within the profession and is likely to be at least tangentially involved in well-publicized cases.[27] As AAUP Associate General Secretary Jordan Kurland says, "We have a monopoly on academic freedom even if we don't hold the copyright."[28] Thus, even though association data is incomplete, analysis of those cases investigated by Committee A and reported in the AAUP's journal between 1970-1980 probably gives a fair indication of the overall pattern of academic freedom infringements.

Between 1970-1980, there were fifty-nine cases, each representing an institution.[29] In prestige terms, cases reported seem to come most often from higher education's middle ranks where fluctuations in faculty and student market make for volatile conditions. Thirty-two (or 62 percent) occurred in the public sector, with the majority at institutions rapidly and recently upgraded from normal school to university status. The twenty-three cases (38 percent) in the private sector took place largely at small, church-related colleges.

While no cases were reported at long-established universities with departments consistently ranked in the top ten, and few from community colleges, this lack of reported violations does not necessarily indicate their absence; it merely suggests they might be handled by means other than the AAUP. At the bottom, faculty located in community and state colleges may rely more on union organization and strict contractual obligation to protect their academic freedom. In the topmost tier, highly rated research universities might have more sophisticated administrators and colleagues might bring more subtle pressures. Most importantly, faculty at the top are able to move elsewhere, often without great loss of prestige. Thus, it is the vast middle, composed of faculty aspiring to attain or maintain the privileges of the most highly ranked universities, on the one hand, and of those too weak and divided about their professional status to organize, on the other hand, who bring cases reported by the AAUP.

As Table I indicates, the fifty-nine cases resulted in the firing of 1,348 faculty members, and in eight having their pay docked. The number of faculty dismissed from each institution varied extremely. On the one hand, thirty cases concerned a single faculty member each; on the other, a single case involved the firing of 1,000. The largest numbers are accounted for by financial exigency in New York state, but groups ranging from five to forty were fired in all the remaining categories with the exception of "other." Each case represents a violation of academic due process or academic freedom since all resulted in censure by the AAUP.

In cases involving large numbers of faculty, tenure status was often not reported. However, most of the 990 in the financial exigency column were fired from CUNY, where a seniority principle was used in making cutbacks. Thus, untenured faculty are probably a great deal more vulnerable than tenured when an institution faces financial crisis. In those cases where rank of fired faculty is known with certainty, tenured and untenured faculty are almost evenly matched overall. However, untenured professors are much more likely to be dismissed for political action than tenured professors, while the tenured are much more likely to be removed when acting against the administration or during a policy shift involving change of institutional mis-

TABLE 1
ACADEMIC FREEDOM CASES REPORTED BY AAUP 1970-1980

Year	No. of Cases	No. Fired	Financial Exigency	Political Action	Policy Shift	Religious Action	Anti Admini-stration	Other	ND
				MAJOR CAUSES, AS INDICATED BY AAUP REPORT					
1970	9	20	0	10	0	0	10	0	0
1971	6	10	0	8	0	0	1	1	0
1972	4	4	0	4	0	0	0	0	0
1973	10	20*	1	15	2	0	1	0	1
1974	3	29	0	16	13	0	0	0	0
1975	6	82	0	0	33	40	9	0	0
1976	6	14	0	1	0	1	9	1	2
1977	4	1118	1116	0	0	0	1	1	0
1978	2	37	36	0	0	0	1	0	0
1979	5	12	1	1	0	0	2	1	7
1980	4	10	4	0	0	0	4	2	0
Totals	59	1356	1158	55	48	41	38	6**	10
			(85%)	(4%)	(4%)	(3%)	(3%)	(.5%)	(.5%)
Tenured		149	87	6	30	2	16	4	4
Un-tenured		151	81	35	18	0	2	2	6
No Answer		1046	990	14	0	39	20	0	0
	59	1356	1158	55	48	41	38	6	10

*docked pay, but not fired
**incompetence, personality, moral turpitude, etc.

sion. There are several possible explanations for these differences. First, and contrary to popular professional wisdom, young untenured professors, perhaps not as fully cognizant of the perils of academe as their well-socialized seniors, may speak and act more openly on political questions. Second, administrators and trustees may feel they face greater difficulties in removing tenured faculty on political grounds and thus tolerate more outspokenness. Third, the tenured may defend their role as guardians of professional prerogatives at the institutional level rather than in the wider political arena. Their concern with institutional politics is perhaps not misplaced since they are more likely to be dispensed with than young faculty when policy shifts call for new skills or credentials. Although risks may vary with age and status, tenure is not a firm guarantee against violations of academic freedom.

Of the fifty-nine reported cases, twenty were successfully closed and removed from the AAUP's censured list. Censure, inaugurated in 1932, is a warning to professors that the institution so listed does not subscribe to AAUP academic freedom and tenure policies. It is usually lifted when two conditions are met: rules and regulations are revised in accord with association policy, and the faculty members fired are offered some form of redress. Reinstatement is exceedingly unusual. Settlements are most often financial, with a year's salary as the standard. However, this can vary and when it does it is usually less rather than more. These twenty successfully resolved cases involved sixty-three faculty members. Many of the remaining 1,293 are unlikely to receive redress since they are caught up in cases involving mass layoffs where such expectations are unrealistic.

ECONOMIC CAUSES: POLICY SHIFT AND FINANCIAL EXIGENCY

During the 1970s, managers at a wide array of postsecondary institutions recognized faculty occupational autonomy by granting them control over due process mechanisms and tenure review. However, academic due process is abrogated when an administration declares a state of financial exigency. In the decade 1970-1980, 85 percent of the faculty who were fired lost their jobs under conditions of financial exigency. Financial exigency accounts for 85 percent of the faculty fired in the last decade. This strikes at the heart of due process and tenure since reorganization and cutbacks are often defined by fiscal agents, administrators, and sometimes by faculty as a management problem thereby legitimizing administrative rather than professional decision making about who should stay and who should go. Further, a climate of austerity is created throughout the American academic system, increasing administrative intervention with regard to credentials, class size, faculty load, and the general shape of academic programs, all areas previously reserved at least theoretically for faculty self-governance.

Administrators sometimes appear to take advantage of the opportunity presented by fiscal crisis and austerity conditions to upgrade or change institutional mission. Firings during policy shifts usually occur when administrators and trustees decide to upgrade their institutions by taking advantage of a buyers' market. With jobs in short supply faculty previously not in reach are hired to replace faculty lacking Ph.D.s or low in productivity, whether in terms of publications or F.T.E. (full-time equivalent) enrollments. In all but one case falling into the "policy shift" category, administrators at growing and ambitious state or private colleges and universities rid themselves of professors who had come to be considered marginal in view of the faculty available.[30] The Bloomfield College case provides an example. After a period of expansion, the administration claimed financial exigency on the basis of a slight drop in enrollments. The tenure system was abolished and eleven tenured and two untenured faculty, most with service preceding the expansion, were fired. Yet at the same time administrators and trustees were negotiating to build a larger campus on a new site and almost immediately engaged twelve new full-time faculty and twenty-four part-timers. The AAUP, elected collective bargaining agent during the fracas, brought suit. The New Jersey Superior Court reinstated both the dismissed faculty and the tenure system.[31] This unusually clear-cut decision may have discouraged upgrading at the expense of faculty with legitimate claims on an institution. No further attempts to take advantage of the buyers' market in this fashion were made in the second half of the decade.

The City University of New York (CUNY) starkly illustrates the problems created by financial exigency. After rapidly expanding in the 1960s, the CUNY system was sharply cut. In the austerity program that followed New York City's fiscal crisis, 1,000 full-time faculty (and roughly 5,000 part-time faculty not included in the figures in Table I) were fired with thirty-day notice in August, 1975.[32] At the American Federation of Teachers (AFT)-organized CUNY, a seniority principle was invoked to guide retrenchment. No full-time tenured faculty were fired although ten faculty who technically did not receive tenure until September first were terminated.

The State University of New York (SUNY), faced with a financial crisis of decidedly lesser proportions, tried to cut back using a different method. General guidelines were provided by the state and each institution was asked to make cuts based on long-term plans. In some instances there was considerable faculty participation, in most very little. Lack of faculty participation was in large part due to insistence by the system's unions that making cutbacks was a managerial function. Professorial participation was thought to give tacit approval and destroy faculty solidarity in resisting retrenchment.

Despite widespread faculty and union opposition, selective cutting occurred. According to the AAUP, retrenchment may have given administrators a chance to dismiss troublesome faculty. There are indications of violations of academic freedom in the SUNY system's procedures. An example is the case of a distinguished senior professor and outspoken critic of the administration. When his small program was abolished, he was not allowed to move to a related department where he regularly taught classes. Similarly, another troublesome professor in an Asian studies department found Chinese language, a specialty represented only by himself, designated a unit for retrenchment. He was fired and the rest of the department retained.

The SUNY administration may also have used retrenchment as a pretext for reorganization. The SUNY system had one hundred and four more faculty members in 1976-1977 than in 1975-1976, the year when cuts were made. The system's average salary dropped from $19,180 to $18,750. The AAUP has accused SUNY of using financial distress to reorganize the system at the expense of well-paid professors.[33]

There has been little active organization within the academic profession on the issue of retrenchment. Management prerogatives have been upheld by the courts in states of financial exigency. Both AAUP and AFT have conceded to administrators their right to manage retrenchment, so long as a plan that is neither capricious nor arbitrary guides cutbacks.

ANTI-ADMINISTRATIVE BEHAVIOR: THE FIGHT FOR OCCUPATIONAL AUTONOMY

A number of faculty are still struggling for a voice in decision making, academic due process and tenure review. The thirty-nine faculty members fired for anti-administrative behavior all engaged in some form of open criticism of their administrations, usually as part of a struggle for a modicum of occupational autonomy. Although not comprising a large percentage of cases, anti-administration dismissals occur more regularly than any others. Administrators, invariably backed by trustees, assert their sense of managerial privilege and retaliate against faculty demands, especially at new state colleges and universities, community colleges, and small private colleges. In only one of the thirteen cases did anything so radical as a demand for union organization precipitate dismissals. Most were what AAUP Associate General Secretary Kurland calls "mean little cases," where administrators casually rid themselves of troublesome faculty and appear affronted when called to task.[34]

The institutional charges made against faculty during investigation give an idea of the contempt in which their right to a voice in governance is held.[35] These ranged from "not fitting in with college philosophy," to "not playing on the team," and included several false claims of financial exigency. These anti-administration cases indicate that some administrators and trustees still see their colleges as private fiefdoms. Here faculty are regarded as "mere employees" and any challenge to the administration—as in the case where a professor protested unilateral administrative alteration of a faculty committee's work on tenure policy—is grounds for termination.[36] Running a college like a plant with a company union, where even AAUP membership must sometimes be kept secret, may account for the sharp rise in collective bargaining in the past decade.[37] As AAUP Associate Secretary and Director of Collective Bargaining Geri Bledsoe put it, a union is often "the only way to curb a rogue president," and all-encompassing contractual protection may be the best way to guarantee job security and academic freedom at institutions disregarding professional custom.[38]

IDEOLOGICAL CAUSES: POLITICAL AND RELIGIOUS ACTION

Despite efforts over half a century and more to clarify professors' political rights, the degree and manner of faculty participation in politics that trustees, administrators, and colleagues will tolerate is not yet firmly fixed and remains difficult to predict at specific institutions. Political cases are not confined to the bottom tier of colleges and universities, but occur as well at institutions not far from the top. In the decade 1970-1980, UCLA, Ohio State, the Universities of Southern Illinois, Maryland, and Arizona State were involved in political cases. If political cases are combined with religious cases to account for all dismissals on ideological grounds, they total 5 percent or almost twice the number of dismissals in any category other than financial exigency. Indeed, according to some calculations, between 1965-1975, professors were fired on overtly ideological grounds at a rate unmatched since the height of the McCarthy era.[39]

Most of the cases reported by the AAUP in the years 1970-1980 stemmed from events that took place between 1969-1971, even though they were often not published for one to three years later due to the sometimes lengthy process involved in exhausting internal university due process procedures and the time needed to complete an AAUP investigation. With one exception, faculty were not involved in events resulting in political cases after 1972. The political cases correspond to those turbulent years when order on campus was often maintained at gunpoint. All but one case involved professors exercising their civil liberties by engaging in overt political activity: making radical social commentary before public audiences, working with controversial organizations or causes, or participating in tension-fraught protests.

Teaching was seldom at issue. Indeed, only two cases touched on professors' classroom performance. Both involved extremely provocative behavior—professors' burning of flag and draft card—ending in immediate dismissal.[40] This relative lack of interference in the classroom is subject to several possible interpretations. First, professors may in the main follow established practice and scholarly format, confining themselves to their subject matter and presenting all sides of controversial materials equitably, thereby avoiding charges of indoctrination or abuse of their position. Second, faculty may vigorously uphold long recognized claims about the private and privileged nature of the exchange between professors and students. For example, faculty who encountered undercover government agents or media representatives in their classrooms often effectively made student-backed complaints to their administrations.[41] Perhaps all members of the university community have a vested interest in sheltering the uncertain and unpredictable transactions between professor and students from the public eye.

The earliest cases that turned on professors' politics usually involved civil rights and took place in the South. Local elites were pitted against national faculty who could appeal to outside audiences and institutions for support, and they were sometimes successful in challenging the status quo. The University of Mississippi provides a good example of the dynamics of civil rights cases. Following the Brown decision, Mississippi's Board of Trustees tried to combat support for integration through a variety of means: banning outside speakers, freezing the salaries of faculty who litigated over speaker censorship, and instituting rules that prevented faculty use of expertise on external projects that might further civil rights. When two Yale-educated law professors announced their intention to continue working on the Office of Economic Opportunity (OEO)-funded Northern Mississippi Legal Services Project despite university warnings, their contracts were not renewed. However, they were able to bring successful suit against the university as well as initiate a joint investigation on the part of the AAUP and the American Association of Law Schools.[42]

Although some professors at Mississippi were fired and others economically penalized, their careers were not irreparably damaged. Institutions representing national norms offered some recourse to professors able and unafraid to tap their resources. Ultimately, a federal appellate court put the university on notice that its procedures would be reviewed until at least token compliance was reached. The dismissed professors found other positions and received financial redress. However, not all professors involved in civil rights cases—especially those who were regionally based and not well connected or familiar with national support networks—were able to solicit aid as effectively as the University of Mississippi faculty.

Unlike the Southern civil rights cases, professors participating in the violent rhetoric that were part of the student movement sometimes found their academic careers ended. Angela Davis's dismissal points to the increasingly radical tenor of the struggle for civil rights and the consequences thereof. In this case, civil rights and student movement concerns were bridged by the linking of minority and third world peoples' issues with the U.S. presence in Vietnam through a radical critique of American society.

Davis, black, young, a woman, and a radical, ran afoul of the Regents in her first semester at UCLA when it became widely known that she was a member of the Communist Party. Using a 1949 law of dubious constitutionality, the Regents suspended her from teaching. However, strong faculty protest accompanied by litigation resulted in rapid reinstatement. But after this point she was always in the public eye. Faculty as well as students attended her classes in large numbers and her outside activities in support of the Soledad Brothers were extensively covered by the media. Davis drew careful line between her professional work and her extramural utterances, b the public did not. Although it was uniformly agreed that she was a co petent, well-prepared instructor who did not use her classroom as a platf for indoctrination, her outside speeches were uncompromisingly revolu ary, well attended, and often scathingly critical of higher education. V she did not incite to specific, immediate acts of violence, thus keeping w the limits of the law, she clearly advocated radical structural change thr extralegal means. Ultimately, the Regents charged her with "lack of priate restraint," and when department, faculty hearing committee, a ministration did not find her guilty, the Regents fired her anyway.[4] underlined the fact that they were well within their rights in doing s they permanently rescinded authority previously delegated to faculty sonnel review. Faculty control of due process is still a privilege, not a right to be taken for granted.

Unlike Davis, most faculty fired in political cases were not celebrated radicals and many were not even well-known activists. However, they were severely disciplined when moved to take a moderate stand by extreme campus political polarization. The case of William Wickersham, who was fired from two higher educational institutions, illustrates this point. A committed pacifist, he did not try to "escape the responsibility of choice," but took a leave of absence from his post at the University of Missouri at Columbia in order to devote himself to peace work. In this he followed AAUP policy recommending that professors who see "an insoluble conflict between the claims of politics, social action, and conscience, on the one hand, and the claims and expectations of their students, colleagues and institutions on the other," either take leave or resign.[44] While on leave he served as a mediator between students and administrators during massive demonstrations following the Kent and Jackson State shootings and was a central figure in media accounts. Despite his acting consistently as a moderating force he was fired. Moreover, the position he then accepted at another college was withdrawn because the trustees at this small, private institution feared adverse reactions from possible donors and parents as a result of the media attention Wickersham had received.[45]

Although Wickersham was the only professor fired at the University of Missouri, other faculty members who canceled classes at the height of the demonstrations had their salaries docked. This form of reprimand followed AAUP introduction on a new policy of sanctions. Up to this point, only dismissal proceedings required due process. In 1971, the AAUP called for full-scale hearings on the imposition of major sanctions and grievance procedures in the case of minor ones. These sanctions range from oral reprimands to suspension from service without prejudice for a stated period.[46] While incorporating sanctions less severe than dismissal in due process proceedings may prevent extreme solutions to problems created by infractions of rules, they also give administrators and trustees greater opportunity to legitimately monitor a wider range of faculty activities. Thus, in the 1970 Teaching Assistants' Association Strike at University of Wisconsin, Madison, faculty were not brought to book for their support, while in 1980 faculty who did not meet classes on campus during the strike were involved in proceedings that ended with over 50 professors threatened with having their salaries docked.[47]

The Morris Starsky case at Arizona State is the last arising from the agitation over the Vietnam war and reveals most fully the forces that can be mobilized against professors who are openly and consistently anti-establishment: the public, the media, Regents, conservative elites, and the FBI. Starsky was a "publicly acknowledged Marxist Socialist" committed to social action. He was active in antiwar demonstrations and labor disputes, served as faculty advisor to socialist and radical student groups, and was active in Socialist Party politics. He had received tenure almost automatically during the rapid expansion of Arizona State in the 1960s, but despite media outcry no one moved against him until the FBI took a hand in his affairs. FBI documents released in the course of a lawsuit brought by the Socialist Worker's Party revealed the bureau, as part of its counter-intelligence program against the New Left (COINTELPRO), decided to use a highly placed contact influential in the state and with the board of Regents to push for Starsky's dismissal. When Starsky cancelled a class to speak at a Tucson rally ending in a disruptive demonstration, he opened himself to charges. Not content with moving the board to bring proceedings, the FBI also tried to influence the faculty hearing committee's deliberations. It mounted a covert operation that included sending committee members anonymous letters charging him with threatening a fellow Socialist Party worker with bodily harm. The faculty committee as well as the administration, however, recommended that Starsky be retained, at which point the Regents intervened and fired him. Although he found a one-year appointment immediately after his dismissal, Starsky's reputation as a troublemaker has since prevented him from holding a fulltime job.[48]

Most professors are unlikely to identify themselves with controversial causes, and thus are not involved in academic freedom cases. Still, the attitude of the many toward the few caught up in controversy is critical since they must defend their colleagues' right to civil liberties. In the twenty-three political cases in the 1970s, there was no reported evidence of any faculty support in twelve, or approximately half. Administrators apparently acted without undue outside pressure and without due process to rid themselves of faculty they defined as risks to their institutions' well-being. There is no record of faculty protest over what was often heavy-handed or abrupt action.

However, in seven cases there was evidence of some faculty support for fired colleagues, and in four additional cases—UCLA, Ohio State, Southern Illinois University at Carbondale, and Arizona State—faculty hearing committees supported by administrators resisted forceful direction by lay boards as well as strong outside pressure to recommend that colleagues involved in political action be retained. In each of these four instances, Regents intervened and fired the professors in question regardless of the opinion of the faculty as a whole. In a fifth instance of strong support, faculty at Concordia Seminary struck when a colleague and the President were suspended. The President had championed the faculty member in question when he was charged with "false teaching" of religious doctrine. The forty striking faculty members were dismissed and established a university in exile.[49]

Radicalism in and of itself was not necessarily cause for dismissal during the period under consideration. Political *action* was the issue in the 1970s.[50] Academic Marxists who addressed their social criticism primarily to each other did not figure in academic freedom cases even as liberals were fired for activism. Ideas alien to the established order were tolerated so long as they did not move men and women to deeds. Civil liberty more than intellectual substance was at issue.

Although research and teaching seldom seem to have precipitated dismissals resulting in nationally reported academic freedom cases in the 1970s, this does not mean that professors working in ideologically questionable scholarly paradigms all survived unscathed by avoiding action. Given the low number of tenured professors involved in political cases, many probationary faculty silently engaged in controversial research may have been quietly removed during tenure decisions. The structure of scholarship lends itself to removal of deviants at this point. First, tenure review is governed by senior faculty in part selected for their adherence to national academic norms that define extremism of any stripe as suspect.[51] Second, professors outside the intellectual mainstream have fewer publication outlets and those that are available are often regarded with disdain by established academics. Third, they may have difficulty attracting students, especially when market conditions make exploration of unworn paths a luxury. Finally, there is little chance of making a convincing case to the courts or the professoriate at large when collegial consensus defies the quality of their intellectual output as lacking. Even when senior faculty are able to control fully the mechanisms of due process and tenure review, the climate of academic freedom may still not be conducive to professors working with alternative intellectual paradigms.

"OTHER" CASES AND WOMEN

Apparently few faculty see themselves as wrongly dismissed for incompetence. Only four of the cases in the category "other" stem from this cause. This could mean that faculty who are incompetent know it and leave the university, or that they are removed by their colleagues after annual reviews or during tenure proceedings. More likely, incompetence is hard to prove in a profession difficult to evaluate, and, with the increase in litigation, such charges are not made unless they can be backed. With peer review, such cases should not appear on the AAUP censured list at all and do so largely because they involve notable violations of due process.

Two women appear in the "other" category, one fired for an irreconcilable personality conflict with a colleague, another for "moral turpitude" in the only case of its kind in some years. "Moral turpitude" has always been a mysterious charge; in a permissive age, what degree of baseness or depravity brings dismissal? In the case in question, a woman made the mistake of living openly with a man other than her husband in faculty housing located next door to the President's residence. Her colleagues found her indiscreet but not guilty of moral turpitude since they were unable to agree among themselves what this might be. However, the President was seemingly convinced that he knew and fired her anyway.[52]

Thirteen women were involved in those cases where gender is known. There seems to be nothing remarkable in their distribution across categories, except that four of the five involved in political cases were black. What is remarkable is the lack of sex discrimination cases. Although the AAUP called for use of procedural standards in instances of sex discrimination that are similar to those used when violations of academic freedom were alleged in 1971, only two cases involving sex discrimination were brought and neither were sustained by Committee A investigations.[53]

AAUP Associate Secretary Lesley Francis sees the lack of reported sex discrimination cases as due to the AAUP's function and the problem of proof. The AAUP is primarily a mediatory agency and does not have the financial resources, personnel, or subpoena powers necessary to mobilize the evidence needed to prove discrimination. However, the AAUP has devised progressive guidelines for sex discrimination complaints and can mediate when a case is still in university due process channels. Further, its policy and *amicus* briefs can successfully support women in sex discrimination cases tried in the courts, as in *Kunda* v. *Muhlenberg College*.[54] What is not clear is whether or not the AAUP allocates an even-handed proportion of its admittedly thin resources to its female constituency.

When women turn to government agencies and the courts, the problem of proof persists. Individual complaints of sex discrimination in hiring, promotion, or tenure fall under Title VII and are investigated by the Equal Employment Opportunity Commission. The complainant's first step in a court review is to make a *prima facie* case of discrimination. Statistical evidence can be offered on this point but may not be sufficient to establish a claim of discriminatory treatment. Though the plaintiff is not technically required to prove intent, she must show that the employer had a discriminatory motive in making the disputed employment decision. If she succeeds in doing this, the employer need only articulate some legitimate, nondiscriminatory reason for the decision. The burden of proof again shifts to the plaintiff to show that the employer's reason is a "mere pretext." Even if statistical evidence of discrimination is impressive, court opinions show that faculty women have found it difficult to meet the levels of proof required.[55] Although there have been some victories, especially in class actions brought by the agencies themselves, the process is costly, time-consuming, and so nerve-wracking that many women may be discouraged from becoming central figures. However, the number of women who brave this process is not known since federal agencies do not publish consistent statistics.[56]

Sex discrimination complaints brought by faculty women have been notably unsuccessful due to the courts' consistent deferral to decisions made by faculty and administrators concerning qualifications for hiring, retention, tenure, and promotion. In general, faculty try to avoid court interference in these decisions, perhaps to protect their due process privileges. At the extreme, the *Blaubergs* case demonstrates a tenured professor's willingness to defend his autonomy in these matters even if it means jail. As with all aspects of academic freedom, peer review controlled by white, male senior faculty may create a climate in which they flourish but others do not.

ACADEMIC FREEDOM IN THE 1980S

Since the professional problems that inform concepts of academic freedom vary with historical circumstance, new issues continuously present themselves. In the 1980s, two phenomena in the changing postsecondary world seem to impinge heavily on academic freedom. Both stem from the continuing resource crisis higher education confronts. On the one hand, administrators faced with tight budgets are exerting closer and more exacting control over faculty workload, often challenging the degree of freedom professors customarily expect to exercise. On the other hand, administrators are encouraging faculty to engage in relationships of a fiduciary nature with external organizations, such as business corporations, even though these often violate professional mores and strain fragile institutions, such as academic freedom.

In their recent monograph, *Faculty Freedoms and Institutional Accountability: Interactions and Conflicts,* Steven G. Olswang and Barbara A. Lee outline a number of the issues related to work load.[57] Traditionally, faculty have been able to decide what they teach and how they will teach it, subject only to the number of courses they are assigned to teach. Their time outside the classroom was presumed to be spent helping individual students, doing research, or serving the community, and was not closely monitored. However, faculty are increasingly being asked to account for one hundred percent of their time, and to document that they devote their full effort to the university.

Clear articulation of work load will bring to the fore questions about the value of academic work. After teaching obligations are met, what is a legitimate expenditure of effort with regard to research? Are unfunded projects that generate no income for department and university as deserving of faculty time as funded projects? Should faculty who work full-time for the university be allowed to engage in private consulting, and if so, to what degree, and how should their activity be monitored? Should they return a percentage of their consulting income to the university? What happens to *gratis* community service, given the increasing emphasis on committing professors' full-time to the institution, or encouraging interaction with the external groups only if income is generated for the institution?

If these decisions are made collegially, with groups of faculty engaged in dialogue with administrators, a fair amount of professional autonomy, which is a necessary condition for academic freedom, will probably be preserved, even while greater accountability is gained. If decisions about the value and assignment of the several components of faculty work load are made unilaterally by administrators, professional autonomy will suffer. The regulation of work load will probably be a key issue in the 1980s, and new forms of academic government may emerge as professors negotiate with administrators over how work load is determined.

Questions about who controls faculty time outside the classroom have become ever more important as academic knowledge becomes increasingly central to economic development. As high technology takes center stage, the differences between basic and applied research are collapsing. Business and government are increasingly interested in university-based research in science and engineering. Since the mid 1970s, many funding initiatives have directed faculty talent toward high technology partnerships with corporations and the state. The National Science Foundation (NSF) has funded an array of "partnership" programs, and corporations have entered into multi-year, multi-million-dollar contracts with universities.[58]

In a period when resources are less readily available, these partnerships are very attractive to universities. They receive funding from the corporate community as well as the state. Professors share in development often all the way to the product stage, and gain a fuller understanding of commercial application. If patent rights are part of the exchange, then universities stand to reap substantial benefits from royalties and licenses.

But university-industry partnerships are not without problems, especially with regard to academic freedom. Corporations often ask for secrecy to protect company information and materials. There are standard clauses providing for delays in publication until patent applications are secured. As partnerships become more prevalent, possible conflicts of interest between faculty, sponsoring company, and university multiply.[59] When the states are involved in providing seed money for joint ventures, legislative committees sometimes review proposed research projects.[60]

By acting entrepreneurially with regard to exploiting industry-university-government partnerships, research universities hope to make substantial economic gains, and perhaps to stabilize funds.[61] However, the commercialization of research flies in the face of professional and scientific codes. In formulating its declaration of principles, the AAUP justified academic freedom by proclaiming that professors would always use knowledge in the public interest, not for self, special, or private interests. Current efforts to profit from basic research turn away from past scientific practice. The ethos of modern science was generally understood to be characterized by universalism, communism, disinterestedness, and organized skepticism. In the words of Robert K. Merton,[62] "communism" meant that "the substantive findings of science are a product of social collaboration and are assigned to the community. They constitute a common heritage in which the equity of the producer is severely limited." The idea of science as part of the public domain "is linked with the imperative for community of findings. Secrecy is the antithesis of this norm, full and open communication its enactment." Should professors become too involved in commercial research, they may have to forfeit the special protection of academic freedom.

Like business, the military has increased its emphasis on university research. The Department of Defense (DOD) now defines its mission so broadly that almost all basic research falls within its purview.[63] DOD funding for universities grew dramatically between 1980 and 1985, from $495 million to $930 million, an increase of 89 percent. The National Science Foundation, which was the second fastest growing source of support for university research, grew only 51 percent during the same period. If DOD funding of off-campus institutes such as MIT's Lincoln Laboratories is figured into the equation, the Pentagon was outspending NSF on academic research in the first half of the present decade. If the Strategic Defense Initiative (SDI), or Star Wars, program receives the funding advocated by the current administration, it could quickly become the federal government's largest research activity.[64]

The problems presented for academic freedom by the increased military spending are many. Because highly technical knowledge has been deemed critical for military preparedness, government and military leaders have a much greater interest in how university knowledge is used. This interest sometimes turns into attempts to appropriate or control knowledge. The federal executive's recent efforts illustrate this tendency. In the name of national security, the President issued Executive Order 12356 in April 1982. The order expands "categories of information subject to classification to include nonclassified research developed by scientific investigators outside the government."[65] It also says that research that is "born free" may, under order, "die classified." In other words, a scientist's work, even if unfunded by the federal government and not drawing on any classified research, may be reclassified by executive agencies and withdrawn from circulation.[66] A more recent directive from the administration requests that the more than 100,000 government employees and 15,000 federal contractors with access to highly classified intelligence information "submit to a government agency for prior review virtually everything they may write, even after they leave government service, before discussing what they have written with or showing it to any other person not authorized to have access to the classified material."[67]

The increasing centrality of academic knowledge has reversed a thirty-year trend and is part of a complicated struggle between the elected head of government, various factions in the bureaucratic branches, and the university. As the AAUP points out, the conflict over national security is also a conflict over control of information. The "likely result is to remove from public and scholarly access additional tens and thousands of items that bear upon one's ability to determine the truth of statements made by executive branch officials, as well as upon the integrity of one's work."[68]

Military funding is not the only object of classification. Commercial high technology also falls under government regulation if it can be used for military purposes. Since most high technology—computers, lasers, materials science, biotechnology—is dual use, this means that faculty involvement in commercial ventures is sometimes monitored, and faculty participation in conferences devoted to high technology has been constrained under the Reagan administration. Increasingly, even exchange programs involving students and scientists from "adversial" nations come under close scrutiny.[69]

CONCLUSION

In sum, academic freedom can perhaps be best defined as the intellectual climate established by senior faculty when they are able to exercise the professional autonomy that comes with control of personnel policies via due process mechanisms, and have the job security that comes with tenure. It has been argued that the mechanisms of academic freedom—academic due process, tenure review, and a modicum of self government—have not been easily won and still require very active maintenance. Academic freedom seems most vulnerable in periods of social turmoil, which are many. In retrospect, the times when academic freedom has undergone severe challenge—the 1890s, the Progressive era, World War 1, the 1930s, the late 1940s and early 1950s, the late 1960s—seems almost as numerous as periods without strife. It is unlikely that professors will be able to work out policy or practice that allows them to avoid defending their academic freedom since "freedom of speech has a very special function in the case of those whose job it is to speak."[70] Moreover, professors need to pay close attention to their occupational context since the professional problems that inform concepts of academic freedom vary with historical circumstance, and new issues continuously present themselves.

NOTES

1. I would like to thank Jordan Kurland, American Association of University Professors' (AAUP) Associate General Secretary and spirit of Committee A, for his careful reading of several versions of this manuscript. While his help has been invaluable, he should not be held responsible for my interpretation of cases and policy. I would also like to thank Ms. Patricia Hyer, graduate student, College of Education, Virginia Polytechnic Institute and State University for her help in preparing the section on women.

2. Helene Wieruszowski, *The Medieval University* (New York: Van Nostrand Reinhold Company, 1966); Richard Hofstadter, *Academic Freedom in the Age of the College* (New York: Columbia University Press, 1955).

3. Walter P. Metzger, "The German Contribution to the American Theory of Academic Freedom," *American Association of University Professors Bulletin* (hereafter *AAUPB*) 41 (Summer 1955): 214-230; John S. Brubacher and Willis Rudy, *Higher Education in Transition: A History of American Colleges and Universities, 1636-1976* (New York: Harper and Row, 1976).

4. Jurgen Herbst, *The German Historical School in American Scholarship: A Study in the Transfer of Culture* (Ithaca, N.Y.: Cornell University Press, 1965).

5. Walter P. Metzger, "Academic Tenure in America: A Historical Essay," in *Academic Tenure,* Commission on Academic Tenure in Higher Education (San Francisco: Jossey-Bass, 1973), 93-159; Matthew W. Finkin, "Toward a Law of Academic Status," *Buffalo Law Review* 22 (1972): 575-601.

6. Walter P. Metzger, *The Development of Academic Freedom in the United States* (New York: Columbia University Press, 1955). For a second interpretation of these cases, see Mary O. Furner, *Advocacy and Objectivity: The Professionalization of Social Science, 1865-1905* (Lexington: University of Kentucky Press, 1975); for yet another interpretation see Edward T. Silva and Sheila Slaughter, *Serving Power: The Making of the American Social Science Expert* (Westport, Conn.: Greenwood, 1984).

7. Arthur Twining Hadley, "Academic Freedom in Theory and in Practice," *Atlantic Monthly* 91 (February 1903): 160. For a fuller account of the attitude of enlightened trustees, usually located at emerging research universities, see Burton J. Bledstein, *The Culture of Professionalism: The Middle Class and the Development of Higher Education in America* (New York: Norton, 1977).

8. For details of academic service to government see David Michael Grossman, "Professors and Public Service, 1885-1925: A Chapter in the Professionalization of Social Science" (Ph.D. dissertation, Washington University, 1973).

9. There were continued violations between the Ross case in 1900 and the Mecklin and Fisher cases in 1913, but for the most part these were not at newly emerging graduate centers and did not make the national news. See Howard Crosby Warren, "Academic Freedom," *Atlantic Monthly* 114 (November 1914): 689-699 for a partial listing.

10. "Report of the Committee on Academic Freedom and Tenure," reprinted from 1915 in *AAUPB* 40 (Spring 1954): 89-112.

11. For a fuller interpretation of this exchange see Sheila Slaughter, "The 'Danger Zone': Academic Freedom and Civil Liberties," *Annals of the American Academy of Political and Social Science* 448 (March 1980): 46-61.

12. Carol S. Gruber, *Mars and Minerva: World War I and the Uses of the Higher Learning* (Baton Rouge: Louisiana State University Press, 1975) and William Summerscales, *Affirmation and Dissent: Columbia's Response to the Crisis of World War I* (New York: Teacher's College Press, Columbia University, 1970).

13. See for example, "Emergency Council of Education," *AAUPB* 4 (April 1918): 4-6.

14. "American Council on Education: Conference on Academic Freedom and Tenure," *Bulletin of the AAUP* 11 (February 1925): 99-102. The ACE was and is an umbrella organization with a number of higher educational associations representing managers among its constituents. Although the Conference was held under ACE auspices and endorsed by a number of member organizations, negotiations over the document were in the main carried out by the AAUP and the Association of American Colleges. For an account of the AAUP's relation in ACE see Ralph E. Himstead, "The Association: Its Place in Higher Education," *AAUPB* 30 (Autumn 1944): 445-447.

15. Slaughter, "'The Danger Zone,'" *Annals,* 46-61.

16. "The 1940 Statement of Principles on Academic Freedom and Tenure," in *Academic Freedom and Tenure: A Handbook of the AAUP,* ed. Louis Loughlin (Madison: University of Wisconsin Press, 1969).

17. William Van Alstyne, "The Specific Theory of Academic Freedom and the General Issue of Civil Liberties," in *The Concept of Academic Freedom,* ed. Edmund L. Pincoffs (Austin: University of Texas Press, 1975), 81-82.

18. Although the 1940 document serves as a sort of Bill of Rights for the profession, it has been subject to clarifying interpretations over time by the association. The most recent was in 1970. See "Academic Freedom and Tenure: 1940 Statement of

Principles and (1970) Interpretative Comments," *AAUP Policy Documents and Reports* (Washington, D.C.: AAUP, 1977), 1-4.

19. Ellen W. Schrecker, *No Ivory Tower: McCarthyism and the Universities* (New York: Oxford University Press, 1986). Unless otherwise indicated the followng account of academic freedom cases in the Cold War is drawn from Schrecker's work.

20. Schrecker, *No Ivory Tower,* 218.

21. Lionel Lewis, "The Cold War and the Campus," unpublished ms., SUNY-Buffalo, Sociology Department, 1986.

22. Paul Lazarsfeld and Wagner Thielens, *The Academic Mind* (Glencoe, Ill.: Free Press, 1958), as summarized in Schrecker, *No Ivory Tower,* 309-310.

23. Other organizations have reported on academic freedom, for example, the AFT and ACLU in the 1930s and the New University Conference in the 1960s, but their reports are sporadic and lack detail. On this point see Lionel S. Lewis, *Scaling the Ivory Tower: Merit and its Limits in Academic Careers* (Baltimore: Johns Hopkins University Press, 1975), 148-149.

24. "Report of Committee A, 1978-1979," *AAUPB* 65 (September 1979): 296. For an explanation of the processing of complaints received by the AAUP see "Report of the Special Committee on Procedures for the Disposition of Complaints under the Principles of Academic Freedom and Tenure," *AAUPB* 51 (May 1965): 210-224.

25. Interview with Irving Spitzberg, Jr., General Secretary, AAUP, December 29, 1980.

26. On this point see Lewis, *Scaling the Ivory Tower,* 148.

27. Irving Spitzberg, Jr., former General Secretary of the AAUP, estimates that the AAUP was contacted in at least 90 percent of the cases in the 1970s; interview, December 29, 1980. Jordan Kurland, Associate General Secretary, indicated by letter, February 23, 1981, that the contact number is roughly 50 percent.

28. Interview with Jordan Kurland, AAUP, December 29, 1980.

29. This and the following data are compiled from the academic freedom cases reported by the AAUP from 1970-1980.

30. The exception was a state college that shifted from a traditional to an experimental mission and back again, accompanied by great tension and twelve dismissals. The AAUP supported litigation with its Academic Freedom Defense Fund and a decision was made in the terminated professors' favor. See "Academic Freedom and Tenure: University of Science and Arts of Oklahoma (formerly Oklahoma College of the Liberal Arts)," *AAUPB* 61 (April 1975): 39-48.

31. "Academic Freedom and Tenure: Bloomfield College (New Jersey)," *AAUPB* 60 (March 1974): 50-66; see also "The Bloomfield College Case: the Decision of the New Jersey Superior Court," *AAUPB* 60 (September 1974): 320-330.

32. "Academic Freedom and Tenure: City University of New York: Mass Dismissals under Financial Exigency," *AAUPB* 63 (April 1977): 60-81. See also James O'Connor, *The Fiscal Crisis of the State* (New York: St. Martin's Press, 1973), and Eric Lichten, "The Development of Austerity: Fiscal Crisis in New York City," in *Power Structure Research,* ed. G. William Domhoff (Beverly Hills: Sage, 1980), 139-171.

33. "Academic Freedom and Tenure: the State University of New York," *AAUPB* 63 (April 1977): 237-260. For AAUP policy on financial exigency see "Termination of Faculty Appointments Because of Financial Exigency, Discontinuance of Program or Department, or Medical Reasons," *AAUPB* 61 (Winter 1975): 329-331.

34. Interview with Jordan Kurland, AAUP, December 29, 1980.

35. Institutions were not required by the AAUP to give reasons for the dismissal of untenured professors until 1972. Even after this was required, many institutions refused to provide information for fear they might be opening themselves to legal suit. See "Development of Association Policy," *AAUPB* 57 (June 1971): 202-205, for the debate that preceded this policy decision. For the problems this has created in AAUP

investigations see William Van Alstyne, "Furnishing Reasons for a Decision Against Reappointment: Legal Considerations," *AAUPB* 62 (August 1976): 285-286.

36. "Academic Freedom and Tenure: Onondaga Community College (New York)," *AAUPB* 57 (June 1971): 167-174.

37. "Academic Freedom and Tenure: Blenn College (Texas)," *AAUPB* 62 (April 1975): 78-82. For the rise of collective bargaining in the 1970s see Joseph W. Garbarino, "Faculty Unionism: The First Ten Years," *Annals* 448 (March 1980): 74-85.

38. Interview with Geri Bledsoe, AAUP Associate Secretary for Collective Bargaining, December 29, 1980.

39. Robert Justin Goldstein, *Political Repression in Modern America, 1870 to the Present* (Cambridge, Mass.: Schenkman, 1978), 522-523.

40. "Academic Freedom and Tenure: Indiana State University," *AAUPB* 56 (March 1970): 52-61; "Academic Freedom and Tenure: Ohio State University," *AAUPB* 58 (September 1972): 306-321.

41. Although the AAUP condemned government and police interference in classrooms by resolution in the 1970s, it did not develop a policy position on domestic monitoring. However, it did debate the relation between universities and the CIA. See "Universities and the Intelligence Community," *AAUPB* 65 (February 1979): 15-26.

42. "Academic Freedom and Tenure: The University of Mississippi," *AAUPB* 56 (March 1970): 75-86.

43. "Academic Freedom and Tenure: The University of California at Los Angeles," *AAUPB* 57 (June 1971): 382-420. See also Bettina Aptheker, *The Morning Breaks: The Trial of Angela Davis* (New York: International, 1975).

44. "A Statement of the Association's Council: Freedom and Responsibility," *AAUPB* 56 (December 1970): 375-376.

45. "Academic Freedom and Tenure: University of Missouri, Columbia," *AAUPB* 59 (March 1973): 33-45; "Academic Freedom and Tenure: Columbia College (Missouri)," *AAUPB* 57 (June 1971): 513-517.

46. See "Report of the Joint Sub-Committee on Faculty Responsibility," *AAUPB* 57 (June 1971): 524-527.

47. This dispute is still in the process of settlement. After the penalty was known, the professors brought suit in federal district court, and it now appears that only those faculty who did not meet classes at all will have their pay docked while those who met their classes off campus to honor picket lines may not be docked.

48. "Academic Freedom and Tenure: Arizona State University," *AAUPB* 61 (December 1975): 55-69, supplemented by an interview with Jordan Kurland. After a one-year appointment at San Diego State, Starsky accepted a position as associate professor and chair of the philosophy department at California State University, Dominguez Hills. But his appointment was cancelled before he assumed his duties due to the President's discovery of the circumstances under which he left Arizona State. Although Starsky received $20,000 from California as redress for the cancelled contract, he never won recompense from Arizona even though two courts affirmed that his First and Fourteenth Amendment rights had been violated. On his attorney's advice he had accepted 60 percent of a year's salary for a terminal sabbatical on leaving Arizona State and the courts held this technically constituted redress. However, the AAUP has continued to press for a settlement and negotiations with Arizona State are continuing.

49. "Academic Freedom and Tenure: Concordia Seminary (Missouri)," *AAUB* 61 (April 1975): 49-59.

50. For clarification of the AAUP's 1940 position on political action see "A Statement of the Association's Council: The Question of Institutional Neutrality," *AAUPB* 55 (Winter 1969): 448; "Academic Freedom and Tenure. 1940 Statement of

Principles and (1970) Interpretative Comments," *AAUP Policy Documents and Reports* (Washington, D.C.: AAUP, 1977): 1-4, and "A Statement of the Association's Council: Freedom and Responsibility," *AAUPB* 56 (December 1970): 375-376.

51. Most senior faculty would have received their primary socialization during the McCarthy era (1950-1960). For a notion of the ideological mind-set in this period see Paul L. Lazarsfeld and Wagner Thielens, Jr., *The Academic Mind: Social Scientists in Times of Crisis* (Glencoe: Free Press, 1958).

52. "Academic Freedom and Tenure: Lynchburg College (Virginia)," *AAUPB* 65 (December 1979): 598-605.

53. "Report of the Council," *AAUPB* 58 (June 1972): 160-163.

54. Telephone interview with Lesley Lee Francis, Associate Secretary, AAUP, January 22, 1981. For AAUP discrimination guidelines see "On Processing Complaints of Discrimination on the Bias of Sex," *AAUPB* 63 (August 1977): 231-236; see also "News: Kunda Decision Affirmed," *AAUPB* 66 (May 1980): 172.

55. *A Program for Renewed Partnership: A Report of the Sloan Commission on Government and Higher Education* (Cambridge: Ballinger, 1980); Bruce A. Nelson and Richard W. Ward, "Burdens of Proof Under Employment Discrimination Legislation," *Journal of College and University Law* 4 (1979-1980): 301-316.

56. B. Haber, "Why Not the Best and the Brightest? Equal Opportunity vs. Academic Freedom," *Forum* 19 (January 1981): 19-25.

57. Steven G. Olswang and Barbara Lee, *Faculty Freedoms and Institutional Accountability: Interactions and Conflicts* (Washington, D.C.: Association for the Study of Higher Education, ASHE-ERIC Higher Education Research Report, No. 5, 1984).

58. Lois Peters and H. Fusfeld, "Current U.S. University-Industry Research Connections," in National Science Board, *University-Industry Research Relationships,* (Washington, D.C.: NSB, 1982).

59. David Dickson, *The New Politics of Science* (New York: Pantheon, 1984); Association of American Universities, *University Policies on Conflict of Interest and Delay of Publications* (Washington, D.C.: Report of the Clearinghouse on Unviersity-Industry Relations, 1985).

60. Scott Jaschik, "Universities' High Technology Pacts with Industry Are Marred by Politics, Poor Planning and Hype," *Chronicle of Higher Education* (March 12, 1986): 15-17.

61. For an excellent discussion of the many issues involved in the complex relationships between research universities, corporations, and federal bureaucracies see Derek Bok, *Beyond the Ivory Tower: Social Responsibilities of the Modern University* (Cambridge, MA.: Harvard University Press, 1982).

62. Robert K. Merton, "Science and Technology in a Democratic Order," *Journal of Legal and Political Sociology* 1 (1942): 115-126.

63. National Science Board, *Basic Research in the Mission Agencies: Agency Perspectives on the Conduct and Support of Basic Research* (Washington, D.C.: National Science Foundation, 1978).

64. W. Hartung and R. Nimroody, "Pentagon Invades Academia," *Council on Economic Priorities Newsletter* (New York: CEP Publication N86-1, 1986), 1-6.

65. Academic Freedom and Tenure, "The Enlargement of the Classified Information System," *Academe* (January/February 1983).

66. Academic Freedom and Tenure, "Government Censorship and Academic Freedom," *Academe* (November/December 1983): 15a-17a.

67. American Association of University Professors, "Academic Freedom and Government Restraints," *Academe* (March/April 1984): 32a.

68. Academic Freedom and Tenure, "Corporate Funding of Academic Freedom,"

Academe (November/December 1983): 18a-22a.

69. David Dickson, *The New Politics of Science.*

70. Fritz Machlup, "On Some Misconceptions Concerning Academic Freedom," *AAUPB* 41 (Winter 1955): 75-86.

6

Economics and Financing
of Higher Education
The Tension Between Quality and Equity

W. Lee Hansen and Jacob O. Stampen

INTRODUCTION

This chapter examines the social and economic changes since World War II
that affect the allocation and distribution of resources to higher education.
The massive expansion of enrollments and the broadened missions of higher
education institutions that began in the late 1950s not only required but also
stimulated a substantial increase in resources allocated to higher education.
However, the past fifteen years have been markedly different. Relatively less
abundant available resources and scaled-back aspirations have been put into
place even though demands on institutions of higher education continue to
increase. How higher education will respond in the face of such belt-tighten-
ing measures remains unclear. To provide some insight into this conflict, we
examine how and why the level and allocation of resources has shifted over a
forty-year period.

One apparent explanation for the shift is the significant changes in the
goals of higher education that have taken place over the past two decades.
Substantially increased attention toward promoting wider access resulted in
less attention to developing high-quality educational programs. These changes
stem from an ongoing concern with social justice, a concern that has always
received strong support from higher education. As a result, the character of
higher education by the end of the 1970s seemed to have been substantially
and permanently altered, with its focus on access, choice, and persistence.

It now appears that this conclusion was premature. Since 1981 we have

The authors acknowledge the research assistance of Marilyn H. Rhodes as well as the financial
support of the National Center for Postsecondary Governance and Finance and the Wisconsin
Center for Education Research.

experienced another dramatic change, evidenced by renewed public concern over quality and related calls for standards that differ markedly from those of the preceding decade. As a result higher education is making a strong bid to raise academic standards so as to improve educational programs, to use its resources more effectively, and to respond judiciously to a widening array of social demands. Partly as a result of these developments institutions of higher education have recently embarked on a major effort, particularly at the state and local levels, to increase available resources.

The path of progress for the higher education sector has not been a smooth one. The pace of change has been erratic at times; the direction has been meandering; and many outside forces have shaped its evolution over the past four decades.

The structure for our analysis is based on a series of questions concerning expenditures in higher education, which reflects society's investment in this area. We then develop criteria that can be used to relate various mandates for change in higher education with social and economic changes. The central focus of the analysis is to identify distinct time periods that can highlight the major forces affecting postsecondary education since World War II. Based on this framework, we proceed to examine the changing investment patterns in higher education, shifts in the allocation of expenditures, and what all of this means for those who pay the costs.

The principal questions that guide our discussion are:

1) How did the various social-political mandates from the past forty years influence societal spending, or investment, in higher education?

2) What were the key events affecting investment in higher education during these forty years?

3) What were the trends in overall expenditures for instruction, tuition and fee changes, and student financial aid?

4) How did these changes affect the sharing of the costs of higher education and the ability of students and their families to finance college attendance?

The data available to address these questions are less than ideal. Routinely gathered federal statistics on higher education have been frequently redefined, thereby making it difficult to document consistently financial trends and changes in higher education activities. Public opinion polls that might capture prevailing views about higher education are sporadic and usually rather vague in the information they elicit. Existing studies and research reports pursue a variety of questions that do not necessarily bear on our topic. For these reasons the variables selected for observation are necessarily broad, and represent a synthesis not entirely free of our own judgments. Nonetheless, the general patterns that emerge seem to offer explanations of changes in higher education that are both plausible and meaningful.

DATING THE PERIODS OF ANALYSIS

In reviewing the past four decades in the history of higher education it is evident that this sector was successively buffeted by a variety of unprecedented forces. Perhaps the most noticeable force was demography. The enrollment surge after World War II that resulted from the GI Bill was followed by a relatively stable enrollment until the late 1950s. After a gradual enrollment increase into the early 1960s, an explosion of enrollments occurred as the baby-boom population reached maturity. This enrollment surge continued but at a somewhat slower pace through the 1970s. Since 1980 overall enrollment growth slowed considerably.

Another key factor has been the efforts of the higher education sector to chart its own course, as reflected in a long series of reports, that articulate the goals and aspirations of the higher education community. Still another force has been that of economists and other social scientists who periodically introduce new concepts, provide fresh insights, and offer novel proposals that stir the air and stimulate thinking about the economics and financing of higher education. Last but not least, political forces always loom large and are revealed most immediately in governmental actions; ultimately, however, these actions reflect an even more powerful force, namely, the changing priorities of the citizenry who ultimately determine the focus of political action and the availability of resources for higher education.

To facilitate our analysis we define four distinct time periods. The first embraces the years between 1947 to 1958, a period of readjustment following World War II, that began with the GI Bill and concluded with the emergence of higher education as a major factor in the development of American society. The second period, 1958 to 1968, reflects the enormous expansion of the higher education sector and its emphasis on the elusive dimension of quality, spurred by concern that American technology was falling behind that of the Soviets. The next period, 1968 to 1981, represents a sharp change of focus. The first part of the period reflects the search for ways to broaden opportunities for students to attend college, initiated by the federal student loan programs in 1965. This search culminates with the federal decision in 1972 to establish a national need-based student aid system that credited the Pell grants (earlier called Basic Educational Opportunity Grants). The latter part of the period, from 1972-73 onward, can best be described as a time for consolidating the system and resolving equity problems; this experience revealed the great difficulties of dealing effectively with these issues. As most readers are aware, the period 1980-81 to the present represents a sharp swing in the opposite direction, with concerns about quality, efficient use of resources, and broadened missions rising to the forefront once again.

These forces and their changing direction over the past four decades reflect the well-known pendulum effect in social and political affairs.[1] It begins with special concerns about equity that led to the GI Bill, followed by concern for quality in the late 1950s and early 1960s. This is followed by the ascendancy of interest in equity and opportunity in the late 1960s and 1970s. By the early 1980s these forces had run their course and we see our apparent reversion to concerns about quality and effectiveness.

We begin by outlining the major forces operating in each of the four periods.

1947 to 1958

This period can best be described as one of readjustment after the Great Depression and World War II. It begins with the rapid increase in enrollments occasioned by returning veterans who resumed or began their college training with the help of the GI Bill. Despite the declining size of the college-age population in the early 1950s, as a result of falling birth rates in the 1930s, enrollments held up reasonably well with the flow of Korean War veterans into college, also under the GI Bill.

Aside from changes on college campuses brought about by the returning veterans, this period was rather uneventful. The social and economic pressures on higher education were minimal. The resources provided, while not substantial by current standards, matched public expectations that access to higher education should be limited to a modest percentage of high school graduates. The one noteworthy report of the period came from the 1947 Truman Commission on Higher Education (otherwise known as the Zook Commission),[2] which suggested that after the veterans completed their schooling larger proportions of the civilian population should be educated. The commission estimated that half of all high school graduates could benefit from higher education. It called for removing the financial barriers to college attendance by providing loans, grants, and work-study opportunities based on financial need.[3]

The period marked the ascendance of higher education to a new level of prominence in American society. Colleges and universities had been instrumental in easing the transition from a wartime to a peacetime economy, many young people who might not have had a chance to attend college did, and institutions of higher education were able to expand and develop. Knowledge of the important contributions of academe during World War II led to society's increased reliance on it, and people came to believe that colleges and universities could be instrumental in resolving other national problems. Meanwhile, many higher education leaders proved to be persuasive spokesmen for education and exercised positions of leadership on national policy issues that had broad social implications.

1957 to 1968

This period can be described as one of enormous expansion and a strong emphasis on quality. The most important element was demographic, with the number of young people reaching eighteen years of age rising from 2.3 million in the fall of 1957 to 2.8 million in the same period of 1964 and then jumping to 3.8 million in 1965.[4] By the early 1960s colleges and universities were scrambling to construct facilities and to recruit new faculty members to deal with this unprecedented growth. The emphasis on quality had come earlier and unexpectedly as a result of the Soviet launching of the Sputnik satellite in 1957. This event dramatized the need for augmenting the nation's human resource base and for focusing particular attention on developing the most talented youth; it led to passage of the National Defense Education Act, which provided limited loans and scholarships.

Meanwhile, economists were developing the concept of human capital, which blossomed in the early 1960s and demonstrated the powerful effects of human "investment" in higher education on economic growth and on individual well-being.[5] Simultaneously, social scientists were identifying the "talent loss" resulting from many highly qualified high school graduates who could profit from college neither attending nor planning to attend college. These developments combined to justify the enormous expansion of resources invested in the instructional programs and the facilities of colleges and universities. They were also instrumental in expanding the amount of organized research activity financed largely by the federal government.

Several national reports proved to be influential in focusing the debate and defining paths for subsequent action. A 1957 report by the President's Committee on Education Beyond High School recommended that planning begin for the projected expansion of higher education and that faculty salaries, which had lagged seriously behind those of other comparable groups, be doubled in real terms by 1970 so as to assure an adequate base for the coming expansion of the college population. Equally important was President Eisenhower's Commission on National Goals, which presented its findings in a 1960 report titled *Goals for Americans.*[6] Among the report's twenty-five educational goals was a call for establishing more community colleges, expanding the number of Ph.D.s, state planning of higher education, low interest loans for college construction, fellowships for graduate students, as well as more student loan funds and higher loan amounts.[7] Though not expressed in so many words, the proposed creation of a vast new network of community colleges as well as an expanded and upgraded system of four-year colleges suggested simultaneous pursuit of the goals of improved quality and wider access.

Some progress was achieved during the first half of the 1960s in reducing the financial barriers to college attendance. Several states developed their own financial aid programs, which later became models for federal programs.[8] President Johnson's War on Poverty legislation in 1964 led to the creation of the Work Study Program and to special grants to help minority students attend college. Additional impetus came with passage in 1965 of the Higher Education Act, which provided subsidized loans for college and university students through the commercial banking system. Despite these advances, the total resources devoted to student aid remained quite small.

The period closes with Lecht's 1966 report that articulated a set of national goals and translated them to quantitative terms for 1970 and 1975.[9] The goals included not only an increase to a 100 percent high school graduation rate, but also an increase to 50 percent in high school graduates going to college; these goals were based on the assumption that state financial resources would be available to permit this expansion. At the same time, colleges were expected to double their loans and scholarships, private firms were expected to subsidize the schooling of more of their employees, and federal resources for loans and work-study programs were expected to increase substantially. While the implications of these goals are clear, the problems likely to arise from trying to attain them were not discussed.

1967 to 1981

The Lecht report marked the end of an era that reflected an almost unbounded optimism about the prospects for higher education. Meanwhile, new forces pushing for greater equality of opportunity moved to the forefront, concern mounted over the "talent loss" resulting from financial barriers to attending college, people became increasingly conscious about poverty and its growth, and the pressures growing out of the civil rights movement focused new attention on equity issues. Taken together, these forces soon pushed concerns about quality into the background.

The opportunities inherent in these developments were quickly recognized by Clark Kerr who was then organizing the Carnegie Commission on Higher Education: he crystallized them in an influential chapter in the 1968 Brookings Institution volume titled *Agenda for a Nation*.[10] Kerr outlined six major issues facing higher education in the 1970s. These included the quest for greater equality of educational opportunity, the problems of financing higher education in view of rising costs, the likelihood of extensive use of new "technology" in learning, the continuing shortages of Ph.D.s and M.D.s, the need for metropolitan universities to develop an urban focus, and the special financial difficulties of black, liberal arts, and state colleges.

To deal with these problems, Kerr pushed for federal solutions through federal funding. This approach no doubt reflected the successes of higher education over the previous decade in garnering federal support for research, college buildings, and special equipment. Yet it also marked a significant departure from the traditional combination of financial support—tuition from students and their parents, state and local tax revenues for public institutions, and voluntary support for private institutions. Rather than push only for institutional support, Kerr called for an expanded program of student financial aid that would increase to fifteen billion dollars annually by 1976. About one-third of this total would go for the continuing support of research, another third would underwrite a system of need-based student financial aid grants, and the remainder would go for construction, institutional support, special programs, and medical education.

This report was followed within a year by two more detailed sets of proposals. One was issued by Kerr's Carnegie Commission on Higher Education[11] and the other emanated from an Advisory Task Force created by the Department of Health, Education, and Welfare under the direction of Alice Rivlin, then Assistant Secretary for Education.[12] These reports proved to be surprisingly similar in their recommendations, calling for a federally-financed system of need-based student financial aid grants, direct institutional grants tied to the number of students receiving support, and various related proposals to deal with special needs. Both reports spent considerable effort to justify their particular recommendations, to estimate their costs, and to assess their likely effects. It is clear that these recommendations constituted a package, with student aid as the centerpiece of an integrated set of proposals. The obvious objective was to promote greater equality of educational opportunity.

Meanwhile, economists were turning their attention to issues of poverty and income distribution as well as their effects on public programs. These studies showed that prevailing policies had the effect of directing the bulk of higher education subsidies to help youths from higher- and middle-income families rather than lower-income families, thereby disputing the conventional wisdom.[13] These findings accentuated the desirability of need-based student financial aid programs to help offset financial barriers to college attendance.

A federal student financial aid system emerged in 1972 with passage of the Basic Education Opportunity Grant (BEOG) program, which provided grants to students based on their financial need.[14] The program was phased in over a four-year period, and thus covered all undergraduates by the 1976-77 academic year. This completed the erection of a federal aid system relying on a combination of grants, loans, and work-study programs to help youths from lower income families overcome the financial barriers to college attendance.

Creation of the national need-based student grant system in 1972 meant the realization of a goal that had first been proposed by the Truman Commission almost a quarter of a century earlier. Expectations for the new program were high for many reasons. But, with the less bouyant economy of the 1970s—periodic episodes of sharp inflation, continuing increases in postsecondary enrollments, and the ascendancy of other social priorities—the financial support for academic programs began to erode, and efforts to improve equity became more diffused at the institutional level. This produced increased stress within higher education, and between it and its outside constituencies. For example, middle-income families finding that their children could not qualify for Pell (formerly BEOG) grants pressured Congress to give them access to student loans. The result was passage of the "Middle Income Student Assistance Act of 1978"[15] which eliminated the requirement that students demonstrate financial need when applying for aid from the subsidized Guaranteed Student Loan program. Borrowing expanded rapidly and soon loans displaced grants as the most common form of student aid.

The large-scale movement of middle-income students into the ranks of aid recipients also became a focus of controversy. Examples of middle-income students buying cars or purchasing certificates of deposit with the proceeds of their heavily subsidized student loans rather than using the money to pay for education became commonplace. On a broader scale there were rumblings about whether America had caught the "British Disease," which conjured up the image of public programs exhausting their ability to assist genuinely needy people but becoming increasingly inefficient by including virtually everyone. At the same time there was a developing sense that government regulation of higher education had become overly burdensome and inefficient.

In terms of student aid, however, the latter part of this period, between 1972 and 1980, reflected efforts to consolidate the gains already made and to work out the inevitable difficulties associated with new public programs. It culminated with the reauthorization in fall 1980 of student aid programs that called for a sizeable expansion of grants and loans well into the 1980s.

Meanwhile, many institutions experienced difficulty maintaining support for instruction. Constant dollar declines in support for students occurred in many states even though per-student appropriations on a national basis actually increased. In part, this was explained by public expectations that higher education should maintain programs aimed at solving a wide array of social programs including health, poverty, and the environment, and by increases in the numbers of administrators needed to assure accountability. In addition, the financial squeeze on many state budgets slowed the flow of resources to higher education even though enrollments were steadily rising.

Throughout this period colleges and universities continued to grapple with a myriad of problems associated with student unrest that began in the late 1960s: calls for educational reform, pressures of increased enrollments, growing proportions of women and minority students, and changing preferences among students in their major fields of study. The trickle of literature on these and related developments swelled into a vast torrent, fed in part by the Carnegie Commission's recruitment of legions of scholars to examine every facet of higher education.

1980 to the Present

The national elections of 1980, which brought the Reagan administration and a Republican majority to the U.S. Senate, marked an abrupt shift from an almost exclusive focus on equity concerns to one emphasizing economic and political reform. The election campaign and its aftermath drew attention to double-digit inflation, the need to cut federal spending and taxes, deregulation, and the need to enhance America's competitiveness. It also drew attention to declining SAT scores, increased drug problems in the schools, and growing illiteracy. More importantly, it downplayed the role of federal policy in attempting to solve these problems. These changes are documented by

Whitt, Clark, and Astuto[16] who find in the years after 1980 a sudden shift of policy focus from concerns about equity to related issues such as academic performance and institutional improvement; they also find a public consensus in support of this shift.

Student financial aid, the major avenue of federal support for higher education, came under sharp attack early in the ninety-seventh Congress (1981), with Senate-led efforts to reduce substantially appropriations for grant programs. Two important changes were enacted: the re-establishment of income requirements in the Guaranteed Student Loan programs and the elimination of Social Security education benefits. Thereafter, a bipartisan consensus in the Congress prevented further cuts.[17]

A Reagan administration initiative, aimed at improving the quality of education, began to gain bipartisan support at the same time that cuts in student aid were halted. An agenda took shape in a series of national reports focusing on elementary and secondary education.[18] The best known of the reports, *A Nation at Risk*[19] renounced pre-existing policies as leading to economic, political, and social decline, exhorting educators and the general public to develop new performance standards in the schools aimed at improving the nation's competitive position. Other similar reports were less dramatic but generally supported the need to raise educational standards, even though none were very specific about how this might be accomplished.[20]

Shortly thereafter a similar series of reports began to appear that focused on higher education.[21] These reports called for renewed emphasis on quality, a sharpened focus on institutional missions, and greater attention to student learning. Since then pressures to monitor quality in higher education have continued to mount, just as they did earlier for elementary-secondary education.

It is too soon to tell whether efforts to enhance the quality of education will be effective. However, it is clear that recent calls for improvement have yet to result in new infusions of resources similar to those occurring in previous eras (e.g., the Truman GI Bill, the Sputnik period, the rapid enrollment expansion of the 1960s, and the significant expansion of need-based financial aid in the 1970s). As in previous periods, several recent national reports call for new resources. As yet, the federal and the state governments have shown little inclination to respond. Instead, attention has been focused on new demands for accountability in using existing resources.

THE ANALYSIS

Having now established the time periods for this analysis, we turn to the data in the hope of learning whether the changing political-social-economic conditions and the accompanying mandates embodied in commission reports had any lasting effect on higher education. We begin by describing the changing dimensions of the nation's investment in institutions of higher education. Expenditures are then examined in an effort to highlight major trends and to reveal the interplay between external and internal forces affecting the allocation of resources within the higher education sector. This paves the way for measuring the burden of costs and how they are shared among students and parents, state and local taxpayers, private donors, and federal taxpayers through the provision of student financial aid.

In large measure official data from the Department of Education and its predecessor the U.S. Office of Education are relied upon. Because of changes in our data collection systems as well as periodic alterations in the definitions of expenditures and revenues, the detailed data are not completely comparable over the forty-year period under study. Nonetheless, the broad categories employed here are consistent. Readers are cautioned that this overall analysis hides differences between public- and private-sector institutions as well as among universities on the one hand, and those between four-year and two-year institutions on the other.[22]

Students

Enrollment growth is described by two different sets of data: total enrollment, for which the data are readily available; and full-time equivalent (FTE) enrollment, which must be estimated.[23] As shown in columns 1 and 2 of Table 1, full-time equivalent enrollment declined as percentage of total enrollment. The results from the steady increase in the proportion of part-time students (column 3), which is attributable to several developments, the most important being the substantial increase of older students (those age twenty-five and over who typically cannot attend full-time).

The overall growth figures for enrollment reflect the tidal wave-like effect of the baby boom as well as the increasing desire of adults either to begin or to return to college. Enrollments edged up only slightly from the late 1940s to the late 1950s, nearly doubled by the late 1960s, almost doubled again by 1981, and continued increasing but at a much slower pace in the early 1980s. The enrollment increases in the 1980s is at odds with many projections from the 1970s, which had anticipated enrollment declines for the early 1980s.[24]

An appreciation for the implications of enrollment growth is provided by examining the percentages of students enrolled in higher education relative to the college-age population (those 18-24: column 4) and to the adult population (18 and above: column 5). The percentage enrolled among those age 18-24 rose steadily from 16 percent in 1947-48 to 43 percent in 1983-84.[25] The percentage enrolled among those age 18 and over rose from 2.6 percent in 1947-48 to 7.3 percent in 1983-84. For both series the big gains occurred from the late 1950s to late 1960s and from then until 1980.

As these data reveal, a substantial expansion in demand for higher education occurred but its uneven rate of growth was heavily influenced by demographic forces.

Table 1
Enrollment in Higher Education Institutes

Year	Total Head Count Enrollment (in thousands) (col. 1)	FTE Enrollment (in thousands) (col. 2)	Part Time as a Percent of Head Count Enrollment (col. 3)	Head Count Enrollment as a Percent of 18-24-Year-Olds (col. 4)	Head Count Enrollment as a Percent of Total Population (col. 5)
1947-48	2,616	2,222	22%	16%	2.6%
1957-58	3,068	2,395	33%	20%	2.5%
1967-68	6,912	4,591	31%	29%	5.4%
1980-81	12,097	8,819	41%	41%	7.4%
1983-84	12,465	9,166	42%	43%	7.3%

SOURCES:

Column 1 Historical Statistics of the United States, Colonial Times to 1957, Series H 316-326, p. 210.

Statistical Abstract of the United States, 1970, Table 185, p. 132; 1981, Table 266, p. 158; 1985, Tabl 252, p. 150.

Column 2 *Fact Book, 1984-85* (American Council on Education, Macmillan Publishing Company, 1984).

Column 3 Calculated using part-time enrollment data. Pre-1980-81 estimated from data in June O'Neill, *Resource Use in Higher Education* (Carnegie Commission on Higher Education, 1971). 1980-81 on from *Digest of Educational Statistics,* 1985-86, p. 101.

Column 4 Calculated using age 18-24 population from U.S. Bureau of the Census.

Column 5 Calculated using Total Population from U.S. Bureau of the Census.

Total Resources for Higher Education

Providing for these ever-growing numbers of students meant raising substantial amounts of new revenue from taxpayers, donors, students, supporters of research, and those who purchased services sold by higher education institutions. The major sources of current fund revenue are shown in Table 2 for 1983-84; for comparison, the table also shows the distribution of current fund expenditures.

The growth of revenues for higher education is substantial. Because of economic growth and inflation the linkage between the growth of revenue and increased enrollment is unlikely to be close over any extended period. More interesting for our purposes is the relationship between higher education's revenue growth and the economy's capacity to support higher education. This is illustrated in Table 3, which shows revenues for higher education as a percentage of gross national product (GNP); revenues averaged about

Table 2
Major Categories of Current Fund Revenues and Expenditures
for Higher Education Institutions, 1983-84 (Millions of Dollars)

Total Current Fund Revenue	$84,417
Tuition and Fees	19,715
Federal Government	10,406
State Government	24,707
Local Government	2,192
Private gifts, grants, and contracts	4,415
Endowment income	1,874
Sales and service	18,468
Other services	2,640
Total Current Fund Expenditures	$81,993
Education and general	63,741
Instruction	26,436
Research and public service	19,223
Scholarships and fellowships	3,302
Auxiliary enterprises and hospitals	16,630

SOURCES: "Higher Education Finance Trends, 1970-71 to 1983-84," OERI Bulletin, U.S. Department of Education, Center for Education Statistics, December 1986, CS 87-303b, pp. 6-10.

1.0 percent of GNP in the 1940s and 1950s, rose to a little over 2.0 percent in the late 1960s, and then stablized at about 2.5 percent of GNP in the 1980s. These results demonstrate the close connection that persists between enrollment levels and the proportion of the nation's total resources required to support higher education. This relationship prevails largely because, at least in the public sector, the funding formulas give considerable if not exclusive weight to enrollments.

The sources of current-fund revenue for institutions of higher education changed in only minor ways as shown in Table 4. The major source is state government, followed closely by tuition and fees, with all three types of funding growing at roughly the same rate. Federal contributions have for the most part been stable, constituting less than a quarter of total revenues.

Higher Education Expenditures

Higher education current-fund expenditures by institutions, as shown in Table 5, represent the other side of the ledger, one that is conditioned by the amount of revenues available. As Howard R. Bowen[26] so aptly explains,

Table 3

Total Current Fund Revenues and Expenditures for Higher Education
Institutes and Gross National Product (GNP) and Annual Percentage
Rates of Increase

	Total Current Fund Revenues (in millions)	Gross National Product (in billions)	Total Current Funds Revenues as a Percent of GNP (in percent)	Total Current Fund Expenditures (in millions)
	(1)	(2)	(3)	(4)
1947-48	$2,027	$235	0.9%	$1,883
% Annual Change	9%	7%		9%
1957-58	4,676	451	1.0%	$4,509
% Annual Change	14%	6%		14%
1967-68	16,910	816	2.1%	16,556
% Annual Change	11%	10%		10%
1980-81	65,585	2,732	2.4%	64,053
% Annual Change	9%	8%		9%
1983-84	84,417	3,402	2.5%	81,993

NOTE: GNP data are for calendar year in which academic year begins.

SOURCES:
Column 1 Biennial Survey of Education, Financial Statistics of Higher Education.
Column 2 Economic Report of the President, 1986.
Column 3 Calculated as indicated.
Column 4 Same as Column 1.

higher education is comprised of essentially nonprofit organizations which, while forced to live within their available resources, seek constantly to increase their revenues in order to better serve their students and society.[27] These current-fund expenditures increase at about the same rate as do current-fund revenues (see Table 2, columns 1 and 3). This similarity is quite understandable in light of the organizational form of higher education institutions. More interesting than the changing level of overall expenditures is how major components of these expenditures grew from period to period.

We see in column 1 of Table 5 that total current-fund expenditures increased from $1,883 million in 1947-48 to $81,993 million in 1983-84, an increase of almost ten-fold. The rate of increase for the 1947-48 to 1957-58 period proved to be substantial, with total expenditures increasing about two and one-half times over the decade and quadrupling over the next two pe-

Table 4
Sources of Current Fund Revenues for Higher Education Institutions
(Millions of Dollars)

	1947-48	1957-58	1967-68	1980-81	1983-84
Total Income	$2,027	$4,641	$16,825	$65,585	$84,417
Tuition and Fees (1)	305	934	3,380	13,773	19,714
Federal Government	526	707	3,348	8,479	10,406
State Government	352	1,138	4,181	20,106	24,706
Local Government	48	129	504	1,790	2,192
Private Gifts, Grants, and Contracts	91	324	848	3,176	4,415
Endowments	87	182	364	1,364	1,874
Auxiliary Enterprises	465	839	2,482	7,288	9,456
Other Income (includes student aid) (2)	24	70	498	8,173	2,640

NOTES:

(1) 1947 to 1967 includes "Student Fees" only.

(2) 1947 to 1980 includes student aid with other income; 1983 includes only "other income."

SOURCES:
For 1947/48 see, Historical Statistics, Colonial Times to 1970, Series H 716-727, p. 384.
For 1957/58 see, op. cit.
For 1967/58 see, op. cit.
For 1980/81 see, Digest of Educational Statistics, 1985-86, Table 137, p. 154.
For 1983/84 see, "Higher Education Finance Trends," OERI Bulletin, U.S. Department of Education, Center for Education Statistics, December 1986, CS 87-303b, p. 6.

riods: the increase was less than a third in the final but appreciably shorter period from 1980-81 to 1983-84.

The data on total current-fund expenditures are not highly illuminating in understanding the impact on higher education of the developments discussed in the first part of this paper. The reason is that total expenditures include funds allocated to carry out activities less central to the educational function of higher education and are in any case often self-financed. To the extent that expenditures for these functions grew more rapidly than total expenditures, this indicates that the residual, which is largely instruction-related expenditures, grew more slowly than the total.

How do we construct estimates of what we have just referred to as instructional or instruction-related expenditures? Several types of expendi-

Table 5
Major Components of Current Fund Expenditures for
Higher Education Institutions and Annual Percentage Rates of Increase

Year	Total Current Fund Expenditures (in millions) (1)	Auxiliary Enterprises, Hospitals (in millions) (2)	Student Financial Aid (in millions) (3)	Organized Research and Public Service (in millions) (4)	Instruction Related Expenses (in millions) (5)
1947-48	$1,883	$492	$40 (est.)	$230	$1,162
% Annual Change	9%	5%	11%	15%	9%
1957-58	$4,509	$775	$113 (est.)	$903	$2,701
% Annual Change	14%	11%	22%	14%	14%
1967-68	$16,566	$2,307	$830 (est.)	$3,312	$10,234
% Annual Change	14%	14%	9%	8%	11%
1980-81	$64,053	$12,721	$2,505	$8,973	$39,854
% Annual Change	9%	12%	9%	.1%	9%
1983-84	$81,993	$18,252	$3,302	$9,222	$51,217

NOTES:
Column 2 includes Auxillary Enterprises, Hospitals
Column 3 includes Student Financial Aid, Scholarships, and Fellowships
Column 4 includes Organized Research, Public Service, and Expansion
Column 5 includes column 1 less the sum of columns 2-4

SOURCES:
Biennial Survey of Education, Financial Statistics of Higher Education.

tures need to be excluded from total current-fund expenditures to arrive at instruction-related expenditures. The first category includes activities that are self-financing, such as auxiliary enterprises (dormitories and the like), hospitals, and related activities. Spending on these activities (column 2) grew at a slightly faster pace than did total expenditures.

A second category includes research expenditures that are heavily financed by outside sources, and also public service expenditures. While research is an integral element in the missions of research institutions, it is not directly related to instruction, especially at the undergraduate level. Research activity builds new knowledge, which is subsequently disseminated through classroom instruction and published journal articles. Research expenditures prove to be a substantial component of total expenditures and, in the 1950s and 1960s spending in this area grew rapidly, with most of this coming because of the growth of research support. By the 1970s, federal interest in research spending waned, having been displaced by spending on new social programs.

A third category of spending to be excluded from total current-fund expenditures is student financial aid, which in recent years has been classified as a part of education and general expenditures; this money is not central to the instructional mission of institutions even though it may be important to the attainment of other objectives. By way of illustration, student financial aid expenditures from institutional sources largely affect the mix of students at individual institutions; they are presumed to exert some effect on overall enrollment levels in the higher education system. Beyond that, they are unrelated to instruction.

Student financial aid expenditures made by and through institutions of higher education increased substantially. They grew from two percent of the total in the 1940s to about four percent in the 1980s. Of course, a more significant amount of financial aid—that provided largely through federal programs—does not flow through institutions but rather is distributed directly to students through Pell grants and various student loan programs.

If we now exclude each of these categories of expenditures by subtracting columns 2-4 from column 1 in Table 5, we arrive at something that can be identified as costs related to instruction, hereafter called "instruction-related" costs or expenditures. These costs represent about 60 percent of total current-fund expenditures.

Instruction-related Costs, Tuition and Fees, and Student Aid

We now focus on the relationship between instructional costs, what students pay in the form of tuition and fees, and the amounts of financial aid received by students. We interpret student financial aid as an effort to promote equity, and we take changes in student financial aid relative to instruction-related costs as an indicator of the trade-off between quality and equity. Tuition and fees help to highlight the dimensions of this trade-off.

The data needed for this analysis are shown in Table 6, which highlights the growth of student financial aid funding by showing noninstitutional aid as well as total student aid. Built into the table are estimates of financial aid provided through veteran's programs (the GI Bill) for 1947-48 and 1957-58 so as to make the data as comparable as possible over time. It is clear that veterans' educational benefits were enormous, being equal to from 74 to more than 100 percent of all instruction-related costs in 1947-48 and from 18 to 24 percent of those costs in 1957-58.

The evolution of student financial aid resources is clear: a dramatic fall took place from the late 1940s to the late 1950s, followed by a moderate increase to 1967-68, an enormous increase to 1980-81, and a slight decline from 1980-81 to 1983-84. Equally striking is the fact that total student aid

Table 6
Instructional-Related Expenditures, Tuition and Fees,
Receipts and Student Financial Aid Funding (Millions of Dollars)

Year	Total Instructional Related Expenditures (1)	Tuition and Fees (2)	Institution-ally Provided Student Financial Aid (3)	Other Student Financial Aid (4)	Total Financial Aid (5)
1947-48	$1,162	670a	40	$824-1,249b	$864-1,289b
% Annual Change	9%	3%	11%	-4% -5%	-4%
1957-58	2,701	934	113	381-520b	494-633b
% Annual Change	14%	14%	22%	8% -5%	13% -10%
1967-68	10,234	3,380	830	821	1,651
% Annual Change	11%	11%	7%	25%	18%
1980-81	39,854	13,773	2,138	15,209	17,347
% Annual Change	9%	12%	5%	-10%	-2%
1983-84	51,217	19,714	2,502	13,593	16,095

NOTES:

a Includes tuition and fees paid for veterans under the GI Bill. This $365 million figure may overstate the "tuition" component because of a surcharge paid directly to institutions to help pay the costs of expanding capacity to accommodate the enrollment of veterans.

b The range reflects our inability to develop a precise estimate of student financial aid provided by the federal government.

SOURCES:
Columns 1 and 3 from Table 5.
Column 2 from Table 4 except for 1947-48 figure. See note.
Column 4 1947-48 and 1957-58 estimated from information in 1948 and 1958 *Annual Reports* of the Veteran's Administration, U.S. Government Printing Office. 1967-68 estimated from data in papers by W. Lee Hansen and Joseph Boyd in *Trends in Postsecondary Education*, Office of Education, 1972. Data for 1980-81 and 1983-84 represent the difference between columns 3 and 5.
Column 5 is the sum of columns 3 and 4 except for 1980-81 and 1983-84. Those data are from Donald A. Gillespie and Nancy Carlson, *Trends in Student Financial Aid*, The College Board, 1985.

funds exceeded total tuition and fee payments in 1947-48 and again in 1980-81. By contrast, student aid funds were only about half of all tuition

Table 7
Sharing the Costs of Higher Education
"Share" as a Percentage of Total Instructional Related Expenditures (costs)

Year	Total	Non-Student (a)	Student	Student Share Net of Instructional Aid	Student Share Net of All Aid
	(1)	(2)	(3)	(4)	(5)
1947-48	100.0	42.3	57.7	54.2	-16.7 to -53.3
1957-58	100.0	65.4	34.6	30.4	16.2 to 11.1
1967-68	100.0	67.0	33.0	24.9	16.9
1980-81	100.0	65.4	34.6	29.2	-9.0
1983-84	100.0	61.5	38.5	33.6	+7.6

NOTES:
(a) Defined as state and local taxpayers and private donors.

SOURCES:
Column 1 Column 1 of Table 6 set equal to 100.0.
Column 2 Column 1 minus Column 2 of Table 6 set as a percent of Column 1.
Column 3 Column 2 of Table 6 as a percent of Column 1.
Column 4 Column 2 less Column 3 divided by Column 1.
Column 5 Column 2 minus Column 5 divided by Column 1.

and fees paid in 1967-68, just when new need-based student aid programs were being launched.

Sharing the Costs of Higher Education

We now take the last step in the analysis, which is to show how the costs of higher education are shared. This is accomplished in Table 7 by rearranging the data from Table 6. Total instructional costs are shared between students who pay tuition/fees and state and local taxpayers and private donors who make up the difference (see columns 1 and 2).

The nonstudent share rose considerably from 1947-48 and then stabilized in the 61 to 67 percent range. The student share of these costs, the exact opposite of the nonstudent share, proved to be surprisingly constant from 1957-58 through 1980-81. By 1983-84 there had been a slight increase because of the rise of tuition levels. The 1947-48 figure shows that students paid an appreciably larger proportion of the costs, by our estimate 58 percent (see note to Table 6).[28]

The student share shown in column 3 of Table 7 is reduced in two ways. The first is through institutionally-provided student financial aid, which has had relatively little impact on the student share (see column 4). The second and most important way is through other types of student aid that, with institutional aid, produces dramatic changes in the student share (see column 5). We find the net student share to be negative in 1947-48 because of the large infusion of student aid provided by the GI Bill. Total student aid reduced the student share by about one-half in 1957-58 and continued to do so through 1967-68. In other words, student aid was equivalent to roughly half of all tuition and fee payments by students.

It needs to be pointed out that student financial aid is designed to do more than simply defray the costs of tuition; it also goes to meet the costs of attendance. Nonetheless, the magnitude of financial aid resources is highlighted by this comparison.

The dramatic effect of the actions taken in the late 1960s and 1970s appears in the data for 1980-81. Total student financial aid grew so rapidly that it exceeded tuition and fee payments by students. With the slower growth of student aid in the early 1980s and continued increases in tuition and fee levels, the student share rose but remained well below the level of the 1950s and 1960s.

The results for 1980-81 do not entirely reflect the equity effects of student aid. At that time Guaranteed Student Loans were awarded without regard to financial need, and hence many middle-income students took advantage of the favorable borrowing opportunities. Were we able to adjust for this, the net student share would probably not have dipped below zero.

The results for 1983-84, which show a rise in the net student share, reflect in considerable part efforts by institutions to offset the slower growth of resources available to higher education institutions from traditional sources (i.e., state tax support and private funds). This led to tuition increases that were required to raise substantially faculty salaries that had been declining in real terms, to increase expenditures for maintenance and modernization of facilities that had earlier been deferred, and allocation of funds to new technology, such as computers.

We conclude that federal student financial aid represented a powerful injection of new resources into the higher education system. By 1980-81 this amount was enough to more than eliminate tuition and fee assessments against all students. Of course, financial aid funds could not have been used in this way because they are directed largely to students who demonstrated financial need. And by 1983-84 student aid still acted as an important offset for student costs of higher education.

CONCLUSION

In summing up this analysis, it is clear that the substantial rise in college enrollments led to the need for increased funds to provide instruction and related services. Meanwhile, current-fund income for institutions of higher education rose relative to GNP, but we know this reflects at least in part enrollment increases. It is expenditures rather than income, however, that determine what happens in higher education, and particularly instruction-related expenditures. We find that these expenditures increased at about the same pace as revenues but their level was somewhat lower because of the need to exclude several categories of expenditures that were not (or were less) directly related to student instruction.

Instruction-related expenditures, tuition/fees, and student financial aid rose substantially overall from the late 1940s to the 1980s. Yet the burden on students through their tuition and fees has remained relatively constant in the 38 to 39 percent range since the late 1950s. Once we take into account student financial aid funds, we find that the student share has been substantially reduced by the infusion of federal funds for student financial aid; great progress was made from 1967-68 to 1980-81, with some backsliding since then. However, it needs to be pointed out that a large proportion of the 1980-81 financial aid was not targeted to low-income students as it was in 1983-84. This raises the possibility that the changes from 1967-68 to 1980-81 and 1980-81 to 1983-84 were exaggerated in their impact on overcoming financial barriers to college attendance.

The usefulness of the periods employed in this analysis derives from their ability to differentiate among the social goals. These goals for the most part reflected efforts to resolve problems outside higher education. The goals carried with them only two demands: to improve quality and to improve equity. We do discern the pendulum effect mentioned earlier. The student share diminishes as equity concerns dominate and increases again when greater attention is given to quality.

What progress has been made in pursuing these goals? On equity it is clear that the cost of college attendance for students with incomes low enough to qualify for student aid declined sharply over the past forty years, and this by itself stands as a major accomplishment. The evidence concerning quality is less clear. It is encouraging that no matter of how one looks at higher education institutions and their programs, levels of investment have been maintained.

What do we conclude and what is the issue for the future? Earlier progress toward improving the quality of higher education in the 1950s and 1960s has been eroded by efforts to improve equity in the 1970s. The gains achieved in pushing equity at the expense of quality, leads us to expect eroding support for equity. If these funds are reallocated to promote quality, they will do so in a much more restricted fashion, benefiting those students who are most able to pay.

The sentiment favoring increased investment in higher education is mounting. Recent debate in Congress and the results of public opinion polls indicate a sharp rise in the perceived importance of higher education.[29] Calls for the involvement of higher education in stimulating economic development and restoring American competitiveness continue to grow. Increased concern is also voiced about improving quality in higher education by raising academic standards. Despite this, most recent discussions about how to improve quality neglect to point out the need for new investment of resources. Without additional resources the only alternative will be to curtail equity.

NOTES

1. David C. McClelland, *The Achieving Society* (New York: Irvington Publishing, 1976).
2. President's Commission on Higher Education, *Higher Education for American Democracy* (Washington, D.C.: U.S. Goverment Printing Office, 1947).
3. Janet Kerr-Turner, *From Truman to Johnson: Ad Hoc Policy Formulation in Higher Education* (Ph.D. dissertation, University of Virginia, 1986).
4. The population of eighteen-year-olds subsequently hovered in the 4.2-4.3 million range from 1975-79 but in 1984 had dropped to 3.7 million.
5. See T. W. Schultz, *Journal of Political Economy,* (October 1962) vol. 46; Edward F. Denison, *The Sources of Economic Growth and the Alternative Before Us* (New York: Committee for Economic Development, 1962).
6. The Report of the President's Commission on National Goals, *Goals for Americans* (Prentice Hall, 1960).
7. Janet Kerr-Turner, op. cit.
8. Lois Rice, ed., *Student Loans: Problems and Policy Alternatives* (New York: College Entrance Examination Board, 1977).
9. Leonard A. Lecht, *Goals, Priorities, and Dollars: The Next Decade* (New York: The Free Press, 1966).
10. Clark Kerr, *Agenda for a Nation,* ed. Kermit Gordon (Washington, D.C.: The Brookings Institute, 1968).
11. Carnegie Commission on Higher Education, *Quality and Equity: New Levels of Federal Responsibility for Higher Education* (New York: McGraw Hill, 1968).
12. Alice Rivlin, *Toward a Long Range Plan for Federal Financial Support for Higher Education* (Washington, D.C.: Department of Health, Education, and Welfare, January 1969).
13. W. Lee Hansen and Burton A. Weisbrod, *Benefits, Costs, and Finance of Public Higher Education* (Chicago: Markham Publishing Company, 1969).
14. Lawrence Gladieux and Thomas R. Wolanin, *Congress and the Colleges* (Lexington, Mass: Lexington Books, 1976).
15. 1978 Amendments to the Higher Education Act of 1965
16. E. Whitt, D. Clark, and T. Astuto, *An Analysis of Public Support for Educational Policy Preferences of the Reagan Administration* (Policy Studies Center of the University Council for Educational Administration, December, 1986). Occasional Paper, No. 3.
17. Jacob O. Stampen and Roxanne W. Reeves, "Coalitions in the Senates of the 96th and 97th Congresses," in *Congress and the Presidency: A Journal of Capital Studies,* vol. 13, no. 2.
18. E. L. Boyer, *High School: A Report on Secondary Education in America* (New York: Harper and Row, 1983); Business Higher Education Forum, *America's Challenge: The Need for a National Response* (Washington, D.C.: Author, 1983); National Commission on Excellence in Education, *A Nation at Risk, The Imperative for Educational Reform* (Washington, D.C.: Government Printing Office, 1983); Na-

tional Task Force on Education for Economic Growth, *Action for Excellence* (Denver: Education Commission on the States, 1983); D. Ravitch, *The Troubled Crusade: American Education 1945-1980* (New York: Basic Books, 1984); T. R. Sizer, *Horace's Compromise: The Dilemma of the American High School* (Boston: Houghton-Mifflin, 1984); The Twentieth-Century Fund Task Force on Federal Elementary and Secondary Education Policy, *Making the Grade* (New York: Author, 1983).

19. National Commission on Excellence in Education, *A Nation at Risk, The Imperative for Educational Reform* (Washington, D.C.: Government Printing Office, 1983).

20. M. S. Smith, *Educational Improvements Which Make a Difference: Thoughts About the Recent National Reports on Education* (Washington, D.C., 1984a). Paper presented to the Federation of Behavior, Psychological and Cognitive Sciences.

21. *A Nation at Risk;* F. Newman, *Integrity in The College Curriculum: A Report to the Academic Community* (Washington, D.C.: Association of American Colleges, 1984); Ernest L. Boyer, *College: The Undergraduate Experience in America* (Princeton: Carnegie Foundation for the Advancement of Teaching, 1987).

22. We begin with 1947-48 because data for 1946-47 are incomplete.

23. We plan to examine differences between public and private institutions in a subsequent paper.

24. Carol Frances, *The Short Run Economic Outlook for Higher Education* (Washington, D.C.: American Council on Education, 1980).

25. To the extent that the percentage of students age twenty-five and above increased, the rise in the college-going rate is somewhat overstated.

26. Howard Bowen, *The Costs of Higher Education* (San Francisco: Jossey-Bass, 1980).

27. For other recent studies of expenditures, see Joseph Froomkin, "The Impact of Changing Levels of Financial Resources on the Structure of College and Universities;" Paul T. Brinkman and Dennis P. Jones, "Colleges and Universities Adjustment to Changing Financial Enrollment and Structure Implementations of Institutional Adjustment Strategies" presented by the National Science Foundation Conference, July 29, 1986; and Durward Long, "Financing Public Universities and Colleges in the Year 2000," in Leslie W. Koepplin and David Wilson, eds., *The Future State of Universities: Issues in Teaching, Research, and Public Service* (New Brunswick, N.J.: Rutgers University Press, 1985).

28. A considerable fraction of the student share was offset because for veterans the federal government paid tuition/fees directly under the provisions of the GI Bill.

29. Gallup Poll (October 17, 1985).

7

Current and Emerging Issues Facing American Higher Education

Clark Kerr and Marian Gade

There have always been problems for higher education and for American society. Crisis and change have been the rule, not the exception. Even during what now looks like the "Golden Age" of the late 1950s and 1960s, the period of the greatest expansion higher education has ever seen, administrators were under constant strain and pressure to meet the challenges that growth brought.

Even before the Golden Age, problems were nothing new. From the beginning of the colonial era through most of the nineteenth century, the struggle was for survival, as the record of colleges founded and failed indicates. Then new universities arose to meet the needs of an industrializing society, a task that occupied the builders of post-Civil War institutions. World War I brought threats to stability that were not entirely allayed by the time the Great Depression hit. World War II saw the beginning of the university-government partnership in research, but reduced enrollments as potential students became soldiers instead. In the late 1940s the GI Bill flooded colleges and universities with students and pressed them to provide new programs, counseling and placement services, and to change administrative mechanisms at an unprecedented rate.[1]

Higher education met all these challenges and many more. It has responded to events in the political and social world, such as wars and depressions, as well as crises of confidence and internal dissension, as during the Vietnam War and the concurrent student movement of the late 1960s and early 1970s.

It is less certain that American higher education can meet the challenges posed by current and emerging issues facing it, although past successes augur well.

1. CHANGING COMPOSITION *AND*
   CHANGING NUMBERS OF STUDENTS

Until now the trend has been one of almost constant growth; sometimes slow and steady with minor fluctuations, as during the first two centuries when the average growth rate was less than 250 students per year. Enrollments rose from about 10 students in 1638 (all at Harvard) to 50,000 in 1870. Sometimes growth was very rapid, as from 1870 to 1890, and from 1960 to 1970, when higher education enrollments in each instance doubled.

Because of declining fertility rates beginning after 1960, the number of young people in the age group from 18 to 24 years, those who make up the traditional college-going age cohort, will drop about 23 percent between 1978 and 1993. After that the children of the "baby boomers" will enter the college-going age cohort, raising enrollments to approximately the 1979 level by the end of the first decade of the twenty-first century. The issue before higher education institutions and planners is, what effect will the falling, and then rising, numbers in the group have upon enrollments? What are appropriate responses?

Estimates of the impact of an age-cohort decline upon enrollments varied widely as the nation entered the period of uncertainty. Enrollments might drop the same amount, about 23 percent, as the group declined. Some observers forecast a much greater enrollment decline, as the economic returns to investment in a college education fell due to a greater supply of such people, so that a smaller proportion of even the traditional college attenders might choose to pursue postsecondary education. Some people expected there to be an actual increase in student numbers, in spite of a declining traditional group from whom to draw students, as persons who have not in the past participated in higher education continue to attend in greater numbers—members of minority groups, foreign students, older persons, and women, for example—and as institutions increase retention rates.[2]

It is necessary, therefore, to take a careful look at the composition of the potential college applicant pool, and not just at overall numbers.

Differential fertility rates among racial and ethnic groups, along with immigration, mean that blacks and Hispanics are enlarging their share of the traditional age cohort. In the past, high school graduation rates and college attendance rates have been lower in these groups than in the white or Asian populations. Blacks and Hispanics increased their graduation and attendance rates from the late 1960s up to 1976, but college entrance attendance rates leveled off and even declined slightly into the mid-1980s, while Asians are attending in increasing numbers. At the same time the composition of the total population is changing so that around the year 2000, nearly one out of every three Americans will be a member of a minority group. The problem facing colleges and universities is to increase the numbers of students drawn from these groups so as to offset the decline in the majority population. (See Table 1.)

TABLE 1
Participation of Women and Minority Groups in Higher Education

Women	1960[a]	1985[b]
Percent of undergraduate enrollment	38.0	52.5
Percent of graduate enrollment	29.0	48.9

Racial and ethnic groups	Black %	Hispanic %	Asian & other %	White %	All races %
Percent of total U.S. population, 1980[c]	11.7	6.4	5.9	83.1	*
Percent of 18-24-year-olds who are high school graduates, 1984[d]	74.7	60.1	n.d.	83.0	81.6
Percent of higher education enrollments, 1984[e]	8.9	4.2	2.8	80.7	96.6**
Percent of 18-24-year-olds in college, 1984[d]	20.4	17.9	n.d.	28.0	27.1

*Totals add to more than 100 percent because persons of Hispanic origin are also counted among other races.
**Omits Native American and nonresident alien students.

[a]U.S. National Center for Education Statistics, *Projection of Education Statistics to 1975-76* (Washington, D.C.: U.S. Government Printing Office, 1966).
[b]U.S. Department of Education, Center for Statistics, as published in *Chronicle of Higher Education*, "Fact-File: Fall 1985 Enrollment," 33 (15 October 1986): 42.
[c]U.S. Bureau of the Census, *Statistical Abstract of the United States, 1986* (Washington, D.C.: U.S. Government Printing Office), Table 32.
[d]U.S. Bureau of Census, *Current Population Reports*, Series P-20, No. 404, "Population Characteristics: School Enrollment—Social and Economic Characteristics of Students: October 1984 (Advance Report)" (Washington, D.C.: U.S. Government Printing Office, 1985), Table B.
[e]U.S. Center for Education Statistics, *The Condition of Education, 1985 Edition* (Washington, D.C.: U.S. Government Printing Office, 1985), Table 2.9.

The college-going propensities of women, too, have changed rapidly. Traditionally less likely to attend college than males, by the late 1970s they constituted over half of undergraduate students in the U.S.

Persons older than the 18-24 age cohort are also attending college in increasing numbers. In 1984, 36 percent of the students were 25 years or older. Over two-thirds of the students in the over-35 age group are women.

Older students tend to be enrolled only part-time, and these nontraditional groups also are heavily concentrated in certain kinds of institutions, mainly in community colleges and comprehensive colleges instead of in four-year liberal arts colleges or research institutions. Both changing numbers and the changing composition of the college attending group are affecting different institutions and different segments of the higher education universe in different ways.

The challenges to institutions set by changing demographic factors are to maintain or raise quality of education while seeking new clienteles; to remain flexible without losing a sense of identity and mission; and to avoid unfair competitive practices that would destroy public confidence in higher education or make it less possible to retain the capacity to serve the larger numbers of students that are expected again after the mid-1990s.

2. QUALITY IN COLLEGE *AND* IN HIGH SCHOOL

As the needs of our technological society become increasingly complex, so too will its need for highly trained and personally competent individuals, able to manage their own lives wisely, to perform productively in the labor force, and to participate effectively in the affairs of the nation and the world. At the same time, there will be fewer young persons available to meet these needs. More disturbing, there is evidence that they may be less, rather than more, prepared than in the past.

The proportion of the labor force in jobs classified as technical, managerial, and professional has risen from 10 to 26 percent (1900 to 1984) and is likely to keep on rising. Job requirements within these occupations intensify as technology becomes more complex and as systems of control become more complicated. Coping skills[3] become more important as society becomes more bureaucratized. People must learn to be discriminating consumers, to invest prudently, to preserve their health, to fill out forms and keep accounts, and to cultivate other skills necessary to survival in an industrialized world. Quality of life will increasingly be measured in ways that require use of mental and artistic skills.[4]

There is increasing evidence that America's schools and colleges may not be preparing young people to participate effectively in this society. A series of reports published in the early 1980s, first on the shortcomings of the nation's high schools and then on the condition of undergraduate education, raised questions about the overall quality of education. Several of these reports are, in our judgment, excessively negative in their appraisal of the performance of American higher education. By 1986, partly in response to the "reform" reports, over half of American colleges were engaged in curriculum reform, mainly addressed to broad educational purposes and the quality of general education.[5]

Concern about quality has also led to increased interest in evaluation or assessment. A number of states have raised admissions requirements for entrance to public colleges, reflecting concern about the quality of education in secondary schools. Some states have mandated tests or other forms of assessment at points throughout the higher education process, such as "rising junior" examinations which students must pass at the end of their sophomore year, or teacher competency examinations which students must pass to become credentialed teachers. Financial incentives are in place in some states to encourage assessment of student learning. These initiatives have caused some observers to fear that forms of assessment used may be simplistic, that tests may encourage institutions to meet only minimum standards instead of providing high quality education, and that some institutions may be penalized for failure to remedy deficiencies beyond their control, such as poor secondary preparation of entering students. In addition, the full value of a college education can only be evaluated years or decades later, and in ways that cannot be measured by standardized tests. The problem facing institutions is to develop forms of assessment that will be helpful in improving teaching and learning within the classroom and, at the same time, will demonstrate to the public and its representatives that students are benefiting as a result of their educational experiences.

In addition to the question of institutional quality there is the question of individual talents and abilities. The decline in the number of persons in the current generation, of course, means that the number of people with high innate talent will drop by the same 23 percent that the age cohort decreases. In addition, test scores of developed ability of students leaving high school and headed for college declined on the order of 5 to 10 percent by 1980 since their high point in the early 1960s; they have inched up slightly in the 1980s. (See Table 2 on p. 135.) About half the decline can be attributed to the larger number of persons taking the tests, many of them from groups in the society that have not in the past participated in higher education; but test scores dropped for all groups.[6]

Scores on standardized tests for college graduates have behaved in more erratic ways, and the proportion of test-takers scoring in the "high ability" group dropped from about 19 to 13 percent between 1966 and 1979. An analysis of 23 types of graduate school admissions tests, including both tests of general learned abilities and tests of advanced achievement in 15 subject areas, found that performance declined on 15 of them from 1964 to 1982, mostly on specific Graduate Record Examination subject area tests. Scores remained stable on four tests and advanced on four. Of the 15 that declined, six showed "large" or "extreme" decreases, but none of the four that increased did so by a large amount. Neither demographic variables nor changes in the numbers of test takers explained the trends. The performance and participation of undergraduate majors from different academic fields was the only variable that helped explain the declines. With the exception of engineering majors, undergraduates who majored in professional or occupational fields—education, business administration, social work, journalism, and other fields that are growing most rapidly—consistently scored lower than did those who majored in the traditional arts and sciences. Those with undergraduate majors in science, mathematics, and engineering outperformed all others on the examinations.[7] Relatively steady average scores for students taking admissions tests for entrance to law, medical, and graduate business and management schools suggest that the better students may be moving into these professions and away from graduate education that would prepare them to teach coming generations of students in high schools and colleges. (See Table 2.)

On the whole, it appears that test scores out of college have dropped to some extent, but the decline has been no greater, and probably less, than that out of high school. The "value added" by college has stayed the same or increased.

The issue for society, and for higher education, is to increase quality to meet increased needs, to close the "quality gap."

Efforts will also be concentrated on reducing the "talent loss." Young people in the top quartile of academic ability, but from families with lower incomes, are still less likely to attend college than are equally talented students from higher income families. One 1980 study showed a 10 to 15 percent difference in college attendance intentions among students in the high ability quartile from families with incomes under $20,000 a year as against those with incomes over $25,000.[8] Financial aid policies at institutional, state, and national levels, as well as recruitment and admissions policies, will need to be reviewed for their potential contribution to reducing the talent loss.

Efforts to retain students in high school for longer periods (i.e., reducing drop-out rates, now about 20 percent overall); to increase high school graduation rates, especially among groups that now fall below the national average; to reduce voluntary absenteeism; and to increase the amount of time actually spent in education and training during the school year are all coming under scrutiny as states and local school districts try to raise the quality of secondary school graduates and reduce the loss of talent. Colleges and universities will be expected to assist in these efforts, both through direct partnership with secondary schools, as in the case of court-ordered linkages between universities in the Boston area and public high schools, as well as through the traditional task of training teachers and administrators for the public schools. How colleges can maintain and increase their own quality, while contributing to higher quality secondary education, will continue to be a major issue in the 1980s and 1990s.

3. SERVING *ALL* OF YOUTH

Just as colleges and universities are becoming resources for the improvement of secondary schools, they are also being asked to serve a larger proportion of the postsecondary population. In 1983, 42 percent of the nation's youth aged 16 to 24 were enrolled in school or college. Fifty-five percent were employed (including many of those who were also students); 11 percent were unemployed; and another 6 percent were neither in school nor in the labor force nor in the armed forces nor homemakers. They had opted out of society. At present, there is no institution in the society responsible for look-

TABLE 2

Average Scores on Standardized Tests, 1966-1986

	SAT[1,a]		GRE		GMAT[2,a]	LSAT[2]	MCAT	
Academic year ending	Verbal	Math	Verbal	Quant.			Verbal	Quant.
1966	471	496	520	528	485	511	524	557
1970	460	488	503	516	474	518	517	566
1975	437	473	493	508	461	520	511	568
1980	423	467	474	522	462	539	b	b
1981	424	466	473	523	467	544		
1982	426	467	469	533	468	553		
1983	425	468						
1984	426	471	472[2]	539[2]				
1985	431	475						
1986	431	475						

SAT = Scholastic Aptitude Test
GRE = Graduate Record Examination
GMAT = Graduate Management Admissions Test
LSAT = Law School Admission Test
MCAT = Medical College Admission Test

(1) All candidates. High school seniors only scores do not differ significantly.
(2) Based on 3-year rolling average for period ending in indicated year.

[a]For all cases attending test administrations during a testing year. Thus, an individual may be counted more than once if he/she was tested more than once in a give year.
[b]The MCAT and its scoring method were changed in 1977 so that subsequent test results are not comparable to 1976 and earlier. Scores on the new test have declined slightly since its first administration in 1977.

SOURCE: For SAT and 1984 GRE: Educational Testing Service, Princeton, New Jersey; for GRE, LSAT, and GMAT, Clifford Adelman, *The Standardized Test Scores of College Graduates, 1964-1982* (Washington, D.C.: U.S. Government Printing Office, 1985), Table A; and for MCAT, U.S. National Center for Education Statistics, *The Condition of Education, 1977 Edition* (Washington, D.C.: U.S. Printing Office, 1977), vol. 3, pt. 1, Table 5.04.

ing after the welfare of youth as a whole, linking strategies to reduce teenage unemployment (which runs over 50 percent for some groups such as black male high school drop-outs) with strategies to create easier transitions from the world of school or college to the world of work. It is likely that educational systems will be asked to take a larger role in developing programs to serve all the youth in an area, not just those who enroll in classes.

The community colleges, which have proven successful in their outreach programs and in establishing cooperative arrangements with industry, businesses, high schools, and other community groups, will be in the forefront of this movement. One proposal calls for community colleges to make "a residual responsibility for youth."[9] They would be available to advise youth on

academic and employment opportunities, to offer job preparation and placement, to refer young people to other community services such as medical and
legal advice, and to make referrals to apprenticeship programs and govern-
ment-subsidized programs.

Whether this proposal is adopted or not, involvement of colleges and
universities with the needs of a larger segment of the postsecondary age
group is likely to increase. This is partly because the "youth problem" will not
go away of its own accord, even with fuller employment, and postsecondary
educational institutions have shown more success in educating and training
young people than have some other institutions. It is partly, too, because the
possibility of declining postsecondary enrollments will create incentives for
colleges and universities to widen their base of recruitment and the range of
services they offer.

4. MEETING THE NEW COMPETITION: SECTORS II, III, AND IV

Although the universe of over three thousand nonprofit colleges and universities, both public and private, is the one that generally comes to mind when
we speak of postsecondary education (this is Sector I), there are other institutional forms that are rapidly expanding their educational functions.

The for-profit, or proprietary segment, Sector II, has existed almost as
long as Sector I and may account for 5 percent as many full-time equivalent
enrollments as Sector I.

Sector III includes educational and training programs offered by organizations such as corporations, trade unions, and the military, whose basic
functions are noneducational. Some estimates place the number of persons
enrolled and the resources expended in Sector III as higher than those in all
four-year colleges and universities, or over 8-million students each year. Estimates of the corporate expenditures on these programs range from a relatively conservative $40-billion a year upwards, amounts approaching those
spent by our nation's four-year public and private institutions in Sector I.[10]

A relatively new development in Sector III, and one that presents a
challenge to more traditional colleges and universities, is the emergence of
corporate colleges that offer accredited degrees. Although the numbers are
still small, this is an important trend, especially in view of increasing doubts
about the quality of the skills possessed by the graduates of Sector I institutions and the "remedial" education many businesses feel it necessary to provide to their employees. Corporations may be moving toward providing not
only such remedial education but a full program of skills and knowledge they
believe necessary for corporate and personal achievement.

Although the "technological revolution" in education has been predicted
for a number of years, recent developments in video discs, low-cost computers, and TV satellites indicate that Sector IV, electronic education, may be
on the verge of substantial expansion.

Beyond all this lies what might be called Sector V, on-the-job informal training, where perhaps up to 50 percent of all skills actually used in employment are learned.

As it is perceived that the schools and colleges in Sector I are unable to meet all the complex needs of the labor market, or to supply all the education people want for personal fulfillment, the other sectors will continue to grow and to offer competition for students, for funding, and for programs. Public policy makers will have to address questions such as how to provide possible "consumer protection" for users of educational products coming from organizations that fall outside Sector I accreditation procedures, and how to provide freedom of choice for students receiving financial aid while at the same time assuring that public funds are wisely spent.

Educational policy makers in Sector I will come face-to-face with the dilemma of how to meet competition from the other Sectors and to serve new needs, while maintaining institutional integrity and a sense of academic mission.

5. STILL THE "HOME OF SCIENCE"?

The flow of young scholars into scientific positions in universities has slowed greatly. This is not so much because of declining enrollments in the research universities, but because of low faculty turnover. The large numbers of faculty members who were hired in the 1960s and early 1970s will not be ready to retire until the 1990s or later, and few new positions will be added. Many potential young scientists will be discouraged from getting a Ph.D. degree at all, or they will look to government or industry for jobs. American society could be seriously weakened in its ability to meet competition from abroad and to respond to new scientific opportunities if some action is not taken to encourage young scientists to enter teaching and research careers and to preserve the university as "the home of science."[11]

The United States, unlike many other nations, concentrates basic scientific research in its colleges and universities. These institutions perform nearly half of all basic research, about $5.6-billion in 1984, two-thirds of which is funded by the federal government. Industry support of basic research in colleges and universities also increased during the 1980s and may continue to do so as more business-university partnerships come into being.

Federal funds for basic research dropped in constant dollars from 1968 to 1975, mainly because of decreased spending in defense and space programs. Funding increased in every subsequent year, growing 34 percent in constant dollars between 1975 and 1984. Within the total allocated to research by the federal government, basic research constituted an estimated 47 percent in 1984 compared to 35 percent in 1975, indicating a recognition on the part of

TABLE 3
Academic Research and Development Expenditures
By Colleges and Universities

	Basic research	Applied research and development
1968	77%	19%
1984	66%	34%

Source: U.S. National Science Foundation, *National Patterns of Science and Technology Resources, 1980,* (NSF 80-308) (Washington, D.C.: U.S. Government Printing Office, 1980), p. 7 (for 1968). U.S. National Science Foundation, *National Patterns of Science and Technology Resources, 1986,* (NSF 86-309) (Washington, D.C.: U.S. Government Printing Office, 1986), p. 65 (for 1984).

the federal government of its continuing primary responsibility for maintaining the nation's basic research capacity.

Within the universities, on the other hand, there has been a shift away from basic and towards applied research. (See Table 3.) Basic research spending in universities and colleges increased 20 percent in constant dollars during the decade of the 1970s; applied research spending increased 74 percent. The question arises whether universities, the principal home of basic research, ought to be shifting resources away from this activity.

The distribution of funds is another issue that arises with respect to federal funding of scientific research in universities. In 1983, the 100 leading universities, in terms of receipt of federal funds for research and development, received over 80 percent of all such funds, a proportion that has held steady since 1970.[12] This pattern results from decisions made during World War II, and followed since, that research funds should go to institutions that have the best scientists and the greatest possibility of extending the frontiers of scientific investigation. Arguments are likely to continue between those who advocate distributing federal research funds only on the basis of excellence, and those who want a wider, more egalitarian system based on geography or some other criterion.

Questions about allocations of funds among fields, among and within institutions, and about the methods used to make allocations will become even more pressing than in the past as public budgets level off and as university funds from nonfederal sources decrease along with enrollments. As long as totals available were rapidly expanding, as in the two decades after World War II, few hard decisions were necessary. Now the temptation to shift more funds into applied or development fields in hope of a quick "payoff" will have to be weighed against the need to support science as a cultural activity in its own right, against the need to ensure a supply of young scientists in the coming decades, and against the ultimate payoff to society of pursuing scientific research in directions dictated by the nature of the disciplines themselves.

Some universities have found themselves involved in clashes with agencies of the federal government over the management and accounting procedures used in connection with research grants and contracts. There has also been increasing federal regulation of the actual content of research, as in the case of federal guidelines prohibiting certain kinds of experiments in "gene-splicing" or "genetic engineering," and in regulation of research methods in experiments using human subjects. The government-university partnership in scientific research appears to be a permanent one, but no longer one in which the federal partner supplies the funds and the university partner takes them, no strings attached. New rules for the partnership will need to be negotiated.

6. PLAN OR MARKET?

One of the important changes that has taken place in American higher education in the past half-century is the shift in both financing and enrollments from the private to the public sector. In 1930, public sources supplied 42 percent of all current income for higher education institutions, and in 1977, the public share was over 63 percent. Private sources of funding dropped correspondingly from 58 to 37 percent. The public share of enrollments, too, has increased. In 1950 students were evenly divided between public and private institutions, but by 1985 the public share had increased to 77 percent of headcount enrollments, and this during a period of greatly increased numbers overall.

Public concern with coordinating and planning for higher education went along with growth of the public sector and increased public financial commitments. In 1980, only one state lacked a mechanism for coordination of all higher education within the state, including the private sector; forty years earlier, only one state had such a mechanism.

Coordinating bodies, which came into existence to plan for orderly growth, will find it harder to plan for decline, where decisions involve taking away resources, reducing personnel, consolidating or eliminating programs, and possibly closing campuses. There are few general rules that can be offered in this period, as there will be tremendous variations in circumstances over which planners have little or no control, and plans will have to be adjusted to them.

Some regions and states, and even parts of states, will continue to grow. The Sunbelt states of the southwest may never notice that the age group has declined in numbers, although economic conditions such as changing prices for oil and minerals may make it harder to fund the larger number of students. Some categories of institutions, such as community colleges, will experience increased growth while other types, such as some small liberal arts colleges, will be struggling for their existence. Some programs will continue to grow and others to decline, as market forces move students into some fields and out of others. For example, the proportion of students with or more, or extreme cutbacks in state funding for economic reasons, would professional school majors rose by over 50 percent in the first half of the 1970s, while social science and humanities majors decreased by 50 percent. First professional degree programs are the fastest growing segment of higher education; degrees awarded increased by 29 percent between 1975 and 1981.

Both market and plan will continue to affect higher education, as students "vote with their feet," taking their interests, and their financial aid packages, to institutions of their own choosing.

Planning has accomplished several things that will help provide guidance in a period of decline. First, many states have clearly defined and differentiated the functions of different segments of higher education, as in the early decision by California to establish a tripartite system consisting of a multi-campus university, a system of state colleges and universities, and a community college sector, each with somewhat different functions, financing and staffing formulas, and admissions standards.

Second, there has by now been considerable experience with developing budgetary formulas for the support of higher education. (See section 8 of this chapter.) Third, most states, over forty of them, have established some form of support for the private sector. These decisions were easier to make during a period of growth, but they will help mitigate the chances of cutthroat competition among institutions and sectors for resources and students during a period of decline.

A central decision will be about how much to rely on the market and how much on planning. There are several arguments, however, for placing more reliance on the market during a period of decline. First, plans are based on political reality, and politically it is almost impossible to reduce drastically or close out a campus or program. The impersonal forces of the student market can accomplish reduction a little at a time, and in a manner that carries legitimacy. Second, planned reductions bring greater state intrusion into the private lives of academic institutions than do planned increases. Increased resources enable participants to do what they want to do, while planned reductions involve coercion by the state. They will bring on protests and claims that academic freedom has been infringed. Again, the slower, more impersonal actions of the student market may be more effective. Third, people react differently to planning than to market forces. Faculty and other staff may respond to planned decline with confrontation, as through collective bargaining, but a reduction in student demand may, on the other hand, bring a response to improve the attractiveness of programs.

A major role for planners could be to utilize the market forces constructively. For example, students will need good information on costs and programs at alternative institutions. The plan may need to place enrollment ceilings on some programs, or assist in shifting faculty and students from one institution or program to another. There should be a plan for dealing with closings or mergers of institutions in both the public and private sectors.

And above all, the plan should provide a set of positive goals for higher education, beyond holding on to past gains. With fewer new students to provide for, attention can be turned to providing the best possible education for those within the system, to meeting the needs of the state and its students.

7. PRESERVING THE PRIVATE SECTOR

The United States and Japan are the only industrial nations in the world that rely on private institutions to supply a substantial part of their higher education. Much of the diversity and flexibility of the American system—its ability to respond quickly to changing numbers of students, changing fields of interests, changing clienteles—stem from the existence of a large private sector. All of the institutions with religious affiliations, and almost all single-sex institutions, fall in the private sector.

Private colleges and universities constitute the majority of all higher education institutions in the U.S. (1,783 private and 1,512 public institutions reported enrollment figures to the National Center for Education Statistics in 1981), but they enroll only 23 percent of all (headcount) students. This compares with 50 percent of the students in 1950, 41 percent in 1969, and about 25 percent in 1970.

Absolute numbers of students at private institutions have been increasing even while the private share has dropped. Headcount enrollment went up by 80 percent between 1960 and 1980, and during the decade of the 1970s, FTE (full-time equivalent) enrollment increased by 16 percent at private institutions, compared to a 24 percent increase at all institutions. It is only in comparison with the public sector's tremendous growth during the same period that the private sector has lost. While lower costs at public institutions may continue to draw students out of the private sector, it is noteworthy that the rapid increase in the public share leveled off in the mid-1970s when public institutions accounted for 78 percent of headcount enrollments; the 1983 figure was 77 percent. Full-time equivalent (FTE) enrollments in 1983 were divided three-fourths in the public sector and one-fourth in private institutions.

Yet there are strains and pressures on private institutions that jeopardize their future, or at least the future of some of them. Private colleges that closed during the decade of the 1970s outnumbered new institutions by almost two to one, and by more than three to one if specialized institutions, mainly religious seminaries, are omitted. Some private colleges merged with other institutions, either public or private; a few were taken over by the public sector. Most of the colleges that closed were very small (under five hundred students), were church-related, and were coeducational. Private two-year colleges were particularly vulnerable; one-fifth of those in existence in 1970 were closed eight years later.

The private research, comprehensive, and highly selective liberal arts colleges appear highly resilient, but, while they are less vulnerable than the two-year institutions and the less selective liberal arts colleges, they, too, will encounter difficulties. In the first place the overall age-cohort decline may hit private liberal arts colleges harder than public colleges. The former have tended to enroll heavily from the traditional age group, offer fewer opportunities for part-time study or for non-traditional scheduling, and are often too small to mount new programs to attract new clienteles without a major change in institutional mission.

Second, private colleges are caught in a cost squeeze to a greater extent than are many public institutions. Tuition and fees at private institutions have provided about half of their current revenues for educational and general purposes for the past half-century, and private gifts have remained steady at about 15 percent of income. Funds generated by endowments, however, have plummeted, from almost one-third of private institutional income in 1930 to less than 10 percent in the late 1970s. Tuition can only be changed once a year, and then at the risk of pricing some potential students out of the market. Inflation, a fact of life for the foreseeable future, raises costs and eats away at the value of endowments. Events outside the realm of higher education, such as the OPEC oil crisis of 1973, raise costs unexpectedly. And in most areas, public education is available at a much lower out-of-pocket cost to consumers, the students, and their families. Public and private tuitions have risen, in recent years, in about the same percentage terms, but since private tuitions started from a much higher base, the dollar difference between tuition at public and private institutions, the "tuition gap," has become larger.

Private institutions can themselves do much to preserve their existence and their quality, but public policy must also be carefully designed to preserve the balance of the system by supporting private higher education institutions, while at the same time making sure they remain independent. Federal financial aid policies that distribute funds to higher education institutions as tuition provide financial support with little interference or control. In addition, federal funds for research, including for physical plant and research libraries, make no distinctions between public and private universities. In fiscal year 1983, about 45 percent of federal R&D funds to universities and colleges went to private institutions.

A survey in 1975-76 showed that most of the states, about forty of them, had some kind of program to provide state support to private institutions, largely in the form of financial aid to students attending those colleges. About one-fifth of state aid took the form of general institutional grants on a formula basis, and about the same amount was spent for specific educational programs, institutions, or purposes.[13] The total state support per FTE student was found to be about 11 percent of state support for students in public institutions. The Carnegie Council, in the study cited above, concluded that a state subsidy amounting to not more than half the educational subsidy to students in public institutions would be a reasonable maximum to provide support for private institutions while preserving their freedom from state control.

8. NEW FINANCIAL FORMULAS FOR RISING MARGINAL COST CURVES

Public as well as private colleges are financially threatened by declining enrollments. Most public institutions are funded on a formula that takes full-time equivalent (FTE) enrollment as its basis. As a result, when more students enroll, the institution receives more money from the state. Well over half of funding for public institutions comes from state sources. Federal sources provide about 16 percent, and local and private sources, including tuition, roughly a quarter. When enrollments decline, less state money is provided. Most states now have more sophisticated formulas that take into account a number of factors besides sheer numbers of students, but no matter what form the formula takes, a number of problems arise when formulas devised during a period of growth are applied to decline.

The basic problem arises because of the difference between "average cost" and "marginal cost" per student. If all the expenses of an institution are added up and the total divided by the number of FTE students, the result is average cost per student. A considerable portion of that cost, however, is fixed and does not vary directly with the number of students. Maintenance of the physical plant, and many administrative costs, some minimum of counseling services, for example, are ongoing regardless of the number of students, within broad limits. More students can be accommodated without increasing them, so that the marginal cost of adding one more student will be less than the average cost per student. A lecture course can accommodate 35 students as easily as 30. If a college is funded on an average cost basis, it will get more money for each new student than it costs to serve that student, and it was exactly that "profit," or difference between average and marginal cost, that allowed much of the improvement of programs that took place during the boom years of the 1960s.

On the other hand, if an institution loses funds equal to the average cost per student as enrollment declines, contraction is very rapid. Fixed costs continue at the same level while numbers and support drop. Some factors that are related to enrollments, such as numbers of faculty, may be difficult to cut back in the short term because of the need to staff most programs on at least a minimum basis, contractual or tenure agreements with faculty, and for other reasons.

In response to such problems, some states have tried to cushion public institutions against budgetary cutbacks due to small variations in enrollment and are experimenting with formulas that will smooth out long-term decline. For example, in the University of California system, only enrollment changes greater than 2 percent of the previous year's enrollment trigger budgetary increases or decreases. Several states have adopted measures of workload that take into account headcount (as well as FTE) enrollment, square feet of building space, projected rates of inflation, and other factors. Other states have adopted a formula relating average and marginal costs, so that some fixed percentage of average cost, rather than the full amount, is deducted for enrollment losses. In a study by John Millett for the Ohio Board of Regents, it was estimated that only one-fourth to one-third of the average cost could be considered to be variable; the remainder is fixed or only semivariable.[14]

Another approach is to adopt different funding formulas for various levels and types of instruction. Upper division and graduate instruction carry larger costs than does lower division instruction; teaching in a laboratory setting is more expensive than are large lecture sections. Such differentiation can reduce the temptation for institutions to eliminate programs that have high average costs as an immediate response to budget cuts. That decision should be made on educational and not purely financial grounds, and sensitive formulas can help ensure good educational decision making.

As states review financing formulas, they also have to take into account what their educational priorities are. Some programs and institutions need special protection because they are essential at some minimum level, such as research. Protection of persons hired under affirmative action programs, who otherwise, as last hired might be first fired, is considered high priority in many states. Education of the handicapped, remedial, and continuing education, are other examples of programs where special categorical funding (rather than an enrollment based formula) has been adopted.

Protection of innovative instructional programs may be a priority as they are likely to be one of the first areas to be cut back under an average cost formula. Some states require institutions to hold some fixed percentage of their enrollment-generated income in a discretionary or priority fund to meet innovative or special needs.[15]

After a five-year period of planning and pilot studies, the State of Tennessee and its Higher Education Commission instituted, in the 1979 budget cycle, a method for making an additional allocation of up to 2 percent of an institution's educational and general funds on the basis of performance criteria. This addition to the basic enrollment-driven formula rewards institutions that are willing to set goals congruent with their academic mission, and to conduct evaluations to appraise how well they meet those goals. It is designed so that institutions compete against standards appropriate for institutions with their mission, and not directly against one another. Financial incentives are used to reward quality improvement, and not just those institutions that start, for instance, with better students.[16]

Other states have also partially detached funding from enrollments, some providing base budgets using formulas that vary with the type of institution, as in Ohio, or that are negotiated, as in New Jersey. Institutions then compete for funds for programs in addition to the base budget. All of these state studies and experiments are aimed at maintaining the mission and integrity of their educational and research programs on a short-term basis and to meet current challenges to quality. A long-term decline in enrollments of 25 percent entail not only cushions to soften year-to-year changes, and categorical funding for priority programs, but examination of the roles and functions of whole programs and institutions, keeping in mind that, by the mid-1990s, we may again be traveling back up the marginal cost curve. Different formulas may well need to be developed for periods of contraction and for times of expansion.

9. THE SURVIVAL OF FACULTY MORALE AFTER THE GOLDEN AGE

Faculty morale in the late 1970s was considerably lower than the buoyant optimism of the 1960s. The reasons why faculty are concerned about the future, and why policy makers need to be concerned, center around faculty compensation, the role of faculty in governance, and declining labor market demand.

Faculty compensation (salaries plus fringe benefits) increased 41.2 percent in constant dollars during the 1960s, but in the 1970s the rate of advance first slackened, then stopped, and finally reversed itself. By 1980, real faculty salaries were over 20 percent below what they had been a decade earlier, because of inflation and lessened bargaining power as faculty hiring decreased. In the early 1980s, with annual increases in faculty salaries ranging around 6 percent and with lower rates of inflation, faculty salaries began to creep up again in real terms, although they are still well below the 1970 level.[17] Not only has faculty compensation failed to keep up with the cost of living, it has also failed to keep pace with compensation in the rest of the economy. Faculty salaries are considerably higher than those earned by the average American worker but are lower than those received by business executives, federal government executives, and others with comparable qualifications.

Collective bargaining agreements between faculty unions and institutional or system administrators are one response to falling real salaries, but they also represent a banding together for protection of job security in an era of decline. However, unionization has not proceeded nearly so rapidly as many expected from the original spurt in the late 1960s and early 1970s. By the end of 1984, about one out of every four college campuses was organized. Collective bargaining agreements covered about 27 percent of all faculty, but less than 5 percent in the private sector compared to 36 percent in the public. Two-year campuses are more heavily unionized than are four-year, 36 percent compared to 24 percent.[18]

Collective bargaining in the private sector was dealt a severe blow by the U.S. Supreme Court decision early in 1980 that the faculty members at Yeshiva University in New York City were, in effect, the managers of the institution and that their "professional interests—as applied to governance at a university like Yeshiva—cannot be separated from those of the institution."[19] Governing bodies of some other private universities and colleges subsequently refused to bargain with representatives of faculty unions, and have been up-held in their refusal by the courts on the basis of the *Yeshiva* decision. One interesting result of the *Yeshiva* decision may be a strengthening of collegial mechanisms of governance, such as faculty senates, as administrators try to increase faculty involvement in governance so that courts will, as in the *Yeshiva* case, rule that they are too involved in management to have separate interests that could be represented through collective bargaining agents.

The academic labor market in many fields has suffered drastic declines, with net additions to faculty ranks falling from about 20,000 per year at the peak to zero in the late 1970s. The prospective decline in enrollments means continued low rates of new hires until at least the early 1990s, and lowered rates of mobility for faculty wishing to change institutions.

Another result of the collapse of the labor market for faculty members is the large bulge of faculty in the age range between about 40 and 55 years, those hired during the unprecedented growth years of the 1960s. These persons, mainly white males, have low mortality rates, are too young for retire-ment until the 1990s, and are heavily tenured in—over 80 percent of faculty members at some institutions have the job security afforded by tenure. Prospects for young Ph.D. recipients looking for teaching jobs in colleges and universities are very poor; students face in their classrooms a faculty increasing-ly distant in age from themselves; more women and minorities are qualifying for nonexistent faculty positions; and the researchers and teachers of the 1990s and the years thereafter, when present faculty will retire and more may be needed to teach in new fields and to deal with a new bulge of students, are not coming up through the ranks.

The combination of these factors has led one set of researchers to call the American professoriate "a national resource imperiled," suffering from de-terioration in working conditions and a decline of morale.[20] Colleges and universities face the challenge of revitalizing their faculties before the next great wave of students hits in the mid-1990s. Many are already experimenting with opportunities for young scholars to take tenure-track positions even before older faculty have retired, finding resources to pay competitive market salaries for faculty in some impacted fields such as engineering, and devising programs to attract graduate students into the "pipeline."

10. DEALING WITH UNCERTAINTY

All of these issues have a high probability of being important in the next ten to twenty years. But the one thing we can be certain about is that there will be a number of other issues, equally important, that we do not now recognize. The signs pointing to them may be there now. We have missed or ignored warnings of impending crises in the past. Allan Cartter noted as early as 1965 that we were turning out more Ph.D.s than the academic labor market could absorb,[21] but few noticed his warnings. The turndown in the fertility rate that resulted in the smaller age cohort coming into college now began in the early 1960s, but was not noticed until a few years later.

Some other issues with tremendous impact upon higher education could not have been foreseen, such as wars or the world political crises that led to high fuel costs. We will continue to have uncertainty that stems from actions of others outside the control of higher education institutions. Policies that increase the intake of young persons into the military or other forms of national service could have a great impact on higher education enrollments. Changes in the nation's economic climate, such as high unemployment, could affect enrollments as young people prolong their educational careers in times of job scarcity. Student movements tend to run in cycles, and there is bound to be another wave of student protest sooner or later, although we cannot now tell what the specific issues will be.

The rate at which these uncertain events occur is likely to increase. The more uncertainty there is in society, the more uncertainties there are for higher education.

11. RENOVATION OF THE ROLE OF LEADERSHIP

Academic administrators have made huge adjustments to changing circumstances in the past several decades. Issues such as those discussed here, as well as those we cannot now anticipate, require ever more effective leadership of higher education as it is tied more closely to society and suffers the shocks that rock the rest of the nation.

But several things have happened to make the position of leadership of a college or university less tenable than in former times. It is easier, and more satisfying, to be the leader of an expanding institution than of a declining one. The "management of decline"[22] requires making decisions that satisfy no one. Increasing regulation from outside, from state boards and legislatures, and from federal agencies, makes it harder to exercise effective leadership. As power to make decisions affecting persons or groups within institutions moves farther and farther away from those affected, the roles of managers and accountants expand, and the role of leadership decreases, becomes diffused. The irony is that responsibility for what goes on in the institution is also more diffused with the introduction of the spirit and mechanisms of "participatory democracy." The push for ever more centralization and accountability results in no one being accountable. The president of a major state university has said, "When no one is in charge, no one is fully accountable. I could once say decisively, 'the buck stops here.' Now it never stops." He went on to say, "If an occasional administrator abuses . . . discretion, it makes more sense to replace the administrator than to remove the discretion."[23]

Leaders who can exercise discretion, adjust rapidly to new developments, handle the sudden crisis, will be more, not less, important in the higher education of the future.

NOTES

1. David Henry, *Challenges Past, Challenges Present: An Analysis of American Higher Education Since 1930* (San Francisco: Jossey-Bass, 1975).

2. In 1974, Howard R. Bowen stated that "A doubling of college attendance is not beyond possibility." *Educational Record* 55 (Summer 1974), 150. In the same year Joseph Froomkin suggested, in the most pessimistic of three scenarios he presented for the year 1985 and beyond, that college enrollments might decline as much as 50 percent from the 1974 level. *Changing Credential Objectives of Students in Post-Secondary Education* (Washington, D.C.: U.S. Department of Health, Education, and Welfare, Contract #0574257, 1974). In its final report, the Carnegie Council on Policy Studies in Higher Education projected an enrollment decline in the range of 5 to 15 percent from 1978 to 1997. *Three Thousand Futures: The Next Twenty Years for Higher Education* (San Francisco: Jossey-Bass, 1980), 34. For alternative strategies to increase enrollment by as much as 3.5 percent between 1980 and 1990, see Carol Frances, *College Enrollment Trends: Testing the Conventional Wisdom Against the Facts* (Washington, D.C.: American Council on Education, 1980).

3. See chapter 3, "Coping," in Stephen K. Bailey, *The Purposes of Education* (Bloomington, Ind.: Phi Delta Kappa Educational Foundation, 1976).

4. For evidence that higher education is correlated with more prudent financial behavior, better care of one's health, and other skills, see F. Thomas Juster, ed., *Education, Income and Human Behavior* (New York: McGraw-Hill, 1975). Also see Howard R. Bowen, *Investment in Learning: The Individual and Social Value of American Higher Education* (San Francisco: Jossey-Bass, 1977). For a summary of these issues, see Charlotte Alhadeff and Margaret S. Gordon, "Supplement E: Higher Education and Human Performance," in Carnegie Council on Policy Studies in Higher Education, *Three Thousand Futures: The Next Twenty Years for Higher Education* (San Francisco: Jossey-Bass, 1980).

5. Reports on secondary schooling include: Ernest L. Boyer, *High School: A Report on Secondary Education* (Princeton, NJ: The Carnegie Foundation for the Advancement of Teaching; New York: Harper & Row, 1983); John I. Goodlad, *A Place Called School: Prospects for the Future* (New York: McGraw-Hill, 1983); National Commission on Excellence in Education, *A Nation at Risk: The Imperative for Educational Reform* (Washington, D.C.: U.S. Department of Education, April 1983). Major examples of reports on higher education are: Association of American Colleges, *Integrity in the Academic Curriculum: A Report to the Academic Community* (Washington, D.C.: The Project on Redefining the Meaning and Purpose of Baccalaureate Degrees, Association of American Colleges, February 1985); William J. Bennett, *To Reclaim a Legacy: A Report on the Humanities in Higher Education* (Washington, D.C.: The National Endowment for the Humanities, November 1984); Ernest L. Boyer, *College: The Undergraduate Experience* (New York: Harper & Row, 1987); and Study Group on the Conditions of Excellence in American Higher Education, *Involvement in Learning: Realizing the Potential of American Higher Education* (Washington, D.C.: National Institute of Education, U.S. Department of Education, October 1984).

6. Advisory Panel on the Scholastic Aptitude Test Score Decline, *On Further Examination* (New York: College Entrance Examination Board, 1977).

7. Clifford Adelman, *The Standardized Test Scores of College Graduates, 1964-1982* (Washington, D.C.: U.S. Government Printing Office, 1985), 21-24.

8. The study is "High School and Beyond," a study of students in 1015 high schools throughout the U.S. carried out for the National Center for Education Statistics by the National Opinion Research Center.

9. Carnegie Council on Policy Studies in Higher Education, *Giving Youth a Better Chance: Options for Education, Work, and Service* (San Francisco: Jossey-Bass, 1979), 25.

10. Estimates range from $10 billion to $100 billion a year for education and training for as many as 16 million workers. Beverly T. Watkins, "Post-Compulsory Education by U.S. Companies May Be a $10 Billion Business," *Chronicle of Higher Education* 21 (22 September 1980): 7. Also see Nell Eurich, *Corporate Classrooms: The Learning Business* (Princeton, NJ: The Carnegie Foundation for the Advancement of Teaching, 1985).

11. Dael Wolfle, *The Home of Science: The Role of the University* (New York: McGraw-Hill, 1972).

12. Previous figures in this section are from NSF 86-309 (see source for Table 3). This figure is from U.S. National Science Foundation, *Federal Support to Universities, Colleges, and Selected Nonprofit Institutions, Fiscal Year 1983*, NSF 85-321 (Washington, D.C.: U.S. Government Printing Office, 1985), 47.

13. Carnegie Council on Policy Studies in Higher Education, *The States and Private Higher Education: Problems and Policies in a New Era* (San Francisco: Jossey-Bass, 1977), 32.

14. Ohio Board of Regents, *A Strategic Approach to the Maintenance of Institutional Financial Stability and Flexibility in the Face of Enrollment Instability or Decline* (Washington, D.C.: Academy for Educational Development, 1979), p. 132.

15. This survey of state experiments with budgetary formulas is indebted to the work of the California Postsecondary Education Commission, "State Budget Formulas for Declining Enrollments in California's Public Segments of Postsecondary Education" (Sacramento, February 1980).

16. E. Grady Bogue, *Allocation of State Funds on a Performance Criterion: The Report of—The Performance Funding Project—of the Tennessee Higher Education Commission* (Nashville, 1980).

17. "Continuing the Upward Climb, The Annual Report on the Economic Status of the Profession, 1985-86," *Academe* 72 (March-April 1986): 3-4.

18. John M. Douglas with Elizabeth A. Kotch, *Directory of Faculty Contracts and Bargaining Agents in Institutions of Higher Education* II (January 1985) (National Center for the Study of Collective Bargaining in Higher Education and the Professions. Baruch College, City University of New York), 3-8.

19. *NLRB* v. *Yeshiva University*, 48 U.S.L.W. at 4179.

20. Howard R. Bowen and Jack H. Schuster, *American Professors: A National Resource Imperiled* (New York: Oxford University Press, 1986).

21. Allan M. Cartter, "A New Look at the Supply of College Teachers," *Educational Record* 46 (Summer 1965): 266-77; and "The Supply and Demand of College Teachers," *Journal of Human Resources* 1 (Summer 1966): 22-38.

22. Kenneth E. Boulding, "The Management of Decline," *AGB Reports* (September/October 1975): 4-9.

23. Harold H. Enarson, "Quality and Accountability: Are We Destroying What We Want to Preserve?" *Change* 12 (October 1980): 9, 10.

Part 2

External Forces

8

The Federal Government
and Higher Education

Lawrence E. Gladieux and Gwendolyn L. Lewis

INTRODUCTION

The federal government plays an important and varied role in American
higher education. Washington provides about twenty percent of all college
and university revenues, and in two types of spending, direct aid to students
and support of university-based research and development (R&D), federal
outlays far exceed those of the states, industry, and other donors.

Deep cutbacks in student aid proposed by the Reagan administration in
the early 1980s dramatized the importance of this support for higher education. In the research arena, concern has been mounting for a decade or more
about whether the federal commitment to academic research is sufficient to
keep the United States among the world's leaders in science and technology.

Federal tax policies also impinge heavily on higher education, affecting
both the financing of institutions and the problems and possibilities confronting students and families in meeting the expense of a college education.
Recent tax reform legislation has highlighted the important stakes for students and institutions.

Federal spending and tax policies generate another pervasive influence
on the higher education system, i.e., the weight of regulations. As a condition
of federal support, Congress and executive agencies of the government impose a variety of rules and mandates on institutions of higher education.

The federal impact on the campuses and on students is substantial,
diverse, and constantly changing. The objective of this chapter is to provide
an overview of the federal government's involvement in higher education.

HISTORICAL DIVISION OF RESPONSIBILITIES
IN THE AMERICAN FEDERAL SYSTEM[1]

That the states have the basic responsibility for higher education—indeed, for education at all levels—is an American tradition. Historically, the Tenth Amendment and the fact that "education" is nowhere mentioned in the U.S. Constitution pointed toward a secondary role for the federal government in this field.

While some of the founding fathers urged a national system of education run by the central government, the majority favored state, local, and private control, perhaps with a national university to cap the system. All proposals to establish such a university in the capital city failed, despite the fervent support of George Washington and several of his successors in the presidency. To this day the federal government does not directly sponsor institutions of higher learning apart from the military academies and a few other specialized institutions. Nevertheless, early federal policy was important in promoting higher education as an adjunct of western migration and public land development in the late eighteenth and nineteenth centuries, and the Morrill Land-Grant College Act of 1862 was instrumental in fostering what are now some of the nation's great public, as well as private, universities.[2]

The federal investment in university-based R&D and in student aid via the GI Bill took off following World War II. Beginning with the Soviet challenge of Sputnik, Congress created a variety of aid-to-education programs in the late 1950s and 1960s, and by the 1970s the federal government became the largest source of direct assistance to individual students for financing their college costs. But fundamentally, federal expenditures have remained supplementary to state and private support of higher learning.

Over the past two centuries the states have moved with varying speeds and approaches to create and expand public systems of higher education and, more recently, to assist (or purchase educational services from) private colleges and universities. Today, the major public support for postsecondary institutions continues to come from the states. Figure 1 illustrates the proportionate contributions of the different levels of government to public financing of higher education, excluding federal aid going directly to students. The states in 1985 provided over sixty-five percent of governmental revenues to colleges and universities, more than twice the federal share.

The traditional division of responsibilities between the federal and state governments was reaffirmed in the early 1970s when Congress debated, and ultimately rejected, proposals for general-purpose federal institutional aid. In passing the 1972 amendments to the Higher Education Act

Congress pulled up short of a plan that amounted to federal revenue sharing with institutions of higher education—across-the-board general operating support distributed on the basis of enrollments. It was unwilling to underwrite

FIGURE 1

Government Sources of Current Fund Revenues
to Higher Ed. Institutions, FY 1985

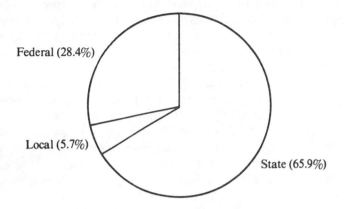

SOURCE: U.S. Department of Education, Center for Education Statistics, *OERI Bulletin,* February, Table 1, based on data gathered in the Higher Education General Information Survey (HEGIS).

the entire system without reference to any national objective other than preserving and strengthening educational institutions. . . . The responsibility for general support of institutions, it was decided, should continue to rest with the states.[3]

The federal government would continue to aid higher education indirectly by supporting programs in areas of special national concern.

This is not to say that the federal government has been unconcerned with the health and capacity of institutions. Certain types of institutions have been the object of special federal attention because of their particular contributions to the national interest. The major research and graduate-oriented universities, particularly their medical schools, comprise one such category. They are supported by grants and contracts from multiple federal agencies. The historically black colleges are another, many of them drawing substantial operating support under Title III of the Higher Education Act.

A few federal programs, such as the National Institutes of Health's Biomedical Research Support Grants and the National Science Foundation's Institutional Development Program, address institutional capacity for research. Other federal funding includes support for institutions that strengthen the arts and humanities, provide occupational and vocational education,

engage international exchanges and studies, those that provide military training, and so on. Although amounts spent in such categories are relatively
small, they are significant for some institutions and certain parts of the
population.

In addition, student aid is in some measure an indirect form of subsidy to
institutions, and it affects virtually every institution in the country. More than
one-third of all postsecondary students are estimated to receive some federal
aid, whether in the form of grants, loans, or employment, as shown in Table
1. The proportion of students receiving aid varies with the type of institution,
but the proportion is significant everywhere, even at low-tuition community
colleges. Some of the historically black colleges and other schools serving
substantially low-income populations have become especially dependent on
federal student aid. Proprietary (for-profit), postsecondary vocational schools
make extensive use of the Guaranteed Student Loan program as well as Pell
Grants for their students. The vigorous politics surrounding congressional
reauthorization and revision of the student aid programs in 1980 and 1986
attest to the high stakes involved for postsecondary institutions. Representatives of the various public and private, two-year and four-year institutions
struggled over the scores of amendments to the allocation formulas; eligibility
criteria; and debated the definitions of student need that determine who gets
what type of aid, where the support would go, and how the assistance would
be transferred from the several billion dollars now spent annually in student
aid programs under Title IV of the Higher Education Act.

TABLE 1
Estimated Percentage of Undergraduate Students Receiving Financial Aid by Type of Institution Attended, 1985

Type of institution	Any aid	Any federal aid	Any non-federal aid
4 year	42.2[a]	34.3	23.7
2 year	47.5	37.8	32.9
Public	36.5	29.3	18.9
Private[b]	60.9	50.6	39.3
Non-profit	53.2	41.2	45.4

[a]The balanced repeated replications measure of the proportion of the estimate due to sampling variability is given for each cell in the original source.

[b]The residual figures for the private for-profit institutions are not presented because their sample size in the survey is inadequate for inference.

SOURCE: Office of Educational Research and Improvement, U.S. Department of Education, *National Postsecondary Student Aid Study: Field Test Results,* July 1986, Table III-2.

But the broad historical delineation of federal and state roles persists in the 1980s. The states retain the fundamental responsibility for higher education, primarily through providing general operating support for public systems of colleges and universities. The federal government provides particular kinds of support to meet perceived national objectives without, for the most part, distinguishing between public and nonpublic recipients of this support. The federal government:

- purchases, services and supports research capacity (R&D);

- fills some gaps (whether in college library support, foreign language and area studies, or health professions development); and

- channels the bulk of its aid directly to students rather than to institutions, with the aim of removing financial barriers facing individuals who aspire to higher education.

MECHANISMS, TYPES, AND DIMENSIONS OF FEDERAL SUPPORT

In the nineteenth century states served as intermediaries under federal legislation for higher education. Proceeds from the sale of public lands provided endowments that helped the states establish and finance the early land-grant institutions, agricultural extension programs, and other forerunners of today's comprehensive colleges and universities. The federal grants to the states were broad and carried few restrictions.

Toward the beginning of the twentieth century the pattern began to change. Federal support became piecemeal and started going directly to the institutions themselves, and not by way of the states. In recent decades, nearly all federal monies have been channeled to institutions (or to departments, schools, and faculty members within institutions) or to individual students.

The federal-state "partnership" in supporting higher education that is frequently referred to is meaningful only in the general sense of the historical roles and governmental division of labor described above. There is, in fact, virtually no conscious meshing of funding purposes and patterns between the two levels of government. By and large the federal activity proceeds independently. As one observer has noted:

With a few modest exceptions, federal postsecondary spending arrangements make no attempt to stimulate state spending, to compensate for differences in state wealth or effort, or to give state governments money to allot as they see fit.[4]

Nor, it might be added, would it be easy to implement a program or funding formula that would effectively achieve any combination of such objectives.

The federal government's distribution of money to higher education is so decentralized and intermixed with other policy objectives that trying simply to enumerate the programs and tally the total investment can be an accounting and definitional headache. It has been estimated that Washington sponsors over 400 programs, administered by some 25 separate agencies and cabinet-level departments, that provide some measure of support for postsecondary education.[5] A sampling of programs suggests the far reaches of federal involvement:

> Purposes vary widely and include, for example, agricultural research, innovative approaches to the education of the handicapped, and training professionals in the study and control of water pollution. Students can receive financial assistance . . . if they are veterans or are willing to study in a field of special interest to the federal government, such as mental health, law enforcement, or urban mass transportation. . . . The Federal Government even provides assistance "in-kind" to postsecondary institutions, ranging from loans of machine tools and dispersal of surplus Government property to provision of films for educational purposes.[6]

The fragmentation of federal support is almost certain to continue. Creation of the U.S. Department of Education in 1979 consolidated only about one-fourth of the 400 programs and less than one-third of total federal expenditures for higher education, not substantially more than were encompassed by the old Office of Education in the U.S. Department of Health, Education, and Welfare. The remaining programs and funds are still scattered across the federal scene, from the Department of Defense and the Veterans Administration to the Department of Agriculture, the National Aeronautics and Space Administration, and the Smithsonian Institution. Fragmentary decision-making about higher education within the executive branch is mirrored in Congress, where committee responsibilities tend to follow agency structures.

Table 2 provides an overview of federal support for higher education. In fiscal year 1985, federal spending totalled about $22 billion, with over forty-seven percent of this amount going for the cost of student aid, almost the same proportion for R&D in higher education, and the balance for assorted categorical assistance and payments to colleges and universities. The more than $10 billion spent for student aid is about two-thirds of the aid generated because the federal government guarantees and subsidizes private loans and requires non-federal matching in certain programs.

Student Aid[7]

Legislative History

From the land-grant college movement to the GI Bill experience following World War II, public policy has progressively extended educational oppor-

TABLE 2
Estimated Federal Financial Assistance to Higher Education in FY1985
(Dollars in Millions)

	Amount	Percent
Student Aid		
Department of Education		
Pell, SEOG, SSIG, NDSL, CWS, & GSL	$ 8,959	
Graduate Fellowships	20	
Veterans Administration	874	
Social Security education benefits	35	
Science/Engineering fellowships, traineeships & training grants	255	
ROTC scholarships and other military assistance	184	
Subtotal	$10,327	47.4%
Research and Development		
Science and Engineering	7,001	
R&D Centers (FFRDCs)	3,071	
Subtotal	$10,072	46.2%
Other Institutional Support		
Special institutions	$ 254	
Programs for disadvantaged students	175	
Occupational and vocational	175	
Aid for institutional development	141	
Military academies	522	
Construction and facilities	52	
Other categorical (Fund for the Improvement of Postsecondary Education, Minorities in Science Improvement, International Education, Cooperative Education, and Libraries)	78	
Subtotal	$ 1,397	6.4%
Total Federal Aid	$21,796	100.0%

SOURCES: American Council on Education, "Sources of Financial Assistance to Postsecondary Education," October 27, 1986; National Science Foundation, "Early Release of Summary Statistics on Academic Science/Engineering Resources," October 1986, Table 8; Department of Education and Department of Defense budget statistics.

tunity to new groups in society. In the past twenty years a major focus of such policy has been federal aid to students, and its growth has been enormous. In 1963 the federal government invested a little less than $200 million in student aid through a fledgling National Defense Student Loan Program and a smattering of graduate fellowships. In the academic year 1985-86, the federal government generated, either through direct appropriations or loan guarantees and subsidies, over $15 billion for students in higher education. That is more than a twenty-fold increase, even after adjusting for inflation. During the same period, enrollments also increased, but by less than three-fold.

The growth of student assistance is especially remarkable in light of the controversy surrounding the issue of federal student aid during the 1950s and early 1960s. Aside from GI Bill benefits, proposals for scholarships to undergraduates, whether based on financial need or academic merit, generated heated debate during the Eisenhower and Kennedy years. Resistance to giving students a "free ride" doomed one such proposal after another in Congress.

The breakthrough came in the mid-1960s. As part of the "Great Society" under President Johnson, the Higher Education Act of 1965 embodied, for the first time, an explicit federal commitment to equalizing college opportunities for needy students. Programs were designed to identify the college-eligible poor and facilitate their access with grants, replacing the contribution their families could not afford to make. Colleges and universities, if they wanted to participate in the new Educational Opportunity Grant Program (later renamed Supplemental Educational Opportunity Grant), were required to make "vigorous" efforts to identify and recruit students with exceptional financial need.

With the 1965 legislation, a new dynamic began to shape the federal role in higher education. Earlier federal support was prompted by various national concerns: fostering a democratic citizenry, sponsoring research in the national interest, meeting perceived personnel shortages, compensating those who had served the country in wartime, and promoting international understanding. Military preparedness was the spark for the National Defense Education Act of 1958. The 1960s put the spotlight on what was, in effect, a moral imperative: removing barriers of inequity that stood in the path of individual opportunity.

Also in 1965, Congress added a new benefit to the Social Security program that allowed children of deceased, disabled, or retired parents eligible for Social Security to receive benefits as dependents while they attended college.

Appropriations for student aid grew in the late 1960s, while other forms of federal support, like construction of academic facilities, gradually faded in importance. Then, in 1972, Congress and the Nixon administration converged with separate proposals that resulted in elaborating and greatly expanding the commitment to student assistance. Amendments to the Higher Education

Act created Basic Educational Opportunity Grants as a floor of direct support for all needy students. Now called Pell Grants, this program in 1986 provided over $3 billion to nearly three million students enrolled in postsecondary education and training.

The 1972 legislation also created the State Student Incentive Grants Program (SSIG) to provide federal matching funds for need-based state scholarship programs. Twenty-eight states preceded the federal government in providing loans and/or scholarships to students, but the federal stimulus of SSIG helped prompt the rest of the states to launch need-based aid programs of their own. During the same period, an increasing number of states also responded to federal incentives to help generate credit financing for students under the Guaranteed Student Loan Program.

Pell Grants and SSIG rounded out the federal commitment to student aid, which during the 1960s had already come to include College Work Study (CWS), National Defense Student Loans (NDSL), Guaranteed Student Loans (GSL), and Supplemental Educational Opportunity Grants (SEOG). Assistance was generally targeted to low-income students. But during the mid-1970s pressure began to mount for broadening the base of eligibility for student aid. Proposals for college tuition tax credits built a head of steam in Congress and, to ward them off, the Carter administration went along with a legislative package that resulted in the Middle Income Student Assistance Act of 1978 (MISAA). MISAA liberalized eligibility for Pell Grants and opened subsidized loans to any student regardless of income or need. Shortly thereafter, Congress let the special allowance to banks participating in GSL float with Treasury bill rates, assuring a highly favorable return for lenders in the program.

The legislative expansion continued through the Educational Amendments of 1980, which further liberalized need analysis for student aid, shielded the GSL program from cost controls, and established an additional loan program called Parent Loans for Undergraduate Students (PLUS).

Then came the 1980 elections and a new administration determined to shrink many domestic social programs. Public and congressional reaction quelled any notion of wholesale cutbacks in student aid. But the growth era in student assistance was clearly over. Many provisions of the 1980 reauthorization law were repealed or delayed, GSL eligibility was tightened, Social Security benefits for students were phased out, appropriations leveled off, and the purchasing power of federal student aid declined.

TABLE 3
Aid Awarded to Postsecondary Students, 1980-81 and 1985-86
(Dollars in Millions)

	Academic Year		
	1980-81	1985-86	Percent Change
	(current dollars)		(constant dollars)
Program			
Federally Supported Programs			
Generally Available Aid			
Pell Grants	$ 2,387	$ 3,652	21.8
SEOG	366	396	-13.8
SSIG	76	76	-19.4
CWS	658	693	-16.1
NDSL	695	751	-13.9
GSL and PLUS	6,201	8,836	13.4
Subtotal	**10,384**	**14,404**	**10.4**
Specially Directed Aid			
Social Security	$ 1,883	$ 0	-100.0
Veterans	1,714	667	-69.0
Other Grants	119	48	-68.1
Other Loans	61	248	224.1
Subtotal	**3,777**	**963**	**-79.7**
Total Federal Aid	**$14,161**	**$15,367**	**-13.6**
State Grant Programs	801	1,374	36.5
Institutionally Awarded Aid	2,138	3,426	27.5
Total Federal, State, and Institutional Aid	**$17,101**	**$20,167**	**-6.2**

SOURCE: The Washington Office of The College Board, *Trends in Student Aid: 1980-1986*, 1986.

Trends and Issues in the 1980s

Between 1980 and 1986, student assistance generated by federal programs declined in constant (inflation-adjusted) dollars by about 14 percent, as shown in Table 3. State and institutional efforts helped to make up for some of the federal losses. The real value of state grant aid grew 36 percent, and the real value of institutionally-funded student aid increased an estimated 28 percent. Even with such changes, the federal government still accounts for the great bulk of funds that help postsecondary students meet their costs of college attendance, contributing more than 75 percent of available aid.

Overall, student assistance from federal, state, and institutional sources declined by six percent in inflation-adjusted dollars between 1980 and 1986. Thus total student aid shrank somewhat in real terms during the first half of the 1980s. At the same time both the distribution among types of students and the composition of the pool of aid funds have been shifting.

First, the funds are being shared by more students each year, particularly as students in proprietary vocational schools increase their participation in federal programs. The percentage of Pell grant dollars going to proprietary school students has nearly doubled during the current decade, from 12 to 23 percent.[8] National data on GSL borrowing by proprietary school students are not available, but state figures show such students' share of these funds growing as well. More than one-third of GSL lending in some states is to students in proprietary institutions.

Second, the most dramatic shift in the composition of the aid pool is the emergence of student loans as the most common form of financial assistance. Loans accounted for 17 percent of aid in 1975-76, 41 percent in 1980-81, and 49 percent in 1985-86. Grant aid has gone from a peak of 80 percent of aid ten years ago, when the Vietnam-era GI Bill was in full use, to 47 percent now. The shift in the grant/loan balance has been the result of three factors: the winding down of Vietnam-era veteran educational benefits that were generally limited to ten years after service, the phasing out of Social Security student benefits beginning in 1981, and the substantial growth of federally-guaranteed and subsidized student borrowing that began in the late 1970s.

In 1986 Congress reauthorized the Higher Education Act for another five years, amending but leaving intact the basic structure of federal student aid under Title IV. While congressional leaders lamented the increase in student indebtedness and said they hoped to re-establish a better balance between loans and grants, the drift toward a system that relies primarily on student debt to finance higher tuitions is not likely to be arrested by the 1986 reauthorization. For its part, the Reagan administration has proposed to shift still more of the burden onto students, through their borrowing, on the grounds that students are the principal beneficiaries of their education.

It can be argued that the federal commitment to equalizing college access has been turned 180 degrees from its origins. In the 1960s the government undertook to remove barriers to the disadvantaged by providing grants and work-study, while helping the middle-class with what were intended to be largely unsubsidized loans of convenience to meet cash-flow problems. But in recent years, as grant dollars have become scarcer, needy students have increasingly had to resort to substantial borrowing to finance their education, a factor very likely related to the decline of minority and low-income college students in the 1980s.

At the same time, ironically, middle-class families are being squeezed out of the Guaranteed Student Loan (GSL) program, which was originally designed for them. Now substantially subsidized in the form of interest paid on behalf of the borrowers during the enrollment period and allowances to private lenders to keep them in the program, GSLs cost the government up to fifty cents on every dollar loaned. Increased federal loan costs since the late 1970s have gradually forced Congress to limit eligibility.

The debate over how college costs should be shared among students, parents, and taxpayers will continue. Policy-makers are concerned about the effect of mounting student debt on students' career choices and on equality of access to higher education.[9] They are looking for remedies, including alternative methods of loan repayment designed to ease the burden for borrowers with low earnings. Variations on the "income-contingent" loan concept are being considered. So, too, is the notion of strengthening the tie between student work and college aid. Various national service plans are advocated by congressional and private sector leaders. Under these, students would receive benefits in return for a commitment to serve the nation or their community, either in the military or in other areas of public need.

Policy-makers are also concerned with the role of the family and the importance of parents' planning and saving well in advance of their children's education. Various incentives for parents to save have been proposed in recent years, but most of the ideas that have surfaced are tied to federal tax policy. Educational savings accounts, or "IRA's for Education," allowing families to set aside tax deferred money or to tap funds already accumulated in individual retirement accounts to pay college costs, are a popular notion. But the recent tax reform movement in Washington dims any early chance for such plans in Congress. Meanwhile, states and institutions are advancing their own strategies, including tuition prepayment plans, allowing parents to invest in a fund that would guarantee prospective college tuition payments for their young children.

While examining the role of parents in the college finance equation, policy-makers need to consider the growing number of older students coming from a variety of life circumstances. More adults are returning to higher education for a "second chance" or retraining and mid-career change. There will be pressure to devise financing policies that better accommodate the "nontraditional" student in the years ahead. No one argues that the parents' financial obligation, an assumption traditionally underlying student aid policy, should last indefinitely, but where to draw the line will be a continuing issue in student aid debates.

Another issue will be tension between the principles of merit and need in awarding student aid. Proposals for merit-based scholarships will continue to surface as particular public needs and personnel shortages are identified. For instance, the White House Science Council Panel on the Health of U.S. Colleges and Universities has recommended that one percent of the country's most able students in mathematics, engineering, and the natural sciences be supported for four years of college at an annual level of $15,000.[10]

Graduate Student Assistance

The bulk of direct federal student aid goes to support undergraduate students, and the policy debates on student aid typically focus on issues of educational access and choice at the undergraduate level. Yet a significant proportion of the aid available through the loan and work-study programs goes to graduate and professional students.

Federal support for graduate students also comes in the form of research assistantships, fellowships, and traineeships, and much of this support is built into the funding of R&D. Table 4 (see p. 166) presents estimates of graduate student support from federal as well as state, institutional, and private sources.

Overall, grant funds have decreased in recent years even though some science fields have experienced growth. Funding of federal fellowships and traineeships declined by 20 percent between 1974 and 1984. Fewer awards are available, and in many cases federal and private funding agencies have reduced the amount of the individual award, in effect covering less of the student's total costs. On the other hand, research assistantships for science and engineering students increased substantially in that period.

With cutbacks, universities have looked to alternative sources. The College Work-Study (CWS) program, for example, is increasingly used to fund teaching assistants; under CWS, the university must provide only 20 percent matching for federal dollars, rather than 100 percent of a teaching assistant's stipend.[11] The most common recourse for filling the gap, however, has been student borrowing. The federal GSL has become an integral part of financing graduate education. Federal loans made up 13 percent of assistance for graduate students in 1974 and 44 percent in 1984. Loans from all sources went from 16 percent of graduate student support in 1974 to 48 percent in 1984.

Traditionally, graduate institutions and departments have awarded aid primarily on the basis of academic merit. But recent financing trends have created a dual system. Research assistantships and what remains of fellowship support from federal and private sources continue to be allocated on merit, whereas the great proportion of subsidized work, loan, and other aid to graduate and professional students is directed according to need without regard to competitive academic criteria.

TABLE 4

Estimated Financial Assistance for Students Enrolled
for Advanced Degrees by Source, 1974 and 1984

(Dollars in Millions)

	1974		1984	
	Amount	Percent	Amount	Percent
Federal Programs				
Fellowships and Traineeships	$ 175	9%	$ 140	2%
Research Assistantships	160	8	460	8
Grants with Service Payback				
Obligations	60	3	180	3
Loans	250	13	2,500	44
College-Work Study	20	1	65	1
Veterans Educational Benefits	300	16	100	2
Subtotal	**$ 965**	**50**	**$3,445**	**60**
State Programs				
Grants	10	1	30	1
Loans	20	1	100	2
Subtotal	**$ 30**	**2**	**$ 130**	**3**
Institutional Sources				
Assistantships	500	26	1,100	19
Fellowship and Tuition Waivers	100	5	300	5
Loans	20	1	80	1
Subtotal	**$ 620**	**32**	**$1,480**	**26**
Private Sources				
Employer Assistance	250	13	500	9
Fellowships	30	2	60	1
Loans	20	1	70	1
Subtotal	**$ 300**	**16**	**$ 630**	**11**
Total Assistance	**$1,915**	**100%**	**$5,685**	**100%**

SOURCE: Arthur M. Hauptman, *Studies in Graduate and Professional Education: What We Know and Need to Know*, Washington, D.C.: Association of American Universities, 1986, Table 18.

Overall, graduate students are experiencing increased difficulty financing their education while at the same time knowing that financial rewards accruing to an advanced degree, especially in traditional academic disciplines, are uncertain compared to alternative careers. Many observers worry about the quality and numbers of students pursuing graduate work and the adequacy of federal policies regarding research and student financing to meet national needs for highly trained personnel in the 1990s and beyond.

The mix of students in the pipeline is already changing. The proportion of American citizens in U.S. graduate programs is declining (from 87.0 percent in 1960 to 74.5 percent in 1985).[12] Their places are being filled by foreign nationals, many of whom wish to remain in the United States upon completing their degrees. This source of replacement may help to meet future national needs (though some call this into question as well). But the issue remains whether current policies are adequate to assure U.S. economic growth, creativity, and international competitiveness into the next century.

Research Support[13]

Federal support of research and development and other aspects of science at colleges and universities goes back further than the federal commitment to student aid. In 1883 the first law was enacted to support agricultural experiment stations. The amounts of federal support for academic science were fairly small, however, until World War II, when wartime needs caused federal spending to skyrocket. The boom in federally sponsored research continued through the 1950s and early 1960s. But beginning in the mid-1960s, annual growth rates (in constant dollars) fell from double-to single-digit levels and actually declined in some years in the late 1960s and early 1970s, and again in 1982.[14] This period of decline coincided with a gradual shift in federal emphasis from long-term investment in research capacity to a more short-term approach of procuring specific R&D products.[15]

Though federal support of academic R&D has not continued to grow at anything like the rates of two and three decades ago, it has increased in recent years and remains a major source of financing for higher education. Moreover, beginning in the late 1970s nondefense R&D support has increasingly emphasized basic over applied research. Since basic research tends to be conducted in universities, this trend has channeled proportionately more federal research funds to higher education.

Unlike student aid, federal research assistance is highly concentrated on a relatively small number of major research universities. In 1985, 100 doctorate-granting institutions received 86 percent of all federal R&D obligations to academia, a proportion that has remained quite stable over the years.[16] Fewer than 600 out of more than 2,000 four-year and graduate institutions grant doctoral degrees in science or engineering and/or have R&D expenditures of as much as $50,000 a year, the criteria used by the

National Science Foundation in monitoring academic R&D finances.

The sources of total academic R&D spending are summarized in Table 5. The primary source is the federal government, which furnished $6.0 billion or 63 percent of all academic R&D funds in 1985. The federal government's contribution increased (in constant dollars) by 10 percent between 1980 and 1985. Contributions from all other sources, except state and local governments, grew much more. The percent increase in industry's contribution (from a much smaller base) has been the most substantial.

TABLE 5
R&D Expenditures at Universities and Colleges
by Source of Funds, FY 1980 and 1985
(Dollars in Millions)

Source	1980	1985	Percent Increase
	(current dollars)		(constant dollars)
Federal government[a]	$4,096	$6,003	10.0
State and local governments	491	665	1.6
Industry	237	538	70.5
Institutional funds	827	1,593	44.5
All other sources	409	704	29.1
TOTAL	$6,060	$9,504	17.7

[a]Does not include amounts for federally-funded research and development centers (FFRDCs).

SOURCE: National Science Foundation, "Early Release of Summary Statistics on Academic Science/Engineering Resources," October 1986, Table 1.

Although the federal investment in academic science increased overall during the first half of the 1980s, investment in different components of research has been uneven. Project support for R&D, including money to purchase research equipment, has increased substantially, but general support for nonspecific purposes related to scientific research and education has continued to decline in constant dollars. So has support for instructional facilities and (as noted earlier) graduate fellowships and training grants. Federal obligations for R&D plant have more than tripled between 1980 and 1985 in current dollars, but still fall far short in real dollars of the amount the federal government invested in this category twenty years ago.

Project grants, long the mainstay of federal research support, are not designed to sustain what the National Academy of Sciences calls the infrastructure of research: "equipment that cannot be justified for any single project, support for preliminary exploration of new ideas, funds needed by beginning scientists to establish a record of performance, and temporary support for experienced scientists who are changing the field of their research."[17] Only a very small part of federal support for academic science is now available in the form of institutional grants for general support of research.

A specific and critical problem affecting the research and teaching capacity of universities and colleges is the deterioration and obsolescence of scientific equipment and facilities. As the National Academy notes, "the government has invested substantially in academic research equipment and facilities, especially during 1950-1965. Neither the government nor the universities made adequate commitments for sustaining these major elements of research capacity."[18] Research facilities, many built during the boom years of federal support, are increasingly out-of-date and inadequate to handle modern equipment.

Because the dimensions of the "infrastructure" problem are difficult to assess precisely, and there has been concern that corrective action could cost billions of dollars, Congress has mandated a biennial NSF survey of science and engineering research facilities in higher education. In 1986 the National Science Foundation issued the first baseline data from this survey, focusing on doctorate-level institutions.[19] Future surveys will cover all four-year institutions.

Some members of Congress concerned about sustaining the academic base of science have proposed a "Universities Revitalization Act," which would devote a portion of R&D funds of specified federal agencies to the replacement or modernization of laboratories and other research facilities at colleges and universities.[20] The National Science Foundation, however, officially opposes this approach, suggesting alternatively that the rate of federal reimbursement of universities' indirect (overhead) costs for research contracts be adjusted to allow for such physical plant and equipment needs.

The Reagan administration has operated from the beginning on the premise that the federal role in R&D should be limited to projects, either long-term or high-risk, that the private sector is not likely to fund.[21] It has also tried to promote closer cooperation among government, industry, and universities in science research. Tax incentives have been provided for private investment in university-based R&D, and nonprofit organizations and small businesses have been allowed to benefit from patents resulting from federally-sponsored research.

While the Reagan administration has supported subtantial increases in overall federal funding of science research, much of the commitment has been concentrated on national defense and on large R&D projects, such as the Strategic Defense Initiative (SDI) and "super computer" research. These increased commitments have not necessarily channeled substantial new funds to universities; a great deal of SDI work, for example, is carried out in nonacademic settings. Meanwhile, the administration has effected large reductions in civilian applied research and development projects, especially in the energy and environmental areas.

Notwithstanding the emphases of the Reagan administration, the broad distribution of academic R&D obligations among federal agencies has yet to shift dramatically in the 1980s. Three agencies continued to dominate support in 1985: the Department of Health and Human Services (HHS), the National Science Foundation (NSF), and the Department of Defense (DoD). About half of all university-based research is in the life sciences, and HHS continues to be the largest contributor of federal funds for science conducted in academic settings, despite repeated Reagan administration proposals to cut funding for the National Institutes of Health. The HHS provided nearly 49 percent of federal R&D support for higher education in 1985, up less than one percent from 1981. DoD provided over 16 percent, also up less than one percent from 1981. The NSF accounted for about 16 percent in 1985, up by nearly two percent from 1981.

A variety of other departments and agencies, from Agriculture and Energy to Transportation and the Nuclear Regulatory Commission, provide the balance of federal funding for academic research and development. While NSF, DoD, and HHS budgets have increased slighty over these years, many of the smaller agencies, such as the Environmental Protection Agency and the Department of Energy, have sustained relatively large losses. According to the American Association for the Advancement of Science, "Trends in funding in these agencies . . . have only limited effect on the overall academic R&D picture, but they do have major impacts in certain institutions and certain fields and subfields."[22]

When the NSF was created in 1950, Vannevar Bush envisioned an agency having broad purview over federal funding of research in the physical sciences, medicine, and defense with a separate science advisory board to evaluate and integrate technical research sponsored by other government departments.[23] This vision is far from the reality of the mid-1980s when more than a dozen mission-oriented "technoscience" agencies separately channel funds to academic institutions for a variety of purposes. Although such diffuse and overlapping deployment of government R&D resources may promote the funding of diverse topics and lines of inquiry, critics point to the lack of a cohesive federal policy as a major drawback that narrows and duplicates research, promotes over-specialization among scientists, and impedes efficient effort on problems of major national significance.[24]

The tide, however, may be turning once again at the federal level, from a preoccupation with short-term procurement back toward one of more long-term investment in science. The increased federal emphasis on funding basic research at universities reflects this trend. Moreover, the NSF may be slated, after all, for a more prominent and central role in funding university-based R&D in the years ahead. The Reagan administration has announced its support for doubling the NSF's budget between 1987 and 1992, consistent with

1986 recommendations of the White House Science Council Panel on the Health of U.S. Colleges and Universities.[25] An NSF boost of such magnitude would likely strengthen academic science and engineering research, broaden to some extent the range of institutions supported, and restore support for undergraduate science education that was dropped from the NSF budget in 1981. Whether Congress will approve such expansion during a time of overall budget retrenchment, however, remains to be seen.

An issue for universities that is likely to be of growing concern in the late 1980s is the possibility of reduced reimbursement of indirect costs on federal research grants. Currently, individual institutions face two separate federal systems (those of the NIH and the NSF) for reviewing grant proposals and paying indirect costs. In 1986, the Panel on the Health of U.S. Colleges and Universities recommended that the NSF method, which reduces costs to the government at the expense of universities, be used by all federal agencies.

Tax Policies

In addition to direct funding of students and institutions, the government indirectly assists higher education through its tax policies. A variety of exclusions, exemptions, and deductions in the federal tax code have over the years benefited education at all levels. Some of these provisions—for example, the nontaxability of scholarships and fellowships, the personal exemptions that parents may claim for students age nineteen and over, and the interest deductions on student loans—affect individuals and families in their ability to save for and pay educational costs. Other provisions affect the income and financial arrangements of colleges and universities; their not-for-profit status allows them, for example, to receive tax-deductible contributions from corporations, foundations, and individuals.

The monetary benefits to institutions and students of such indirect assistance are called "tax expenditures," which are measured by the estimated amount of federal revenue that would be collected in the absence of such provisions. Prior to the enactment of the Tax Reform Act of 1986, estimated tax expenditures for higher education totalled over $4 billion annually.

Indirect support for university research was provided by the 1981 tax legislation, which gave tax credits to industry for investment in cooperative, applied research projects with universities and enhanced deductions for gifts of research and research training equipment. The allowed credit was for increases in such spending over the previous three years. Critics of the 1981 bill argued that R&D funding at colleges and universities would not benefit much from such an incremental approach.

The Tax Reform Act of 1986 balanced the treatment of corporations' investments in basic and applied research. The revised tax credits reflected a growing recognition that basic research requires long-term, relatively constant support and is done best in the universities, and that corporations require encouragement more for basic than for cooperative, applied research.

The Tax Reform Act of 1986 contains many additional changes for 1987 and beyond. Some of the law's new provisions have direct implications for educational institutions.

- The tax deduction for gifts of stocks and other appreciated property, accounting for 40 percent of all giving at private colleges and universities, will be tightened.

- The tax deduction for charitable gifts by non-itemizers is terminated, thus affecting giving to all non-profit institutions. According to Professor Charles Clotfelter of Duke University, the 1986 tax reform will reduce giving to colleges and universities by 25 to 30 percent in 1988 from the level that could otherwise be anticipated.[26]
- Rules for tax-exempt financing are changed, potentially affecting both construction of educational facilities and bond financing of student loans.

- The federal deduction for state and local sales taxes is eliminated. Currently, many states rely on sales taxes to finance education at all levels. The loss of this deduction could reduce support for the use of sales taxes to finance public education.

Other changes as a result of the 1986 tax reform will affect students and parents.

- The elimination of tax-deductible Clifford Trusts and changes in taxation of income transferred to children under the age of fourteen will limit the use of these methods as a means of saving for educational purposes. For the great majority of families, however, a transfer of income remains a viable college savings technique with a tax advantage.

- An individual will no longer be able to take a personal exemption on his or her own tax return if eligible to be claimed as a dependent on another's return. Thus, full-time students under the age of nineteen who currently are benefiting from such an exemption will no longer be able to claim it.

- The deduction for consumer interest, incuding interest on education loans to students and parents, is phased out between 1987 and 1992. However, home mortgage interest remains deductible, and taxpayers will be able to deduct interest payments on home equity loans used to meet educational expenses.

- Scholarships, fellowships, and federal financial aid grants to graduate and undergraduate students will be counted as taxable income to the extent these awards, either individually or together, exceed the cost of tuition and related expenses. Those most likely to be affected are married students with spouses earning income, athletes receiving full scholarships, and paradoxically, some of the neediest students (those with the large grants). On the other hand, for many students the increase in the standard deduction will mitigate the impact and leave them with little or no increased liability.

The overall magnitude and direction of changes in tax expenditures induced by the new law are yet to be determined since it must be interpreted by Treasury Department regulations and possibly further amended by Congress. All the above changes are likely to reduce tax expenditures for higher education. Two other changes affecting higher education, the reinstatement of the non-taxability of employer-provided educational assistance and enhanced tax incentives for corporations investing in university-based research, are likely to raise tax expenditures.

REGULATION (AND SELF-REGULATION) OF HIGHER EDUCATION

Concern about the impact of federal regulations on the internal affairs of universities was one of the most controversial issues in government-university regulations in the late 1970s. One analyst wrote in somewhat apocalyptic tones: "Not only legislatures and Federal agencies but the courts as well are willing to scrutinize every exercise of discretion on the basis of a complaint. This is the twilight of autonomy and authority. The prevailing tides of opinion currently are egalitarian and legalistic and they are joined in a simplistic view of society and the likelihood of its improvement."[27]

During the 1980s this issue has receded somewhat. The Reagan administration's widely publicized support for regulatory relief (getting the government "off the backs of the American people") has altered the climate of regulation. Regulatory enforcement has slowed in some areas, and over the years colleges have learned to accommodate bureaucratic requirements of the federal government, tempering the conflict experienced previously. Some institutions have actually bargained with the federal government to lessen their regulatory burden. For example, Yale and Stanford have accepted lower indirect cost reimbursement on federal research contracts in exchange for a reduction in reporting requirements.[28]

Federal regulation of higher education derives from two principal sources: (1) the requirements of accountability that accompany the receipt of federal funds; and (2) the dictates of social legislation as well as executive orders and judicial decisions stemming from such legislation.[29]

To the degree that government officials insist on accountability for the proper expenditure of funds and that congressional mandates addressing a range of social problems remain in force, there will be complexity and strain in the relationship of government and higher education. Tensions are inherent, given on the one hand the traditions of academic autonomy and on the other the mandates of Congress, the missions of federal agencies, and the responsibility of those agencies for the stewardship of taxpayer dollars.

The academic community has long been wary of entanglement with government, but only a few (mainly independent, religiously affiliated) institutions have consistently refused funds from Washington. The great majority of colleges have found by experience that accepting federal patronage does exact a price that is both monetary (the costs of compliance) and nonmonetary (the intrusion and distraction of external controls).

Although regulatory pressure has generally eased in the 1980s, it has intensified in some areas. Faculty appear to face a mounting burden of record-keeping and accounting on research contracts; complications in assessing overhead charges have led to detailed "faculty effort reporting" and other forms of "micromanagement" by federal agency program officers that are said to impede creativity and efficiency. (In response to such concerns, five federal agencies have recently initiated a demonstration project in conjunction with the research universities in the state of Florida under the auspices of the Government-University-Industry Research Roundtable of the National Academy of Sciences. The project's aim is to streamline the research grant and contract system and reduce red tape for the universities.)

In the administration of federal student aid, institutions and their students must cope with increasingly complex procedures for verifying the accuracy of data on application forms. And the 1986 tax reform law may impose additional record-keeping obligations, related to taxation of fellowships, scholarships and other awards to students.

The federal government affects higher education through a variety of statutes and regulations administered across almost all federal agencies. Some mandates, such as those of the Environmental Protection Agency (EPA) and the Occupational Safety and Health Administration (OSHA), affect all types of organizations equally, while others, such as the Buckley Amendment on privacy rights of students and Title IX barring sex bias, are specific to educational institutions.

The organizational decision-making style of academic institutions differs considerably from that of both the federal government and other organizations, such as businesses, that are recipients of federal support. These differences, not surprisingly, create clashes in expectations. Colleges and universities have a collegial or democratic mode of shared leadership and decision-making that promotes "amateur administration," according to one analyst.[30] This mode relies on consensus building, a slow process that increases costs considerably in comparison with institutions that are more traditionally hierarchical and bureaucratic in structure. In addition, although colleges and universities benefit from their tax-exempt status for many purposes, they are unable, unlike profit-making organizations, to reduce the expense of federal compliance by deductions from taxable income.

Two other areas of increasing costs to colleges and universities related to government action are social security taxes and unemployment insurance contributions required of employers. Since college and university budgets are made up disproportionately of personnel costs, higher education is more heavily affected by the rapid rise in these taxes than are some other sectors. (In early 1987 the Reagan administration proposed extending social security coverage to the earnings of full-time students; both student and employer would be subject to the social security tax under the proposal.)

An arena of ongoing regulatory debate and litigation has been the desegregation of public postsecondary education systems. Fourteen states are currently under court order to develop and implement plans to end segregated systems of postsecondary education—or face termination of federal funds. Several states that have chronically failed to gain federal approval are embroiled in litigation.

One major court action of the 1980s, the Grove City case, appears to have had a broad effect in slowing federal antibias enforcement. Previously, laws forbidding bias as a condition for receipt of federal funds had been interpreted to apply to the entire institution receiving the funds. In 1984 the Supreme Court ruled that Title IX prohibiting sex discrimination in federally assisted programs, and by implication other anti-bias statutes, applied only to the Grove City College student aid office because Pell grants were the only federal aid accepted by the institution. Pending in the 100th Congress is the Civil Rights Restoration Act, which would revise relevant statutes to make clear that they apply to the entire institution.

Challenges to Self-Regulation

Notwithstanding Washington's substantial regulatory impact on higher education, it is important to note that the federal government has in important respects traditionally relied heavily on *self-regulation* by colleges and universities. Two major examples are the role of voluntary accreditation in determining the eligibility of institutions for federal assistance, and the use of "peer review" for awarding federal research dollars. Both mechanisms have come under challenge in recent years, however.

Since the Korean War GI Bill, various federal laws have called on the Commissioner (now Secretary) of Education to publish a list of accrediting agencies whose decisions would be acceptable as a proxy for the educational and fiscal soundness of institutions receiving federal funds. Thus, the government has sought quality assurance without probing directly into delicate areas of academic decision making. But since the late 1970s serious questions have been raised about the adequacy of this approach, and the Department of Education has begun to tighten the criteria for approving accrediting agencies. A 1986 report by an advisory group to the department urged much closer attention in the accreditation process to standards of quality and "truth in advertising" by institutions to assure they deliver the kind of education promised to prospective students.

Likewise, the traditional, heavy reliance on nongovernment scientists to review the merits of research proposals is being challenged—from several directions. Critics charge that this "peer review" system has become a self-perpetuating "old boys' network" that stifles innovation in academic science and allows a small group of universities to monopolize the bulk of federal research funding. Institutions not in this group tend to chafe at the "unfair advantage" of those who staked out the territory first and are perceived to control peer review. Some institutions have, in effect, skirted the "agreed-upon" peer review systems and have gone directly to Congress seeking earmarked funds for research and research facilities.

In response to congressional concerns, the General Accounting Office has studied the distribution of research money to universities, including the impact of peer review.[31] While the study is limited and inconclusive, it tends to support the claims of those who say that the pattern of funding that results from peer review is reasonably fair. The Department of Defense and the National Science Foundation have been examining the fairness issue as well.[32] Whatever the outcome of such studies, "pork-barrel science" will continue to be debated, with at least some institutions likely to break ranks and search for project funding commitments through the political process.

A third example of federal reliance on self-regulation by the academic community is in the conduct of "need analysis" to determine student eligibility for certain forms of financial assistance. Congress and the Department of Education have traditionally allowed colleges to use private systems, such as the College Scholarship Service, for awarding federal campus-based student aid. Here again, such delegation of authority to nongovernmental agencies is being questioned. In recent years, Congress has taken an increasing interest in the specific criteria for measuring family and student financial need. Beginning in 1988, colleges will be required to use systems of need analysis written directly by Congress into Title IV of the Higher Education Act.

DATA COLLECTION AND POLICY ANALYSIS

When first established by Congress in 1867, the Department of Education (later to become the U.S. Office of Education, which in turn became the Department of Education in 1979) was charged primarily with collecting "statistics and facts to show the condition and progress of education in the several States and Territories," and "diffusing such information respecting the organization and management of schools and school systems and methods of teaching."[33] The Commissioner of Education was required to give an annual report on the facts, along with results of studies and his recommendations.

This statistics-gathering function continues to reside with the federal government. When the National Center for Education Statistics (now the Center for Education Statistics) was formed in 1965, it "assumed responsibility for all the general purpose data gathering within the then Office of Education and for helping states, through a program of grants, improve their own data-gathering and statistical capabilities."[34] It was established as a research arm for education in the federal establishment, parallel to the National Center for Health Statistics, the Agricultural Reporting Service, and the Bureau of Labor Statistics.

Most investment in the effort to collect information has emphasized data for elementary and secondary education, but today higher education relies on the Department of Education and the Center for Education Statistics for data on characteristics of students and institutions. Many college and university administrators complain about the burden of completing surveys from the center, but recognize that it is essential to have comparable baseline data on finances, curricula, students, and other aspects of higher education.

The Center for Education Statistics, however, has remained relatively small and its budget meager compared to the centers it was established to parallel. In 1985, total government (local, state, and federal) spending on health ($150 billion) was less than for education ($180 billion), but spending for federal health statistics was over nine times that for education statistics. In response to criticisms raised in a full-scale evaluation of the center by the National Academy of Sciences in 1986,[35] the staff of the center has been expanded and proposals have been made to increase funding for the center, while at the same time sharpening the center's mission and upgrading the quality, timeliness, and policy relevance of its output. Congress, however, has been reluctant to grant the request for additional funding for education statistics while the Reagan administration is proposing deep cuts in other programs of the Department of Education.

One response to criticism that the center's studies lack usefulness to policy makers has been the National Postsecondary Student Aid Study. Begun in 1986, this ambitious survey is intended to yield comprehensive data related to the federal government's largest single investment in education. The study investigates patterns of student support from all sources—federal, state, private, institutional, and family—to help inform future policy debates on how to divide the responsibility for paying college costs.

Another mechanism of the U.S. Department of Education for serving higher education has been support of centers and laboratories conducting educational research. The Cooperative Research Act of 1954 established a mix of individual research projects and stable research centers devoted to large-scale, long-term consideration of major problems in education. The National Center for Higher Education Management Systems (NCHEMS) was the one center devoted to higher education issues, until 1985 when a congressionally-mandated five-year recompetition instituted new topical areas for research and relocated some centers. Two of the eleven new centers focus on higher education: the National Center for Research to Improve Postsecondary Teaching and Learning, located at the University of Michigan, and the National Center for Postsecondary Governance and Finance, located at the University of Maryland-College Park. In 1990 new topics will be selected and another competition for the centers will be held.

THE SECRETARY OF EDUCATION'S "BULLY PULPIT"

An analysis of the federal government and higher education in the 1980s would not be complete without reference to a phenomenon quite apart from the tangible, operational activities of the federal establishment: the role of the nation's chief education official, and to an extent the president himself, in shaping the broader public debate on education.

While the transformation of the U.S. Office of Education into the Department of Education almost a decade ago did little to consolidate or streamline all the bureaucratic bits and pieces in the executive branch that affect education, cabinet status has boosted the visibility of education as a national issue. The department is far from being a national ministry of education—the American tradition of state and local control rules that out. But recent experience demonstrates that the secretary is in a strategic position to shape public attitudes (and spark controversy) on educational issues of the day.

Terrell Bell accepted appointment as Secretary of Education in 1981 knowing he would be presiding over a department that President Reagan, in the 1980 election campaign, promised to abolish. But congressional opposition forestalled any such plan. The 1983 release of *A Nation at Risk,* the report of the National Commission on Excellence in Education, catapulted the secretary to prominence in the media and to a lead role in the education reform movement.[36] The Reagan administration, far from proposing to downgrade the organizational status of education in the executive branch, embraced the cause of reform. Education and its importance to the nation suddenly commanded attention (if not support for federal spending) from the White House. In 1984 another Department of Education-sponsored report, *Involvement in Learning,* put the spotlight on the need for strengthening undergraduate as well as elementary and secondary education.[37]

William Bennett, who had written his own report on undergraduate learning as director of the National Endowment for the Humanities, succeeded Bell as Secretary of Education in 1985. Bennett immediately signalled that he intended to use his office as a "bully pulpit," speaking directly to the public. He has, indeed, been the most visible, vocal, and activist education secretary or commissioner in history, not so much with respect to the day-today management of the Department of Education, but in the larger public arena.

In fact, most of the issues on which Secretary Bennett has cajoled the public and harangued the education establishment—from student discipline and moral values in the schools to college costs, the curriculum, and quality of education at all levels—are not matters over which the department or the federal government has much, if any, direct authority or influence. He has criticized colleges for raising -tuition faster than general inflation, yet aside from exhortation on this issue, the secretary has little practical leverage on pricing decisions in higher education.

Likewise, on the matter of the quality and outcomes of higher education, the secretary has castigated college leaders for failing to assure that students learn anything before they graduate. But, again, he is left with limited tools for influencing educational practice. He has some leverage (as noted earlier) through strengthening federal criteria for recognition of college accreditation agencies and through incentive grants for research and innovation in student learning techniques (from the Fund for Improvement of Postsecondary Education, for example). His greatest power remains, however, the "bully pulpit."

Under another administration and another secretary, education may not attract quite the attention and controversy at the national level that it has in the mid-1980s. But neither does education seem likely to slip from cabinet status into the backwaters of Washington bureaucracy and out of the national spotlight in the near future.

THE OUTLOOK FOR THE FEDERAL ROLE IN HIGHER EDUCATION

Gauging the prospects for federal support of students and colleges in the decade ahead is akin to reading tea leaves. The post-Reagan era is fast approaching, and much will depend on election results. But whoever is in the White House and whatever the complexion of future Congresses, the fundamental struggle over federal spending, taxes, and national priorities will continue. On behalf of higher education there is reason for both caution and optimism regarding the outcome.

On the one hand the federal fiscal dilemma looms, with annual deficits hovering at $200 billion and a cumulative national debt that exceeds $2 trillion. Debts of such magnitude clearly constrain the potential for federal creativity and largesse in addressing the nation's educational needs. The federal government may not meet precisely the fiscal targets established by the Emergency Budget Control and Deficit Reduction Act (Gramm-Rudman-Hollings) through fiscal year 1991. But under any circumstance there is likely to be continued downward pressure for at least the remainder of the 1980s on both direct spending and tax expenditures for higher education.

Favoring the outlook for higher education, on the other hand, are the renewed concern for U.S. competitiveness and the recognition that our long-run economic and technological position in the world is directly linked to the training of the future work force and the strength of research and teaching in American colleges and universities. This recognition may or may not lead to real increases in the federal investment but should at least help to protect current levels of support from some of the ravages of deficit reduction immediately ahead and erosion over the long term.

The federal government will undoubtedly continue to make important contributions to enhancing the academic enterprise and equalizing educational opportunities in America. As in the past, federal support will supplement the basic funding provided from state and private sources, and it will spring from objectives (like economic competitiveness) other than supporting education for its own sake. Funds (and attendant regulations) will continue to flow from a variety of agencies in Washington. Such support is untidy, piecemeal, and not without headaches for institutions, students, and states. But the pattern serves a variety of national purposes and may, in fact, ultimately better serve to protect institutional diversity, students' freedom of choice, and independent thought in American higher education than would an overarching federal policy.

NOTES

1. This section is based upon Lawrence E. Gladieux and Janet S. Hansen with Charles R. Byce, *The Federal Government, the States, and Higher Education: Issues for the 1980s* (New York: The College Entrance Examination Board, 1981).

2. For the historical development of federal involvement with higher education, see George N. Rainsford, *Congress and Higher Education in the Nineteenth Century* (Knoxville, Tenn.: University of Tennessee Press, 1972). The two private universities benefitting from the Morrill Land-Grant College Act are MIT (established 1861) and Cornell University (1865).

3. Lawrence E. Gladieux and Thomas R. Wolanin, *Congress and the Colleges: The National Politics of Higher Education* (Lexington, Mass.: Lexington Books, 1976), 226.

4. Chester E. Finn, Jr., "A Federal Policy for Higher Education?" *Alternative* 8 (May 1975): 18-19.

5. Pamela Christoffel and Lois Rice, *Federal Policy Issues and Data Needs in Postsecondary Education: Final Report to the National Center for Education Statistics* (Washington, D.C.: U.S. Department of Health, Education, and Welfare, 1975), p. 4.

6. Ibid., 4-5.

7. Much of this section is based upon Lawrence E. Gladieux, "Student Financial Assistance: Past Commitments, Future Uncertainties," *Acadame,* Bulletin of the American Association of University Professors, Volume 72, Number 6 (November-December, 1986).

8. The Washington Office of the College Board, *Trends in Student Aid: 1980-1986,* Table 8 and unpublished data from the Office of Student Financial Assistance, U.S. Department of Education.

9. For a thorough analysis of the possible effects of increased student borrowing, see Janet S. Hansen, *Student Loans: Are They Overburdening a Generation?* (New York: The College Board, 1987).

10. White House Science Council, Panel on the Health of U.S. Colleges and Universities, *A Renewed Partnership: An Examination of Federal Government-University-Industry Interactions in U.S. Research and Higher Education in Science and Engineering* (Washington, D.C.: Executive Office of the President, February 1986).

11. Arthur M. Hauptman, *Studies in Graduate and Professional Education: What We Know and Need to Know* (Washington, D.C.: Association of American Universities, 1986), 6.

12. Susan L. Coyle, *Summary Report 1985: Doctorate Recipients From United States Universities,* (Washington, D.C.: National Academy Press, 1986), Table C, 6.

13. Part of this section draws upon a paper prepared by Janet S. Hansen for the National Conference of State Legislatures, "Federal Support of Postsecondary Students and Research," October 29, 1983.

14. National Science Board, *Science Indicators: The 1985 Report* (Washington, D.C.: U.S. Government Printing Office), Table 5-20, 279.

15. *A Renewed Partnership,* 11-12.

16. National Science Foundation, "Early Release of Summary Statistics on Academic Science/Engineering Resources," October 1986, Table 1.

17. National Academy of Sciences, Ad Hoc Committee on Government-University Relationships in Support of Science, *Strengthening the Government-University Partnership in Science* (Washington, D.C.: National Academy Press, 1983), 8.

18. Ibid., 101.

19. National Science Foundation, *Science and Engineering Research Facilities at Doctorate-Granting Institutions* (Washington, D.C.: September 1986).

20. *A Renewed Partnership,* 14.

21. John T. Wilson, *Academic Science, Higher Education, and the Federal Government, 1950-1983* (Chicago: University of Chicago, 1983), 90.

22. American Association for the Advancement of Science, Intersociety Working Group, *AAAS Report XI: Research & Development, FY 1987* (Washington, D.C.: AAAS, 1986), 16.

23. Deborah H. Shapley and Rustum Roy, *Lost at the Frontier,* (Philadelphia: Institute for Scientific Information Press, 1985), 39, and W. Henry Lambright, *Governing Science and Technology,* (New York: Oxford University Press, 1976), 202.

24. Ibid.

25. *A Renewed Partnership.*

26. "A Tax Course Not Taught in School," *U.S. News & World Report* (November 17, 1986): 61.

27. Robert A. Scott, "More Than Greenbacks and Red Tape: The Hidden Costs of Government Regulations," *Change* 10 (April 1978): 16.

28. *A Renewed Partnership,* 48.

29. Wilson, 104-106.

30. Scott, 16.

31. United States General Accounting Office, *University Funding: Patterns of Distribution of Federal Research Funds to Universities,* (Washington, D.C.: February 1987), 48-49.

32. Colleen Cordes, "Three Government Agencies Scrutinize the System of Awarding Research Money by Peer Review," *The Chronicle of Higher Education* (January 28, 1987): 6.

33. Daniel B. Levine, ed., *Creating a Center for Education Statistics: A Time for Action* (National Academy Press, Washington, D.C.: 1986), 5.

34. Ibid., 6.

35. Ibid.

36. National Commission on Excellence in Education, *A Nation at Risk: The Imperative for Educational Reform* (United States Department of Education: April 1983).

37. Study Group on the Condition of Excellence in American Higher Education, *Involvement in Learning* (National Institute of Education: October 1984).

9

State Governments

John D. Millett

State governments in the 1980s continued to be the principal providers of higher education services in American society. These services—usually identified as student instruction, research and development, public service (including technological transfer and cultural patronage), equality of educational opportunity, and constructive criticism of social institutions and processes— enrolled 12.4 million students in the autumn of 1986, spent around $100 billion in 1986-87, and awarded around 1.7 million degrees in 1986. By far the greater part of this activity occurred in colleges and universities sponsored and supported by state governments.

It is important to a clear understanding of the higher education system in the United States to draw a sharp distinction between state governments as political structures and state government sponsored and supported colleges and universities as enterprises of higher education. Most colleges and universities classified as "public" institutions of higher education have been created by state government constitutions or laws. The federal government has been involved only in the establishment of military academies and a public university and several private or independent institutions in the District of Columbia. Public institutions are often given the legal status of bodies politic and corporate, and in fact, most public institutions do operate as public corporations drawing financial support from various sources of income. State governments may regulate various aspects of the operation of public and even private institutions, but public institutions operate in practice with an identity separate and apart from state government.

There are 1,500 public institutions of higher education in the United States. There were over 1,800 private institutions as of 1985. These institutions were classified by the U.S. Department of Education as follows:[1]

	Public	Private	Total
Doctoral-granting	109	62	171
Comprehensive	254	164	418
General baccalaureate	118	590	708
Specialized	67	518	585
Two-year	919	349	1,268
New	33	148	181
	1,500	1,831	3,331

In terms of enrollment and degrees granted, the difference between public and private institutions is much more pronounced than the numbers of institutions might suggest. In 1986, of a total enrollment of 12.4 million students, 9.6 million or 77 percent of the students were enrolled in public institutions.[2] Some 85 percent of all associate degrees; around 70 percent of all bachelor's degrees, master's degrees, and doctoral degrees; and about 45 percent of all first professional degrees (primarily law, medicine, dentistry, optometry, veterinary medicine, and pharmacy) were granted by public institutions of higher education.[3] Of the nearly $100 billion of current funds income available for higher education institutions in 1986, some 63 percent was provided to public institutions.[4] Of the sources of income for both public and private institutions, 29 percent came from state governments, 23 percent from tuition charges, and 12 percent from the federal government. For the public institutions 45 percent of their total income came from state governments, 15 percent from tuition, 10 percent from the federal government, and only around 3.5 percent from local governments (mostly for two-year institutions). If we exclude income from auxiliary enterprises, state governments provided 50 percent of the income of public institutions.

The relationship of state governments to both public and private institutions is a critical one. For public institutions their principal source of income, their primary policies and programs, and their basic structure of governance are determined by state governments. For private institutions of higher education, although as a whole they derived only about 2 percent of their income from state governments in 1986, there was an increasing concern about the tuition gap between public and private institutions, about the availability of student financial assistance, about possible increases in institutional assistance, and about state government regulation (most evident and perhaps most onerous in New York State).

The agenda of state governments in their relationship to public institutions and in their relationship to private institutions underwent some revision during the 1980s. Some issues remained as troublesome in the 1980s as they had been in the 1970s. For the purpose of this discussion we shall concentrate our attention upon five particular issues confronting state governments during the decade of the 1980s: (1) the changing environment, (2) the financing of

institutions, (3) the quality and assessment of public institutional performance, (4) the problem of access and choice in student enrollment (including
financial assistance to private institutions), and (5) the governance of public
institutions.

THE CHANGING ENVIRONMENT

The political environment of both public and private institutions of higher
education experienced considerable change during the 1980s. This change
was publicly observed especially in connection with the federal government,
but it was nonetheless evident and even more dramatic in its institutional
impact at the state government level. Two concerns of the 1970s receded in
importance during the 1980s: enrollment loss and inflation. But other concerns came to the fore: the situation of the economy in each one of the fifty
states, and the role of higher education in relation to economic development.

During the 1970s the prospective decline in the traditional college-age
cohort eighteen to twenty-two years of age to take place in the 1980s was
widely publicized. The implication of these forecasts was that a similar decline
would take place in higher education enrollments. From 4.3 million eighteen-
year-olds in 1980, the number was expected to decline to 3.7 million young
persons in 1985 and to 3.3 million by 1995. In this fifteen-year period there
would be a decline of 23 percent in the number of eighteen-year-olds in the
United States. The projected decline was expected to vary depending on
region and state; in some regions and in some states the decline was forecast
to be 40 percent or higher.[5]

By the autumn of 1986, a decline in higher education enrollments corre-
sponding to the decline in the number of eighteen-year-olds had failed to
materialize. Total enrollments in the 1980s stabilized between 12.2 and 12.4
million students; the higher number was the enrollment in 1986. Public institutions of higher education had one percent more students in 1986 than in
1985. The experience varied among institutions, and there were changes. The
ranks of female undergraduates were increasing and at public institutions
they outnumbered the male students. The number of part-time students was
increasing, especially women over twenty-four and thirty-four years of age.
The number of part-time students twenty-five years and older enrolled in
higher education increased nearly twenty percent between 1980 and 1985.
Enrollment trends appeared to be most favorable for public institutions that
were selective in admission and for public institutions that were located in
urban areas. In any event, as of 1986-87, one concern expressed by state
governments in the 1970s had become a matter of minor interest.

Economically, the decade of the 1970s, especially after the oil embargo of
1973, had been a period of mounting inflation. State governments had had to
cope with escalating prices, particularly the price of energy. The consumer

price index increased in 1974 more than 12 percent over 1973 figures, 1978's figures were 9 percent over those of 1977, figures for 1979 were 13 percent over 1978, and in 1980 they were 12 percent over 1979. Beginning in 1982 the annual increases in the consumer price index was around 4 percent.[6] In their support of higher education state governments experienced lesser inflationary pressures than they had known in the 1970s.

But there were new economic difficulties with which state governments had to cope in the 1980s. The two most troublesome concerns were the continued slowdown in patterns of economic growth and the need for economic development. Both of these concerns had a major impact upon state government support for higher education, especially the support of public institutions.

In terms of dollars of constant purchasing power, a slowdown in the growth of gross national product began in the 1970s. This slowdown continued in the 1980s. After a recession in 1974 and 1975 a growth rate of about 5 percent per year took place from 1976 through 1978; in 1979 the growth rate dropped to 2.5 percent. In 1980 there was a recession, followed by a growth of 1.9 percent in 1981. In 1982 there was another recession, followed by growth rates of 3.5 percent in 1983, 6.5 percent in 1984, 2.3 percent in 1985, and 3 percent in 1986.[7]

While some considerable economic recovery was experienced in the industrialized states from 1983 through 1986, a different problem arose for state governments. This problem resulted from the twin efforts of the federal government to reduce both expenditures and income tax rates. Curtailment in federal government expenditures reduced state government income and produced new pressures on state budgets if current levels of service were to be maintained. The efforts which resulted in so-called "simplification" of the federal income tax brought about a general public opposition to tax increases. Indeed, some state legislatures hastened to eliminate a "windfall" increase in state income tax collections geared to the federal definition of gross taxable income and of allowable deductions. In state government elections in 1986, candidates for executive and legislative positions, regardless of party affiliation, were inclined to promise no increases in state taxation.

In spite of such economic growth as occurred in the 1980s, unemployment remained relatively high and employment of workers in heavy industries tended to decline. Poverty continued to be extensive in urban centers and in many instances appeared to be perpetuated by a cycle of children often born out of wedlock and of parents who were unemployable. The change in employment opportunity in the industrialized states presented complexities in the care of a displaced and nonworking population. The burden of this care made increases in state government support of higher education a questionable action.

The principal economic impact of higher education upon American society in the 1980s continued to be the preparation of educated talent for the

American labor force. Yet here again there were changes, the major ones of which took place in the composition of the labor force between 1950 and 1973 and began to slow down thereafter. As a consequence, surpluses of educated talent started to appear. In the 1980s, apart from some engineering specialties, information systems specialists, and certain specialists in business management, there appeared to be overages of degree recipients in terms of available employment opportunities. There were even declarations about surpluses in the health professions, including medicine and dentistry. It was estimated that out of about one million graduates with a bachelor's degree, appropriate employment opportunities existed only for about 800,000 graduates.[8] The role of higher education generally and of public higher education in particular in providing educated talent to the American labor force was not nearly so critical in the 1980s as it had been in the 1960s.

In the meantime, a somewhat different preoccupation with higher education became evident in state governments, i.e., one concerned with the potential of higher education to stimulate economic growth through scientific research and technological transfer, two areas that had done much to assist agricultural production and health care delivery. State chief executives and legislative leaders began to ask for and to expect contributions from higher education in the development of new industrial products and new production processes. In many different ways, and in varied relationships, institutions of higher education endeavored to respond to this new, or at least this more loudly voiced, expectation. State governments in many instances may have expected more than could be reasonably asked of higher education. But some higher education support began to be directed toward specific concerns of economic development, and public institutions of higher education were challenged to offer evidence of direct contributions to economic growth.

The 1980s witnessed a new interest on the part of institutions of higher education in strategic planning. In 1983, a book by George Keller was published which tended to encourage further attention to the process of higher education in responding to its political and economic environment and to the social expectations that emerge therein.[9] Such planning on the part of public institutions was demanded, or at least stimulated, by state governments. In addition, those governments began to make their own studies of higher education structures, programs, and costs.

In at least half of the fifty states during the first five years of the 1980s, executive or legislative action had undertaken formalized studies of higher education operations. Apart from some concern with educational quality, these studies generally concentrated attention upon statewide governance of public institutions of higher education, upon the scope and effectiveness of statewide planning for higher education needs, upon the possible duplication of programs and the costs associated with the operation of multiple public institutions in a state, and upon the costs of programs.

For the most part, as of the end of 1986, it must be said that most of these state government sponsored studies resulted in very little change. Some adjustments in a few instances were made in the administrative arrangements for statewide governance. But executives and legislators proved to be little interested in reducing access to public institutions of higher education, in closing or merging public institutions, or in reducing the programs offered by higher education. There continued to be complaints on the part of state government officials about the costs of remedial education, about the costs of medical education and of teaching hospitals, about "unnecessary" duplication of program offerings, and about higher education costs in general. Yet no state government was inclined substantially to curtail its higher education programs or costs. They feared the possible political, economic, and social consequences of any such action.

STATE GOVERNMENT FINANCING OF HIGHER EDUCATION

State government support of higher education increased generally throughout the last half of the 1970s and into the first half of the 1980s.[10] Institutions of higher education reported income from state governments for various fiscal years as follows:

Fiscal Year	Thousands of Dollars
1975	12,260,885
1980	18,378,299
1984	24,706,990

Although private institutions as of 1975 reported receiving nearly $300 million from state governments and nearly $550 million in 1984, the proportion of state support for these institutions declined somewhat. As of 1975, private institutions of higher education received about 2.5 percent of state government appropriations for institutional support; in 1984 the proportion was 2.2 percent.

The doubling of state government support for institutions of higher education between 1975 and 1984 reflected the ravages of inflation in the economy rather than a substantial increase for improved or expanded operations. In terms of dollars of constant purchasing power, the nearly $25 billion of state government support in 1984 was barely 8 percent more than that provided in 1975. The increase in total enrollment in public institutions between the autumn of 1974 and the autumn of 1983 was 31 percent. Thus, the record of state government support in this time period failed to match both the inflation in costs and the increase in enrollment. State government support tended to be more responsive to the economic circumstances of each state than to the needs of public institutions of higher education.

State governments spend some funds in support of higher education that do not necessarily flow through public and private colleges and universities. Primarily such funds are spent for student financial assistance that is distributed directly to eligible students; in 1986-87 such expenditures were estimated at $1.5 billion.[11] Other funds may be spent for the operation of state government coordinating and advisory boards and for debt service on academic facilities. Of $32.4 billion appropriated by state governments in the fiscal year 1987 for higher education purposes,[12] about 90 percent went for the operation of institutions of higher education, public and private.

State governments do not support the total operations of public colleges and universities. Apart from the problem of student tuition charges, which we shall consider later, state governments generally provided no funds for the operation of student residence and dining halls; these costs were borne by students. Such costs could be sizeable for students, since most state universities founded in the 1800s were not located in the major urban areas of a state but were located in smaller communities.

Financial assistance to students provided by the federal government and by state governments was not usually reported as an operating expenditure by public institutions. On the other hand, state universities did provide assistance to students from endowment funds, private gifts, and general income. Public institutions reported nearly $1.3 billion spent for student aid in 1984, of which nearly $600 million came from general income and over $700 million from restricted sources; some of these expenditures may have come from the general support provided by state governments.[13] Student financial assistance has been a major contribution of the federal government to the operation of higher education institutions; this assistance appeared in institutional accounts as the payment of tuition and the payment of room and board charges.

It was reported that in the fiscal year 1985 there were 91 institutions of higher education each of which spent more than $30 million for separately budgeted research.[14] Among these 91 institutions were 60 state universities and four state health science centers. The separately budgeted research expenditures of these 64 state institutions amounted to $4.8 billion, of which $2.7 billion came from the federal government, only some $480 million from state and local appropriations, and some $1.5 billion from other sources including industry, endowments, private gifts, and the sale of services.

Although direct state government support of research was limited in amount, and much of this support earmarked for agricultural research, state government institutional support was basic in building and maintaining state universities and separate health science centers with major research potential. The 64 state institutions as listed for 1985 were to be found in 36 different states.

Public institutions reported expenditures of $2.5 billion in 1984 for public service.[15] Apart from appropriations earmarked for support of agricultural extension services, most of the income for this program area was obtained

TABLE 1
Appropriations of State Tax Funds for Higher Education 1986-87

	Appropriations in Millions of Dollars	Two-Year Gain, Percent	Ten-Year Gain, Percent
Alabama	557	11	122
Alaska	207	-11	219
Arizona	480	27	160
Arkansas	273	10	138
California	4,563	18	150
Colorado	423	10	105
Connecticut	369	22	153
Delaware	97	14	123
Florida	1,278	24	194
Georgia	714	17	169
Hawaii	221	18	126
Idaho	126	12	82
Illinois	1,391	18	100
Indiana	661	20	109
Iowa	405	3	92
Kansas	351	4	102
Kentucky	469	15	128
Louisiana	542	-3	151
Maine	125	37	194
Maryland	570	17	133
Massachusetts	816	27	248
Michigan	1,229	22	107
Minnesota	747	15	130
Mississippi	327	-5	113
Missouri	476	19	101
Montana	103	-4	116
Nebraska	217	2	78
Nevada	102	30	142
New Hampshire	56	31	145
New Jersey	899	19	227
New Mexico	234	2	185
New York	2,721	15	117
North Carolina	1,172	22	187
North Dakota	124	11	155
Ohio	1,208	25	145
Oklahoma	386	5	153
Oregon	336	19	90
Pennsylvania	1,109	12	68
Rhode Island	117	12	108
South Carolina	520	15	147
South Dakota	73	19	86
Tennessee	608	23	169
Texas	2,141	-9	133
Utah	257	9	152
Vermont	47	12	132
Virginia	901	26	185
Washington	610	9	97
West Virginia	241	10	93
Wisconsin	667	8	83
Wyoming	112	7	194
Total and Weighted Average	32,337	14	134

SOURCE: *Grapevine*, October-November, 1986

from nonstate government sources, especially the federal government, private grants, and charges for services. Here again, the potential for public service activities depended in part upon the quality of state government general support of individual institutions.

The state government appropriations in support of higher education for the fiscal year 1986-87 are shown in Table 1, along with the percentage of two-year and ten-year gains. The figures in themselves tell us very little, except that states vary in population size, in the condition of their economies, and in their higher education interests. An increase of 91 percent over the ten-year period was necessary in order to provide in 1986-87 the same level of support as was provided ten years earlier, with no allowance for enrollment increases, higher energy costs, and demands for expanded and improved services. Even so, the appropriations are overstated for several states—at least twenty had to reduce these appropriations because state government income was less than expected.[16]

A more meaningful comparison of state government support is provided by Table 2 (see p. 192). The first two columns present tax capacity (defined as the average state government tax structure in the fifty states) and tax revenues on a per capita basis. It will be observed that state government tax revenues vary greatly from state to state, from a high in Alaska to a low in Tennessee. The state governments vary also in the proportion of their tax receipts allocated to higher education, from a high of 14 percent in Alabama to a low of under 5 percent in New Hampshire. In terms of appropriations per full-time student equivalent, there are considerable variations around the $3,875 average for the United States in 1986, from a high of $14,000 in Alaska to a low of under $2,300 in New Hampshire.

An important financial support decision for state governments is that of how to divide financial support of public institutions between state taxpayers and students (and their families). State universities inherited, from the nineteenth century and the early twentieth century up to World War II, a tradition of low tuition charges to students. Public institutions sought to provide wide access to students through low costs. Circumstances changed after 1945. To some extent state universities were encouraged to increase their charges as a result of federal government student financial aid programs as embodied in the Veterans Benefits Act of 1944, the National Defense Education Act of 1958, and the higher education acts of 1965 and 1972. As the economic circumstances of families improved, especially in the 1960s, and as higher education needs expanded, state governments permitted tuition charges at state universities to increase, relying more and more upon student financial assistance (both federal and state) to ensure that students were not denied access to higher education because of economic circumstances.

As tuition charges by state universities increased, state governments became concerned about the availability of educational opportunity to many students. State governments began to seek a policy determination of the "ap-

TABLE 2

	Tax Capacity Per Capita	Tax Revenues Per Capita	Allocation to Higher Education	Appropriations Per Student
Alabama	$ 977	$ 865	14.0%	$ 4,055
Alaska	3,146	5,080	7.4	14,038
Arizona	1,285	1,221	10.4	3,398
Arkansas	1,009	848	9.6	3,527
California	1,574	1,442	12.0	4,666
Colorado	1,612	1,299	7.1	2,617
Connecticut	1,665	1,606	5.2	4,436
Delaware	1,573	1,246	11.0	4,011
Florida	1,371	1,002	8.3	3,484
Georgia	1,159	1,041	8.4	3,958
Hawaii	1,468	1,527	12.4	6,697
Idaho	1,082	925	12.5	4,205
Illinois	1,200	1,361	7.5	3,384
Indiana	1,108	1,082	8.5	3,299
Iowa	1,134	1,260	8.8	3,390
Kansas	1,311	1,241	10.4	3,476
Kentucky	1,023	907	9.2	3,547
Louisiana	1,357	1,070	7.6	2,938
Maine	1,232	1,204	6.8	3,408
Maryland	1,298	1,383	7.9	3,318
Massachusetts	1,442	1,534	7.0	5,057
Michigan	1,161	1,559	7.9	3,622
Minnesota	1,252	1,638	8.8	3,777
Mississippi	905	857	10.6	2,515
Missouri	1,154	992	8.5	3,261
Montana	1,343	1,249	9.4	3,459
Nebraska	1,337	1,201	7.7	2,725
Nevada	1,928	1,191	7.5	3,828
New Hampshire	1,455	1,005	4.8	2,283
New Jersey	1,494	1,621	5.8	4,569
New Mexico	1,402	1,146	11.4	3,929
New York	1,286	2,043	6.0	5,174
North Carolina	1,160	1,006	13.7	3,465
North Dakota	1,397	1,281	10.8	3,072
Ohio	1,148	1,220	7.1	3,016
Oklahoma	1,442	1,112	9.1	3,055
Oregon	1,239	1,242	9.3	3,362
Pennsylvania	1,141	1,216	6.4	3,676
Rhode Island	1,140	1,389	7.6	4,397
South Carolina	996	941	11.3	4,406
South Dakota	1,147	939	7.5	2,768
Tennessee	1,062	843	11.4	4,025
Texas	1,555	1,047	9.7	3,085
Utah	1,075	1,111	11.8	3,871
Vermont	1,264	1,170	4.6	1,912
Virginia	1,259	1,113	9.3	3,222
Washington	1,311	1,317	9.2	3,476
West Virginia	1,128	1,024	7.5	2,986
Wisconsin	1,141	1,540	9.1	3,514
Wyoming	2,282	2,505	9.2	6,664
U.S. Average	$1,305	$1,305	8.6%	$ 3,785

SOURCE: Kent Halstead, *State Profiles: Financing Public Higher Education 1985-86*. Tax capacity and tax revenues are 1984 estimates. Allocation and appropriations are for 1985-86.

propriate" charge to students. In some states this charge was fixed at 25 percent of average instructional cost, in other states the desirable charge was fixed at one-third of the average costs, and in certain states the proportion was even higher. For 1985-86 Halstead estimated the average tuition charge to be $1,116, although the range of charges was from nearly $4,000 in Vermont and over $3,000 in New Hampshire to under $500 in California and under $1,000 in Arizona, Florida, Hawaii, Idaho, Illinois, Louisiana, Mississippi, Montana, New Mexico, North Carolina, Oklahoma, Texas, Utah, and Wyoming.[17]

No state as of 1987 had found an answer to the question: Just how much should higher education cost a state? State universities and other public institutions each year or each biennium pushed for incremental additions to their previous appropriations. Various arguments were advanced to justify these requests. Appropriation increases were needed to keep pace with inflation or to catch up with past inflation, to meet rising costs of energy and supplies and equipment, to pay larger salaries to recruit and retain able faculty members, to improve the quality of services by increased infusion of resources, to respond to the demand for expanded services, to equalize salaries among men and women and to pay women "comparable worth," to advance the recruitment of minority students and to provide the necessary financial aid, and to improve services to students including developmental (remedial) education. One argument used by some institutions was to equalize the expenditures of comparable or "peer" institutions in other states. All of these arguments to some degree in individual circumstances had validity. Faculty members in state universities continually claimed that they were undercompensated, and administrative officers continually claimed that their institutions were underfunded. State governments each year or each biennium had to confront and respond to the case for increased appropriations for higher education.

State government support for higher education was a political decision to be made in terms of available income or increased income, in terms of competing claims for other services such as public schooling and welfare, in terms of the executive and legislative perception of the importance of higher education to the state, and in terms of interest group pressures including pressures from student organizations in states where such organizations existed and were effective. To a considerable degree the case for higher education support rested upon a demonstrable impact upon social mobility and economic performance. Unfortunately, this impact was often more a declaration of faith rather than a demonstration of fact.

QUALITY AND ASSESSMENT

The decade of the 1970s was the time of the Carnegie Commission and Carnegie Council studies and reports on the condition of higher education in the United States. Largely pragmatic and optimistic in their approach, these reports found only such flaws in the performance of higher education purposes as could be remedied with a few adjustments at appropriate places in the operation.

The decade of the 1980s was different. A large number of reports from federal government agencies and from other agencies sounded a critical warning about the performance of higher education. In general, the criticism was that higher education had deteriorated in quality while it was expanding its enrollment during the 1960s and 1970s. Only a few of these reports need to be mentioned here: *A Nation at Risk* (1983), *America's Competitive Challenge* (1983), *Academic Preparation for College* (1983), *Involvement in Learning* (1984), *To Reclaim a Legacy* (1984), and *Integrity in the College Curriculum* (1985).[18] These reports and others argued that academic preparation for college study in American high schools had deteriorated, that coherence and comprehension in undergraduate curricula had been sacrificed to student interest in preparation for employment, that standards of student performance had been reduced at the undergraduate level, that students were too little involved in advancing their educational performance, that the United States was losing its competitive edge in scientific knowledge and technological development, and that the assessment of student performance in higher education was generally lacking in American colleges and universities.

Without undertaking to evaluate any of these reports—they deserve the same critical scrutiny that they purport to devote to higher education as a social undertaking—we may note that they have had extensive publicity and that they have aroused a good deal of public discussion. The criticisms of undergraduate curricula raise issues that must be addressed by college and university faculties. State government responses by 1987 had been addressed to two issues: the high school curriculum and the assessment of college achievement.

Before discussing these two responses, we need to note the problem of trying to define quality in higher education. The reports previously mentioned offered different definitions of quality in American higher education; student development of full potential for learning (whatever that statement may mean), better preparation of high school students for college study, greater student participation in the learning process, institutional assessment of its contribution to student learning, a "better" curriculum for accomplishing the general education objective of a college or university, and evidence of an improved capacity for American competition with other economies (notably those of Japan and West Germany). There was only the most general kind of guidance to be found in these guidelines.

State governments responded first of all by insisting that admission to state universities should be based upon the completion of a college preparatory curriculum by high school graduates. One part of this action was insistence upon cooperation between state boards of education and state boards of higher education. The imposition of more rigorous admission standards was then taken by boards of trustees or boards of regents of state universities. The new standards generally involved four (Carnegie) units of English, three units of mathematics, three units of social studies, two units of science, two units of a foreign language, and perhaps other units in art, the world of work, and non-Western civilization. Thus, legally the changing pattern of academic preparation for state university admission was taken by governing boards rather than by state legislation. Nonetheless, the imposition of higher standards came as a response to state government expectations, sometimes voiced by a state coordinating board and sometimes voiced by state government executives and legislators.

A second kind of state government expectation was expressed through the National Governor's Association in 1986. The governors issued a report entitled *Time for Results,*[19] in which they committed themselves to provide the leadership needed to obtain results over the following five years in the better schools movement. The report presented the study and recommendations of seven task forces each made up of a group of governors. Six of these task forces were concerned with issues facing the public schools. The seventh was a task force of eight governors on college quality.

The report of the Governors' Task Force on College Quality began by citing the studies of higher education in the 1980s and then asserting that "Today's graduates are not as well educated as students of past decades."[20] The report went on to say that improvement in undergraduate education would require the coordinated effort of state policy makers, institutional governing boards, administrators, and faculty members. "As the primary source of funds for public higher education, the states have a major stake in the quality of postsecondary institutions. . . ."[21] The task force insisted that state attention must be directed to the outcomes of the higher education system. Assessment, the report argued, was an area in which colleges and universities should invest "significant time and resources."[22]

The Governors' Task Force on College Quality presented an "action agenda" of six recommendations. (1) Governors, state legislatures, state coordinating boards, and institutional governing boards should clearly define the role and mission of each public higher education institution in the state. (2) Governors, state legislatures, coordinating boards, governing boards, administrators, and faculties should reemphasize—especially in research universities—the importance of undergraduate education. (3) Each college and university should implement "systematic programs that use multiple measures to assess undergraduate student learning." (4) Governors, state legislatures, and statewide coordinating boards should adjust funding formulas for public colleges and universities to provide incentives for improving undergraduate student learning based upon the results of comprehensive assessment programs. (5) Governors, state legislatures, coordinating boards, and governing boards should reaffirm "their strong commitment to public higher education for students from all socio-economic backgrounds." (6) The higher education accrediting community should require colleges and universities to collect and utilize information about undergraduate student outcomes.[23]

As stated by one observer, "assessment is here to stay."[24] Some eleven states by the beginning of 1987 had undertaken by law or by state coordinating board action to develop a statewide assessment effort. Other states could be expected to take similar action. Yet despite the considerable agreement that some kind of assessment effort was desirable, there was little agreement about how to accomplish the desired result. An early disposition to rely upon standardized tests for measurement of student learning began to disappear in the face of some evidence that there was considerable difference in test results along racial and ethnic lines. Increasingly, tests were being considered as diagnostic rather than as academic hurdles, and as indicators of desirable curricular change. Some states enacted legislation requiring public institutions to demonstrate improvement in student knowledge, capacities, and skills between entrance and graduation but left the determination of how to accomplish this demonstration to state higher education boards and individual public institutions. In other states, selected "lead institutions" were encouraged and supported to experiment with assessment practices. Some concern had apparently arisen that assessment measures would be externally imposed rather than institutionally developed. The concern with assessment can be expected to achieve its objective only if the measures adopted result in curricular change and improved instructional procedures.[25]

In the past, state colleges and universities were inclined, like higher education institutions generally, to assert their quality in terms of input resources: expenditures per student, selectivity in student admission, faculty qualifications, faculty salaries, student/faculty ratio, student services and facilities, capital plant resources, library resources, and general academic reputation. Although few if any institutional administrators or faculty members would assert that these input indicators were unimportant, the advocates of assessment measures insisted that resources did not demonstrate actual learning achievements by students. It was evident late in the 1980s that institutional claims upon increased state government support would have to be bolstered by demonstration of student learning accomplished with those resources.

There was some concern on the part of administrators of public institutions that the attention directed in the 1980s to the issue of the quality of institutional operations was in part motivated by a political need to justify reduction in governmental support. This concern was especially directed toward federal government efforts to reduce outlays for student financial assistance and the support of nondefense-related research. Even at the level of state government interest in higher education, the issue of quality could become an excuse for steady-state or reduced support. As of 1987, there was no evidence that any such action based upon quality standards had been taken or contemplated by any state government. In fact, administrators were generally quick to point out that improved quality in the learning process would require increased resources. In any event, as of the late 1980s a new dimension had been added to the state government interest in higher education, the dimension of learning measurement or assessment.

ACCESS AND CHOICE

In issuing their 1986 report, the state governors were careful to affirm a commitment to access to public institutions of higher education regardless of socioeconomic status. The governors rejected any supposed connection between broadened access to higher education in the 1960s and 1970s and a decline in the quality of student outputs. Rather, they argued that access without quality was a denial of educational service to students. The governors then limited their comment to encouragement for boards and institutions to define the prerequisites of academic preparation for "successful" college study and to provide school districts with their records in preparing youth for college study. Just as governors avoided any effort to define quality in higher education, they carefully stayed away from any mention of existing practices among public institutions of higher education in the selectivity of student access.

In fact, while state governments have committed themselves to a policy and practice of open admission to higher education opportunity to all high school graduates, only some six states ever enacted laws insisting upon such open admission to every public institution. Moreover, even in these open admission states, limitations upon the enrollment size of particular institutions and a concern with the "over-popularity" of some institutions and the "under-popularity" of others resulted in some admission differentiation. Only in California was differential access defined by law: the University of California was directed to admit only high school graduates in the upper 12.5 percent of their high school class, the California State University system to admit only high school graduates in the upper one-third of their high school class, and the community college system to admit any high school graduate. Even in the absence of so exact a specification as the California law of 1960, many states did in effect have structured access to higher education based upon institutional status, reputation, and other factors.

Earlier, public institutions were classified according to their degree-granting records under criteria utilized by the Center for Education Statistics of the U.S. Department of Education. In a modification of this structure a study by the National Center for Higher Educational Management Systems subdivided the doctoral-granting institutions into research universities and other universities.[26] The 109 public doctoral-granting institutions were divided into 51 research universities and 58 other universities. In general, if we ignore specialized health science centers and certain other specialized professional institutions, we may say that state governments support a four-tiered structure of public institutions: research universities, other universities, comprehensive universities, and community colleges.

This structure reflects more than a certain prescribed set of missions and degree programs (according to number of degree programs and of degrees granted by level of study). The structure tends also to embody, with some exceptions, a system of access. This structure generally ranges from highly selective access on the part of many research universities and some other universities to open admission on the part of community colleges. Among a total of 413 state universities responding to a questionnaire, one study found 72 percent to be selective, 12 percent to be competitive, and 15 percent to be open-door in 1985.[27] Selective institutions were defined as those requiring incoming students to meet some specified level of academic achievement other than high school graduation; competitive institutions were even more selective, admitting only a limited number of individuals; open-door institutions admitted any high shool graduate.

A different study classified some 2,785 institutions into four categories as follows:[28]

Access Category	Number of Institutions	Distribution of Freshman Enrollment
Open	1,258	66%
Liberal	714	15
Traditional	354	8
Selective	459	11

Selective access was defined as admission from the upper third of a high school graduating class; traditional access was defined as admission from the upper half of a graduating class; liberal was defined as admission of some students from the lower half of a high school class; and open access was admission of all high school graduates. Unfortunately, this study did not divide the 2,785 institutions into public and private sponsorship.

A different study classified public institutions by the average Scholastic Aptitude Test composite score for entering freshmen by nine score levels.[29] The date of these data was not indicated. If we divide the average test scores of entering freshmen into three categories—over 1,000 as generally promising, 750 to 999 as promising, and under 750 as less promising—we find the following distribution of public institutions:

SAT Average Scores	Doctoral-granting Universities	Comprehensive Universities	Community Colleges
1,000 and over	37	50	4
750 to 999	57	291	813
Under 750	0	61	80
	94	402	897

Insofar as community colleges were concerned, these data indicated that open-door institutions could and did attract students whose average test scores placed them in the promising categories, even though other less promising students might also be admitted. For state universities, these data indicated a differentiated structure by access based upon admission test scores.

The fact remains that students differ from one another in terms of ability for college study, motivation, and effort. Students may also differ by socioeconomic class. State governments by design or by historical development have tended to sort out students according to ability or academic promise in different kinds of public universities and colleges. The practice has been criticized by one scholar on the grounds that the least promising students may thus be denied the same learning opportunity as more promising students.[30] On the other hand, this sorting does provide one approach to the effort to achieve a quality educational opportunity for students of promising academic ability.

There can be no doubt that state governments are concerned to provide access to some type of higher education institution for every high school graduate. One economy move, which as of 1987 had not recommended itself to any state government, was to eliminate open access to higher education. The concern for quality was a concern for instructional improvement within open-door institutions even as much as for improvement in more selective institutions.[31]

In the expansion of public institutions of higher education in the 1960s many state governments sought to establish and expand universities as well as community colleges in major urban areas. Two purposes were thereby served: expanded opportunity for part-time students and elimination of residential cost. A new concern then appeared in the late 1970s and in the 1980s. Should state student financial aid programs undertake to meet residential costs for students who would prefer not to enroll in a predominantly commuting institution? And a second concern was whether or not state financial aid programs should permit students, if they so chose, to enroll in private institutions where tuition costs were sometimes three and four times the cost of a public institution. State governments found limitations to what they could afford to provide, even though many did try through student aid programs to lessen the gap between public and private tuition cost.

Both access and choice remained problems for state governments even as they had in the 1960s and 1970s. With all the good will toward students in residential and in private institutions, state governments were hard pressed to meet these concerns along with others. In the meantime, state governments were reminded by the comprehensive universities that they needed substantial additional resources in order to equalize educational opportunity for larger numbers of minority and less promising students.[32]

GOVERNANCE

Traditionally, the principal agency of campus governance for colleges and universities in the United States, both public and private, has been a governing board of part-time, unpaid laypersons. The early state universities were established under the jurisdiction of a board of trustees, although in some instances the board was designated as regents and even as visitors and curators. These boards were usually appointed by governors for six-, seven-, or nine-year terms, sometimes longer. When colleges of agriculture and mechanical arts were established after the U.S. Congress passed the Morrill Act of 1862, in some instances the new institutions were placed under a state board of agriculture. As teachers colleges were created in the late nineteenth century, they were often governed by state boards of education. As landgrant institutions for black students were organized after the 1890 federal legislation, they were also established usually under boards of trustees.

A consequence of these developments was the emergence in every state (except Wyoming) of multi-campus public institutions. There were state universities, separate land-grant colleges (in 20 states), separate black land-grant colleges (in 16 states), and various teachers colleges, some of which in the "old south" were designated for black students. This structure underwent substantial expansion after World War II because of enrollment growth. The land-grant colleges became separate and prestigious state universities. Some state universities created new campuses in urban areas, in order to serve more students and to increase their political influence. The teachers colleges became state colleges or state universities, although usually not offering the doctoral degree. State legislatures created new state colleges or universities. The number of "senior" public institutions ranged from two or three in states like Alaska, Arizona, Delaware, Hawaii, Iowa, Montana, Nevada, New Hampshire, and Rhode Island, to ten or more in states like Alabama, California, Colorado, Georgia, Illinois, Indiana, Louisiana, Maryland, Massachusetts, Michigan, Minnesota, Missouri, New Jersey, New York, North Carolina, Ohio, Oklahoma, Pennsylvania, South Carolina, Tennessee, Texas, Virginia, West Virginia, and Wisconsin.[33]

The existence, the push for expansion, and the competition of multiple public institutions of higher education presented state governments with a special problem: how were the states to organize an administrative arrangement to bring about some cultural direction of planning, program offerings, and funding for several, even many, public institutions of higher education? The problem emerged in some states in a critical way during the Great Depression of 1929 to 1939, or during the agricultural depression of the 1920s. In other states the problem did not become critical until after World War II. Because of this problem, state governments began to establish administrative agencies to bring about some order from the chaos of unrestrained growth and expansion.

State government administrative arrangements have been primarily of two types: a statewide governing board or a state coordinating board. There is some variety among the states in the authority and status of both kinds of arrangements and, as of 1987, it is fair to say that no state government was entirely satisfied with either arrangement. During the 1980s at least half of the states conducted studies intended to bring about some kind of change in the governance/administrative structure of state colleges and universities. In some instances in the 1970s state government experience with a coordinating arrangement was considered to be so unsatisfactory that a statewide governing board was created; this change occurred in Massachusetts, North Carolina, Utah, and Wisconsin. In the 1980s, proposals to establish a statewide governing board were considered in three or four states but were not adopted by the states involved. Tinkering with the structure and authority of coordinating boards was a continuing preoccupation of state governments.

As of 1987, 22 state governments had created statewide governing boards. The date of the earliest such board was 1890 and the most recent date was 1980. Eight statewide governing boards had been set up before World War II and 14 had been set up in 1945 or thereafter.[34] There were 140 public doctoral-granting, comprehensive, and general baccalaureate institutions as well as a number of specialized institutions subject to governance by a statewide governing board. In 14 states the authority of the statewide governing board also extended to all two-year institutions. In the other eight states there was a separate state board dealing with community or junior colleges.[35]

Before we turn to some mention of state coordinating boards, we must observe one other special characteristic of state governance arrangements for public higher education. This arrangement was the multi-campus structure, which embraced two or more "senior" institutions but was not statewide in scope. Indeed, as of 1987 the prevailing governance pattern for state colleges and universities was the multi-campus system, either statewide or less than statewide. Within the 19 states having various kinds of coordinating boards, there were 237 doctoral-granting, comprehensive, and general baccalaureate institutions that were parts of multi-campus systems. Perhaps the best known of these multi-campus systems were the University of California with eight campuses (plus two specialized campuses), the California State University system with 19 campuses, the State University of New York with 19 campuses (other than health science and two-year institutions), and the

City University of New York with 10 campuses (other than one specialized institution and several two-year institutions).

Of the total of 481 public state colleges and universities mentioned at the beginning of this chapter, 377 were parts of multi-campus systems, either statewide or less than statewide, and only 114 had a separate board of trustees concerned solely with the one doctoral-granting, comprehensive, or general baccalaureate institution. Separate boards of trustees for individual institutions predominated in the states of Alabama, Kentucky, Michigan, Missouri, New Jersey, Ohio, Oklahoma, South Carolina, and Virginia.

The twenty-seven state coordinating boards have been classified in various ways according to the authority vested in them.[36] For practical purposes they may be divided into three groupings, plus the unique New York Board of Regents. Coordinating boards included (1) boards with a strong role in executive budget-making in nineteen states, (2) boards with considerable influence with the legislative branch of state government in four states, (3) boards with a general planning role only, and the New York Board of Regents with its unique status and authority over programs of both public and private institutions.

No matter what the arrangement—statewide governing board, strong coordinating board, legislative advisory board, or planning agency—state governments were inclined to find fault with whatever was the current pattern. Chief executives and legislative leaders were inclined to expect more from higher education boards than they were competent to deliver. From the perspective of state government, a statewide governing board should be state oriented; often they became primarily spokesmen for the institutions they governed. Statewide governing boards had authority to define the role and mission of an institution, to allocate instructional and other programs among institutions, to determine general policies and practices, and to control budgets. Necessarily statewide governing boards were cautious in their approach to such power because of concern for executive and legislative reactions.

State coordinating boards might approve new degree programs and arrange the equitable distribution of available funds among institutions, but only a few boards could discontinue academic programs at public institutions and none of the boards could merge institutions or control institutional budgets. These boards were dependent upon executive and legislative action on many higher education issues; coordinating boards had no authority to appoint or remove campus presidents.

Both statewide governing boards and state coordinating boards encountered opposition and sometimes hostility from individual state colleges and universities and their presidents. A statewide governing board had the authority to appoint and remove campus presidents, but these boards were reluctant to act when a president had considerable political influence. Coordinating boards could do no more than remind multi-campus and single-campus governing boards that they had common interests to advance. Governing boards, including statewide governing boards, had unique constituencies that included campus faculties, campus staffs, students, alumni, and local communities where campuses were located. The constituency of a coordinating board was the executive and/or legislative branch of state government. Unfortunately, conflict rather than cooperation often marred state board and campus relationships.[37]

Governors and legislators often wanted statewide governing boards and coordinating boards to make decisions on "hot" issues: program duplication, the location of institutions, access and quality, desirable mergers, competition among institutions for students and funding, and the constant pressure for increased financial support. Yet chief executives and legislatures wanted such issues to be resolved without political conflict, an impossible expectation. It was unreasonable for state governments to believe that state boards of higher education could somehow make decisions that state governments wished to avoid. No matter what the governance structure, public higher education remained political in its essential outlines.

State governments generally did not endeavor to define internal campus governance. Nor did state governments usually interfere with the selection of institutional presidents and faculty members. These and related matters were left to the discretion of governing boards. State governments did often expect state colleges and universities to conform to state financial management, to state purchasing practices, to state civil service procedures, to state building laws and arrangements, to state "sunshine" laws, and to state legal requirements in the prosecution and defense of cases at law. Some progress had been made in various states such as Ohio, New York, Kentucky, and Colorado in relaxing the law and practice of state administrative supervision in the period from 1960 to 1985. Much remained to be accomplished in many states in this effort at management autonomy.[38]

CONCLUSION

State governments are the principal providers of higher education services in the United States. Private colleges and universities—especially the best known, the best funded, and the best achievers of quality—set standards that state governments cannot ignore and sometimes endeavor to emulate. Public higher education responds to economic, social, and political expectations concerning the benefits to be derived from colleges and universities. These expectations vary from time to time but also have a continuing core consistent with a society characterized by a mixed economy, liberal democracy, and social pluralism.

There was no escape from the fact that public higher education depends for its principal financial support upon state governments. The conditions of the state economy, the demand for higher education services, the concerns of political leaders—these circumstances have much to do with the financial well-being of public higher education.

Governing boards of lay trustees afford major protection to public colleges and universities against political interference with faculty appointments and tenure, censorship of speech and writing, and violation of academic freedom. Yet, governing boards have to be aware of the political environment within which they exist and from which they derive their sustenance. In a political economy of limited resources no public campus can decide for itself the scope of its mission, the extent of its program offerings, and the magnitude of its claim upon state government funding.

NOTES

1. Center for Statistics, *Accredited Higher Education Institutions in 1984-85,* (Washington, D.C., Office of Educational Research and Improvement, U.S. Department of Education, September 1986).

2. Center for Education Statistics, *Statistical Highlights,* "Projected Decline in College Enrollments Not Materializing," (Washington, D.C., Office of Educational Research and Improvement, U.S. Department of Education, December 1986).

3. Center for Statistics, Office of Educational Research and Improvement, U.S. Department of Education, *Digest of Educational Statistics 1985-86.* (Washington, D.C.: U.S. Government Printing Office, 1986), 123bb.

4. Estimates based upon data from Center for Education Statistics, "Higher Education Finance Trends, 1970-71 to 1983-84," *Bulletin* of the Office of Educational Research and Improvement, (U.S. Department of Education, December 1986).

5. David W. Breneman, *The Coming Enrollment Crisis: What Every Trustee Must Know* (Washington, D.C.: Association of Governing Boards of Universities and Colleges, 1982).

6. *Economic Report of the President Transmitted to the Congress,* February 1987 (Washington, D.C.: U.S. Government Printing Office, 1987).

7. Ibid.

8. Estimate of the author based upon data from the Bureau of Labor Statistics, U.S. Department of Labor.

9. George Keller, *Academic Strategy* (Baltimore: The Johns Hopkins University Press, 1983).

10. "Higher Education Finance Trends, 1971-72 to 1983-84," op. cit.

11. *The Chronicle of Higher Education* (February 11, 1987).

12. Edward R. Hines, *Grapevine,* October-November 1986 (Normal, Ill.: Center for Higher Education, Illinois State University).

13. "Higher Education Finance Trends," op. cit.

14. *The Chronicle of Higher Education* (December 10, 1986).

15. "Higher Education Finance Trends," op. cit.

16. *The Chronicle of Higher Education* (February 18, 1987).

17. Kent Halstead, *State Profiles: Financing Public Higher Education 1985-86* (Washington, D.C.: Research Associates of Washington, 1986), 34.

18. The National Commission on Excellence in Education, *A Nation at Risk* (Washington, D.C.: U.S. Government Printing Office, 1983); Business-Higher Education Forum, *America's Competitive Challenge,* a report to the President of the United States (Washington, D.C.: American Council on Education, 1983); The College

Board, *Academic Preparation for College* (New York: The College Board, 1983); Study Group on the Conditions of Excellence in American Higher Education, National Institute of Education, *Involvement in Learning* (Washington, D.C.: U.S. Government Printing Office, 1984); William J. Bennett, *To Reclaim a Legacy* (Washington, D.C.: National Endowment for the Humanities, 1984); Project on Redefining the Meaning and the Purpose of Baccalaureate Degrees, *Integrity in the College Curriculum* (Washington, D.C.: Association of American Colleges, 1985).

19. *Time for Results,* The Governors' 1991 Report on Education (Washington, D.C.: National Governors' Association, 1986).

20. Ibid., 155.

21. Ibid., 156.

22. Ibid., 159.

23. Ibid., 160-163.

24. Peter T. Ewell, "Assessment: Where Are We?" *Change* 19 (January/February 1987): 23.

25. Ibid.

26. Melodie E. Christal, *Higher Education Financing in the Fifty States: Interstate Comparisons, Fiscal Year 1984* (Boulder: National Center for Higher Education Management Systems, 1986).

27. Report of a Survey of Undergraduate Admission Policies, Practices, and Procedures, *Demographics, Standards, and Equity: Challenges in College Admissions,* published by American Association of Collegiate Registrars and Admission Officers, the American College Testing Program, the College Board, Educational Testing Service, and National Association of College Admissions Counselors, November 1986.

28. Fast Response Survey System, *College Level Remediation,* FRSS Report No. 19, Center for Statistics, Office of Educational Research and Improvement, U.S. Department of Education, October 1986.

29. Alexander W. Astin, *Achieving Educational Excellence* (San Francisco: Jossey-Bass 1985), 7.

30. Ibid.

31. On improvement at the community college level, see John E. Roueche and George A. Baker III, *Access and Excellence: The Open Door College* (Washington, D.C.: The Community College Press, 1987).

32. Report of the National Commission on the Role and Future of State Colleges and Universities, *To Secure the Blessings of Liberty* (Washington, D.C.: American Association of State Colleges and Universities, 1986).

33. John D. Millett, *Conflict in Higher Education* (San Francisco: Jossey-Bass 1984), 10-11.

34. For this history the standard studies are Lyman A. Glenny, *Autonomy of Public Colleges* (New York: McGraw-Hill Book Company, 1959); and Robert O. Berdahl, *Statewide Coordination of Higher Education* (Washington, D.C.: American Council on Education, 1971).

35. *State Postsecondary Education Structures Handbook 1986* (Denver: Education Commission of the States, 1985).

36. Ibid., 4.

37. Millett, op. cit.

38. On the general subject of state government/institutional relationships see Paul L. Dressel, *The Autonomy of Public Colleges,* New Directions for Institutional Research, No. 26 (San Francisco: Jossey-Bass 1980).

10

The Courts

Walter C. Hobbs

It is fashionable among academics today to decry the alleged increased involvement of the courts in higher education's affairs. The traditional deference, it is said, long paid by courts to decisions made by academic experts, has been replaced by a judicial activism that not only inhibits the autonomy of the academy but, worse yet, jeopardizes academic freedom that is autonomy's chief justification.

The view is widespread. But is it valid? This chapter will summarize the complaints, review the countercriticisms, examine the doctrine of "academic abstention" (judicial deference to academic expertise), describe the functions of the courts, and discuss the impact of judge-made law on three core academic concerns.

We shall conclude the chapter by taking the (minority) view that to the very slight extent judicial deference to academe has lately been eroded, the consequence has been a modest limitation on institutional autonomy in favor of a major reinforcement of the legal bases of academic freedom. In that outcome, higher education—not to be confused with colleges and universities, let alone with academic administrators only—has the better end of the bargain. Both individuals within the academic enterprise and the enterprise per se have been and are today the beneficiaries of a strong judicial bias toward academic liberty, a bias that operates generally to limit incursions by others, including the courts, on the autonomy of the academics, but that refuses even to academics the liberty to infringe academic liberty.

COMPLAINT: THE COURTS INTRUDE TOO MUCH

In an eloquent and lengthy passage we only excerpt here, Fishbein speaks for many an academic who is persuaded the courts have hobbled academic administration by heaping inappropriate and dysfunctional procedural requirements on the everyday activity of college and university personnel:

[T]he due process requirements that the courts have imposed upon public universities have had an unfortunate consequence, namely, that today students and faculty alike appear to have a legal cause of action no matter how minor the dispute. Almost every [administrative decision] is thus escalated to the level of a constitutional issue, and there is commonly a race to the door of the federal courthouse by every dissatisfied party. . . . In other words, everything becomes a federal case. As a result, . . . relationships between students and administrators, between students and faculty and between faculty and administrators become increasingly adversarial. . . . This is an appalling development. . . . It is regrettable that so many aspects of life at public universities have been remolded in a legalistic, highly procedural fashion. It means, of course, that the administrator in the public university must undertake his or her daily tasks in the company of a lawyer.[1]

Six years earlier, O'Neil reviewed challenges posed to campus autonomy by various elements of government including the courts and offered the following comment concerning the costs incurred by colleges and universities by reason of court activity:

Judicial intervention . . . poses a significant threat, as witness the . . . suits brought against campus administrators and governing boards as a result of campus disorder. All but one of the cases [O'Neil had described] were ultimately dismissed—but not without considerable costs in legal fees, time and energy, and a virtually certain chilling effect upon future administrative behavior.[2]

More recently, the Sloan Commission on Government and Higher Education worried about not only the inhibition of effective academic management born of caution in the face of the likelihood of litigation, but also the changes that litigation itself produces in interpersonal relations:

The Commission views the reliance on litigation as counterproductive since it reinforces adversary relations. . . . The adversarial cast of the trial process fosters tensions that may continue for years, tensions inimical to [academic productivity].[3]

In sum, say the complainants, the willingness of the courts to review and, at times, to reform the decisions made within academe is inflicting on colleges and universities costs both direct and indirect. Resources of time and money that would ordinarily go to support teaching, scholarship, and the ancillary services on which these central activities depend are being diverted instead to lawyers' and court stenographers' fees and the various other expenses incurred when defending against a lawsuit. Institutional personnel, moreover, become skittish about exercising their creative judgment, preferring rather to "play it safe" than to run the risk of legal challenge to themselves and to their institution. Most seriously of all, the collegiality that is the warp and woof of the academic fabric is brought to the tearing point by the adversarial character of the litigation encouraged by the judicial willingness to be involved in academic disputes.

On the face of things, the complaints are at least plausible. Lawsuits are indeed expensive; anyone who has been involved in litigation will do—or refrain from doing—almost anything to avoid getting to court again, and the character of the dispute process before the bench forever changes relationships among former friends.

RESPONSE: THE COMPLAINTS ARE OVERDRAWN

Edwards sharply disagrees both with the particulars of the complaints and with the thread of the argument.[4] His response addresses each element of the complaint, and he appends a countercomplaint of his own:

a. *Monetary costs*—Quoting the U.S. Supreme Court in *Cannon* v. *Chicago* (441 U.S. 677 [1979]) and implicitly generalizing to all of academe, Edwards recites *Cannon*:

> Although victims of discrimination on the basis of race, religion or national origin have had private Title VI [of the Civil Rights Act of 1964] remedies available at least since 1965, . . . [the university has] not come forward with any demonstration that Title VI litigation has been so costly or voluminous that either the academic community or the courts have been unduly burdened.[5]

The Court's observation is consistent also with the Sloan Commission's findings concerning the cost to academe of the regulatory process: in a study prepared expressly for the commission, Kershaw found that (in Edward's words) "many of the institutions surveyed viewed the monetary costs of dealing with the Federal Government as a bargain."[6] From other reports as well, Edwards concludes "that the financial benefit derived from governmental assistance outweighs the financial costs of regulation."[7]

b. *Nonmonetary costs*—The fear that academic administrators and/or faculty will be coerced by judge-made law (not to be confused with legislation) to reach and implement decisions that dilute academic quality plainly irritates Edwards. Statutory law might have produced such effects, for

> There is nothing in . . . national policy . . . to support the exemption of [college and university] employees—primarily teachers—from [coverage by the Civil Rights Acts]. Discrimination against minorities and women in the field of education is as perverse as discrimination in any other area of employment. (House of Representatives Rep. No. 238, 92d Congress, 2d Sess. [1971].)[8]

But the courts have not seen fit to give force to that congressional intent. As the U.S. Circuit Court of Appeals for the Second Circuit has put it (*Powell* v. *Syracuse University*, 580 F.2d 1150 [1978]):

[M]any courts have accepted the broad proposition that courts should exercise minimal scrutiny of college and university employment practices. . . . This anti-interventionist policy has rendered universities virtually immune to charges of employment bias, at least when that bias is not expressed overtly.[9]

If there is any substance to the oft-heard claim that the judicial presence hangs like Damocles' sword over the wary decision-maker in academe, that person need only peek up to see that the sword swings for, not against, the institution and its administrators. It is the plaintiff, usually female or minority, not the defendant college, who stands to learn from the litigation: "faculty status is not won in the courtroom."[10]

c. *The death of collegiality*—The short answer here is that neither litigation nor the courts themselves kill collegiality; they only constitute the evidence of a death already transpired. One can not prevent conflict by choking off its channels,[11] for conflict will find a path to follow or, like lava, create its own. Nevertheless, whatever academics may do to one another in their internecine warfare, Edwards notes that the courts—unfairly the putative culprits here—abstemiously avoid to the extent possible playing any role in wrecking collegiality. As a matter of law, indeed, spoken by the U.S. Supreme Court, "traditions of collegiality [demand] that principles developed for use [elsewhere] cannot be 'imposed blindly on the academic world.'"[12]

d. *A countercomplaint*—Edwards appreciates the frustration that academics feel who have long perceived themselves as immune to judicial prescription and proscription and are now experiencing the reality of judicial power. But not only does he contend that that power is sparsely used and its effects greatly exaggerated when scrutinized against hard data, he goes on as well to suggest that in given matters the courts ought to do more than they do—not more expansively, certainly not more harshly, but simply more pointedly in response to appeals for redress of academe's injustices. Under current law, public institutions can dismiss an untenured faculty member for false and damaging reasons without affording him/her opportunity of rebuttal, simply by not making public the basis of dismissal. But what will the person do when asked by the next employer why he/she left the college? Similarly, a person who believes that he/she has been discriminated against for promotion by reason of race or gender must show that the institution's stated reasons for nonpromotion (e.g., poor teaching performance, inadequate research) are pretext, rather than being able to throw on the institution the burden of demonstrating they used legally permissible grounds. The imbalance of advantage in such instances, where the individual must make the entire case while the institution may simply stand pat, says little to Edwards on behalf of the judicial system's sensitivity to fairness in the resolution of academic dispute.

JUDICIAL DEFERENCE: THE DOCTRINE
OF "ACADEMIC ABSTENTION"

Fundamental to the foregoing debate is the question whether the courts should, can, and/or do refrain in given circumstances from exercising their considerable powers, yielding to others who enjoy expertise in the matter at hand the final substantive determination of the issue. Courts do refuse, for example, to reach a judgment whether a surgical procedure used by a physician was the best approach that might have been taken to a plaintiff-patient's malady. Neither will courts decide questions of scholarly competence, such as whether a given researcher's experiment was well designed or a given teacher's syllabus was sound.

The vocabulary of law refers to the principle of judicial deference to academic expertise as "the doctrine of academic abstention." It is not a novelty in the law, for courts traditionally have in fact deferred to expertise in all esoteric areas: such deference is the bedrock, for example, on which rests the judicial review of administrative agency actions such as the promulgation of pure food standards.[13] But it is important to distinguish judicial deference to the expertise of others from the exercise of judicial power in matters well within the courts' undoubted competence, e.g., the question whether an institution has complied with standards duly promulgated by a government agency. Whether the standards should have been imposed on academe was a question for the legislative branch to decide; whether the standards are substantively valid is a question for the agency (and ultimately the legislature) to decide, so long as no arbitrariness can be shown in their actions; but whether the college or university has in fact complied with the standards is a question no court need avoid.

The simple reality that a court will not substitute its own judgment in an esoteric matter for the judgment of a trained professional such as a physician or an educator, or for the judgment of an agency established by a legislature, does not mean there is nothing else for courts to decide. Courts are especially sensitive to the *procedural* care that experts show to those they affect. The student whose grade was a disappointment will seek in vain for a court to raise it, but if arbitrariness can be shown in the evaluation *process* that led to the grade the student will find in the court a champion quick to require the academic professionals to behave fairly. Judicial deference, in other words, does not mean complete judicial abstinence.

Neither does deference rest on a legal doctrine of institutional autonomy. To date at least, there is no such doctrine. Judicial deference to any party at all, academic or other, is a function of the court's self-acknowledged incapacity to address esoteric concerns, not of some imagined legal monopoly of the experts in that area. Where a court is precluded by law from addressing a matter, e.g., "has the Rev. Dr. Smith, theologian of a given denomination, embraced a heresy?" there the court is not exhibiting deference: it is legally powerless to act (in this illustrative instance by the First Amendment's "wall" between church and state). But courts *can* constitutionally evaluate a student's work and order that his/her grade be changed. They simply don't—not because colleges and universities are legally autonomous, but because courts understand the wisdom of leaving professional judgments to professionals.

Judicial deference is most commonly confused with the court's jurisdiction of a case. In the federal jurisprudence of the United States (and in the vast majority of the states), courts sit to decide cases and controversies. They are not at liberty to refuse to decide cases properly brought before them, nor are they empowered to solicit or compel parties to seek redress from them. To the extent there was a detectable period in history when little or no academic dispute was decided by the courts, it is not because courts were refusing to decide such cases in deference to academic expertise; it is rather because academics were not bringing their quarrels before the bar. Likewise, any increase in the incidence of academic litigation tells us little about judicial activism; chiefly it tells us that academics are becoming more litigious.

The incidence of academic litigation has clearly increased over the past decade and a half since the mid-1960s. But as is elaborated in the last section of this chapter, with one instructive exception there has been no perceptible decline of judicial deference to academic expertise, the conventional wisdom in many quarters to the contrary notwithstanding. Courts have made clear that public universities, under the requirements of the U.S. Constitution's Fourteenth Amendment, which covers all public entities, must provide procedural safeguards to students about to be suspended or expelled for misconduct, and to tenured faculty about to be discharged. But the courts have maintained deferential silence concerning the criteria on which such dismissals are decided, inquiring only into the character of the procedures by which a person may be deprived of a significant interest—which hardly bespeaks an unsophisticated meddler intruding on the domain of the academic professionals.

The sole exception to the general practice of judicial deference to academic expertise, the archetypical instance in which the courts have unhesitantly substituted their own judgment for the positions taken by colleges and universities, has arisen when in the name of institutional autonomy constitutionally impermissible limits have been placed on the exercise of academic freedom by faculty and students. In such cases, the doctrine of "academic abstention" has been ignored, judicial deference has been eschewed, and the courts have landed foursquare on the side of academic freedom against institutional autonomy.

THE FUNCTIONS OF COURTS

Government in the United States finds its theoretical underpinnings in the twin principles that (1) sovereignty lies in the people, not in a monarch or other ruling body, and (2) an effective system of "checks and balances" protects the people against abuse of power by the government that they create. As to the latter principle, government comprises three branches—the legislature, the executive, and the judiciary—each of which enjoys primacy within its own sphere of responsibility, but the exercise of the power of each is limited by the counterpart powers of the other branches. Legislatures declare social policy and enact statutes to implement it; the executive, however, may veto the enactments or may implement them less vigorously than the legislature contemplated. The courts may invalidate the legislation either for its unconstitutional character or for its impermissible application in given instances. Legislatures may override vetoes, and they typically have opportunity to review prospective judicial appointees nominated by the executive, preventing the coming to the bench of those they deem unfit.

All these safeguards and more are rooted in the constitutions of the federal government and of the several states. The federal government is one of limited jurisdiction: only such matters as are enumerated in its constitution fall within its power, all others being retained by the states or the sovereign people. But within that limited scope, the constitution and laws of the United States are "the supreme law of the land," binding on all judges in every state regardless of state law (Article VI, Constitution of the United States). By contrast, the governments of the several states are governments of general jurisdiction and, save for matters included in the federal power and therefore covered by the aforementioned "supremacy clause," state governments may authoritatively address any topic of interest.

When in 1787 the Continental Congress submitted the proposed federal constitution to the states for ratification, it was understood that several matters too controversial for initial inclusion would be taken up immediately upon formation of the new government. The Congress of the United States was convened in March 1789, and by December 1791 the first ten amendments to the Constitution, often called the Bill of Rights,[14] had been adopted. But in the first test of the amendments' power to protect a citizen against the action of state government, the U.S. Supreme Court held they were not applicable at the state level.[15]

Following the War Between the States, the Thirteenth Amendment was adopted rendering slavery unconstitutional, together with the Fourteenth Amendment requiring evenhandedness in the treatment of all persons within the reach of state power: "No state shall . . . deprive any person of life, liberty or property without due process of law; nor deny to any person within its jurisdiction equal protection of the law."

The Fourteenth Amendment's provisions, fashioned in the aftermath of emancipation, were designed to secure to former slaves legal rights long enjoyed only by free persons, and initially the U.S. Supreme Court insisted upon maintaining that focus.[16] In later years, however, the doctrines of due process and equal protection were interpreted literally to include "*any* person" regardless of race or former condition of servitude, regardless even whether he/she were a citizen of the United States. Moreover, beginning in the 1930s and continuing through the 1960s, the Court incorporated—piecemeal and never completely, but substantially nonetheless—many of the protections of the Bill of Rights against abuse of power by state government as well as by the federal, by interpreting the term "liberty" (in "No state shall deprive any person of liberty . . . without due process of law") to include many of the liberties guaranteed by the first ten amendments.

Two fundamental implications for academic law derive from the foregoing review. One concerns the respective boundaries of federal vis-a-vis state jurisdiction in academic matters, and the other concerns the relative limits imposed by the federal Constitution on governmental vis-a-vis independent (on "public" as distinguished from "private") higher education.

Education is nowhere mentioned in the federal Constitution. By reason, therefore, of the principle (made explicit in the Tenth Amendment) that all matters not enumerated in the federal Constitution are reserved to the states and/or to the people, the federal government is without power to address educational matters per se. To reach education—which, of course, it does— the government must address itself to aspects of education constitutionally within its power, e.g., by funding various programs within education under the provision of the preamble to the Constitution that government is to "promote the general welfare"; or by prohibiting school authorities from infringing a person's First Amendment right of free expression; or by requiring educational management to engage in collective bargaining with employees in order that labor disputes not impede commerce among the states (Article I, Section 8, Constitution of the United States).

The jurisdictions of the two court systems—federal and state—mirror the enumerated constitutional powers, but with important qualifications. As courts of general jurisdiction, state courts enjoy wide latitude in what issues they are legally authorized to decide, whereas federal courts are limited to hearing disputes involving some federal issue. A zoning dispute, for example, over the legality of operating a college pub on a given street corner may go only to a state court, but a dispute over whether a person has been discriminatorily refused employment in that pub in violation of the equal protection clause may go to either a state or a federal court. State courts, that is, may hear disputes grounded in federal claims; but they may not decide those disputes on the basis of state law if it is inconsistent with the federal. The federal courts, on the other hand, may not entertain any suits between residents of the same state quarreling over a matter devoid of any element of federal law, e.g., again, a zoning ordinance.

Most litigants prefer to take federally based claims to a federal court for disposition, especially when the federal law runs counter to the mores of the locality. Consequently, as the momentum of the civil rights movements of the 1950s and 1960s built to a crescendo in the late 1960s and early 1970s, the pattern of primarily state court activity in academic litigation gave way to chiefly federal activity instead, leading many an observer to conclude the federal courts were activist. As indicated above, however, courts sit to hear cases, and hear them they must. Activity, therefore, i.e., the relative incidence of cases that come before a bench, is a function primarily of social forces over which the courts exercise negligible control. Activism, on the other hand, i.e., the forsaking of the traditional judicial deference to academic expertise in favor of the courts' own judgments, has yet to be demonstrated. We shall return to the question more fully below.

The second implication for higher education of the "separation of powers" principle in American government concerns the legal distinctions drawn between the public and private sectors of academe when they come before the courts. In chapter 2 of this volume, Duryea discusses the role of the celebrated *Dartmouth College* case in refashioning the concept of institutional autonomy in American higher education. The divorce of state control of colleges and universities from their creation by the state via the chartering process gave rise, on the one hand, to institutions governed by independent boards of private citizens and (later), on the other hand, to institutions governed by boards of state officials acting under authority either of statute or of the state constitution.

Private institutions can not be reached by the Bill of Rights or the due process or equal protection clauses, because such institutions are neither part of the federal government nor part of a state's, the only entities addressed to those constitutional provisions. If one wishes to draw a private college or university within the prescriptions and proscriptions of those constitutional demands, the task must be accomplished by building bridges from the state to the institution by means of the doctrine of "state action." One of two tests will suffice: if a state has so pervasively insinuated itself into the activities of the institution that, for all practical purposes, the state and the college are interdependent partners, then the college—though formally private by reason of its charter and the composition of its governing board—will be deemed a public institution for purposes of constitutional analysis; the University of Pittsburgh is a case in point.[17] Or if an institution acts on behalf of the state to secure the latter's interests, then in whatever matter it so serves it too will be deemed for constitutional purposes a public institution; the colleges under contract to New York State, such as Cornell University's College of Agriculture and Life Sciences, and Alfred University's College of Ceramics, are cases in point: these institutions are "public," though sister colleges within the university are not.

Absent evidence of "state action," however, the private institution is free of constitutional constraints. But that is not to say it is at liberty to be a law unto itself. It means only that the legal grounds of any challenge to the college's actions must be found elsewhere than in the Bill of Rights or in due process or equal protection. The most common two such grounds are the law of contract and the statutes, rules, and regulations enforced by government administrative agencies. Together they comprise the basic arsenal of the litigant who seeks to vindicate his/her rights as a "consumer" of higher education.[18] Separately they constitute the primary legal wherewithal of the litigant who seeks redress for losses sustained when an institution fails, say, to honor the terms of his/her employment contract, or when the institution discriminatorily refuses to promote the person on grounds of gender. However, if the success rate of such suits is indicative of the power of these weapons, the legal arsenal is full of BB guns and noisemakers.[19]

THE IMPACT OF THE COURTS ON ACADEME

To this point in the discussion, we have persistently gainsaid the prevalent view that judicial activism has placed institutional autonomy in check, both directly by the substitution of the judgment of the court for academic expertise, and indirectly by the chilling effect it has had on the exercise of administrative discretion. It is time for demonstration instead of assertion.

Several core interests of academe have been brought before the bench sufficiently to provide a clear statement of where and why, if at all, courts are willing to second-guess academics: the admission and retention of students; the appointment, promotion, and dismissal of faculty; and the freedom of faculty and students to inquire into and advance whatever points of view they wish.

Students

Cases now speak the law of (a) standards of admission; (b) discipline for misconduct; and (c) bases of academic dismissal. None of them impinge upon the power of institutions to establish effective criteria in any of the three areas of student affairs.

a. In private institutions, "a State through its courts does not have the authority to interfere with the power of [the] school to make rules concerning the admission of students."[20] In public colleges and universities, no particular admissions standards have ever been judicially required, and only two—race and physical condition—have ever been considered. As to race, it is a permissible but not mandatory criterion,[21] and as to physical ability or disability, "[n]othing in the language or history of [the Rehabilitation Act of 1973] reflects an intention to limit the freedom of an educational institution to require reasonable physical qualifications for admission."[22]

b. Students in public institutions may not be suspended or expelled for misconduct without opportunity to hear the charges placed against them, to defend themselves against those charges before an impartial tribunal, and to purchase a written record of the proceedings.[23] No substantive standards of the validity of such charges beyond "reasonableness" have been required. Nor is such "due process" required when lesser penalties are inflicted. No student in any private institution is afforded any such protection except the requirement of reasonableness, unless the institution chooses to extend it.

It is commonly presumed in academic circles that the doctrine of *in loco parentis,* i.e., the institution stands "in the place of the parent" with respect to the student, is dead. As a practical matter, the presumption is probably sound; *in loco parentis* is dead at many, if not most, colleges and universities. But it was the institutions, not the courts, that sounded its death knell. No reported opinion by a court of any jurisdiction has yet repudiated the legal validity of the doctrine.[24] Nor is it implicitly overruled by the requirement of minimal due process in cases of suspension or expulsion for misconduct any more than a true parent's legal power over a child is dissolved simply because in most jurisdictions parents are no longer immune to suit by their children for conduct that visits a legal injury on the minor.

c. If the procedural requirements in disciplinary action are minimal, they are virtually nil in cases of academic termination. In *Horowitz,*[25] the landmark case in the matter, the U.S. Supreme Court held that "the significant difference between the failure of a student to meet academic standards and the violation by a student of valid rules of conduct . . . calls for *far less* stringent procedural requirements in the case of academic dismissal" (emphasis added). "Far less" stringency than is required in disciplinary actions is tantamount to astringency.

In addition, and more important to the issue of institutional autonomy, the Court continued:

> [W]e decline to ignore the historic judgment of educators [and] to further enlarge the judicial presence in the academic community. . . . We recognize . . . that a hearing may be "useless or even harmful in finding out the truth as to scholarship."
>
> "Judicial interposition in the operation of the public school system of the Nation raises problems requiring care and restraint." . . . Courts are particularly ill-equipped to evaluate academic performance. The factors discussed [earlier] with respect to procedural due process . . . warn against any such judicial intrusion into academic decision-making.

In short, the challenges brought in the last decade to institutional policy and practice toward students may have made for greater activity in the courts, but the courts themselves have not used the opportunity thus provided them to become more activist in their treatment of academic issues. Their sole imposition was procedural only, limited narrowly to instances of disciplinary suspension or expulsion, and avoiding admissions and academic evaluations questions virtually completely. Nor were they any more rigorous procedurally than to require that a charged party who could be suspended or expelled have the opportunity to know and rebut if he/she can the charges on which the discipline is laid, and to secure at the individual's own expense a written record of the proceedings. Institutional autonomy is hardly threatened by such judicial involvement in academic dispute. A reasonable person might even think it strengthened.

Faculty

The power of courts to impose criteria alien to the academic profession on the faculty appointment/retention function is probably more unsettling to academe than the counterpart judicial power in student admission/retention. But academics have no more reason to date to fear intrusion by the judiciary at this level than has been experienced in student affairs. No court has ever required any institution to hire a given candidate for a faculty position. Moreover, (a) nonrenewal of term contracts by an institution can be decided with impunity, for no reasons whatever need be provided; (b) in any controversy whether unlawful discrimination prevented one's promotion, the burden of proof rests with the plaintiff faculty member, not with the defendant institution; and (c) faculty in private institutions who participate extensively in university governance are precluded from compelling the administration to negotiate a collective bargaining agreement with their union.

a. The law of faculty termination in public institutions (contract law controls the issue in private colleges and universities) was enunciated by the U.S. Supreme Court in two companion cases handed down in 1972, *Roth*[26] and *Sindermann*.[27] No untenured faculty member need be provided a hearing at which to contest his/her nonrenewal of contract unless (i) there are grounds on which to believe the nonrenewal may be in impermissible reprisal for his/her exercise of a constitutionally protected right such as public criticism of the university administration; or (ii) the reasons for nonrenewal are defamatory or would otherwise injure his/her reputation such that employment elsewhere is prevented. Defamation and/or the staining of one's reputation, however, must be public to trigger a hearing. If the institution refrains from publicizing such grounds of the nonrenewal, no opportunity to rebut the reasons need be provided.[28]

As to impermissible reprisals for the exercise of constitutionally protected freedoms such as expression or association, institutional administrators responsible for such unconstitutional behavior who knew or should have known the unlawful character of their action can be held personally liable in money damages to the plaintiff.[29] It is here that some critics contend that judicial awards of such damages have a chilling effect on other administrators' willingness to exercise their judgment in whether to renew an incompetent but outspoken faculty member's contract. The argument is not compelling. The penalty is for behavior that not even the most rabid advocate of absolute institutional autonomy can justify, namely, the deliberate or exceedingly careless infringement of another person's right of expression. The penalty does not apply when the actual grounds of renewal are the candidate's professional performance, but only when the administrator has infringed the individual's rights. That will never trouble the truthful decision-maker.

When the faculty member about to be dismissed is tenured, then in the public university he/she must be provided a hearing, if requested, "where he could be informed of the grounds for his nonretention and challenge their sufficiency."[30] But the Court imposes no definition of "sufficiency" on the university; the standards to be met for retention still are formulated by academics to whom the Court pays judicial deference. And when the grounds for dismissal of the tenured faculty member are not his/her professional performance or other personal characteristic but rather the financial exigency of the institution, no procedural protection is afforded: it is "peculiarly within the province of the [college] administration to determine which teachers should be released, and which should be retained. . . . [I]t is not the province of the court to interfere and substitute its judgment for that of the administrative body."[31]

b. Much of the concern over judicial intrusion into the faculty employment process focuses on the courts' interpretations of the "affirmative action" requirements of the Civil Rights Acts of 1866, 1871, and 1964, as enforced by the regulatory process. *Sweeney*[32] suggests the concern is probably misplaced (from candidate to institution) and at least unnecessary. There the U.S. Supreme Court held the aggrieved candidate must first establish a plausible showing that he/she was denied promotion on grounds of gender or race, following which the institution need only "articulate some legitimate, nondiscriminatory reason for the employee's rejection" (hardly an insuperable barrier to overcome). That done, the burden returns to the plaintiff to show that the institution's alleged reasons are sham, a mere pretext to disguise the true and discriminatory reasons, an almost impossible task.

The institution, of course, has control of the essential information in the matter—minutes of committee meetings, memoranda, personnel who participated in the decision process, resources with which to store and retrieve the data—but the Court has nonetheless seen fit to allocate the significant burden in the case to the individual. Under ordinary procedures in litigation, a plaintiff may conceivably secure much of the information necessary to his/her argument through pretrial "discovery." In Georgia, however, a professor who had participated in committee deliberations concerning one such case refused to disclose his vote and his reasons therefor, claiming it was his academic freedom to remain silent (a novel twist on the concept). The court disagreed, found him in contempt, fined him one hundred dollars a day for thirty days in an unsuccessful effort to loosen his tongue, then jailed him for ninety days more. Academic critics of the court suggest that in the interest of the preservation of the integrity of institutional processes (i.e., autonomy) alternatives to such extreme measures ought first have been exhausted: not all members of the professoriate are likely to display such heroic obstinacy as this gentleman. Only when it becomes clear that unarguable injustice will flow from a rigid adherence to the principle of institutional autonomy should that principle be judicially breached for the higher good. By such a time, however, the institution itself should have cast its fortunes with justice over secrecy. At this writing, the issue has been taken on appeal from the trial court to the appellate level.

c. The faculty of Yeshiva University in New York City formed a union and sought through the regulatory process of the National Labor Relations Board to compel a reticent Board of Trustees to negotiate a labor agreement with the union. The trustees insisted that Yeshiva faculty were "managerial employees" excluded from the coverage of the National Labor Relations Act, and the U.S. Supreme Court concurred.[33] Of greater general importance to higher education than the Court's interpretation of what actually took place at Yeshiva University is their stated view (quoted earlier in this chapter) that "traditions of collegiality [between faculty and administrators] continue to play a significant role at many universities [and therefore] principles developed for use [elsewhere] *cannot be 'imposed blindly on the academic world'"* (emphasis added). Courts, that is, may not treat academe as but one more enterprise; instead, says the Supreme Court, they must accommodate higher education's distinctive traditions of collegiality in their resolution of academic disputes.

On point of faculty, then, we see no greater evidence of judicial activism than was exhibited in respect of students. Tenured faculty in public institutions are owed a hearing, if requested, at which to challenge the sufficiency of the grounds on which they are about to be terminated (other than financial exigency; no protections are afforded in such cases). The Court does not, however, delimit the character of permissible grounds. That substantive determination is left to academe. And where it is plausible that the basis of one's nonrenewal/nonpromotion is impermissible by reason of statute, e.g., discrimination on grounds of gender, the burden rests nonetheless with the challenger to make the case, not with the institution to show they have acted lawfully. As to collegiality, the tradition so evident in the historic faculty role in institutional governance may not be sacrificed to principles of labor relations developed in other sectors of the economy. In such data as these, one finds no showing of judicial impairment of institutional autonomy.

Academic Freedom

At last the critics hit pay dirt. The courts do quite blatantly intrude on autonomy in the matter of academic freedom. The difficulty, however, is of course that they do so in defense of the value that academe professes to cherish above all others. Several cases make the point, but two will suffice here.

The constitutional foundation of academic freedom is in the First Amendment's provisions that Congress (and now the states) "shall make no law . . . abridging the freedom of speech or of the press; or the right of the people peaceably to assemble." In a loyalty oath case that reached the U.S. Supreme Court in 1967, the Court held:

> Our Nation is deeply committed to safeguarding academic freedom, which is of transcendent value to all of us and not merely to the teachers concerned. That freedom is therefore a *special* concern of the First Amendment, which does not tolerate laws that cast a pall of orthodoxy over the classroom (emphasis added).[34]

Quoting from an earlier case,[35] the Court continued:

> The essentiality of freedom in the community of American universities is almost self-evident. . . . Scholarship cannot flourish in an atmosphere of suspicion and distrust. Teachers and students must always remain free to inquire, to study and to evaluate, to gain new maturity and understanding; otherwise, our civilization will stagnate and die.

One can hardly conceive a more potent, more authoritative affirmation of the legal vitality of academe's *raison d'être*. But in nourishing academic freedom thus, the Court knowingly and deliberately intruded upon the autonomy of the governing authorities in a state university who had required a loyalty oath of the faculty.

Later the Court similarly intruded upon the autonomy of a particular institution, this time to safeguard the academic freedom of a group of students.[36] The students had been denied official recognition by a state college as a local chapter of Students for a Democratic Society (SDS), on grounds that their professed independence from the politically radical and often disruptive national organization was doubtful, and SDS philosophy was antithetical to college policy. Consistent with established case law, the Court held that even if the group were not independent of the national SDS, their association with an unpopular organization would not be a legally valid basis on which their First Amendment rights of expression and association may be denied. Only action or specific intent to engage in or to further unlawful action—not the advocacy of ideas, no matter how repugnant—may be proscribed. And the burden falls upon the college to demonstrate a legal basis of any refusal to extend official recognition, not upon the student group to show they are entitled to enjoy their First Amendment freedoms.

Three quotes from the several opinions in the case provide glimpses into the justices' views of institutional autonomy and the role of the judiciary. From the majority opinion:

> [W]here state-operated educational institutions are involved, this Court has long recognized "the need for affirming the comprehensive authority of the States and of school officials, consistent with fundamental constitutional safeguards, to prescribe and control conduct in the schools." . . . Yet, the precedents of this Court

leave no room for the view that because of the acknowledged need for order, First Amendment freedoms should apply with less force on college campuses than in the community at large.

From the concurring opinion of a justice who had also joined the majority opinion:

> It is within . . . the academic community that problems such as these should be resolved. The courts, state or federaĺ, should be a last resort. . . . [But] in spite of the wisdom of the [trial] court in sending [this] case back to the college, the issue . . . was not adequately addressed in the [college's] hearing.

And from the concurrence of another such justice who had also joined the majority opinion:

> [T]he fact that [this case] had to come here for ultimate resolution indicates the sickness of our academic world, measured by First Amendment standards.

Strong stuff! The U.S. Supreme Court's preference is that higher education conform its behavior on its own initiative to the fundamental constitutional principles that sustain its claim to academic freedom. But if academe elects not to do so, the Court will unabashedly exercise its considerable power to require conformance, no matter what unfettered authority a given party might otherwise enjoy.

CONCLUSION

There is no evidence that courts today are more activ*ist* than were their counterparts of an earlier day. To be sure, they are undeniably more active in the adjudication of academic dispute. But that is not because courts are exercising an invalid "roving commission" to go about setting wrongs right. They are hearing more cases today because more are being brought to them. Especially are plaintiffs appealing to the federal judiciary for relief from various alleged harms, as the statutory and regulatory fallout of the civil rights movement continues to stimulate litigation in academic matters as well as elsewhere.

Activity, however, is not to be confused with activism. Today's courts, though busier in academic concerns than were their predecessors, are no more likely than were their forebears to substitute their own judgments for judgments reached by experts within academe. To the contrary, despite the anguished cries of more than a few academics, deference to institutional determinations is still the rule. The doctrine of "academic abstention" is as robust as ever. Where the courts might plausibly be considered "activist" (especially if one has a high tolerance for hyperbole) is in the vindication of constitutional rights—especially the First Amendment freedoms of expression and association—of academic plaintiffs. But to the very minor extent that the activism has infringed upon institutional autonomy, the loss is heavily outweighed by the strength it has brought to the legal bases of academic freedom.

We recognize that one might reasonably contend the legislatures and regulatory agencies of government have gone "too far" in their invasion by statute and promulgated rule of institutional self-determination. That is not, however, an issue discussed in this chapter, nor is it one on which we here take a position. Courts, in any event, are not to be lumped willy-nilly together with the other branches of government. For better or for worse they have become increasingly involved in academic dispute, but consistently they have maintained a very sensitive deference to academic judgment.

NOTES

1. Estelle A. Fishbein, "The Academic Industry—A Dangerous Premise," in *Government Regulation of Higher Education,* Walter C. Hobbs, ed. (Cambridge, Mass.: Ballinger, 1978), 57-58.
2. Robert M. O'Neil, *The Courts, Government and Higher Education* (New York: Committee for Economic Development, 1972), 10.
3. The Sloan Commission on Government and Higher Education, *A Program for Renewed Partnership* (Cambridge, Mass.: Ballinger, 1980), 10, 55.
4. Harry T. Edwards, *Higher Education and the Unholy Crusade Against Governmental Regulation* (Cambridge, Mass.: Harvard University Institute for Educational Management, 1980).
5. Ibid., 39.
6. Ibid., 17.
7. Ibid., 20. Perhaps, retorts the critic. But when I must raise $10,000 to render reports that none of my $100,000 categorical grant may be used to prepare, or to improve physical facilities for which I receive no grant, then it's costing me money I don't have and must generate to comply with government regulation.
8. Ibid., 20.
9. Ibid., 29.
10. Sloan Report, *Program for Renewed Partnership,* 61.
11. Walter C. Hobbs, "The 'Defective Pressure-Cooker' Syndrome: Dispute Process in the University," *Journal of Higher Education* 45 (November 1974).
12. National Labor Relations Board v. Yeshiva University, 444 U.S. 672 (1980).
13. Walter C. Hobbs, "The Theory of Government Regulation," in *Government Regulation,* 4-5.
14. The rights are actually enumerated in the first eight amendments.
15. Barron v. Mayor and City Council of Baltimore, 8 L. Ed. 672 (1833).
16. The Slaugherhouse Cases, 16 Wall. 36 (1873).
17. Braden v. University of Pittsburgh, 552 F.2d 948 (1977).
18. Joan S. Stark, ed., *Promoting Consumer Protection for Students* (San Francisco: Jossey-Bass, 1976).
19. Edwards, *Higher Education and the Unholy Crusade,* 19.
20. Steinberg v. Chicago Medical School, 354 N.E.2d 586 (1976).
21. Regents of the University of California v. Bakke, 438 U.S. 265 (1978).

22. Southeastern Community College v. Davis, 442 U.S. 397 (1979).

23. Dixon v. Alabama State Board of Education, 294 F.2d 150 (1961); Esteban v. Central Missouri State College 277 F.Supp. 649 (1967), afmd., 415 F.2d 1077 (1969).

24. Richard C. Conrath, *"In Loco Parentis:* Recent Developments," (Ph.D. dissertation, Kent State University, 1976).

25. Board of Curators of the University of Missouri v. Horowitz, 435 U.S. 78 (1978).

26. Board of Regents v. Roth, 408 U.S. 564 (1972).

27. Perry v. Sindermann, 408 U.S. 593 (1972).

28. Bishop v. Woods, 426 U.S. 341 (1976).

29. Wood v. Strickland, 420 U.S. 308 (1975).

30. *Sindermann case.*

31. Levitt v. Board of Trustees of Nebraska State Colleges, 376 F. Supp. 945 (1974).

32. Board of Trustees of Keene State College v. Sweeney, 439 U.S. 24 (1978).

33. *Yeshiva case.*

34. Keyishian v. Board of Regents of the University of the State of New York, 385 U.S. 589 (1967).

35. Sweezy v. New Hampshire, 354 U.S. 234 (1957).

36. Healy v. James, 408 U.S. 169 (1972).

11

Private Constituencies and Their Impact on Higher Education

Fred F. Harcleroad

Postsecondary institutions have opened and endured in the United States for thirty-five decades. All except those established very recently have been modified over the years and changed greatly in response to pressures from external forces. Particularly in the last century and a half, literally thousands of diverse institutions have opened their doors, only to close when they were no longer needed by (1) sufficient students, or (2) by the public and private constituences that originally founded and supported them. Those in existence today are the survivors, the institutions that adapted to the needs of their constituencies. Even Harvard closed for what would have been its second year (in 1639-1640) after Nathaniel Eaton, its first head, was dismissed for cruelty to students and stealing much of the college funds. After being closed for the year government officials determined that the Massachusetts Bay Colony still needed a college to train ministers and advance learning. A new president, Henry Dunster, reopened the college in 1640, and by changing regularly, and sometimes dramatically, it has remained in operation ever since. Two small examples illustrate this impact. As Massachusetts grew and secularized, ministerial training at Harvard was only one function, so it was placed in a separate divinity school. Also, by the late 1700s required instruction in Hebrew was replaced by student choice, a beginning of our current elective system.

The varied set of external forces affecting postsecondary education in the United States has grown out of our relatively unique, three-sector system of providing goods and services for both "collective consumption" and "private" use. First, the *voluntary enterprise sector,* composed of over six million independent nonprofit organizations, often has initiated efforts to provide such things as schools, hospitals, bridges, libraries, environmental controls, and public parks. They are protected by constitutional rights to peaceful assembly, to free speech, and to petition for redress of grievances. These formidable protections plus their record of useful service led to their being nontaxable, with contributions to them being tax free. Second, the *public enterprise group,* composed of all local, state, and federal governments, administers the laws that hold our society together. Third, the *private enterprise sector,* composed of profit-seeking business and commerce, provides much of the excess wealth needed to support the other two sectors. This pluralistic and diverse set of organizations implements very well the basic ideas behind our federated republic.

Our constitution provides for detailed separation of powers at the federal level between the presidency, the Congress, and the judiciary. The Tenth Amendment establishes the states as governments with "general" powers and delegates "limited" powers to the federal government. "Education" is not a "delegated" power and, therefore, is reserved to the states, where their constitutions often treated it almost as a fourth branch of government. In addition, the Tenth Amendment reserves "general" powers to citizens who operate through their own voluntary organizations, their state governments, or state-authorized private enterprise. Consequently, only a few higher education institutions are creations of the federal government (mostly military institutions, to provide for the common defense), but over 99 percent are creations of states, voluntary organizations, or profit-seeking business.

External groups, associations, and agencies from all three sectors impact on the many varied types of institutions of postsecondary education. This very diverse group of organizations includes everything from athletic conferences and alumni associations to employer associations and unions (or organized faculty groups that function as unions). Of course, the corporate boards that administer all of the private colleges, universities, and institutes authorized to operate in the respective states belong in this group. Their power to determine institutional policies is clear and well known. However, many other voluntary associations can, and do, have significant effects on specific institutions or units of the institutions. To illustrate their potential, these five selected types of organizations will be described in some detail to indicate their backgrounds, development, and possible areas of impact on institutional autonomy and academic freedom. They are:

1. Private foundations;
2. Institutionally based associations;
3. Voluntary accrediting associations;
4. Voluntary consortia;
5. Regional compacts.

PRIVATE FOUNDATIONS

The first beginnings of private foundations in the United States took place over two centuries ago. As a precursor, Benjamin Franklin led in the establishment in Philadelphia of a number of voluntary sector organizations, including the American Philosophical Society in 1743, an association with many foundation characteristics. In 1800 the Magdalen Society of Philadelphia, possibly the first private foundation in the United States, was established as a perpetual trust to assist "unhappy females who had been seduced from the paths of virtue." In the 1890s and early 1900s the Carnegie foundations, followed shortly by the Rockefeller foundations, set a pattern that continues to this day. These foundations established a high standard of operations and valuable service. Few academics realize that their current TIAA pensions were developed and are presently administered by a foundation resulting from Andrew Carnegie's feeling of public service responsibility. Decades before it became legal to tax incomes and before such "contributions" became tax deductible, he gave several million dollars to set up the first pension fund for college teachers.

Today, private foundations vary greatly in form, purpose, size, function, and constituency. Some are corporate in nature, many are trusts, and some are only associations. Many of them can affect postsecondary institutions through their choice of areas to support. They can be classified into five types as follows: (1) community foundations, often city wide and based on a variety of bequests or gifts (local postsecondary institutions, often, can count on some limited support from such foundations for locally related projects); (2) family or personal foundations, often with very limited purposes; (3) special purpose foundations (including such varied examples as the Harvard Glee Club, and a fund set up to provide every girl at Bryn Mawr with one baked potato at each meal); (4) company foundations, estabished to channel corporate giving through one main source; and (5) general foundations or general research foundations (incuding many of the large, well-known foundations such as Ford, Kellogg, Johnson, Lilly, and Carnegie, plus recent additions such as Murdock, MacArthur, and Hewlett). Only 90 percent of private foundation grant funds to higher education come from such general purpose foundations. A number of sources report that higher education receives between 35 and 40 percent of the total giving by foundations. The actual number of grant-making foundations probably approximates 28-30,000. They provide significant help to higher education institutions, and by their choice of the areas they will finance they entice supposedly autonomous colleges to do things they might not do otherwise. Institutional change continues to be a prime goal of foundations as it has been for most of the past century. Thus, although their grants provide a relatively small proportion of the total financing of institutions, they have had significant effects on program development and even on operations. Important support has been provided for such critical activities as the upgrading of medical education, the development of honors programs, and the international exchange of students. Grants from foundations have been instrumental in the establishment of new academic fields such as microbiology and anthropology and the redirection of the fields of business and the education of teachers. Significant support has been provided particularly for the increasing opportunities for minority students' attendance at both undergraduate and graduate levels, and especially in professional fields. Complaints that the private foundations limit their significant funding efforts to "establishment" activities fail to recognize the many critical social changes in which private foundations have led the way. Often, foundation funds have encouraged colleges and universities to take forefront positions in some social causes.

It is important to stress, however, that private foundations affect institutional freedom only if the institutions voluntarily accept the funds for the purposes prescribed by the foundation. Redirection of programs, and even private institutional goals, is possible and has occurred on occasion. Nevertheless, the private foundation model has been so successful that government has adopted it in forming and funding such agencies as the National Science Foundation, the Fund for the Improvement of Postsecondary Education, and the National Endowments for the Arts and for the Humanities. Clearly, private foundations have been and undoubtedly will continue to be important external forces affecting postsecondary education.

INSTITUTIONALLY BASED ASSOCIATIONS

Voluntary membership organizations of this type are almost infinite in possible numbers. Although formed by officials from institutions for their own purposes, the associations often end up having either indirect or direct effects on the institutions themselves. Several large and quite powerful associations represent many of the institutions. The American Council on Education, probably the major policy advocate for postsecondary education at the national level, plays a critical coordinative role as an umbrella-type organization composed of a wide spectrum of institutions. Seven other major national institutional organizations include (1) the Association of American Colleges, (2) the American Association of Community and Junior Colleges, (3) the American Association of State Colleges and Universities, (4) the Association of American Universities, (5) the Council For the Advancement of Small Colleges, (6) the National Association of Independent Colleges and Universities, and (7) the National Association of State Universities and Land-Grant Colleges. These organizations represent most of the public and private, nonprofit postsecondary institutions of the United States, with some institutions belonging to two or three of them. A recent study of the effectiveness of these diverse organizations, as judged by their presidents and by selected national observers, attested to their importance with regard to federal policies and budgets related to higher education.[1] All are based in Washington and, in general, were considered important in representing differing interests of the varied groups of institutions. A majority of the study respondents favored the current, pluralistic system of organizations but with stronger coordination and a more united front on key issues affecting postsecondary education in all departments of government and related congressional committees. The strength of these national associations will continue to grow along with taxes, the federal budget, and federal purchase of selected services from their member institutions. Even though most of the postsecondary institutions are state chartered and many basically are state funded, the increasing power of the federal tax system will make such national associations even more necessary.

Many specialized voluntary membership associations contribute in diverse ways to the development and operations of functional areas within institutions. For example, both the American College Testing Program and the College Entrance Examination Board (its service bureau, the Educational Testing Service, is not a membership organization) provide extensive information resources to their member institutions and program areas. These data are vital for counseling and guidance purposes, admissions of students, student financial aid programs, and related activities. In addition, different administrative functions (such as graduate schools, registrars, institutional research units, and business offices) have their own extremely useful representative associations. Likewise, most different academic fields and their constantly increasing subdivisions or spin-offs have set up specialized groups. Prime examples are engineering and the allied health professions, both with dozens of separate associations. Many of these academic organizations affect institutions and their program planning in very direct ways. In particular, the associations that set up extensive detailed criteria for membership in the association often influence very directly the allocation of resources. Of the several thousand membership organizations* in this category, sixty to seventy of them, from architecture to veterinary medicine, probably exert the greatest influence since those programs or academic units admitted to membership are considered "accredited." The following section will provide more detail on this group.

A small sampling of these varied types of organizations will illustrate their services and emphasize their significance. Very brief and highly condensed, they show in a limited way their potential impact.

1. *The American Council on Education* includes separate institutions and other associations, with approximately 1,500 members. It serves as a key coordinating entity for development of major policy positions, especially in regard to federal legislation and regulatory agency activity. Through its Office of Educational Credit and Credentials it prepares and distributes such important guidebooks as the *Guide to the Evaluation of Educational Experiences in the Armed Services.* This guide is updated

---

*See Gale's *Encyclopedia of Associations* for a comprehensive list that includes many from higher education.

periodically and serves as a "bible" for most registrars' offices. Another comparable ACE publication is *The National Guide to Credit Recommendations for Non-Collegiate Courses.* The extensive overall service and publications program includes reports from the policy analysis service and many special studies on current critical issues in higher education.

2. *The National Association of College and University Business Officers* plays a critical role in all institutional administrative areas. For example, *College and University Business Administration,* which it compiles, updates and publishes, provides the national standards for public accounting in higher education. It conducts extensive surveys on administrative practices and needs, and an active nationwide workshop and seminar program. NACUBO leads in analysis of many other related areas. A critical instance was its central role in establishing the agreement for royalty payments to be paid by colleges and universities for their use of copyrighted music.

3. *The Council for the Advancement of Small Colleges* began in 1955, formed by a group of presidents of small independent colleges. This voluntary, member-directed association now has close to three hundred members and a significant, comprehensive program of services. Before joining the council some member institutions operated without planned budgets, accreditation, or fund-raising programs and with only limited accounting records. During its early years many CASC institutions took advantage of its workshops, seminars, handbooks, and consultants and earned regional accreditation. CASC has secured many millions of dollars to operate programs for the constituency. Many of its special services are supported by useful publications such as its *Handbook for College Administration.* It has a modular Planning and Data System for colleges at various stages of data collection and usage and a related consulting service. Special efforts for the 1980s center on an executive development program for presidents and their spouses, faculty development programs that include "alternate" career programs, and a continuing federal funds service. Recent publications include a *Federal Affairs Handbook* and *A Marketing Approach to Student Recruitment.*

4. *The American Association of State Colleges and Universities* represents three hundred and forty-two public four-year colleges and universities, over 60 percent of the total, plus thirty-three coordinating or governing boards for these institutions. Since its beginnings two decades ago the association has been a leading stimulator of all facets of international education. Its many presidential missions to such countries as Egypt, Israel, Greece, Poland, The Peoples Republic of China, Cuba, Argentina, Taiwan, Malaysia, and Mexico have fostered continuing educational exchange and on-campus programs. It has taken national leadership in developing cooperative, interassociation and interinstitutional programs and networks such as the Servicemembers Opportunity Colleges (with

many AASCU institutions involved), the Urban College and University Network, and the Academic Collective Bargaining Information Service. Its Office of Federal Programs monitors current funding programs and priorities and has been instrumental in increasing AASCU institutions' participation in this ever-increasing source of funds. Its Office of Governmental Relations analyzes pending legislation, develops policy analysis papers, prepares testimony on major national issues, and monitors state developments affecting public higher education. The Office of Program Development assists institutions in various areas of current program development. Recent important areas of assistance have been allied health professions, environmental manpower needs, urban affairs, and public services. Its Research Center for Planned Change works actively with over two hundred and fifty of its member institutions and their chief academic officers, emphasizing future planning, academic program evaluation systems, faculty exchanges between institutions, and innovative educational ideas for new clientele. An extensive seminar, conference, and publication program supports this extensive alignment of institutional services. Overall, the association has had a profound effect on these institutions and their graduates, over one-fourth of those earning baccalaureate degrees and one-third of those earning masters degrees in the United States.

These vignettes from a few associations illustrate the significance and impact of this type of voluntary association. Each of them contribute in varied ways to the diverse needs of their member institutions, or to the program units within them. However, since these organizations continue to be the creatures of their founding members, their efforts do not seem to have noticeable effects on institutional autonomy or academic freedom. Quite the contrary, they seem to be buffering agencies that assist in this regard.

VOLUNTARY ACCREDITING ASSOCIATIONS

The voluntary membership organizations in this critical and important group did not exist a century ago. However, by that time the problems and confusion that led to their establishment had started to surface. Five key factors contributed to the turbulent state of affairs in the period from 1870-1910: (1) the final breakdown of the fixed, classical curriculum and broad expansion of the elective system; (2) new academic fields were being developed and legitimized (such as psychology, education, sociology, and American literature); (3) new, diverse types of institutions were being organized to meet developing social needs (such as teachers colleges, junior colleges, land-grant colleges, research universities, and specialized professional schools); (4) both secondary and postsecondary education were expanding and overlapping, leading to a basic question, "What is a college?"; and (5) there was a lack of commonly accepted standards for admission to college and for completing a college degree.[2]

To work on some of these problems the University of Michigan as early as 1871 sent out faculty members to inspect high schools and admitted graduates of the acceptable and approved high schools on the basis of their diploma. Shortly thereafter pressures developed for regional approaches to these problems, in order to facilitate uniform college entrance requirements.

In keeping with accepted American practice and custom groups of educators banded together in various regions to organize private, voluntary membership groups for this purpose. In New England, for example, it was a group of secondary schoolmasters who took the initiative. In the southern states it was Chancellor Kirkland and the faculty of Vanderbilt University. Six regional associations have developed throughout the United States starting with (1) the New England Association of Schools and Colleges in 1885. It was followed (2) in 1887, by the Middle States Association of Colleges and Schools; (3) in 1895, by the Southern Association of Colleges and Schools; (4) in 1895, by the North Central Association of Colleges and Schools; (5) in 1917, by the Northwest Association of Schools and Colleges; and (6) in 1923, by the Western Association of Schools and Colleges. Criteria and requirements for institutional membership (which now serve as the basis for institutions being considered "accredited") were formally established by these six associations at different times: (1) in 1910, by North Central, with the first list of accredited colleges in 1913; (2) in 1919, by Southern; (3) and (4) in 1921, by Northwest and Middle States; (5) in 1949, by Western; and (6) in 1954, by New England. Thus, at the same time that the federal government instituted regulatory commissions to control similar problems (the Interstate Commerce Commission, 1887, the Federal Trade Commission, 1914, and the Federal Power Commission, 1920) these nongovernmental, voluntary membership groups sprang up to provide yardsticks for student achievement and institutional operations.

Regional groups dealt in the main with colleges rather than with specialized professional schools or programs. The North Central Association finally determined to admit normal schools and teachers colleges, but on a separate list of acceptable institutions. Practitioners and faculty in professional associations gradually set up their own membership associations. These groups established criteria for approving schools and based on these criteria made lists of "accredited" schools and program units. In some cases, only individuals with degrees from an "approved" school could join the professional association. Later, some membership groups made the approved program unit or school a basis for association membership. In any case the specialized academic program and its operational unit had to meet exacting criteria, externally imposed, to acquire and retain standing in the field.

The first of the specialized or programmatic discipline-oriented associations was the American Medical Association in 1847. However, approving processes for medical schools did not start until the early 1900s. In 1905-7 the Council on Medical Education of the AMA led a movement for rating of medical schools. The first ratings in 1905 were a list based on the percentages of failures on licensing examinations by students from each school. This was followed in 1906-7 by a more sophisticated system based on ten specific areas to be examined and inspections of each school. Of 160 schools inspected, classified, and listed, 32 were in Class C, "unapproved," 46 were in Class B, on "probation," and 82 were in Class A, "approved." The Council on Medical Education was attacked vigorously for this listing and approving activity. The recently established Carnegie Foundation for the Advancement of Teaching (1905) provided funds for Abraham Flexner and N. P. Colwell to make their famous study (1908-1910) of the 155 schools still in existence. Obviously, five already had closed. By 1915, only 95 medical schools remained, a 40 percent reduction, and they were again classified by the AMA Council of Medical Education, with 66 approved, 17 on probation, and 12 still listed as unapproved. This voluntary effort led to the ultimate in accountability, the merger and closing of 65 existing medical schools. In the process medical education was changed drastically, and the remaining schools completely revised and changed their curricula—a process still continuing to this day. This provides an excellent example of the work of an external voluntary professional association, with financial support from a private foundation, that took the initiative and acted on its own to protect the public interest. Thus, in some cases intrusions into "autonomy" can have beneficial results.

The success of the AMA did not go unnoticed. The National Home Study council started in 1926 to do for correspondence education what the AMA after seventy years had done in medical education. Between 1914-1935 many other professional disciplinary and service associations were started in the fields of business, dentistry, law, library science, music, engineering, forestry, and dietetics plus the medically related fields of podiatry, pharmacy, veterinary medicine, optometry, and nurse anesthesia. From 1935-1948 new associations starting up included architecture, art, bible schools, chemistry, journalism, and theology, plus four more medically related fields, medical technology, medical records, occupational therapy, and physical therapy. Between 1948 and 1975 the number of specialized associations continued to expand rapidly, for programs from social service to graduate psychology and from construction education to funeral direction. Medical care subspecialties also proliferated, particularly in the allied health field, which included over twenty-five separate groups.

All of these external professional associations affect institutional operations very directly, including curricular patterns, faculty, degrees offered, teaching methods, support staff patterns, and capital outlay decisions. In many cases priorities in internal judgments result from the outside pressures. Local resource allocations, thus, often are heavily influenced by accreditation reports. For example, the law library, a chemistry or engineering laboratory, and teaching loads in business or social work may have been judged substandard by these external private constituents. If teaching loads in English or history also are heavy or physics laboratories inadequate will they get the same attention and treatment as specialized program areas with outside pressures? In such cases these association memberships are not really "voluntary," if the institution is placed on probation or no longer an "accredited" member, and sanctions are actually applied. Often, students will withdraw or not consider attending a professional school or college that is not accredited. States often limit professional licenses to practice in a field to graduates of accredited schools. Federal agencies may not allow students from unaccredited institutions to obtain scholarships, loans, or work-study funds. The leverage of a voluntary association in such cases becomes tremendous, and the pressure for accredited status can be extremely powerful.

Presidents of some of the larger institutions, starting in 1924, have attempted to limit the effects of accrediting associations and the number of these independent organizations with which they would work. Through some of the institutionally based associations described in the previous section they established limited sanctions and attempted to restrict the number of accrediting associations to which they would pay dues and allow on-campus site visits. These efforts to limit association membership and accreditation failed repeatedly to stem the tide. Shortly after World War II, in 1949, a group of university presidents finally organized the National Commission on Accrediting, a separate voluntary membership association of their own. It was designed to cut down the demands and influence of existing external associations and to delay or stop the development of new ones. The numbers of new ones dropped for a few years but pressures of new, developing disciplines on campus soon led to the many new organizations of this type since the 1950s.

In 1949, the regional associations also felt the need for a new cooperative association and set up what became the Federation of Regional Accrediting Commissions. In 1975 the two organizations, FRACHE and NCA, agreed to merge and they became major factors in the founding of the new Council on Postsecondary Accreditation. COPA also included four national groups accrediting specialized institutions, plus seven major, institutionally based associations. They in turn endorsed COPA as the central, leading voluntary association for the establishment of policies and procedures in postsecondary accreditation. By 1980 COPA had recognized fifty-two accrediting associations that met its standards. These associations "approve" or "accredit" approximately 4,000 different institutions of all types and kinds, varying by level (undergraduate, nondegree, or graduate), by form of governance (private/profit seeking, private/tax exempt, or public/tax supported), and by curricular emphasis (professional, liberal arts/general education, or vocational). In addition COPA and the separate accrediting associations increasingly are pressured for recognition of educational programs offered by government agencies, businesses, church groups and unions.

The six current goals of COPA are to:

1. foster educational excellence by developing criteria and guidelines for assessing educational effectiveness;
2. encourage improvement through continuous self-study and planning;
3. provide assurance of clearly defined and appropriate objectives and conditions under which they can be achieved;
4. provide counsel and aid to established and developing programs and institutions;
5. encourage educational diversity;
6. protect institutions' educational effectiveness and academic freedom.

The relationship of voluntary accrediting associations to the state and federal governments also is a major factor in current considerations of academic freedom, institutional autonomy, and institutional accountability. The states, of course, charter most of the institutions, and by so doing establish their missions, general purposes, and degree levels offered. However, the states also license individuals to practice most vocations and professions. In many fields the licensing of individuals is based on graduation from "accredited" programs. Thus, a form of sanctions has developed and membership in the involved, specialized, professional associations, supposedly voluntary, becomes almost obligatory. In the federal area, "listing" of institutions by federal government agencies had little or no effect prior to World War II. However, the entrance of the federal government into the funding of higher education on a massive basis since World War II has drastically changed the overall uses of accreditation. Reported abuses of the Servicemen's Readjustment Act of 1944 (GI Bill) led to a series of congressional hearings, which led in turn to major additions related to accreditation in Public Law 550, the Veterans Readjustment Act of 1952. Section 253 of that law empowered the Commissioner of Education to publish a list of accrediting agencies and associations that could be relied upon to assess the quality of training offered by educational institutions. State approving agencies then used the resulting actions of such accrediting associations or agencies as a basis for approval of the courses specifically accredited.

Extensive legal arguments about the resulting powers of the Department of Education still continue. However, greater institutional dependence of "eligibility" for funding is now based on membership in much less voluntary accrediting associations. The courts normally have ruled that accreditation by accrediting associations is not quasi-governmental action. Nevertheless, there has grown up an important new concept called the "triad." The triad involves delicate relationships between the federal government and eligibility for funding, the state government and its responsibilities for establishing or chartering institutions and credentialing through certification or licensure, and voluntary membership associations that require accreditation for membership.

Thus, these voluntary associations have come to represent a major form of private constituency with direct impact on internal institution activities. The possible multiple sanctions from state licensing of graduates, loss of eligibility for funds from federal agencies, and problems caused by peer approval or disapproval enhance the importance of these sometimes overlooked educational organizations.

VOLUNTARY CONSORTIA[3]

Formal arrangements for voluntary consortia based on interinstitutional cooperation among and between postsecondary institutions have been in operation for over half a century. The Claremont Colleges (California) started in 1925 with Pomona College and the Claremont University Center and were joined by Scripps College in 1926. The Atlanta University Center (Georgia), sometimes called the "Affiliation," started shortly thereafter in 1929, including Morehouse College, Spelman College, and Atlanta University. Over the decades both of these gorups have added additional institutions to their cooperative arrangements and proven that voluntary consortia can be valuable for long periods of time. Some early examples from 1927-29 illustrate the reality of the cooperation between Morehouse and Spelman. In those years several faculty were jointly appointed to both faculties. Upper division students could cross-register and take courses offered by the other college. Also, they operated a joint summer school with Atlanta University. In 1932, a new library was built and the three libraries consolidated into a joint library serving all of the institutions. Thus, although they remained separate institutions they sacrificed some autonomy to extend the academic offerings and services available to their students.[4]

In the years since these early beginnings, hundreds of institutions have developed informal and increasingly formal arrangements for interinstitutional cooperation. In 1966, a national survey conducted by the United States Office of Education determined that there were 1,017 consortia operating in the United States and that the evidence indicated that a number of consortia were not reported. The list included all types of consortia, from simple bilateral arrangements dealing with a single area of service to large complex consortia performing many services and contributing in many areas of education.[5] In 1967, the staff of the Kansas City Regional Council For Higher Education, a leading consortium, published the first directory of consortia, with a list of 31 having these exacting criteria: (1) it is a voluntary formal organization; (2) it has three or more member institutions, (3) it has multi-academic programs, (4) it is administered by at least one full-time professional, and (5) it has a required annual contribution or other tangible membership support. Twelve years later the 1979 Consortium Directory listed 126 general-purpose consortia with "at least six to eight separate services or programs; several administer as many as 30 or 40 different activities over a one year period."[6] Well over 1,000 institutions are involved in these consortia alone. Thus, today consortia represent a major development in American higher education and a significant factor in current planning and development of institutions.

The big push for the development of consortia in the 1950s, 1960s, and 1970s was based on the need to maximize the use of resources to meet the challenge of increasing enrollments, expanding research efforts, and increasing demands on the higher education community for additional services. The demands of the 1980s and 1990s appear to be just the opposite. The demands for efficiency in the use of the plant, facilities, and the faculty again require interinstitutional arrangements in order to make optimum use of facilities that are available. For both state-supported colleges and universities and for private independent institutions, there appears to be a continuing need for more cooperation among various types of educational institutions, including shared use of facilities and joint programs.

The need for this type of organization in the 1980s and later is well illustrated by the development of a number of statewide efforts to establish official, but voluntary, regional councils. States such as New York, Pennsylvania, and California have established regional councils for planning and interinstitutional communication between interested institutions, both public and private. In these cases regionalism revolves more around the planning of available curricular programs, rather than the extensive operational cooperation in most consortia. However, the interest in states in this method of operation, and the inclusion of both private and public institutions on a voluntary basis, represents a major and somewhat comparable departure. As another method of bringing about cooperative effort between both types of institutions, it has valuable implications for the future of all consortia. If the proposed regional councils could be expanded to include the many diverse activities of existing consortia, they could contribute greatly to demands for efficiency and effectiveness.

The importance of voluntary consortia to concerns regarding institutional autonomy becomes evident with the enumeration of their varied activities. An extensive study of twenty-nine consortia by the Academy of Educational Development divided their activities into seven major areas: (1) administrative and business services, (2) enrollment and admissions, (3) academic programs, (4) libraries, (5) student services, (6) faculty and (7) community services. In each of these areas, they found significant and extensive cooperative efforts that had been carried on by many institutions in several consortia.[7] Also, they found that consortia were geographically widespread with programs in all seven of the categories.

Advocates of consortia activity normally stress the educational advantages that accrue from their programs. Voluntary consortia have proven to be an ideal planning vehicle for joint programming of public and private colleges and universities or private colleges acting alone. In fact, a recent restudy of McGrath's fifty private-colleges' sample found that:

> Interinstitutional cooperative arrangements served as a method of providing new educational programs and as a method of retaining old programs for the least expense. Cooperative efforts were found to provide expanded capabilities while requiring a minimum of resources in faculty, facilities, and money. Cooperation was a management method which provided opportunities for students to participate in high cost programs through the use of shared resources.[8]

How very significant financial savings also are often obtained undoubtedly will become more important. In some cases, existing programs have been able to continue without cutbacks, due to economies based on consortium arrangements In others, actual savings accrue that can be used to meet growth costs in other areas. A few selected examples illustrate their fiscal and planning importance.[9]

- Cross-registration provided derived value of instruction to several groups of institutions in 1977-1979—including Atlanta University Center, $1,518,000; and Five Colleges, Inc., $1,889,000 (in Amherst, Massachusetts).

- Cooperative academic programs save significant sums at, for example, the Claremont Colleges, Inc. where three colleges operated a joint science department with joint faculty and joint use of a single science laboratory complex.

- The Washington Metropolitan Area Consortium of Universities, in 1978, combined their purchases of liquid helium and liquid nitrogen through the physics department of Georgetown University and reported a saving of $500,000 from their total research budgets for that period.

- The Union of Independent Colleges of Art (nine institutions in the Kansas City area) made a preliminary study of the cost effectiveness in their joint admissions program alone. Direct cash benefits to each institution were found to be more than $62,986 each, with each college paying fees of only $8,256 per college. A joint film center saved $124,460.

- The Hudson-Mohawk Association of Colleges and Universities (with fifteen members) shared information on fuel oil prices. Three of the members in 1972 reported reduced costs by $20,000 in one year by using this data in their bargaining with suppliers. In February, 1978 they reported savings of over $50,000 during the summer of 1977 on fuel oil, paper and other office supplies. A cooperative surplus sale raised $12,450.

- The Worcester, Massachusetts, Consortium combined their oil purchases and the single supplier cut 10 percent to get the entire bid. The consortium members (including both public and private, two-year and four-year institutions) saved $30,000.

These examples of savings are representative of the actual financial savings possible through joint institutional planning.

Liberal arts colleges led the way for several decades in the establishment of consortia, and Patterson found in 1970 that approximately 75 percent of member colleges were private, nonprofit institutions. However, by 1975, 40 percent were public.[10] Recent federal and state support of cooperative ventures of this type have increased consortia in numbers and membership. For example, the Illinois Higher Education Cooperative Act of 1972 provided some state support for voluntary combinations of private and public institutions, including some from out of state, that applied for funds on a competitive basis. The Quad-Cities Graduate Center in Rock Island, Illinois, administered by Augustana College, combined the offerings of ten public and private colleges and universities in Iowa and Illinois to provide graduate degree programs to several thousand graduate students. Funding is provided by both states and the result is a major, free-standing graduate school drawing strength from its ten members. Several other states such as California, Connecticut, Massachusetts, Minnesota, Ohio, Pennsylvania, and Texas have used the consortium approach for specific, sometimes limited purposes. This trend toward public financing of consortia, thus, becomes another key factor to consider in future institutional planning, along with limited efforts to promote regional, intrastate planning.

In the past, consortia have been developed to provide for interinstitutional needs both in times of growth and in times of decline. They are uniquely capable of handling mutual problems of public and private institutions, and thus, provide a powerful deterrent to further governmental incursions into private and sometimes public institutional operation. At various levels of formality, consortia currently are being used by significant numbers of institutions of all types to adjust to changing curricular and funding necessities. As governmental controls continue to increase and to affect institutional autonomy and academic freedom, voluntary consortia provide another way to plan independently for future operations and program development.

REGIONAL COMPACTS

Regional compacts, although they are nonprofit, private organizations, are quasi-governmental. Groups of states created them, provide their basic funding, and contract for services through them. Still, they operate much like private organizations and receive considerable funding from other sources, including private foundations. Some of their studies, seminars, workshops, and policy studies affect very directly the institutions in their regions.

Soon after World War II three regional interstate compacts developed to meet postsecondary education needs that cross state lines. Originally they concentrated on student exchange programs for the medical education field; however, in the past 25 to 30 years their areas of service and influence have expanded considerably. Although established, funded, and supported basically by state governors and legislatures, their indirect effects on institutional programs and operations can be very, very significant. Listed in order of establishment, they are:

1. Southern Regional Education Board (1948)
2. Western Interstate Commission for Higher Education (1951)
3. New England Board of Higher Education (1955)

These three compacts cover thirty-three states, leaving out the Midwest, New York, Pennsylvania, and Delaware. Efforts are underway to establish one in fifteen states of the Midwest. Between 1978 and 1980 the Minnesota, South Dakota, North Dakota, and Ohio legislatures approved its establishment. In order to begin operations, six states had to adopt the plan. If established, it would provide for interstate student exchanges at in-state tuition rates, cooperative programs in vocational and higher education, and an area-wide approach to gathering and reporting information needed for educational planning.

The Southern Regional Education Board includes key governors, legislators, and other key figures, some from higher education, from fourteen states, Alabama, Arkansas, Florida, Georgia, Kentucky, Louisiana, Maryland, Mississippi, North Carolina, South Carolina, Tennessee, Texas, Virginia, and West Virginia. In its thirty years of operation, it has played a major part in the development of such important areas as equal opportunity for all students in higher education and expanded graduate and professional education. Its research and information program has been vital in state and institutional planning. Its regular legislative work conferences, planned by its Legislative Advisory Council, have been very influential in setting policy and funding directions in the region.

The Western Interstate Commission for Higher Education now has members from thirteen states, Alaska, Arizona, California, Colorado, Hawaii, Idaho, Montana, Nevada, New Mexico, Oregon, Utah, Washington, and Wyoming. It was planned originally (1) to pool educational resources, (2) to help the states plan jointly for the preparation of specialized skilled manpower, and (3) to avoid, where feasible, the duplication of expensive facilities. The student exchange program in the fields of medicine, dentistry, veterinary medicine, and later in dental hygiene, nursing, mental health, and other specialized fields, has been a major effort. Regional conferences on critical topics, annual legislative workshops, and extensive research studies and publications also are regularly carried on by WICHE. One of its developments, the program in higher education management and information systems, created so much demand for participation in the other thirty-seven states that it was "spun-off" to become the National Center for Higher Education Management Systems. WICHEN, its special Council for Nursing education, has operated continuously since 1957 and has been a key research, consultation, and planning source for the development of degree programs in the field of nursing. In 1978, an extensive study of future needs for nurses and differing types of nursing services was completed. These findings are important for academic decision making related to nursing programs in most of the western states.

Two recent studies were of critical importance to institutional academic planning in the region. One was a study of needs for optometry education, in which there are only three schools in the thirteen states, and projected shortages of optometrists in twelve of the states. Second, WICHE had a two-year grant from the Carnegie Corporation of New York during 1978-1980 to study the expansion of regional cooperation in graduate and professional education. Its purpose was to encourage sharing of graduate resources through establishment of an information system about such programs. Decision-makers were provided with a stream of data based on a regional perspective. Two major planning issues were addressed:

1. Do western-state graduate students have adequate access based on current interstate mobility? and
2. Can lower tuitions for out-of-state students be justified by improved resource sharing of graduate facilities?

With decreasing graduate enrollments and a need for programs to assure a reasonable flow of young doctorates into both academic service and newer, expanded areas needing doctoral graduates, this latter study was an important one and provided considerable guidance on needed academic decisions related to graduate professional programs.

The New England Board of Higher Education serves six states, Connecticut, Maine, Massachusetts, New Hampshire, Rhode Island, and Vermont. It administers such programs as (1) the regional student exchange program, (2) the New England Council on Higher Education for Nursing, (3) a library information network, and (4) an academic science information center. A major study of the past few years was the analysis of need and recommended location of a school of veterinary medicine, a very controversial topic.

Clearly, regional interstate compacts provide critical research data and have considerable impact on academic program decision making. In some cases their findings directly affect the location of an academic program at a particular institution or the source and size of the student body for an existing program. Expansion or contraction of an expensive program often is a critical planning decision. In areas such as this an external regional compact can greatly affect an individual college or university. Since regional compacts provide a unique blending of legislators, governors, officials of executive agencies, and key officials from institutions of higher education, these organizations will continue to fill a vital communication link in interstate planning.

CONCLUSION

During the first two centuries of American higher education's existence religious tenets and basic social agreements resulted in a relatively fixed, classically oriented program of studies. However, as the society began to open up, to industrialize and expand, it demanded greater change in its colleges. When this was slow to occur new institutions met these needs and many existing ones closed. Normal schools, engineering schools, military academies, and universities were copied from Europe and adapted to American needs between the 1830s and 1900. However, even these were not sufficient to meet democracy's needs. New types of institutions were developed, unique or almost unique to America. The land-grant colleges of 1862 and 1890, the junior colleges of the early 1900s, the comprehensive state colleges of the 1930s-1960s and the post-world war community colleges all represent essentially new types of institutions. Private constituency groups often pressured state or local governments to establish them. In some cases private constituency groups pressured Congress into funding some of them, including both the 1862 land-grant colleges, and particularly the 1890 land-grant colleges. The critical point, again, is that in the United States new institutions replace existing ones that do not change.

Private constituencies such as the five types detailed here can and do have significant impact on institutional autonomy and academic freedom. Much of this impact is positive, supportive, and welcome. However, those that provide funds can affect institutional trends and directions by determining what types of academic programs or research efforts to support. For example, in the late 1960s and early 1970s significant financial support from Carnegie strongly influenced most of the twenty-five institutions that offer the Doctor of Arts degree for prospective college teachers. Ford support for learning by television led many institutions to test this method of delivery of learning materials. As federal and state funds tighten up even more in the years ahead funds from alternate sources will become even more attractive. Acceptance of grants moves institutions in the direction dictated by fund sources, and faculties are well advised to consider this possibility as the "crunch" of the 1980s and 1990s becomes greater in more and more institutions.

Finally, the very real benefits provided to institutions by private organizations have been stressed previously. Many membership organizations, of course, have been created to provide such anticipated benefits. In some cases these have been greater than anyone could have foreseen. Probably the most dramatic examples have come from private accrediting associations in relation to state political efforts to limit seriously the autonomy and academic freedom of their own public institutions. In 1938, the North Central Association dropped North Dakota Agricultural College from membership because of undue political interference. The U.S. Court of Appeals upheld the action of NCA and the state government basically backed away from its prior method of political interference in internal institutional affairs. In the post-World War II period, likewise, sanctions of the Southern Association basically stopped on-campus speaker-ban legislation in North Carolina and, after 1954, contributed strongly to the development of open campuses in other states in its region.

Private organizations related in some way to postsecondary education clearly continue the great tradition of direct action by voluntary citizen associations in America. Increasingly, they stand in the middle between control-oriented federal and state agencies and both private and public institutions. Governments, literally, have abandoned the self-denying ordinance" that in recent decades kept the "state" at a distance from the essence of many of its institutions. The nurturing of supportive and helpful private constituencies, therefore, becomes even more critical in the final decades of the twentieth century.

NOTES

1. Joseph Cosand, et al., *Higher Education's National Institutional Membership Associations* (Ann Arbor, Mich.: Center for the Study of Higher Education, University of Michigan, 1980).

2. Fred Harcleroad, *Accreditation: History, Process and Problems* (Washington, D.C.: American Association for Higher Education, 1981).

3. Some of the sections on voluntary consortia and regional compacts are adapted from Fred Harcleroad, "Effects of Regional Agencies and Voluntary Associations," in *Improving Academic Management*, Paul Jedamus and Marvin Peterson, eds. (San Francisco: Jossey-Bass, 1980), chapter 6.

4. Florence M. Read, *The Story of Spelman College* (Princeton, N.J.: Princeton University Press, 1953), 217-9, 235, 247.

5. Raymond S. Moore, *Consortiums in American Higher Education, 1965-66* (Washington, D.C.: U.S. Government Printing Office, 1968).

6. Lewis Patterson, *Survival Through Interdependence* (Washington, D.C.: American Association for Higher Education, 1980).

7. Barry Schwenkmeyer and Mary Ellen Goodman, *Putting Cooperation to Work* (Washington, D.C.: Academy for Educational Development, 1972).

8. George Lepchenske and Fred Harcleroad, *Are Liberal Arts Colleges Professional Schools? A Restudy* (Tucson, Ariz.: Center for the Study of Higher Education, University of Arizona, 1978), 17.

9. Lewis Patterson, *Survival Through Independence,* 28-30.

10. Lewis Patterson, "Evolving Patterns of Cooperation," *ERIC Higher Education Research Currents* (June 1975), 1.

Part 3

The Academic Community

12

Stark Realities: The Academic Profession in the 1980s—and Beyond

Philip G. Altbach

This chapter has a simple theme: the American professoriate emerged from a period of unprecedented growth and increased status in the 1970s into much less favorable circumstances.* The decade between 1975 and 1985 saw a dramatic downturn in the fortunes of the academic profession and while the latter 1980s has seen a modest turnaround, the basic situation has not changed. It is the purpose of this essay to describe the background and analyze current realities and future prospects. The present is made all the more difficult by the period of affluence and power that preceded it. The professoriate is beset on all sides and finds itself unable to defend its hard-won gains. Declines in enrollments, decreased mobility for academics, demands for fiscal and often for programmatic accountability from government and other authorities and a decade in which academic salaries actually declined when measured against inflation are all part of the crisis.

The prognosis for the medium term future does not hold out much cause for optimism since these trends seem fairly long-term in nature. In *American Professors: A National Resource Imperiled,* Howard R. Bowen and Jack H. Schuster argue that the deterioration of the professoriate is a threat to American higher education and that remedial steps are required.[1] The deep depression of the 1970s has, at least temporarily, been replaced by a modest upturn in that enrollments have not slid as far as expected and retirements have opened up some positions for younger academics. However, the basic configuration of circumstances has not altered. That most academics have not been dramatically affected by the crisis in that their positions remain secure and their working conditions have not dramatically deteriorated does not make it any less serious. At present, most academics—with the dramatic exception of younger scholars who are unable to find academic jobs or who cling tenuously to temporary or part-time positions—have been insulated from the grim realities of "reduction, reallocation and retrenchment."[2]

The academic profession is at the very heart of the academic enterprise.

If the professoriate is in trouble, the post-secondary education system is threatened. Excellence depends on the professoriate and recent plans for upgrading higher education will flounder unless the academic profession is in a position to implement them. All of the other academic structures that have been so intricately built up in the past several decades—student affairs offices, administrative hierarchies, and even statewide coordinating boards—theoretically function to make the central tasks of the faculty—teaching and research—more effective. The centrality of the role of the professoriate is often forgotten in the bureaucratized university, and if it is possible to reassert this centrality, it may be possible to keep at least a part of the gains of the recent past and to maintain a long tradition of academic power. More important, the effectiveness of the profession in teaching and in research can be maintained or enhanced. If the current situation continues, it seems clear that the professoriate will indeed be imperiled.

The American academic profession, it must be remembered, is large and diverse. In 1970, there were 474,000 persons employed full- or part-time in teaching positions in American colleges and universities. By 1985, the number had increased to 663,000, although this was a decline from a peak of 713,000 in 1982. Diversity is a hallmark of the American academic profession. First of all, the academic system is stratified. About a quarter of the profession teaches in community colleges. Among four-year institutions, there is also a great deal of diversity, and working conditions vary considerably. The tremendous increase in part-time academics, who now number about thirty-two percent of the total professoriate, adds to the diversity.

Only thirty years ago, the academic profession was largely white, male and Protestant. It has grown increasingly diverse, with major gains having been made by Catholics and Jews. The middle-class domination of the profession has weakened somewhat. Women now constitute thirty percent of the professoriate, although they earn less than their male compeers and tend to be clustered in the lower ranks of the professoriate.[3] Racial minorities number about nine percent of the profession.[4] Academics are divided by discipline, type of institution, orientation and other factors. Yet, despite these differences, there is a common sense of an academic profession in America and a vague community of concerns among the large and diverse professoriate.

Precisely because the professoriate finds itself at the center of an increasingly complex institutionalized nexus, it is subject to pressures from many directions. Increasingly complicated accounting procedures measure professorial "productivity" but as yet have been unable to consider the basic issue—that of the educational outcomes of teaching. A deteriorating academic job market has raised standards for tenure and promotion at the same time that outlets for scholarly communication, at least in book form, have somewhat declined. Student "consumerism" in the 1970s and demands for "social relevance" in the 1960s have disrupted the traditional curriculum and the professoriate has yet to put the curricular pieces back together. Because the bulk of the expenditures of any academic institution consists of staff salaries, the working habits, remuneration, and other aspects of the professoriate have been subjected to increased scrutiny. Legislators demand accountability, administrators seek to create order out of what has traditionally been a disorderly yet creative institution, students make often contradictory demands, and the conditions for academic promotion and mobility have become less favorable. These are a part of the crisis of the professoriate.

The academic profession, despite these problems, retains considerable power over academic institutions and is still a power in its own right. Disunited, dispirited, and in disarray, the professoriate remains central not only to the academic function but to the structures of the bureaucratized university. The curriculum remains basically in the hands of the faculty, despite some half-hearted efforts to involve students in the 1960s and some governmental interference. Government involvement has become an increasingly serious issue at all levels in academe. Federal agencies influence curriculum through grants and awards. State agencies engage in program review and approval and in some ways traditional faculty control has been significantly eroded.

The processes of academic promotion and hiring remain in professorial hands despite "tenure quotas" and bureaucratization strengthened by unions in some institutions. Faculty governance, especially in the established and research-oriented colleges and universities, remains a force to be reckoned with. The department, the basic building block of most academic institutions, remains in the hands of the faculty.

Yet academics have been particularly ineffective in articulating their centrality. Entrenched power, a complicated governance structure, and the weight of tradition have helped to protect academic power in a difficult period. But the professoriate itself has not articulated its own ethos.[5] The rise of academic unions has certainly made a contribution in terms of salaries but has created an adversarial relationship in some institutions.[6] The unions, with the partial exception of the American Association of University Professors, have not defended and articulated the professorial role.[7]

This essay, then, sees the American professoriate in an ambivalent role. Beset from all sides, the faculty nevertheless retains prestige, considerable authority, and a central if often unrecognized role. Academics themselves, insulated to some degree from harsh realities by layers of administration, do not in many cases recognize the nature of the dilemma.[8] If the crisis is to be profitably considered, it must first be placed in context and then analyzed.

THE HISTORICAL CONTEXT

The academic profession has been conditioned by a complex historical development. As E. D. Duryea points out, universities have a long historical

tradition and the academic profession, to a considerable degree, is the re-
pository of this tradition.[9] However imperfectly, the professoriate retains a
vision of a long historical development. The glories of the medieval universities, of Oxford and Cambridge, and the rise of the German universities are all
part of this tradition. The traditions of the academic profession developed
slowly.[10] The medieval origins were instrumental for the recognition of the
self-governing nature of the professorial community and infused a certain
amount of autonomy into the operation of universities. Much later, the reforms in German higher education in the nineteenth century greatly increased
the power and prestige of the professoriate, while at the same time linking
both the universities and the profession to the state. Professors were civil
servants and the universities were expected to contribute to the development
of Germany as a modern industrial state. Research, for the first time, became
a key element in the role of the universities.[11] The role and status of the
academic profession at Oxford and Cambridge in England also had an impact
on the American professoriate, since the early American colleges were pat-
terned on British models.[12]

These models, plus academic realities in the United States, helped to
shape the academic profession in the United States. For our purposes, the
most crucial period of development begins with the rise of the land-grant
colleges and of the innovative private universities around the turn of the
twentieth century.[13] Several aspects of the development of the modern American university are of crucial importance for the growth of the academic
profession. The commitment of the university to public service and to "relevance" meant that academics were, of necessity, involved to some extent with
societal issues, with applied aspects of scholarship, and with training for the
emerging professions and for skilled occupations involving technology. Following the German lead, the innovative private universities (Chicago, Hopkins, Cornell, and Stanford, soon to be followed by the great state institutions
such as Michigan, California, and Wisconsin) emphasized research and graduate training. The doctorate became a requirement for entry into at least the
upper reaches of the profession. The prestige of elite universities gradually
came to dominate the academic system and the ethos of research, graduate
training, and professionalism permeated much of American academe. As
these norms and values gradually permeated the American academic enterprise, they have become widespread and form the base of professional values
in the 1980s.

The hallmark of the post-World War II period has been massive growth
in higher education. As noted earlier, faculty numbers tripled in a little more
than twenty years. Student enrollments grew just as dramatically, with many
institutions adding graduate programs. While the dramatic growth of the first
three postwar decades has ended, the implications of this growth remain
quite important for the academic profession.

It is fair to say that expansion characterized higher education in almost every respect. Growth became the norm, and departments, academic institutions, and individuals based their plans on continued growth. Part of the problem in adjusting to the current period of diminished resources and little growth is the very fact that the previous period was one of unusual expansion. Indeed, it can be argued that the period of postwar growth was the abnormal period and the current situation is more "normal."[14] The legacy of the period of expansion is thus significant.

Expansion has shaped the vision of the academic profession. The postwar period saw unprecedented growth, but it also introduced other changes. The basic fact was a "sellers' market" in which individual academics were able to sell their services at a premium. In almost every field there was a shortage of qualified teachers and researchers.[15] Average academic salaries improved dramatically and the American academic moved from a state of semipenury into the increasingly affluent middle class.[16] The image of Mr. Chips was replaced by the jet-set professor. As universities, and particularly those prestigious graduate-oriented institutions leading the "academic procession," were increasingly involved in research, they had greater access to funds for research.[17] The space program, rapid advances in technology, and a fear in 1958 that the United States was "falling behind" in education all contributed to greater spending by the federal government for higher education. Expansion in enrollments meant that the states invested more in higher education and that the private institutions also prospered.

Academics benefitted substantially from this situation. Those obtaining their doctorates found ready employment, with different institutions often bidding for their services. Rapid career advancement could be expected. Mobility was easy, and an individual faculty member could easily move if dissatisfied with his or her institution. This contributed to diminished institutional loyalty and concern. In order to retain faculty, colleges and universities lowered teaching loads and the average time spent in the classroom declined during this period. Both salaries and fringe benefits increased. Access to research funds from external sources increased substantially, not only in the sciences but also in the social sciences and, to some extent, in the humanities. This development also made academics less dependent on their institutions and gave them an independent source of funds. Those few academics with substantial access to external funds were able to build institutes, centers, and in general to develop "empires" within their institutions.

Rapid expansion also meant unprecedented growth in the profession itself, and this has had lasting implications. An abnormally large cohort of young academics entered professorial ranks in the 1960s. With the end of the period of growth, this large cohort has, in effect, inhibited entry to new entrants and has created a "bulge" of tenured faculty members who will not retire for perhaps twenty years. Many of this cohort participated in the campus turmoil of the 1960s and were affected by it. And many graduated from universities of lesser prestige and may not have been fully socialized into the traditional academic norms and values.

This extraordinarily large academic generation is now causing a variety of problems related to its size, training, and experiences. This generation now dominates the American system. It was socialized at a time when academic conditions were improving, professorial mobility was great, and when rapid advancement was the norm. These expectations were dashed with the changing circumstances of the 1970s, with the result that morale is low and adjustment has been difficult.[18] The size, shape, and opinions of this generation will dominate the profession for another decade or more and is one of the most important legacies of the period of expansion.

A final influence of the recent past is the turmoil of the 1960s. A number of elements converged in the turbulent sixties to produce an unprecedented crisis in American higher education. The university, once peripheral to the society, became a key social institution. It was called on to help solve such social problems as access to education and mobility, and academic experts could be found at the frontier of most every social problem. It is not surprising, therefore, that higher education became involved in the most traumatic crises of that period—the Vietnam war and the civil rights struggle. The anti-war movement emerged from the campuses and was most powerful there.[19]

But the campus crisis went deeper than the antiwar movement, although that was the major stimulant. A new generation of students (and some would argue faculty as well), to an extent unsocialized into the norms of higher education and from a more diverse social-class group, has entered higher education. The faculty, which had turned its attention from undergraduate teaching to research and advanced instruction, allowed the undergraduate curriculum to fall into disarray. Overcrowded facilities were common. And the overwhelming malaise caused by the war, racial unrest, and related social problems produced a powerful combination of discontent.[20] The crisis brought unprecedented, and highly critical, public attention to higher education. The faculty, unable to deal constructively with the crisis and feeling itself under attack from students, the public, and the authorities, was quickly demoralized. Faculty governance structures proved unequal to the task and administrators tried, often without much success, to deal with the crisis. It is fair to say that the crisis of the 1960s left the professoriate demoralized and with a sharply diminished public image. The legacy of this period, in many ways, has been a powerful and generally negative influence on the campus.

The history of the very recent past and the impact of twentieth-century trends have been key influences on the development of the academic profession and have shaped its size, attitudes, training, and orientations. In a sense, American higher education is now reaping the fruits of a complicated but highly eventful series of developments at a time when resources are limited and there is little leeway for maneuver.

THE SOCIOLOGICAL CONTEXT

While this is not an essay on the sociology of complex organizations, it is important to locate the professoriate in its institutional and societal contexts.[21] Academics are at the same time professionals and employees of large bureaucratic organizations. They are certified by obtaining the doctorate and have a self-image that is close to that of independent professionals. Unlike such professionals as physicians and lawyers, academics work in complex organizations—colleges and universities—and are subject to many bureaucratic constraints. The rules and regulations of academic institutions, from stipulations concerning teaching loads to policies concerning the granting of tenure, govern the working lives of the professoriate. Despite the existence, in many institutions, of the infrastructures of collegial self-government, academics in many cases feel increasingly alienated from their institutions. Indeed, with the constraints of the 1980s, this alienation is bound to increase. One of the dilemmas of the coming period is to reconcile traditional ideas of autonomy with the demands of bureaucratic controls.

Academics continue to have considerable autonomy over their basic working conditions. The classroom remains virtually sacrosanct and beyond bureaucratic controls. Except at academic institutions at the low end of the status hierarchy, professors have considerable control over the use of their time outside of the classroom. They choose their own research topics to a considerable degree and, until recently, had considerable geographical mobility. This sense of autonomy, built up carefully over the past half-century and linked to the historical traditions of the profession, has been an important part of the self-image of the profession, especially for the top half of the academic hierarchy.

As colleges and universities have become increasingly bureaucratized and as demands for "accountability" have extended to professorial lives, this sense of autonomy has come under pressure. For one thing, the trend that decreased the average teaching load for academics, evident through the 1960s, has been halted. In addition, administrators, under pressure from governing boards and governmental authorities, have tried to subject academic life to more bureaucratic procedures. Student demands during the 1960s for "relevance" and for better teaching also spurred efforts to "regulate" the professoriate. Without question, there is now considerable tension between the norm (some would say myth) of professional autonomy and a self-image of independence and pressures for accountability and to conform to "rules." There is little doubt that the academic profession will be subjected to increased rules in the coming period as the pressure for financial survival is intensified.

The basic organizational reality of the professoriate engenders a certain amount of ambivalence. Academics, unlike the *privatdozent* of the traditional German university, do not depend directly on student fees for their survival.[22]

254   Part 3: The Academic Community

They are employed by institutions and, in the case of the public colleges and universities, are only quite indirectly dependent for their promotion, professional status, or income on their direct role—teaching. Basic judgments on such crucial matters as promotion and tenure and, at least traditionally, on salary increments, have been more related to research and publication than to teaching (at least in the universities) and such decisions are generally made by academic peers. Yet, important academic decisions are reviewed by a bewildering assortment of committees, administrators, and ultimately by governing boards. Increasingly, these levels of legal authority are becoming more important as arbiters of academic decision making. The ambivalence has always been present, but it was muted during the period of the rise of professorial power. At present, what might be seen as the inherent contradictions in the academic role are becoming more apparent.

Professorial myths—of collegial decision making, individual autonomy, and of the disinterested pursuit of knowledge—have come increasingly into conflict with the realities of complex organizational structures and bureaucracies. While many of the fondest dreams of the profession came close to reality during the period of postwar growth, some have argued that increasingly close links to external funding agencies diminished autonomy through the selective granting of research funds.[23] The tension between self-perception and the historical tradition of autonomy on the one hand and the realities of work in a complex organization, particularly in a period of considerable stress, on the other is one of the important conflicts faced by the academic profession.

The American academic system is enmeshed in a series of complex hierarchies. These hierarchies, framed by discipline, institution, rank, and specialty, help to determine working conditions, prestige, and in many ways one's orientation to the profession. As David Riesman pointed out two decades ago, American academe is a "meandering procession" dominated by the prestigious graduate schools and ebbing downward through other universities, four-year colleges, and finally to the community college system.[24] Most of this procession attempts to follow the norms, and the fads, of the prestigious graduate institutions. Prestige is defined by how close an institution, or an individual professor, comes to the norm of publication and research, of participation in the "cosmopolitan" role of links to a national profession rather than to "local" institutional norms.[25] While some segments of the academic system, such as the community colleges, have few links to the prestigious "national" universities, the system as a whole is characterized by adherence, at least in form, to national norms. Even in periods of fiscal constraint, the hold of the traditional academic models remains very strong indeed. Within institutions, academics are also enmeshed in a hierarchical system, with the crucial differences between tenured and untenured staff a key to the hierarchy. Disciplines are also ranked into hierarchies, with the traditional academic specialties in the arts and sciences along with medicine, and, to some extent, law. Other applied fields, such as education, agriculture, and others are considerably lower on the scale. These hierarchies are very much a part of the realities of the academic profession.

Just as the realities of postwar expansion shaped academic organizations by reducing teaching loads, increasing the prestige of the professoriate, and, in many institutions, expanding the power of the profession over working conditions, internal governance, and the direction of higher education, altered circumstances will inevitably change the organizational and sociological aspects of academic life in ways that will affect the professoriate. For example, there has been a noticeable rise in administrative authority as the professoriate has lost some of its bargaining position. Colleges and universities have increasingly turned to part-time faculty as a means of maintaining institutional flexibility and avoiding granting tenure. As academic institutions adjust to a period of declining resources, there will be subtle organizational shifts that will inevitably work against the perquisites of the academic profession. Universities, as organizations, adjust to changing realities and these adjustments will work against the professoriate.

THE REALITIES OF THE 1980s

There is little question but that the American professoriate is in a period of difficulty, and that prospects for the immediate future do not seem especially favorable. Yet, the profession retains many of its hard-won gains and the basic configuration of American higher education is unlikely to change dramatically. It is the purpose of this section to describe some of the realities of the current period, with particular stress on the relationship of the academic profession to the internal dynamic of colleges and universities and the impact of the broader society.[26]

Demographic Changes and the Decline of Community

The professoriate has expanded and it has also changed. These changes have significant implications for the future of the profession and for American higher education. The "age bulge," discussed earlier, means the large cohort of academics who entered colleges and universities during the 1960s and 1970s take up a disproportionate share of jobs, especially when openings have been restricted in recent years.[27] Mobility within academe has become limited. It is much harder for a mid-career academic to find another position if he or she becomes dissatisfied or desires a change in location. The "safety valve" of job mobility has been severely restricted. For a decade, there have been relatively few retirements, further restricting mobility and inhibiting entry to the profession at the lower levels.[28] Thus, for those in the profession, horizons have been diminished. As options have become limited, it is not clear whether academics have become more "local," in Gouldner's terms, concerning themselves with internal college issues and less with the broader "cosmopolitan" and intellectual concerns of the profession.[29]

Fewer entry-level academic jobs has also had a major impact. Perhaps the greatest long-term result is a "missing generation" of younger scholars. The combination of the enlarged academic cohort of the 1960s and the decline of new positions in the 1970s has meant that in many fields, very few younger scholars are being hired. The impact on the age structure of the profession is considerable. Further, a generation of fresh ideas is being lost. Enrollments in graduate school in many fields, especially in the traditional arts and sciences, has dramatically declined, and the most able undergraduates no longer choose an academic career. According to some demographic projections, there will be another shortage of trained doctorates in the next decade, causing different but nonetheless serious strains on the profession and on postsecondary institutions.[30] Complicated demographic pressures are a serious cause for concern.

Not only has the profession expanded, but it has changed in its composition. The largely white Protestant configuration of American academics has yielded to an influx of minorities and women. Jews and Catholics entered the profession in larger numbers than ever before following World War II.[31] More recently, and in part in response to the civil rights movement, the women's movement, and affirmative action pressures, the numbers of racial minorities and women have also increased. These developments have changed the nature of the profession. No longer is there a generally held consensus about the values and norms of the profession. There is more diversity and sometimes dispute among academics. Resistance, particularly to affirmative action, has been widespread, and it has been heightened by the deteriorating job market.[32] Differences in attitudes and orientations are evident among academics of different ages, institutions, and disciplines. Social scientists tend to be more liberal than those in professional schools. Those in high-prestige institutions are more liberal than those lower on the academic pecking order. Commitments to teaching and research vary. Women tend to have slightly different orientations toward the profession than men.[33] Variations within the profession have made a common viewpoint difficult, if not impossible.

Sheer size has also made community more difficult. As institutions have grown to include well over 1,000 academic staff and have substituted elected senates and other governance arrangements for the traditional general faculty meeting, a sense of community has become more difficult. Even academic departments in larger American universities can number up to fifty teaching staff. Committees have become ubiquitous and the sense of participation in the academic enterprise has declined. The bureaucratization discussed earlier has also contributed to this decline in a sense of community. This has been paralleled at the national level, where at one time the American Association of University Professors spoke for a relatively united profession. Now, the

AAUP is challenged by such organizations as the American Federation of Teachers and the National Education Association, as well as a range of large and articulate groups representing the various academic disciplines.

Tenure and Unions

The rise of the academic union movement is a direct reflection of the pressures of the academic profession. As the professoriate has seen its economic status eroded (after more than a decade of substantial gains in "real income," academic salaries began to decline in terms of actual purchasing power in the early 1970s), professional prerogatives threatened by bureaucratization and, in general, perquisites and autonomy less secure, sections of the profession turned to unions as a means of protecting status and advantages. It is fair to say that the American professoriate has turned to unionization reluctantly, and despite present difficulties, academic unions remain quite rare in the prestigious institutions. The number of campuses represented by academic unions was 682 in 1980. Of this number 254 were four-year institutions. This constituted about 17.8 percent of the 3,055 academic institutions in the United States. If community colleges are excluded, only 10.8 percent are unionized. Further, none of the members of the prestigious Association of American Universities was unionized. Thus, while academic unions tend to be concentrated in the middle and lower tiers of the system, the union movement has been one of the major responses to deteriorating conditions and uncertainties experienced by the profession. The growth of the academic union movement has slowed in the past few years, probably as a response to the realization that unions have been unable to solve the basic problems of the profession. The Supreme Court decision in the *Yeshiva* case, which makes unionization at private institutions quite difficult, will further inhibit the expansion of the movement. Despite recent setbacks, academic unions are a lasting and important part of the contemporary postsecondary education scene. Their rise has been directly related to the problems experienced by the academic profession in the past decade.

Unions were, in the early period, quite effective in raising salaries, but they have been less successful in protecting professional concerns. The worries of many academics have turned from purely economic issues to matters of protecting job security, tenure, and the like. To date, academic unions have been only marginally successful in such matters. Neither the rhetoric of the American Association of University Professors nor the trade-union tactics of the American Federation of Teachers has kept academic institutions, and sometimes legislatures, from raising teaching loads and in general contributing to a deterioration in academic life styles.

Tenure has been very much related to the rise of the union movement and with efforts to maintain job security.[34] Originally intended to protect the academic freedom of individual academics, the tenure system has grown to represent the key means of promoting academics and then granting them permanent employment. The tenure system has come under attack from a number of quarters. It has become more difficult for an assistant professor to attain tenure (and usually promotion to associate professor) as standards have been raised. The system, which at one time protected junior staff by indicating a maximum number of years that one could remain in a lower academic rank, now places immense pressure on assistant professors to meet increasingly stiff promotion criteria within six years. In addition, a growing number of institutions have instituted tenure quotas in an effort to maintain a balance between the various academic ranks. This places additional pressures on junior staff.

Retrenchment—the firing of academic staff without regard to tenure—has been one of the major fears of academics.[35] Institutions, under increasing pressure from declining enrollments, fiscal cutbacks, and changing student interests, have tried to cut costs and to reallocate academic resources to meet a changing market. Academic institutions have engaged in retrenchment only after careful consideration and, so far, rather infrequently. But there has been some retrenchment, and in a number of institutions, cuts have been made without regard to tenure, seniority, or other traditional protectors of job security. Institutions have eliminated departments or programs with relative impunity.[36] The courts have generally ruled that colleges and universities have the right to engage in this kind of reallocation of resources or response to fiscal crisis without regard to the protection of tenure but have demanded a careful definition of fiscal exigency. Thus, the traditional protection of the tenure system for permanent academic appointment has been severely vitiated by the problems of the 1970s and 1980s, and academics are beginning to realize that they have, in fact, relatively few legal protections for their job security.

There is no doubt that the intertwined issues of the growth of academic unions, the protection of traditional tenure and the related concept of academic freedom, and the general decline in the status and standards of academic life will have an impact. Some have raised the question that if it is possible for administrators or governing boards to fire professors for fiscal exigency, can the financial issue be used to make firings for other reasons? The issues are complex and, without question, place additional strains on the academic profession. What was once a profession with considerable job security has become much less secure in terms of employment. While most academics at present have few fears of losing their jobs, there is little doubt that the realities of the 1980s will bring a consciousness of insecurity more to the profession.

Accountability and Autonomy

Academics have traditionally had a high degree of autonomy, particularly in their classrooms and research, and only minimal accountability. While most academics are only dimly aware of it, the thrust toward accountability has begun to affect their professional lives. It is likely that this trend will intensify. Institutions, often impelled in the case of public universities by state budget offices, require an increasingly large amount of data concerning faculty work, research productivity, the expenditure of funds for ancillary support, and other aspects of academic life. What is more, criteria for student-faculty ratios, levels of financial support for different types of postsecondary education and for productivity of academic staff have been established. The new sources of data permit fiscal authorities to monitor closely how institutions meet established criteria and adjustments in financial allocations are then quickly implemented. Most of these aspects of accountability are only indirectly perceived by most academics, but they nonetheless have a considerable impact on the operation of universities and colleges, since resources are allocated on the basis of formulas that are measured through the new means of accountability.

If autonomy is the opposite side of the accountability coin, then one would expect academic autonomy to have significantly declined. But, at least on the surface, this has not as yet happened in the United States. Basic academic decisions remain in the hands of departments for the most part, and individual faculty members, despite some pressure and a few changes, have not felt basic change in this area. Most academics retain most of the sense of autonomy that has characterized the past several decades, although many are beginning to worry. Yet, some change is evident, particularly in the less prestigious sector of postsecondary education. There have been pressures on academics in low-enrollment fields to participate in retraining programs. Pressure to have a minimum number of students in class has increased in many institutions. Academic planning, traditionally far removed from the individual professor and seldom impinging on one's academic career, has become somewhat more of a reality as institutions seek to streamline their operation and worry more about enrollments. Yet, basic individual autonomy remains fairly strong.

Academic Freedom

American higher education at present enjoys a fairly high degree of academic freedom. There have been few public pressures aimed at ensuring political or intellectual conformity from professors and the concept of academic freedom seems fairly well entrenched. During the 1980s, some pressure has come from student organizations such as Accuracy in Academe (AIA), a conservative organization concerned with so-called liberalism in the professoriate. But the profession, and virtually all administrators and governing boards, have rejected AIA pressure. The 1980s, however, has been a fairly apolitical period on campuses and thus there have been few problems. This situation is in sharp contrast to the 1950s, when McCarthyism had a considerable impact in the universities and campus administrators did not, in general, effectively protect the academic freedom of the faculty.[37] During the politically volatile period of the Vietnam war, academic freedom was generally defended in America, and few questioned the rights of academics to speak out on the war or related political issues. The record, however, was not entirely spotless. The firing of Bruce Franklin at Stanford University, for example, was a case in which the political views and the political actions of a professor were called into question. A number of junior faculty were not given tenure during this period because of their antiwar activism as well.[38] There is little evidence that retrenchment, tenure quotas and the like have been used in any substantial way for political reasons. There have been few calls, from government officials or the public, for "loyalty" from the campus. At least for the present, the multiple crises of the "steady state" have not substantially impinged on the academic freedom of the professoriate. While one might hope that some lasting gains have been made since the dark days of the 1950s, it will take another political crisis in the country to prove the point.

Students

The two basic elements of the academic equation are students and faculty. Students have greatly affected the current status of the academic profession. Increases in student numbers during the 1950s and 1960s were, of course, the major cause for change at that period. Recently, declines in enrollments at some institutions and changes in the configuration of student interest in many colleges and universities have greatly affected the academic profession. During the 1960s, the student activist movement had several impacts on the professoriate. For the first time, militant students attacked the university and the academic profession, and this demoralized many academics. Demands for relevance in the curriculum, for political consciousness and participation by professors, and for "participation" in governance all related to the profession. Despite considerable pressure, campus unrest, and demonstrations, the lasting impact of the student movement on the American university has been minimal.[39] Yet, the effect on the morale of the faculty can hardly be overestimated. Many academics felt guilty about their lack of involvement and lost confidence in the traditional curriculum. Administrative handling of student protest polarized and disoriented the faculty.

In the late 1970s, student interests and concerns changed, but their impact on the academic profession continues.[40] Changing student interests and concern with vocational rather than social relevance have meant a substantial shift in student academic interests. While students have not been interested in activist or ideological politics, they have been concerned with environmental issues, and with matters directly concerning their own special interests. The academic profession has regained some of its self-confidence, and the current interest at many institutions in the reform of the undergraduate curriculum is an indication of this trend among academics.

Students have a direct and indirect impact on academics. Student interests and attitudes affect the classroom and enrollments in different fields of study. Student opinions of the faculty affect morale and orientations. And a highly political atmosphere on campus, as existed during the 1960s, engendered a sympathetic reaction among some academics and concern among most.

CONCLUSION

The portrait presented in this essay is not a very optimistic one. The academic profession has been under considerable pressure but it is basically intact. Some of the gains made during the postwar period of expression have been lost but such losses are probably inevitable in view of the changed circumstances, the deterioration in the employment market, and economic problems for higher education. Further, comparisons with the period of unprecedented expansion during the 1950s and 1960s heighten the sense of crisis since this was an era of abnormal growth that benefitted the academic profession.

The professoriate stands at the center of any academic institution and in a way is insulated from indirect interaction with the many of higher education's external constituencies. Academics do not generally deal with trustees, legislatures, or parents. Their concerns are with their own teaching and research, and with their direct academic surroundings, such as the department. Yet, these constituencies have a major effect on the careers and conditions of the academic profession.

It is possible to summarize some of the basic trends that have been pointed out in this essay. While some of these factors have moderated in the past several years, they remain basically operative and are likely to influence the future of the academic profession.

- A decline in federal research expenditures has made research funds in many fields very difficult to obtain.

- Financial difficulties for scholarly publishers have reduced the opportunities for book publishing, thereby placing added stress on younger scholars who are faced with ever higher qualifications for tenure and promotion.

- Students have turned to vocational interests and their curricular choices have caused strains in such fields as business, engineering, and pre-medicine and have severely curtailed enrollments in foreign languages and the social sciences.

- Demands for accountability for expenditures from governmental authorities and elsewhere have inevitably extended to measuring faculty productivity in various ways.

- Fiscal problems combined with stable or even declining enrollments in many academic institutions have caused major financial problems for higher education, affecting the faculty in reduced travel budgets, sometimes higher teaching loads, and salary increases that have not kept pace with inflation.

- In a climate of increased accountability, academic administrators have gained increasing power over their institutions and, inevitably, over the lives of the professoriate.

- A decline in public esteem for higher education, triggered first by the unrest of the 1960s and enhanced by widespread questioning of the academic benefits of a college degree, has caused additional stress for academics and has contributed to financial exigencies.

- The academic employment market permits relatively few younger scholars to enter the profession and promises to reduce salaries further and limit mobility for those currently in the profession.

Given all of these stresses and the variety of forces, within and outside of the colleges and universities, combining to weaken the status of the academic profession, it is surprising that the basic working conditions of American academics have remained relatively stable. The basic structure of postsecondary education remains virtually unchanged despite many pressures for reform. Academic freedom, despite some challenges, remains largely intact. Despite criticisms of the tenure system, and its increasingly weak legal basis, most tenured academics can have a reasonable assurance of lifetime employment. Academics retain basic control over the curriculum, generally control their academic departments, and have a reasonable influence on institutional governance. Thus, despite serious problems, the profession remains intact as it enters the 1980s. The future does not hold promise of much improvement, but if the academic profession can maintain its self-confidence and a vision of quality and the academic role, it has a good chance to maintain itself in a period of considerable difficulty.

Without question, the "glory days" of the postwar period will not reappear in the near future. A combination of circumstances including demographic changes, increasingly conservative policy makers at both the state and federal levels who do not see education as a high priority, a decline in the public esteem given to higher education, and less stress on research as a national priority directly affects colleges and universities and the professoriate. How, then, can academics face the challenges of the coming period?

At one level, the academic profession needs to represent effectively its interests to external constituencies. Most academic unions have taken on the tactics and rhetoric of traditional trade unions and tend not to work with university representatives in an effort to convince the public of the value of higher education and of the key role and importance of the profession.

Curiously, only the American Association of University Professors has effectively retained a professional image, and it has lost some of its membership. At the same time, unions do have a role in attempting to protect the hard-won prerogatives of the profession. Academic unions, a relatively new phenomenon, have not fully developed an articulate approach to issues of academic governance, representation of the faculty, and a public stance helpful to higher education. The unions are a powerful new force in higher education. If they can effectively represent the professoriate to the various external constituencies, they can play a powerful role.

The profession mostly reacted to the challenges of the postwar period. It was glad to accept more responsibilities, move into research, and take money from external agencies. It dropped much of its responsibility to students (at least in the universities) as research came to dominate the academic scene. The curriculum lost its coherence in the rush toward specialization. Now, it is necessary to develop a central thrust to the academic enterprise and to restore a sense of mission. The current "general education" movement may be a move in this direction. It is always more difficult to induce change as a result of conscious planning and concern than it is to react to external circumstance. But the present period demands that the profession examine closely its mission and role.

NOTES

*I am indebted to Lionel Lewis, Robert Berdahl and S. Gopinathan for their comments on an earlier draft of this essay. For further discussion of these themes, see Philip G. Altbach, "The Crisis of the Professoriate," *Annals of the American Academy of Political and Social Science,* 448 (March, 1980), pp. 1-4 and Philip G. Altbach, *Comparative Perspectives on the Academic Profession* (New York: Praeger, 1977).

1. Howard R. Bowen and Jack H. Schuster, *American Professors: A National Resource Imperiled,* (New York: Oxford University Press, 1986). See also Martin J. Finkelstein, *The American Academic Profession: A Synthesis of Social Scientific Inquiry Since World War II,* (Columbus: Ohio State University Press, 1984) for a compilation of data from the research on the academic profession.

2. Kenneth P. Mortimer and Michael I. Tierney, *The Three R's of the Eighties: Reduction, Reallocation and Retrenchment,* (Washington, D.C.: American Association for Higher Education, 1979).

3. It is significant that, despite affirmative action programs, the proportion of women in the academic profession has not dramatically increased.

4. See Verne A. Stadtman, *Academic Adaptations* (San Francisco: Jossey-Bass, 1980), pp. 46-74 for an overview of the academic profession.

5. Edward Shils, "The Academic Ethos Under Strain," *Minerva* 13 (Spring 1975): 1-37.

6. Robert Birnbaum, "Unionization and Faculty Compensation: Part II," *Educational Record* 57 (Spring 1976): 116-118.

7. See E. D. Duryea and R. S. Fisk, eds., *Faculty Unions and Collective Bargaining* (San Francisco: Jossey-Bass, 1973) and E. C. Ladd, Jr. and S. M. Lipset, *Professors, Unions and American Higher Education* (Berkeley, Calif.: Carnegie Commission on Higher Education, 1973).

8. E. C. Ladd Jr., and S. M. Lipset, *The Divided Academy: Professors and Politics* (New York: McGraw-Hill, 1975).

9. E. D. Duryea, "The University and the State: A Historical Overview," in this volume, 17-37.

10. See A. B. Cobban, *The Medieval Universities* (London: Methuen, 1975), 196-217.

11. Joseph Ben-David and Awraham Zloczwer, "Universities and Academic Systems in Modern Societies." *European Journal of Sociology* 3, no. 1 (1962): 45-84.

12. Frederick Rudolph, *The American College and University: A History* (New York: Vintage, 1965).

13. For a comprehensive view of the development of the modern American university, see Laurence R. Veysey, *The Emergence of the American University* (Chicago: University of Chicago Press, 1965).

14. This theme is developed at greater length in David Henry, *Challenges Past, Challenges Present* (San Francisco: Jossey-Bass, 1975).

15. The academic job market of this period is captured well in Theodore Caplow and Reece McGee, *The Academic Marketplace* (New York: Basic Books, 1958).

16. See Logan Wilson, *American Academics, Then and Now* (New York: Oxford University Press, 1979).

17. Jacques Barzun, in a chapter entitled "Scholars in Orbit," has some biting comments on jet-set faculty. See Jacques Barzun, *The American University* (New York: Harper and Row, 1968).

18. See Landon Y. Jones, *Great Expectations: America and the Baby Boom Generation* (New York: Coward, McCann and Geoghean, 1980) for a general discussion of the impact of the baby boom of the post-World War II period.

19. The turmoil of the 1960s is covered well in S. M. Lipset, *Rebellion in the University* (Chicago: University of Chicago Press, 1976) and in Michael W. Miles, *The Radical Probe* (New York: Atheneum, 1971). Faculty activism is discussed in Edward E. Ericson, Jr., *Radicals in the University* (Stanford, Calif.: Hoover Institution Press, 1975).

20. See David Riesman and Verne Stadtman, eds., *Academic Transformation: Seventeen Institutions Under Pressure* (New York: McGraw-Hill, 1973).

21. For a broader discussion of these themes, see Talcott Parsons and Gerald M. Platt, *The American University* (Cambridge, Mass.: Harvard University Press, 1973).

22. In the traditional German universities, the rank of *privatdozent* was given to academics who were paid directly by their students. If few students attended lectures, income was very limited. In a sense, the increasing number of part-time teachers in American higher education are perhaps linked to this marginal academic role. See Alexander Busch, "The Vicissitudes of the Privatdozent," *Minerva* 1 (Spring 1963): 319-341.

23. Robert Nisbet has argued in *The Degradation of the Academic Dogma* (New York: Basic Books, 1971), that academe has suffered greatly because it gave up its basic orientation toward disinterested teaching and scholarship in order to gain the advantages of government and foundation largesse. Autonomy, he argues, was lost at that point. For a somewhat similar argument from a different point of view, see Edward T. Silva and Sheila Slaughter, "Prometheus Bound: The Limits of Social Science Professionalization in the Progressive Period," *Theory and Society* 9 (1980): 781-819.

24. David Riesman, "The Academic Procession," in D. Riesman, *Constraint and Variety in American Education* (Garden City, N.Y.: Doubleday, 1958), pp. 25-65.

25. Alvin Gouldner, "Cosmopolitans and Locals: Toward an Analysis of Latent Social Roles, I and II," *Administrative Science Quarterly* 2 (December 1957 and March 1958): 281-303 and 445-467.

26. For an overview, see Carol Herrnstadt Shulman, *Old Expectations, New Realities: The Academic Profession Revisited* (Washington, D.C.: American Association for Higher Education, 1979).

27. See Landon Y. Jones, *Great Expectations.*

28. At least at one major university, there has been an influx of professors entering law school. The meaning of this development is unclear, but it might well signal a dissatisfaction with academe.

29. Alvin Gouldner, "Cosmopolitans and Locals."

30. The data on this topic is mixed and, given the accuracy of previous projections, subject to considerable question.

31. Stephen Steinberg, *The Academic Melting Pot: Catholics and Jews in American Higher Education* (New York: McGraw-Hill, 1974).

32. E. C. Ladd, Jr. and S. M. Lipset, *The Divided Academy,* discuss the variations in opinions and values of the academic profession.

33. See Oliver Fulton, "Rewards and Fairness: Academic Women in the United States," in *Teachers and Students,* Martin Trow, ed. (New York: McGraw-Hill, 1975), 199-248. See also Bonnie Cook Freeman, "Faculty Women in the American University: Up the Down Staircase," *Higher Education* 6 (May 1977): 165-188.

34. Bardwell Smith, ed., *The Tenure Debate* (San Francisco: Jossey-Bass, 1973).

35. See Marjorie C. Mix, *Tenure and Termination in Financial Exigency* (Washington, D.C.: American Association for Higher Education, 1978).

36. Kenneth P. Mortimer and Michael Tierney, *Three R's of the Eighties.*

37. See Ellen Schrecker, *No Ivory Towers: McCarthyism and the Universities,* (New York: Oxford University Press, 1986).

38. Joseph Fashing and Steven F. Deutsch, *Academics in Retreat,* (Albuquerque, N.M.: University of Mexico Press, 1971).

39. Alexander W. Astin, et al. *The Power of Protest,* (San Francisco: Jossey-Bass, 1975).

40. For a discussion of the current student scene, see Arthur Levine, *When Dreams and Heroes Died,* (San Francisco: Jossey-Bass, 1980). See also, Arthur Levine, "The College Student: A Changing Constituency," in this volume, 267-276.

13

The College Student:
A Changing Constituency

Arthur Levine and Eric Riedel

Today's college students are different from the students who attended our universities only a little over a decade ago. First of all, there are more of them. Their number has risen from a little under 8 million in 1969 to almost 12.5 million in 1986, an increase of 50 percent.[1]

Second, their enrollment patterns have changed. Many more students than in the past are attending school part-time, in excess of 40 percent today. The majority of undergraduates work in addition to going to college. Two out of every five are enrolled in nighttime classes. And transfer and drop-out rates have risen appreciably. In short, current students are more mobile, less tied to a single institution, and college is a less central part of their lives.[2]

Third, the composition of the student body has changed. High-achieving young people from wealthier families with better educated parents are, as in the 1960s, most likely to attend college. However, increases have been registered in the proportion of students from traditionally underrepresented minority groups—blacks, women, the handicapped, and adults twenty-five years of age and over, among others.[3] Today's students are, as a result, more diverse in needs and more diverse in desires than their predecessors.

Fourth, and finally, student character has changed. When student personnel administrators from nearly 600 colleges and universities were given a list of fifty-two words and phrases and asked to describe how students on their campuses had changed since 1969-70, they said that today's students were more career-oriented, better groomed, more concerned with material success, more concerned with self, and more practical.[4] Today's undergraduates want slightly different things out of life than the generation of the sixties and, as a consequence, they are demanding somewhat different things of college.

These changes are important. Their ramifications extend not only to the campus, but to the publics of higher education as well.

THE POLITICS OF A CHANGING CONSTITUENCY

Not long ago a faculty member at Bradford College was talking to her students. She said every generation, by virtue of living in the world at the same historical moment, has shared events that bind them: for the generation born after World War I, there was the Depression; for the youngsters born a little later, there was Pearl Harbor or perhaps the death of Franklin Roosevelt; for her own generation, it is the assassination of John Kennedy. She said that we all know where we were when we heard the news. She asked the members of the class where they were. The students looked at her. She looked at them. Silence. Finally, a young woman in the back said—"We weren't born yet."

The majority of today's college freshmen were born in 1969. They were born after the New Frontier ended, after Lyndon Johnson's Great Society, and after the assassinations of Martin Luther King and Robert Kennedy. They were born the year men landed on the moon. They were four when the Vietnam War ended. They were five when Watergate reached its painful conclusion. The dominant events in our lives are at best history to them. The emotions they stir in us—optimism, hope, triumph, anger, pain, sadness—do not stir in them.

For the most part, the present generation of college students knows two presidents—Jimmy Carter and Ronald Reagan. They know about a turbulent economy and a tough job market. They know about the splintering of the American family, international tensions, terrorism, and the threat of nuclear war. They think things were bad during the Carter years and that things are comparatively better now.

There is a sense among today's undergraduates that their world is falling apart, that there is little left to hold onto. In the late seventies, one of the authors described the resulting mood among college students as a "Titanic mentality"—a shared sense that the ship, call it the U.S. or the world, was going to sink. Forced to ride on a doomed vessel, students decided to go first class—seek all the goodies to make the voyage as luxurious as possible as long as the ship is still afloat. They had turned inward and could be described as inceasingly self-concerned. They were far more optimistic about their personal futures than about our collective future together.

In recent years, there have been important changes, though the Titanic imagery remains accurate. Current students are somewhat less pessimistic than their predecessors, though the majority still say they are apprehensive about the future. In 1975, more than three out of four students expressed this opinion. Today, the number has fallen to three out of five (according to unpublished Carnegie Foundation Student Surveys).

The area in which anxiety remains high, however, is the job market. And here it is very high. A casual conversation with students on almost any college campus shows that work is their primary focus. But survey data make it crystal clear: three out of four students are worried about their job prospects; two out of five would take a job right now rather than waiting for graduation to take the same job or leave college if it was not helping their job chances (according to unpublished Carnegie Foundation Student Surveys).

The work-world anxiety is matched by an increasing concern with obtaining the material rewards of life. The overwhelming majority of college students say it is essential or very important not only to be well off financially, but to be *very* well off. This number has risen from less than half in 1969 to two-thirds in 1975, to three-quarters in 1985 (Carnegie Foundation Student Surveys). At Bradford we have an event each year called Freshman Inquiry in which all students are asked to write an essay about their future plans, freshman experience, doubts, questions, and hopes and meet with a faculty, student, administrative panel to discuss plans. One young woman wrote that after college she wanted to be the chief executive officer of a multinational corporation, a U.S. Senator, the head of a foundation that gave scholarships to higher education, and work for nuclear arms control. She was asked what she needed from college to achieve these goals. She said, "A killer instinct." She was asked about social responsibility. No response. She was questioned about nuclear arms control, thinking there was the chink in her armor. She dismissed the point by saying, "Sure, if there is a nuclear war I'm not going to get to run a multinational corporation." Another student at a midwestern college put it far more simply. She said "Money is nice, poor is not nice and I like nice."

All of this translates into a unique brand of politics for the current generation. It could be characterized as the politics of me.

More traditional political perspectives are fading. Between 1969 and 1984 the percentage of freshmen who considered it essential or very important to keep up with political affairs dropped from 51 percent to 38 percent. Today's undergraduates are for the most part apolitical.

They describe themselves as more conservative than the students of the sixties and seventies. In 1969, 81 percent of college freshmen said they were middle-of-the-road to liberal. Today middle-of-the-road to conservative accounts for 76 percent of students. Yet student attitudes belie this trend. They increasingly favor liberal issues such as women's rights, and oppose conservative planks such as the death penalty (see Table 1).

At bottom, one suspects that what students are actually saying is that they have been through a lot of changes and simply want stability. They want a chance to achieve their individual and personal dreams. This is the heart of their politics.

POLITICAL AND PERSONAL ATTITUDES AND ACTIVITY

Students are seeking something they can hold on to; something stable and secure that will assure them of the material returns they want. Political

270 Part 3: The Academic Community

TABLE 1
Political Attitude

Political Orientation	1969	1975	1985
—Left to liberal	44%	36%	24%
—Middle of the road	37%	39%	37%
—Conservative	19%	26%	38%

*　　*　　*

	1969	1975	1985
—Capital punishment should be abolished	—	36%	41%
—Only volunteers in army	65%	70%	48%
—Women given preference with men of equal ability and qualities	—	26%	41%
—Private corporations too concerned with profits, not enough with responsibility	79%	76%	—
—Too much concern with rights, not enough with responsibility	54%	60%	56%

SOURCE: Carnegie Foundation Student Surveys

activity is not considered a particularly effective way of making things better for themselves because "better" is defined from an individual rather than a collective perspective. While the liberal/conservative/middle-of-the-road mix has changed, the overall level of political involvement according to most polls is down. Traditional political party politics do not interest most college students, though in the Republican versus Democratic on-campus battle the GOP claims 980 clubs to the Democrats 150.[4] "Through organizational and marketing savvy, the Republicans have translated this vapid materialism into an electoral majority. Republicans have discovered the formula that sells on campus: concentrate on economics and national self-esteem and avoid social issues that might force kids to curtail their vices."[5] Whatever the reason, the few issues that stir most students are primarily self-serving: student aid and military involvement.

Exceptions to the general trend exist; most notably the involvement of college students in activities concerning South Africa. For the most part South Africa has been an issue only on the campuses of research universities and elite liberal arts colleges. Apartheid stirs a response in activist students reminiscent of the campus civil rights activism of the early sixties. At that time some students joined with black leaders in advocating black access to the American dream. Similarly, some students today are sympathetic to the call for equal opportunity expressed by South Africa's overwhelmingly non-white majority. That the anti-apartheid/divestment rallying cry poses no real threat to American student economic interests is a fact. And the initiative on a number of campuses, say deans of students interviewed, has come from blacks who see South Africa as a way of attracting attention and ultimately addressing conditions at home. "What's in it for me?" is still the common denominator. Deans of students around the country report far lower participation in anti-apartheid demonstrations than in comparable 1960s civil rights activities.

Ethnic affinity groups (e.g., Hispanics, Arabs, Slavic countries, and all other imaginable geographic divisions) are active on many campuses, but even these groups' activities are only occasionally political, and many students join because of what the group will do for them academically and socially. Also, where activities have a political purpose, uniting the constituency is difficult, and frequently an organization will divide into subgroups. For example, at one small midwestern college the Black Student Association divided into two groups when most of the women members tired of male insensitivity to their concerns; and thereafter the two groups divided again over institutional policy on South African divestment. At last report further differentiation was imminent on integrationist versus segregationist grounds.

On another campus, the Spartacus Youth League has splintered into four subgroups: the Trotskyite League, the Labor Education League, the Labor Youth League, and the Spartacist Club. And, on the same campus, the most active, visible, and organized student group is the Collegiate Marketing Club, a group that brings to campus corporate speakers, television personalities, and the like.

Groups have fractured and fragmented. "There are 70 groups on campus where ten years ago there were 40," reports one university dean of students. "Even the traditional student government has been very erratic in bearing responsibility for things like appointments to standing committees." Instead, students will get together on an ad hoc basis to respond to a particular matter. Adhocracy appears to have replaced traditional governance on campus.

Major ideological groups on campus have virtually disappeared. According to one California community college dean of students, "students see ideological groups as a luxury! They don't want to take the time to indulge in ideological issues because they see the economic situation as grim; they don't think they'll ever be able to buy a house; and they don't know if they'll be able to get a job." When it comes to campus groups, the primary student concern is "me," and membership is measured against an individual yardstick calibrated on the basis of what membership will do for the individual *now*.

Another factor of contemporary student attitudes and activity is that students are interested in things that will help them "get away from the press" of life. An admissions officer at a major private research university in the

Midwest notes that "in addition to intramurals, there is a fledgling fraternity movement on campus; a particularly remarkable phenomenon since this university has never had fraternities!" Wellness programs, aerobic groups, jogging clubs, and weightlifting are some of the healthful escapes that have grown in popularity and participation. Personal fitness activities are important for growing numbers of students just as less salt, more fibre, cruciferous vegetables, reduced animal fat, and vegetarian menus are regulars in many campus dining halls. It remains to be seen how the trend toward individual fitness effects traditional, group-oriented intercollegiate athletic programs.

Others, in their search for stability, have turned self-destructively inward to escape pressures and uncertainties that they perceive to be greater than those faced by any previous college student generation, and here is the darker side of the "me" generation. Amongst college-age youth depression, suicide, and eating disorders have emerged as major concerns for student development services on college campuses, in addition to the more familiar, but still destructive reality of alcohol and other drug abuse.

As one dean put it, "If you can't manipulate the external environment, manipulate the internal environment." Chemical substances to alter moods are readily available throughout society, and college students are certainly a population at risk. Despite a nearly universal twenty-one-year-old drinking age, alcohol/drug awareness programs, and growth of activities by Students Against Drunk Driving (SADD), BACCHUS (a nonprofit organization that promotes responsible drinking by college students), and National Collegiate Alcohol Awareness Week (NCAAW), abuse of alcohol and other drugs continues to be a serious problem.

In addition to drugs, sexually transmitted diseases like Herpes, Chlamydia, AIDS, ARC (AIDS-Related Complex) are permanent and potentially lethal illnesses that make late adolescent/young adult sexual activity decidedly dangerous. Sexual activity that for some students in previous generations afforded escape (with the not infrequent consequence of unplanned pregnancy) is now a path of potential destruction, a new phenomenon for the post antibiotic generations. "When you have sex with someone these days you are having it with everyone they've ever had sex with."

The popularity of science fiction literature, the revival of fraternities and sororities, and the abundance of self-help/self-improvement books on campuses reflect the lighter side of this inward escape. Indeed, the popularity on the college lecture circuit of humorists, self-improvement experts, and successful business figures contrasts sharply with the reform and revolution spokespersons of the sixties and seventies.

To the extent that student interest in politics has decreased, interest in business has increased. The corporate world is perceived as "the" environment that will provide the material goods students seek. In academe this translates into large numbers of students enrolling in pre-business courses, a trend to which higher education institutions respond by adding more business, management, and administration courses to their curricula.[6] Registrants for the Graduate Management Admission Test (GMAT) have increased dramatically, and pressure from students (and their parents) demanding places in pre-business and pre-professional courses has had a substantial impact in general education circles. Institutions have hastened to launch departments and expand offerings, and there is an uneasy tension between the humanists and social scientists on the one hand and business faculty on the other.

INVOLVEMENT IN INSTITUTIONAL GOVERNMENT

Despite this enormous impact on the current curriculum by students, the omnipresent sixties' demand for "student power" has vanished. It is completely gone. Current students are not eager to participate in institutional government. Only a minority are interested in student control or voting on discipline problems, the content of courses, and degree requirements. In fact, only slightly more than half want such a role in residence halls. These numbers have decreased continuously for the past three decades. Along with this has come a slight drop in student voting in campus elections. (See Table 2.)

TABLE 2
Students and Governance

Role of undergraduates in governance (Control or voting)	1969	1975	1985
—Bachelors degree requirement	29%	25%	18%
—Provision to content of courses	42%	32%	24%
—Residence halls	77%	70%	55%
—Student discipline	73%	64%	48%
* * *			
—Usually vote in student elections	—	44.1%	38.6%

SOURCE: Carnegie Foundation Student Surveys

This comes at a time in which a labyrinth of committees exist on college campuses, a legacy of the sixties. Students sit on most of them with the usual exceptions of budget and personnel. Yet, a number of campuses report difficulty in filling the student seats. In fact, several student-body presidents around the country complained bitterly to us or felt put upon having to furnish their colleges with a never-ending supply of students to sit on discipline committees. One threw his arms in the air and asked plaintively, "Where am I supposed to get them all? I'm no superman."

Perhaps the answer is that current students are far more pleased with college than their predecessors (Carnegie Foundation Student Surveys). They do not want college to change. They are decidedly opposed to the most discussed reforms of past years. They do not want a more elective curriculum, less emphasis on grades, more general education, less specialization, or a year of mandatory service. They eschew the universal cry of prior years that college is irrelevant. (See Table 3.)

TABLE 3
What Do You Want from College?

	1969	1975	1984
—Detailed grasp of a specialized field	62%	68%	74%
—Training and skills for a job	59%	67%	75%
—Get along with people	76%	66%	56%
—Formulate goals and values for life	71%	62%	59%

SOURCE: Carnegie Foundation Student Surveys

Despite all of this, college students remain a power in campus governance. They are probably more powerful than previous student generations.

One reason is numbers. The number of traditional college-aged students is plummeting. Institutions of higher education need desperately to keep the classrooms full. As a result higher education has changed from a seller's to a buyer's market, in which the student is increasingly powerful.

The second reason is money. More than seven out of ten colleges require students to pay a student activities fee. At a rock bottom minimum, this amounts collectively to more than one-quarter billion dollars a year. This kind of money can buy a great deal. It can be and has been borrowed by institutions to tide them over during cash flow problems. It can be and has been used to provide services that universities can no longer afford, owing to shrinking budgets. It can be and has been used to fight colleges in the courts, in the legislatures, and in the media; in some cases, student resources exceed those that the institution itself can commit. Also, it can be and has been used to achieve ends that a college desires but itself lacks the political muscle to realize.

Money is making students more powerful despite restrictions on how it can be spent. Students are to a greater extent than ever calling the tune on campus. For example, the Florida state senate voted in 1979 to give students who are charged a credit-based construction fee veto power over all building projects at the nine state universities in which their money is used. This authority previously belonged to the state regents.

Off campus the same is true. Student money is being courted and in some cases it is even being listened to. For instance, a flurry of activity resulted when student governments at several California colleges and universities considered removing their money from the Bank of America because of its investments in South Africa. Bank of America officials hurriedly trekked around the state to explain bank policies and urge students not to withdraw their accounts. When the bank said that it would not or could not sever its ties with South Africa, several schools, including San Jose State University, severed their ties with the bank.

CONCLUSION

Current college students are more powerful politically both on and off campus than any student generation of the past. The reasons are several:

- The doctrine of *in loco parentis* is moribund on most campuses, struck dead by the courts.

- The eighteen-year-old vote and the rise of student lobbies in state capitols means more clout for students.

- The conclusion of the post-World War II era of growth and the onset of hard economic and demographic times for colleges have produced an educational marketplace that favors the buyers of education (students) in contrast to the growth years that favored the sellers (institutions).

- Financial aid programs have been increasingly targeted at students rather than institutions, which strengthens the hand of the user of educational services to the detriment of the supplier. Moreover, high default rates on federally guaranteed loans have increased the U.S. government's interest in consumer problems.

- Relative to the 1960s, students have greater access to university officers and more opportunities to participate in institutional affairs. A glance at current student newspapers and those of years past bears this out.

- The growth in enrollments of nontraditional students who are older, married, and employed means that more students have competing demands outside of college and that students must be more selective in their commitment of limited discretionary time and money. They are more consumerist in orientation.

- Students are more self-interested today and more politically astute.

- Public confidence in higher education has declined substantially since the 1960s.

In short, this is the first generation both to have the vote and to live in a time when *in loco parentis* is dead. The ultimate irony, though, is that, as the basis of student power expands with increasing enrollment, so does diversity, which brings to the current generation increasing division and less in common to work for politically speaking, particularly outside the educational realm. The me-ism that divides students politically will pass with time, but it seems quite likely that the diversity will increase for the next decade, with a concomitant decline in student political coherence and effectiveness.

In aggregate, the college students of this nation might be described as a sleeping giant, but as individuals these students are more powerful than ever before. And they are beginning to realize this. When college students are asked what advice they would give a high school senior planning to attend higher education, consumer advice tops their list. "You're doing the paying, make sure they give you what you want." More than ever before the college student is in the catbird seat. What will happen remains to be seen. In the continuing skirmishes between government and higher education, college students are unlikely to be a prominent ally of either combatant. They can be expected to support whomever is on their side on a particular issue. In fact, it would not be surprising if consumerism became the rallying cry of students in the years ahead and the dominant theme governing college and university education, both on and off campus for a long time to come.

NOTES

1. *The World Almanac and Book of Facts 1987* (New York: Newspaper Enterprise Association, 1987).
2. Carnegie Council on Policy Studies in Higher Education, "National Undergraduate Survey" (Berkeley, 1976).
3. *The World Almanac and Book of Facts 1987* (New York: Newspaper Enterprise Association, 1987).
4. *The Chronicle of Higher Education* (December 3, 1986).
5. *The New Republic* (December 1, 1986).
6. Ernest Boyer, *College: The Undergraduate Experience in America* (New York: Harper and Row, 1987).

14

Comparative Reflections on Leadership in Higher Education

Martin Trow

I

In this chapter I want, first, to explore in somewhat general terms what we mean by "leadership" in universities, what its major dimensions may be; second, to contrast the American university presidency with its counterparts in other European countries; and third, to sketch the historical sources of the unique role of the university president that we have developed in America.

Finally, I will try to identify some of the structures and institutional mechanisms through which the American university president does in fact take initiatives, deploy resources, and exercise leadership. (The male pronoun will here be used conventionally to refer to both sexes.) One caveat: many of these observations about the presidency of American universities also apply to four-year colleges, and particularly to the best of them. But this chapter will focus on the role of the presidency as it can be seen in the great American research universities, perhaps thirty or so in all. Moreover, when I refer to university "presidents," I will be speaking mainly about chief campus officers, though in some multi-campus universities—for example, those in Illinois and California—the chief campus officer is called "Chancellor." The special problems of the heads of multi-campus systems deserve a lecture, or a library, of their own.[1]

Leadership in higher education in large part is the taking of effective action to shape the character and direction of a college or university, presumably for the better. That leadership shows itself chiefly along symbolic, political, managerial, and academic dimensions. *Symbolic* leadership is the ability

---

This chapter is a revision of the Ninth David D. Henry Lecture, University of Illinois at Urbana-Champaign, October 1984.

278 Part 3: The Academic Community

to express, to project, indeed to seem to embody, the character of the institution, its central goals and values, in a powerful way. Internally, leadership of that kind serves to explain and justify the institution and its decisions to participants by linking its organization and processes to the larger purposes of teaching and learning in ways that strengthen their motivation and morale. Externally, a leader's ability to articulate the nature and purposes of the institution effectively helps to shape its image, affecting its capacity to gain support from its environment and to recruit able staff and students.[2] *Political* leadership refers to an ability to resolve the conflicting demands and pressures of many constituencies, internal and external, and in gaining their support for the institution's goals and purposes, as they are defined. *Managerial* leadership is the familiar capacity to direct and coordinate the various support activities of the institution; this includes good judgment in the selection of staff, the ability to develop and manage a budget, to plan for the future, and to build and maintain a plant. *Academic* leadership shows itself, among other ways, as the ability to recognize excellence in teaching, learning, and research; in knowing where and how to intervene to strengthen academic structures; in the choice of able academic administrators; and in support for the latter in their efforts to recruit and advance talented teachers and scholars.

Any particular university president need not excel personally in all these dimensions of his office; leaders vary in how their talents and energies are distributed among these facets of academic life. Some are largely "external presidents," presenting the image of the institution to its external constituencies and seeking their support, while giving to a provost or dean the main responsibility for academic affairs and to a vice-president for administration the chief responsibility for internal management. Other presidents spend more of their time and attention on internal matters.

But however a leader fills the several dimensions of the role—in the definition of its character and purpose, in its quest for resources, in the management of its organization, or in the pursuit of ever higher levels of academic excellence—effective action in all areas requires that the president have the legal authority and resources to act, to choose among alternatives, even to create alternatives, in short, to exercise discretion. Without that discretion and the authority and resources behind it, a president or chancellor cannot exercise leadership, whatever his personal qualities.

So a discussion of leadership in American higher education must involve, first, a comparison of the potential for leadership—the power and opportunities for discretionary decisions and action—of American college and university presidents as compared with their counterparts abroad; second, some suggestions as to why those differences exist—an historical reference that allows us to see more clearly how and why our institutions and their presidents are as they are; and third, a somewhat closer examination of how American college and university presidents exercise power, and a look at some of the institutional characteristics and mechanisms that allow them to take initiatives.

II

The American university presidency in recent years has received bad press. Some of the most influential theorists about the organization and governance of higher education argue that colleges and universities are really ungovernable, and that leadership in them is impossible. James March in his various writings, alone and with collaborators, has stressed the sheer chaos and unmanageability of organizations within higher education, institutions characterized by "garbage-can decision processes," in which problems are more often evaded than solved. Colleges and universities, in his view, are prototypical "organized anarchies," characterized by ambiguous goals, unclear technology, and fluid participation.[3] Since their goals are ambiguous, nobody is sure where the organization is going or how it will get there. Decisions are often by-products of activity that is unintended and unplanned. They are not so much "made" as they "happen"—they are events in which problems, choices and decision-makers happen to coalesce to form temporary solutions. From this point of view, "an organization is a collection of choices looking for problems, issues and feelings looking for decision situations in which they might be aired, solutions looking for issues to which they might be the answer, and decision-makers looking for work."[4] Such inept, leaderless organizations must be unable to initiate anything or to innovate. As Cohen and March put it somewhat epigrammatically, "anything that requires the coordinated effort of the organization to start is unlikely to be started. Anything that requires a coordinated effort of the organization in order to be stopped is unlikely to be stopped."[5] And if the university cannot be led or moved, then consistently enough in their view,

> the presidency is an illusion. Important aspects of the role seem to disappear on close examination. In particular, decision making in the university seems to result extensively from a process that decouples problems and choices and makes the president's role more commonly sporadic and symbolic than significant.[6]

Similarly, George Keller cites Cohen, et al., approvingly when he says that "Universities love to explore process and methodology but hate to make decisions. . . . Decisions in a university often get made randomly—by deans, legislators, a financial officer, the president."[7]

But oddly enough, all of Keller's illustrative cases show just the contrary, whether he is talking about planning for cuts at the University of California; the survival of a private college in Maryland; responses to cuts at the University of Minnesota; Carnegie-Mellon; or Teachers College, Columbia. These institutions are not exceptions. While each of course is unique, with its own configuration of problems and leaders, the capacity of American colleges and universities to adapt to new circumstances, whether a demographic crisis, budget cuts, cultural and religious change, or technological explosions, is on the whole astonishing; and most of the gloomiest prophecies in recent decades have not been fulfilled. To take only one example: for at least a decade we have been told that starting in 1979 enrollments in American colleges and universities would begin to decline, impelled inexorably by a decline in the size of the college-age cohorts, a decline nationally of some 23 percent between 1979 and 1992 when these cohorts would be at their lowest levels. And according to these forecasts, the population of college-age youth would not start to grow again until perhaps 1995. It is true that the number of high school graduates peaked in 1979 as predicted; by 1984 the size of the graduating class had already fallen some 13 percent below the 1979 peak. But to almost everyone's surprise, enrollments in colleges and universities nationally did not fall; on the contrary, they actually grew by 6 percent between 1979 and 1984 overall during this time of shrinking college-age cohorts.[8]

Of course there are variations by region and by type of institution. But nevertheless, American colleges and universities have shown a remarkable capacity to respond both to recession and to declining age cohorts, and have continued to attract growing numbers. I would suggest that much of this capacity to respond creatively and successfully to difficult, and in some cases to life-threatening, circumstances must be attributed to the ability of institutional leaders to innovate, to motivate, and above all to lead. Our task is to learn more about the nature of that effective and creative leadership and how it works, rather than to assert in the face of much contrary evidence that it is impossible.

The thoughtful 1984 report of the Commission on Strengthening Presidential Leadership,[9] is also rather gloomy about the state of the college and university presidency. In the course of giving sound advice to institutions, presidents, and governing boards, the report identifies and discusses some recent and current developments that the commission believes have made the college and university presidency less attractive now to able people than it was formerly. Its authors are especially concerned with the growing constraints on the presidency ("more barbed wire around smaller corrals," as one of their informants put it). Oddly enough, though they reach the somber conclusion that "the American college and university presidency is in trouble," they note that "about one-fourth of all presidents [whom they interviewed] are quite satisfied with their situations (some are even euphoric); about one-half are clearly more satisfied than dissatisfied most of the time; and about one-fourth are dissatisfied—some even in despair."[10] But upon reading this report one is struck by the fact that many of the problems that university presidents face, including some of those that have grown in difficulty recently, arise out of the very strength and centrality of the role, a role that has no real counterpart outside the United States.

III

However constrained American college and university presidents may seem to observers, however weak and ineffective they may appear to students of university organization, they look very strong by contrast with the power and influence of their "counterparts" abroad. The question may be raised as to whether they *have* any true counterparts abroad. Certainly in any genuine sense they do not. The weakness of the "chief campus officer" (the rectors, vice-chancellors, or presidents) of European institutions of higher education, arises out of the history and development of those universities. They arose, as we know, initially as guilds of masters, in some places with important initiatives from students. European universities retained their character as corporate bodies of academics that in modern times came to be regulated, funded, and in varying degrees governed by agencies of the state. The basic power relationship in European higher education has been between the guild of academics and its chairman (the rector) on one side and the relevant church authorities or governmental ministries on the other. Their discussions have centered on the issues of autonomy and support. The leading university academic officer, whether he is called rector, vice-chancellor or president, was and still is largely a chairman of the corporate body, and on the continent and in the British ancient universities was until recently elected by the guild from among its own members. On the continent, he is still elected, though now from a wider and more politicized electorate.

Since the Second World War there has been much talk in European academic circles about the desirability of strengthening the hand of the chief officer, making him more like his American counterparts, and indeed sometimes an effort has been made to do so merely by changing his name from "rector" to "president." But I do not think that European countries or institutions have actually gone very far in that direction, beyond the change of name. The broad reforms of higher education introduced since 1968 in almost all European countries have had the effect less of strengthening the president or rector than of weakening the professoriate, "democratizing" governance internally by giving more power and influence to the nonprofessorial staff and to students; and externally, by increasing the influence of politicians, civil servants, and organized economic interest groups on institutional and regional governing boards. The literature on these reforms and reorganizations is not about more powerful institutional leadership, but about more and more complex internal group politics, with central government trying to retain and extend its influence on the nature and direction of the institutions in the face of their claims to traditional autonomies and their newly expanded participatory democracy.[11]

The comparative perspective on American higher education and its leadership is one of American exceptionalism, of a sharp contrast between the role of institutional leadership here as compared with that in almost every other modern society, as well as one of quite astonishing success. We can understand better the highly particularized character of the American college and university presidency if we look at it in historical perspective. The strength of the university presidency in this country, as compared with its overseas counterparts, arose out of the weakness of the academic profession in America throughout most of our history in conjunction with the tradition of noninvolvement by the federal government in education generally, and in higher education particularly.

These two factors—the weak academic guild and weak central government—are also related to the strength of lay boards as the chief governing bodies of colleges and universities. The lay board originated at Harvard, the first American university. The founders of Harvard, community leaders most of whom had studied at the University of Cambridge, had intended to carry on the English tradition of resident faculty control. The senior academic members of the Oxford and Cambridge colleges, the "dons," comprised then, as now, a corporate body that governed each of the constituent colleges comprising those ancient universities. But in the colonial United States there simply were no scholars already in residence. Harvard had to be founded and not just developed. Without a body of scholars to be brought together who could govern themselves, the laymen who created the institution had to find someone to take responsibility for the operation of the infant university, and that person was the president. He was in fact the only professor to begin with, and he both governed and carried a major part of instruction himself, with some younger men to help him. And this pattern lasted for quite a long time in each new institution—long enough to set governing patterns throughout our history. Harvard was established for more than eighty-five years, Yale for some fifty, before either had another professor to stand alongside its president. For a very long time, both before and after the American Revolution, many colleges and universities relied wholly on the college president and a few tutors who would serve for a few years and then go on to another career.[12]

To this set of historical facts we may attribute the singular role of the college and university president in American higher education. He combined in himself the academic role with the administration of the institution. The members of the lay governing boards from the very beginning have had other things to do, and have delegated very large powers to the president whom they appointed, a president who did not until this century have to deal with a large or powerful body of academic peers. The American college and university president still holds his office wholly at the pleasure of the external board that appoints him. Most of the rest of the academic staff have tenure in their jobs. But the president of a college or university never has tenure, at least not as president (though he may return to a professorship if he has such an appointment in the institution). That lack of tenure in office partly accounts for the broad power the board delegates to him; they can always take it back, and often do.

For a long time in American history there were very few who made academic life a career; as long as that was true there was no real challenge to the authority of the president so long as he had the support of the lay board that governed the institution. This of course is quite unlike arrangements in most other countries. European universities, as we know, arose out of guilds, the corporations of doctors and masters and other learned men in Paris, Bologna, and elsewhere. And where they arose differently, as in the modern universities, the academics in their faculties claimed the same powers as their counterparts in the ancient universities. In America, by contrast, colleges and universities were created by a lay board and a president. This has had an enormous impact on the development of our institutions.

The near absolute authority of the American college president has been lost in most of our universities over time, especially with the rise of the research university and the emergence of a genuine academic profession in the last decade of the nineteenth century. In this century, and especially in the stronger universities, a great deal of autonomy over academic affairs has been delegated to the faculty and its senates. But the American college or university president remains far more powerful than his counterparts in European institutions, whose formal authority is shared with the professoriate, the junior staff, government ministries, advisory boards, student organizations, and trade unions. The European rector or vice-chancellor really is a political man, a power broker, a negotiator, a seeker for compromise without much power or authority of his own.

IV

The role of the faculty in the governance of the leading colleges and universities in the United States is substantial and important, but it is as much a source of presidential power as a limitation on it. The two generations of presidential giants—White at Cornell, Eliot at Harvard, Angell at Michigan, Gilman at Hopkins, Harper at Chicago, Van Hise at Wisconsin, Jordan at Stanford, Wheeler at California, among others—the men who governed the great American universities between the Civil War and the First World War, essentially created the American academic profession, a development that coincided with the emergence and growth of the great research universities. Those creative presidents flourished, however, before their universities had large numbers of specialized scholars and scientists with high prestige in American society as well as national and international reputations in their disciplines. Those presidents recruited distinguished scholars and scientists, paid them decent salaries, rewarded their scholarship and research, and thus created the faculty of the modern research university, a body of men and women who could meet them, collectively at least, as equals. The American academic profession and its instruments—the senates on campus and the

American Association of University Professors (AAUP) and various disciplinary associations nationally—were the institutionalized expression or reflection of those scholars and scientists brought together in the new research universities by this generation of great university presidents. It was the growth of that body of academics, increasingly aware of their collective importance to the university and to its supporters and constituents outside the university, that gave rise to the modern university faculty, determined to be treated as members and not merely as employees of the university. They thus came to be included in the governance of the universities, in a role that stressed their right to be consulted on matters of importance to them.

In the leading universities, both public and private—though matters are quite different in the second- and third-tier universities—what has evolved is a system of shared governance, marked by a degree of cooperation and mutual trust that has survived the political stresses of the 1960s, the demands for greater accountability from state governments of the 1970s, the growth of federal law and regulation, the consequent elabortion and formalization of procedures, record-keeping and reporting, and the explosion of litigation against the university over the past two decades. Despite all of these forces and the internal stresses they have engendered, academic senates and committees in the leading universities still gain the willing and largely unrewarded participation of active and leading scholars and scientists in the process of governance by consultation. The nature of this shared governance by consultation is extremely complicated and subtle, never adequately captured in the description of the formal arrangements that differ on every campus. Moreover, the power of the faculty varies sharply depending on the status of the university and of its faculty.

It is sometimes suggested that a strong academic senate reduces the power of the president or chancellor. I believe, on the contrary, that a strong senate enhances that power. An academic senate is, above all, an instrument for the defense of academic and scholarly standards in the face of all the other pressures and demands on the university and on its president. Senates function on the whole through committees; committees are, or can be, excellent bodies for articulating and applying academic values to a variety of conditions and issues that arise. Though committees are splendid at saying no, they are poor instruments for taking initiatives or implementing them. By being consulted routinely on a wide variety of initiatives emanating from the office of the president, the senate may in fact give wise and useful advice. But above all, it makes itself and faculty sentiments felt by giving or withholding its approval and legitimacy to presidential initiatives. Without that consultation and support, the relation of president and faculty would be largely adversarial—which is what we often see where the senate has been replaced by a faculty union, or where the faculty and president are deeply at odds. And there the power of the president is certainly diminished.

Of course, there are frictions between senate and president; the relationship at its best is marked, in Jacques Barzun's words, by "the good steady friction that shows the wheels are gripping." In such a happy relationship, faculty members recognize that just as the effectiveness of the president depends in large part on a strong senate, so also does the strength of the senate depend on a strong president. It is *not* a zero sum game. For much of the senate's power is exercised through its advice to and influence on the president: where *he* has little power, *they* have little power. Effective power then lies outside the institution altogether, in the hands of politicians or ministries, as in European nations or some American states.

V

I have suggested that on historical and comparative grounds that the president of a leading American college or university can exercise leadership: symbolic, political, intellectual, and administrative. But what are his resources for the exercise of leadership, especially when looked at in a comparative perspective? What I will say here is familiar to all, and yet is often dismissed or discounted by commentators except when they are actually describing specific leaders and policies.

First, a president has substantial control over the budget of his institution and its allocation, even though his discretion is constrained by the very large fraction of the budget that is committed to tenured faculty salaries and to support services that must be funded if the institution is to continue functioning. In a public university, he usually works with a block grant; thus he can view the budget as a whole and make internal adjustments subject to the above constraints. By contrast, most European institutions are funded by central state authorities on what is closer to a line item budget—sums are earmarked for particular chairpersons and the support staff around them, and to particular services, such as a library. The rector or president ordinarily has little power over these internal allocations of funds. Moreover, in the United States it is now widespread practice, if not quite universal, that faculty vacancies resulting from death or retirement revert to the president's office and are not the property of the departments where the vacancy occurred. This reversion of resources permits the president and his associates over time to modify the internal distribution of faculty places in response to changing student demand or market demand, to developments in the disciplines themselves, or to his own ideas about the right mix of fields and subjects.

Academic autonomy is related, if not perfectly, to the multiplicity of funding sources.[13] Here again, by contrast with their European counterparts, American universities are funded in a variety of ways, which in itself gives presidents a certain power to bargain from strength in the face of demands from one or another funding source. Even such public universities as the University of California are not state-supported so much as "state-aided."

The University of California gets about 40 percent of its current operating budget from state sources; about 15 percent from federal grants and contracts; about 13 percent from fees, tuition, gifts and endowment; and about 30 percent from various enterprises such as teaching hospitals, educational extension, and sales of educational services.[14]

But in addition to the sheer multiplicity of sources, some of them are more discretionary than others. The use of unearmarked private contributions, research overhead funds, some of the return on the endowment, is largely at the discretion of the president or chancellor, though over time, of course, those discretionary funds become encumbered by expectations if not by formal programmatic commitments. Programs and people supported by such discretionary funds come to expect that they will continue to be supported. But presidents and their staffs can vary the levels of those commitments, especially if they do so incrementally, and thus maintain a genuine degree of discretionary power over their allocations.

Even where discretion is not total, it may be large within a category. For example, "student services" is a very broad rubric indeed, and gives a president equally broad discretion for shaping the mix of such services as between a learning center, medical services, counseling services, intramural athletics, recruitment and admissions, and various forms of remedial education and outreach to the secondary school system, among others. The very size of student support services in American universities, as compared with those overseas, increases the power of presidents; where academic staff is largely tenured, and their programs and departments difficult to modify except slowly and incrementally, the president has far greater (though never total) freedom to restructure support services whose staff members are not tenured (though increasingly unionized). These large support staffs report to someone directly in the president's office, and they constitute a substantial body of resources and people whom the president can draw on in support of his own priorities, again within certain political, legal, and normative constraints. A large staff provides the resources to put behind the president's own ideas about a stronger development office, or larger affirmative action programs, or whatever it is he may think important.

But the discretionary resources built into student services are only part of the staff resources available to American university presidents. In the United States, the great authority of lay governing boards, much of it delegated to the president, together with the relatively smaller role of central government, ensured that as the public universities grew and needed larger administrative staffs, those staffs would be extensions of the president's office rather than civil servants responsible to a faculty body or to state authorities. As a result, the strong president, supported by his own large administrative staff, has been able to preserve much autonomy and power inside the university. Having his own internal staff allows the college or university president to deal with state authorities with equal skill and expertise, rather than as a scholarly amateur against a body of professional planners and managers. Several points need to be made about this large internal staff:

Many staff people (and most of those at the upper levels) owe their appointments to the president they serve, and hold those appointments at his discretion. In some institutions there are "untouchables" on the staff, who have independent ties to the board or powerful alumni; these sometimes constitute a problem for new presidents.[15] But on the whole, few members of the administrative staff have any formal or informal security of employment, and even they owe their advancement, and sometimes their jobs in periods of contraction, to the sitting president. They are for the most part his employees, in a part of the university that much more closely resembles the hierarchical structures of bureaucracies than the collegial structures of departments and research centers. Presidential leadership is often found in programs that rest largely on this administrative staff rather than on the reshaping of the academic programs directly; and that, I think, is because that is where so many of his discretionary resources lie.

These support staffs under the president's direction and leadership can also develop programs that further increase his discretion. For example, strengthening a development office, increasing the effectiveness of market research and student recruitment, writing better proposals for government or foundation grants, all increase the discretion of top administrators. These activities and funds can provide the staff support for new academic programs, new links to secondary schools, remedial courses, creative connections with local industry, and other colleges and universities. They give the president the needed resources to create priorities, to be an entrepreneur and to take advantage of opportunities as they arise.

In the United States the president of a college or university is the link between "the administration" and its support services on the one hand, and the faculty and its programs of teaching, learning, and research on the other. And here again the American college and university differs fundamentally from its overseas counterparts. Almost everywhere else, alongside the rector or president stands a registrar, a "curator," an administrative officer who is not appointed by the president, and who is not really responsible to him but is appointed by the lay governing council or by a government ministry. In the United Kingdom, a vice-chancellor plays a large part in the appointment of the registrar, but the appointment is rather like a senior civil service post, and ordinarily continues beyond the term of any sitting vice-chancellor. And that sharp separation of the academic (and symbolic) leadership from the day-to-day management and administration of the institution enormously reduces the authority and discretion of the chief campus officer of European universities, as compared with his American counterparts.

In addition to the support staff I have spoken of, the American college or university president also appoints the chief academic officers; the vice-president for academic affairs, the provost, the deans, and through them the department chairmen, who are both heads of their departments and administrative officers. The president appoints them, and he can replace them. Of course he cannot do so frivolously or too often without loss of respect and credibility. Nevertheless, the fact that the president appoints the senior academic administrators, unlike his counterparts overseas (and the British case is intermediate in this regard), gives him a degree of leverage over changes in the academic program: for example, the opportunity to influence the balance of subjects, the sub-disciplines represented, and above all the quality and character of new appointments.

Another consequence of the fact that the president appoints his senior administrative colleagues, his cabinet so to speak, is that he largely defines their areas of authority and responsibility; they are not inherent in the job or office, or in fixed regulations of the institution or ministry. University presidents in the United States (unlike their European counterparts) can and indeed often do change the administrative structures under them in the service of their own purposes and conceptions of the interests of the institution. And that restructuring—ordinarily at the beginning or early in the tenure of a president—may be one of his most creative acts. Moreover, presidents can modify the charge and scope of responsibility of any given academic administrator in response to the interests, talents, and capacities of the individual whom they appoint to a post, as well as to new problems and opportunities that develop around it. In addition, leaders can create decision-making structures *ad hoc,* in response to different issues that arise.

If we ask what is the decision-making process at a college or university, we have to answer, "it depends on the issue." Different people and interests are brought together to solve or address different problems. But who is brought together to address what problems is determined chiefly by the president, and that indeed is an important area for the exercise of his discretion and the demonstration of his capacity for leadership. Should a senior academic officer be brought into a discussion of changes in admission procedures, which often conceal changes in academic standards? Should faculty members or academic senate committees be involved in decisions about the athletic program? Should a university financial officer be involved in discussions about a change in the requirements for graduation? What interests, what expertise, what individuals and perspectives should be brought together to deal with a particular problem; at what point will a greater diversity of perspectives not improve and inform a decision, but paralyze it? Those are among the most consequential judgments and decisions that a college or university president makes.

There is another mechanism of presidential power and initiative, one that lies directly at the heart of the academic enterprise, but which I think has not been adequately studied or discussed by students of American college and university life, and that is the power of a president to take a department or program "into receivership." Various observers have emphasized that colleges and universities are organizationally "bottom-heavy," in that expertise, both with respect to teaching and research, is located among the faculty members and in the departments. This is certainly true, and under ordinary conditions college and university presidents are wise not to interfere in the private life of departments, in what and how they teach, what they study, who they appoint, and who they promote. The autonomy of departments, rooted in their expertise, is an important constraint on the power of administrators, including presidents.

But in American colleges and universities, that autonomy can be over-ridden and set aside when something goes wrong: when, for example, factional fights within a department make it ungovernable, or prevent new appointments from being made, or block all promotions; or other tendencies and events lead to a decline in the unit's standing in the periodic national ranking of departments, or a fall-off in its external research support, or a degree of politicization that affects the quality of instruction, or a loss in the department's ability to attract able students or junior staff. These are among the reasons that lead presidents to take departments into receivership. When they do, they take the government and management of the unit out of the hands of the department members themselves, and of their chairman, and put it in the hands of others, with a clear understanding on how to proceed and what to do. The caretaker may be a person from another related department, or from the same discipline in another university, or even a committee of leading scientists and scholars from within the same institution. In my own university, this has happened to five or six departments over the past decade, including most recently to all of the biological sciences in some twenty-five departments and schools.[16]

The surprising thing is that when a department is "put into receivership," there is remarkably little resistance or opposition within the faculty—probably because it happens rarely enough and in extreme cases, so that there is a general consensus that something really has gone wrong. That is to say, it can be treated as an exceptional case, and the treatment of that case is not going to be an attack on the ordinary processes of academic governance in which the faculty plays a major role. Something has gone wrong, and the president or his senior advisers intervene to help put it right, so that the action is in the service of the fundamental values of the faculty anyway. It does not happen very often, but it is extremely important that it can, and there are times when departments know "we can't let things go on like this or they will come and take us over." Like all drastic sanctions, the power to put departments into receivership is a powerful threat as well as an act, and affects behavior even when it is not employed.

Control over the budget and especially over the discretionary resources in "student services"; the relatively large staff appointed by and responsible to the president; his power to set the institution's priorities, define problems, and specify who is to solve them; his power to take departments into receivership—these are some of the organizational resources and mechanisms for intervention and change by which presidential leadership can be exercised in American research universities.

VI

To sum up, this chapter is an effort to get beyond the descriptions of universities as "organized anarchies" engaged in "garbage-can processes of decision making." I believe those conceptions of the university stand in the way of a clearer description and understanding of what leadership in higher education consists of and how it functions. But if they are not true, if indeed the presidency of great research universities is as strong and effective as I claim, why has it had such bad press in recent years; why is it seen as weak, ineffective, and unattractive? Some speculations, if not explanations, may be helpful here.

First, much of the gloomiest writing about university leadership addresses the situation of weaker second- and third-rank institutions. In the American system, marked by a very high level of competitiveness among institutions for students, for faculty, for resources, for prestige and rank, the power of the leading universities as models, both as organizations and as normative communities, is very great. All universities judge themselves by the standards and criteria of the leading universities, and share their high expectations regarding research, graduate work, and institutional autonomy. But those second- and third-ranking institutions do not command the resources of the leading ones: their financial support, both public and private, their libraries and laboratories, their eminent faculties, all the traditions of autonomy that the leading institutions have gained over the years. It may be that the difficulties of university presidents in most institutions commonly arise out of the tension between their high aspirations and inadequate resources, and their resulting sense of relative failure when they compare themselves to Harvard, Stanford, Berkeley, Michigan, or Illinois.

In addition to the costs of this kind of "relative deprivation" are the often frustrating experiences of university presidents even in the leading institutions. The corral does sometimes seem smaller, the barbed wire higher than it was, or at least as it is remembered.[17] It may be that the presidency of a research university is a more effective than attractive position. In one of the most poignant commentaries on the role, the report of the Commission on Presidential Leadership quotes one president as follows:

> On any issue I will enjoy an incredibly high 90 to 95 percent of faculty support. Even so, five percent are dissatisfied with my decision, and they remember. On the next issue, I'll again enjoy the same 90 to 95 percent support, but the five to ten percent of dissenters will be a different group, and they, too, will remember. Eventually one manages to make at least one decision against the convictions of virtually every member of the faculty. By recognizing and providing an outlet for

such accumulated discontent, the formal evaluation process merely increases the speed by which courageous decision makers are turned over. This does nothing for attracting the best people into the jobs.[18]

This "accumulation of discontent" threatens to make the aggregate of many small successes into one big failure. And the inexorable erosion of support that this process describes casts its pall over both the role and the office.

Moreover, university presidents are most likely to underplay their power and effectiveness, and exaggerate the importance of the process of "shared governance" of which they are a part, than they are to claim undue credit for their achievements. In this democratic, indeed populist, age, the towering figures of the heroic age of the university presidency would surely find themselves under attack as authoritarian, power-driven, and without a sensitive concern for the interests of their varied constituencies in the university.

One example: Clark Kerr was, as we all know, a very strong chancellor of the University of California, Berkeley, from 1952 to 1958 and an equally strong chancellor of the University of California system from 1958 to 1967. In both roles he had an enormous impact on the institutions that he led—for example, he shaped the quite distinct characteristics of the new campuses of the university that were established during his tenure as president. And yet, in his seminal book, *The Uses of the University,* perhaps the most illuminating essay on the modern research university (and after some nostalgic references to the giants of the past), Kerr observes that in his own time a university president is likely to be "the Captain of the Bureaucracy who is sometimes a galley slave on his own ship."[19] And he quotes Allan Nevins's observations that the type of president required by the new university, the "multiversity" as Kerr called it, "will be a coordinator rather than a creative leader . . . an expert executive, a tactful moderator. . . ." In Kerr's own words, "he is mostly a mediator."[20]

This, I suggest, is at odds with the realities of university leadership both as Clark Kerr employed it and as it now exists. Of course, leadership may be more visible and dramatic during periods of growth and expansion, and not all presidents carry to the role the talents that Kerr did. Of course, coordination and mediation were important parts of the job, both then and now. But boldness, the undertaking of initiatives, the acting by a president on and through the institution in the service of his own conception of its nature and future—in my view, all of that does not have the weight and emphasis in Kerr's analysis of university leadership that it did in his own exercise of leadership. Kerr's analysis reflects his concern (reflected again in the report of the Commission on Strengthening Presidential Leadership that he chaired) regarding the decline of institutional leadership as a result of the growth of countervailing forces and complex power centers within and around the university. I believe his analysis also reflects his sense that modern university leaders, if they are to be effective, must keep a low profile, must appear to be finding "a sense of the meeting," rather than imposing themselves on the institution and taking important initiatives within it. If we compare the modern university president to those of the heroic age, we find today more problems, more restraints, even more resources, more of everything except authority. The exercise of authority is today often "authoritarian," and successful presidents have learned the trick of exercising authority without appearing to do so: to lead while appearing to follow, facilitate, mediate, or coordinate.

Of course the interplay among the characteristics of the person who occupies the office, the role, and the university's institutional environment is tremendously complex, and successful leadership today requires high skills and careful attention to the process of governance. And finally, even when the presidency is successful, expectations rise, troubles multiply and opposition accumulates: it is perhaps inevitably a case of "doing better and feeling worse."

This may be why presidents tend to underplay their own effectiveness. But why do observers and analysts do likewise? I have already set forth some of the reasons, but there is one other, and that is the apparent anarchy of intertwined purposeful policies in universities. I suspect that observers have been looking at the university president's role as if it were a cross-section of a thick cable, made up of many-colored strands or wires, each strand representing another program or activity, and all together in cross-section representing a heterogeneous collection of issues, solutions, and problems, showing little coherence or purpose. But in the research university this model is misleading. For if this rope is cut along the dimension of time, we see that each strand extends backwards and forwards, moving along in its own coherent, purposeful, even rational way, each marked by its own set of purposes that are largely insulated from other strands even as they intertwine.[21] So what appears as a random or haphazard collection of events, problems, evasions, and solutions when viewed in cross section at a given moment, looks more like a set of purposeful programs each being pursued in relative isolation within the boundaries of the same institution when viewed along the dimension of time. And the variety of these programs in their purposes and participants will be greater the more comprehensive and varied the role of the university in society at large.

It is this multiplicity of activities, governed by different norms and purposes in different ways, that defines the comprehensive university. And it is of some interest to consider how these activities, apparently governed by different and even incompatible values, can be pursued on the same campus, under the general authority of the same president. The key lies in the institutional insulations of activities governed by different values, and the ways in which these activities are brought together in the office of the president. One common situation finds presidents serving what appear to be the mutually incompatible values of academic excellence and social equity, the latter taking the form of increased access to the institution of underrepresented groups. In

Berkeley currently, the commitment to excellence is represented by a major reform of the biological sciences very much keyed to strengthening modern currents in biology, both in research and teaching. This involved a major intervention by the chancellor with the advice and support of leading biologists on campus, an intervention that required the creation of new institutional forms and the temporary but substantial reduction of the power and autonomy of the existing biological departments to control their own faculty recruitment, graduate training, and the like. At the same time, other units of the chancellor's office were engaged in major efforts to upgrade the secondary education of minority groups in the cities surrounding Berkeley, from which many of its undergraduates are drawn. These activities come together in the office of the chancellor, and only there, although they are carried on quite separately and in many ways are highly insulated from one another. It is doubtful if any of the distinguished biologists involved in the renewal of their discipline at Berkeley know very much about the outreach programs into the Oakland secondary schools, or the outreach staff know anything about developments in the biological sciences on campus. In the particular circumstances of Berkeley at the moment—and I suspect this is true much more widely—it is necessary for the university to serve the values of both excellence and equity, and to be seen doing so. How that is done depends very much on the sensitivity of a university leader both to his external political environment and to the internal groups and values with whom he must work, most notably the faculty.

There is of course an apparent contradiction in the values that govern these two kinds of programs. But these two strands of policy, differently colored and serving different ends and values, are not competitive but supportive, closely intertwined as they move along the dimension of time. It is, I suggest, the task of university leadership to tend both of these strands of university policy, and to weave them together. And if that is done effectively, it may not be visible to observers of the office of the president or chancellor, observers who may be more impressed by the illogic or inconsistency of the values served than by the skills and initiative that enter into their accommodation within the same institution. Of course, incoherence and the loss of institutional integrity always threaten the American research university, which says yes to almost all claims on its energies, resources, and attention. But it is precisely the nature of leadership in American universities, the broad conceptions of power and the resources at its disposal, that enable the president or chancellor to give coherence, character, and direction to an institution so large in size and aspiration, so various in its functions and constituencies, so deeply implicated in the life of learning and of action, with links to so many parts of the surrounding society. These great research universities are among the most successful institutions in the world. They could not be if their presidents were unable to give them direction as well as the capacity for responding to what is almost always an unanticipated future. It is in the office of the president that the necessary resources and opportunities lie.

VII

Problems with which we have the resources to cope can also be seen as opportunities. The great research universities currently face a series of such problems (or opportunities) that are uniquely the responsibility of their presidents, however useful their aides and staff members may be. Each of us will have his or her own short list of grave problems that face university presidents, and these lists will change over time, but my own list would include at least the following, though not necessarily in this order of importance:

(i) There is the problem each president faces of accommodating to or reconciling demands for broadened access by students from historically underrepresented groups with the maintenance of the highest standards in teaching and research. This is the familiar tension in education between equity and excellence, both served in different ways within the same institution, and to differing degrees by different institutions.

(ii) There is the problem of the evolving relations between research universities and industry. The question presents itself as how to serve industry while using its funds, research facilities, and know-how for the university's own purposes, at the same time maintaining the unique qualities— the very integrity—of the university as a place committed to the pursuit of truth in an atmosphere of open inquiry and free communication.

(iii) There are the problems created for the university by the very rapid growth of scientific knowledge, and the impact of that growth on the organization of the schools and departments of science and technology, and on the physical facilities in which science is done within the university.

(iv) Closely linked to the third is the problem of maintaining a flow of new scientists and scholars into departments and research labs, without institutional growth and with a largely tenured and aging faculty that is not retiring in large numbers until the 1990s or later.

(v) On the other side of the campus, there is the problem of sustaining the humanities and the performing arts—that is, of maintaining the crucial balance of subjects within the university—in the face of the expansion of scientific and technological knowledge, and the growing attractiveness of professional training, especially at the undergraduate level.

(vi) Finally, there is the problem upon which perhaps all others depend: the defense of freedom of speech and of academic freedom on campus in the face of intense pressure from vocal minorities of students and faculty who, unlike the rest of us, do not have to pursue the truth since they already possess it, and who are loathe to permit others with whom they disagree to express and propagate what they view to be error and pernicious doctrines. (The theological language here is intentional.)

What a list! Yet we expect presidents to cope with large problems, as no other national university system does, because in fact our society gives them the authority and the resources to cope. There are never enough resources, in their view, yet by and large they do cope. It is still in part a mystery how they cope so successfully when so much of the theory of organizational leadership tells us they cannot and should not be able to do so.

But I think that the office of the university president has not been properly appreciated; it has been the object more of compassion and criticism than of understanding. The university presidency deserves understanding, though I suspect that incumbents will continue to speak of it deprecatingly and, with good reason, as fraught with difficulties and constraints. And meanwhile, under their leadership in that extraordinary office, our research universities go on from strength to strength.

NOTES

1. On multi-campus systems, see Eugene Lee and Frank Bowen, *The Multicampus University: A Study of Academic Governance* (New York: McGraw-Hill, 1971).

2. On the distinction between organizations and institutions, and the role of leadership in defining purpose and mission, see Philip Selznick, *Leadership in Administration* (Evanston, Ill.: Row, Peterson, 1957), esp. 5-28.

3. M. Cohen and J. G. March, *Leadership and Ambiguity* (New York: McGraw-Hill, 1974), 3.

4. Ibid., 81.

5. Ibid., 206.

6. Ibid., 2.

7. George Keller, *Academic Strategy* (Baltimore: Johns Hopkins, 1983), 86.

8. Martin Trow, "American Higher Education: Past, Present and Future," in G. W. Lapidus and G. E. Swanson, eds., *Social Welfare and the Social Service: USA/USSR*, Berkeley, 1986.

9. The Commission on Strengthening Presidential Leadership, *Presidents Make a Difference* (Washington, D.C.: The Association of Governing Boards, 1984).

10. Ibid., xix and xviii.

11. See Guy Neave, "Strategic Planning, Reform and Governance in French Higher Education," *Studies in Higher Education,* 10, no. 1 (1985); and Alain Bienayme, "The New Reforms in French Higher Education," *European Journal of Education,* 19, no. 2 (1984). See for example, Maurice Kogan, "Implementing Expenditure Cuts in British Higher Education," in Rune Premfors, ed., *Higher Education Organization* (Stockholm: Almqvist and Wiksell, 1984).

12. See Frederick Rudolph, *The American College and University* (New York: Alfred A. Knopf, 1962), 161-166.

13. See Martin Trow, "Defining the Issues in University-Government Relations," *Studies in Higher Education,* 8, no. 2 (1983).

14. Private communication, University of California Budget Office.

15. Clark Kerr and Marian L. Gade, *The Many Lives of Academic Presidents: Time, Place & Character* (Washington, D.C.: Association of Governing Boards of Universities and Colleges, 1986), 27.

16. See Martin Trow, "Leadership and Organization: The Case of Biology at Berkeley," in Rune Premfors, ed., *Higher Education Organization* (Stockholm: Almqvist and Wiksell, 1984).

17. The phrase is drawn from the Commission on Strengthening Presidential Leadership, op. cit.

18. Ibid., 54.

19. Clark Kerr, *The Uses of the University* (Cambridge, Mass. Harvard University Press, 1963), 33.

20. Ibid., 36.

21. This image, and the next few paragraphs, are drawn from my essay "Leadership and Organization: The Case of Biology at Berkeley," op. cit., 166-167.

15

It's Academic:
The Politics of the Curriculum

Irving J. Spitzberg, Jr.

Never have so many said so much to achieve so little. This could be the judgment history will render about curriculum reform in American higher education in the 1980s. To understand this judgment, one will need to appreciate the structure of American higher education, the nature of academic decision making, and the social and technological environment in which academic change takes place. This chapter will provide an analysis of the politics of the curriculum. It will focus on the campus-based political system as it affects academic matters and the complex interrelationship between the campus and its larger social context.

THE HISTORICAL CONTEXT

A thumbnail sketch of the twentieth-century history of the university and college curriculum will provide the foundation of my subsequent analysis.[1] In the late nineteenth century a group of small colleges and rudimentary land grant universities began the process of professionalization: they separated the professional and the practical from the arts and sciences. At the same time, the arts and sciences themselves were becoming professionalized through the development of graduate facilities at a few institutions. On the eve of the twentieth century, the scholars plowed the fields of the disciplines and planted the seeds that would produce the husks of disciplinary dominance. As often happens with Harvard's role in the history of American higher education, its construction of the elective system directed professionalization into the undergraduate curriculum.

After the world fell apart during the First World War, there was a temporary reaction to the fragmentation and destruction as the world searched for an understanding of the cataclysm that had occurred. This search led to the reconstruction of a core in the undergraduate curriculum—e.g., the contemporary civilization sequence at Columbia University and the Hutchin's era at the University of Chicago.[2] It provided a new interest in the relationship among the arts, sciences, and social studies at the graduate level. Throughout American higher education Western civilization courses tempered electives and various Chinese menus of distribution requirements.

Just after the Second World War, the Harvard "Redbook" provided a justification for the distribution requirements that would characterize American higher education through the mid-1960s. Here the Chinese menu would charge its ideological dues and the twentieth-century enlightenment of the 1950s, with its faith in and fear of technology, would define undergraduate education as a sequence of exposures very much like the achievement of the perfect sun tan.

In the context of the turmoil brought on by the civil rights movement of the 1960s and the war protests of the 1970s, one also observed the campus revolutions. The appeal of the authority of the curriculum eroded with all other features of authority. This third moment of societal disruption and campus change differed from the earlier ones in that it destroyed the existing structure of the curriculum and left only a market basket full of products. The most anti-market social and political movement of the twentieth century had left the American curriculum at the direct mercy of the academic market. The faculty producers of the products essentially threw up their hands and said "Let them eat cake." They then were quite surprised when the consumers only wanted cake, even while the faculty producers were still producing the same pork and beans that had been their staple for years.

The American undergraduate curriculum had become a supermarket where each department offered its wares and the institution was only a sum of its parts. As in most economic markets where the structure is really oligopolistic, the big and elite departmental winners got bigger and at the same time more selective, and the small departments that accepted all comers and were not presently in demand lost on a large scale. The irony was that many of those departments most active in the revolution were the biggest losers—e.g., sociology and philosophy.

The political agenda of active participation in decision making succeeded in only one part of college life—in decisions about the curriculum—where the decision-making process, in theory governed by faculty, essentially abdicated to a market of student consumers without adequate advising and information-disseminating systems to inform decisions. The faculty, in their corporate and collegial guises, viewed the risks of campus political system judgments about value priorities as too great for the parts; yet the reward of leaving the decisions to the individual students was great for some and nonexistent for others.

By the end of the 1970s the impact of laissez faire on the undergraduate curriculum was clear in the redistribution of enrollments to professional and preprofessional courses from the arts and sciences. The change was not only in selection of majors where everyone either became preprofessional or a business major; it was also in choices of electives that served similar vocational ends. These changes had serious implications for many faculty and for the graduate schools. The surplus of Ph.D.s in many arts and sciences disciplines in the 1970s in response to high expectations but in spite of larger market forces illustrates the impact of these changes. The subsequent real decline in faculty salaries and general social support for higher education were equally traumatic legacies of the abdication of curricular responsibility in higher education. Faculty could tolerate market decision making when it did not risk the very existence of parts of the campus; when the market put at risk the core disciplines of the university and their respective faculties, then the need to reassert campus judgment about the curriculum became clear.

This account of the recent history of the curriculum suggests that major changes have correlated with—though not necessarily followed from—important social changes, often political disruptions, in the larger society. Even when there was a clear and landmark event or sequence of events such as a war or the civil rights movement, the campus changes always emerged from campus politics, never directly from external intervention. The most recent changes, to which we now turn our attention, have flowed even more from within the university than from the larger society.

THE NATIONAL POLITICS OF THE CURRICULUM IN THE 1980s

The 1980s version of the politics of the curriculum actually began in the mid-1970s with the appointment of Henry Rosovsky as Dean of Faculty at Harvard University. He and Harvard President Derek Bok, along with a cadre of senior faculty, decided to begin a long process of reconsideration of the Harvard curriculum that culminated in 1979 when the faculty reintroduced a form of distribution requirements that focused on the skills they wished students to have at graduation. The jury is still out on the impact of that change; its impact on the larger universe of American higher education is clear.

In the early 1980s, while the federal government, the states, and individual households were cutting budgets and coping with inflation, American higher education had already begun its own reconstruction. It resurrected distribution requirements on many campuses as a way of regulating the free market that had concentrated enrollments in management, engineering, and computer science. Campuses also restored a faculty role in decision making, although that had eroded so that only the curriculum was an arena where the faculty could exercise authority. Serious financial pressures imposed by federal budget cutting and weak state budgets severely constrained this decision-making process. These discussions reflected even more the territorial imperative of the departmental structure of the university where faculty control reigned supreme.

In this setting, Secretary of Education Terrell Bell appointed a distinguished panel of citizens to assess the state of elementary and secondary education. The panel reported in 1983 in the now famous document *A Nation at Risk*.[3] Its report characterized the public school system as so weak as to threaten the security of the United States. The report's hyperbole generated a national reconsideration of quality in public education, in part because of its clever and catchy conclusionary statements and in part because President Reagan decided that it offered an agenda he could adopt that would not cost the federal government money.

A Nation at Risk became the bible for educational reform at the local and state level. A number of governors sponsored substantial educational reform focusing on quality as the major political issue in their states. They also became interested in the quality of university education and made improvement of universities part of their overall educational plans. In both Arkansas and Tennessee, as well as many other states, the reform of teacher education became a state political issue. Florida and Georgia initiated testing programs for students mid-way in their college careers as well as for teachers. It is important to understand that these higher education initiatives flowed from *A Nation at Risk* and not from any higher education reports.

The panel report had profound impact on the public educational system because of the overt connection between all public school systems and local and state politics. The bully pulpit of the federal government had in fact ignited strong interest in the decentralized political system of public education. The role of this report in mobilizing public opinion was not unique in the history of public education—e.g., the Conant reports in the 1950s, after the Soviet Sputnik rocket was launched, had a comparable impact—but the fact that *A Nation at Risk* had its impact without federal money, yet because of federal politics, offers an idiosyncratic lesson about the politics of reports. If a report serves a larger political purpose, its impact can be great. Indeed, the power of a report generated outside of the educational system—higher or elementary and secondary—is completely dependent upon the political investment in it. And in some ways it is easier for a report on public education to have substantial effect than one that seeks to address its message to colleges and universities, because the nonpartisan politics of elementary and secondary education is still quite public and accountable, whereas the tradition of autonomous university boards of trustees and the standard of shared governance make the impact of external reports much more indirect than in the public schools.

A Nation at Risk had a threefold impact on campus: First, in a few states, it led to the imposition from outside of testing programs (e.g., Florida and Georgia, generally, and many other states in regard to teacher education). In many states the increases in funding for public schools also occasioned increases in state funding for higher education. Finally, the report seemed to spawn a number of subsequent reports focusing specifically on higher education, although many of these efforts were already in process when the panel's report was publicly presented. The national report is of such importance because it concentrated American attention on educational questions for the first time in two decades and because the interest that it mobilized focused on an agenda that also included universities and colleges through the impact of the subsequent reports. It is to these latter reports that we now turn.

Three general reports targeting undergraduate education followed within months after *A Nation at Risk.* First, then National Endowment for the Humanities Chairman William Bennett and a study group of advisors looked at the teaching of the humanities. Bennett wrote his report, *To Reclaim a Legacy,* that asserted the importance of revitalizing the humanities by strengthening the understanding of Western civilization.[4] Bennett asked that institutions agree on a core of texts that every student should read. He had his own list that became the touchstone for his report and the center of controversy in selection. Bennett's "great books of Western civilization" became the catch phrase that characterized his arguments in campus discussions about the undergraduate curriculum. The high visibility of the Bennett report helped catapult its author into the position of Secretary of Education when Terrell Bell resigned.

After *A Nation at Risk,* Secretary Bell appointed a small group to review higher education and the implications of the earlier report. This group, chaired by Dr. Kenneth Mortimer of Pennsylvania State University, published *Involvement in Learning,*[5] which considered not only the curriculum but also the pedagogy and priority (or lack thereof) of teaching as well as the co-curricular environment for learning in universities and colleges. This latest report came to be known as the report that prescribed greater student engagement with the learning process. It called for more writing, speaking, and creativity and fewer large lectures and impersonal learning settings. The higher education community identified Mortimer's group report with pedagogical method more than recommendations for curricular structure.

The third report following *A Nation at Risk* was from the Association of American Colleges (AAC). Professor Frederick Rudolph, the distinguished historian of the undergraduate curriculum, drafted *Integrity in the Undergraduate Curriculum,*[6] which listed six skill areas that set the standards for high-quality undergraduate education and found that faculty had not given priority to these necessary skills in the structure of the undergraduate curriculum. The AAC report abjured text-centered recommendations or the use of Chinese menus. It emphasized the importance of a planned course sequence in undergraduate education as a tactic to offer greater coherence to the market-driven reality in colleges across the country.

These three reports provided the canon for the debate about the undergraduate curriculum as it evolved in the mid-1980s. Their impact was twofold: first, together they created momentum for campus discussion of the undergraduate curriculum at a level of visibility unseen since the late 1950s; second, they provided the footnotes for the particular discussions on individual cam-

302   Part 3: The Academic Community

puses, although they did not—either one or all—dominate the reconstruction of the undergraduate curriculum that continues to proceed at this writing. Since all three were conclusionary and rhetorical rather than based upon substantial research and analysis about current campus reality, the actual debates focused on parochial realities of given campuses.

The three reports together framed the poles of the debates and offered appropriate justifications for nearly any argument mounted on behalf of new curricular structure, although they all ruled out the recent approach of institutional abdication of judgment. Their rhetoric was their strength in that there was an aphorism for all seasons; it was also their weakness. Martin Trow concluded that these reports did more harm than good "because these reports, by substituting prescription for analysis, misled our supporters and the general public into believing that these difficult problems are simpler than they are. . . ."[7]

An important distinction between the impact of these reports and *A Nation at Risk* was that no consensus about the details of reform emerged in higher education. The substance and potential resource implications of this debate have meant that on most campuses the systemic inertia has limited change to the reintroduction of the Chinese menu as it emerged on most campuses after the Second World War. The campus-based politics of the curriculum has been characterized by negotiations among departments about the hours devoted to general education and hours devoted to the major. These deliberations have resulted in a balance of power not unlike the treaties negotiated by Metternich or Kissinger.

Two national associations of states published reports on the state role in higher education. The Education Commission of the States published *Transforming the State Role in Undergraduate Education,* which counseled state interest but restraint in improving colleges.[8] The National Governors' Association Task Force on College Quality published *Time for Results: The Governors' 1991 Report on Education,* which commented not only on the schools but also on the state interest in higher education.[9] Although these reports focused on state initiatives to monitor quality in higher education, they both distinguished between the more direct intervention possible in public elementary-secondary education and the need to respect campus autonomy in higher education.

A new and different report is stirring the waters in the American higher educational pond, although it is premature to assess its impact. Ernest Boyer, President of the Carnegie Foundation, has written *College,* a book that, unlike the previous reports, is a research-based critique of the undergraduate experience.[10] Boyer published an earlier report, *High School,*[11] which provided a research-based analysis and a set of recommendations that complemented *A Nation at Risk* and contributed to the debate about public education. *College,* in addition to its research base, is distinctive in two other ways: like *A Nation at Risk,* and unlike most of the other higher education reports, Boyer has written for a general audience of parents, students, and policy makers as well as for the academic community itself. He considers not only the curriculum but also emphasizes the co-curricular components of the undergraduate experience and makes substantial recommendations about the need for improvement throughout undergraduate education.

The debate about the curriculum in higher education in the 1980s has focused on undergraduate education, in part because the policy debate had ignored it and in part because the political economy and the disciplinary sociology had created a campus structure that made it difficult to look at the undergraduate curriculum as a whole. It took a political debate outside of the particular campus to force each institution to confront the institution-wide issues, although the confrontation itself necessarily takes place on each campus. Even though the debate has been enriched off campus, it is essential to see that the higher education system itself has provided the brainpower for the enterprise. The panels that have fueled discussion have included faculty and administrators from higher education to a much greater degree than those commissions reporting on the schools had involved teachers and principals. The culture of campus autonomy has not been breached in so far as campus insiders have actually written the outside reports.[12] The substantive focus on undergraduate education is part of a cycle of discussion about education that has arisen from the campus but has taken place in forums in the larger political system. It is only a matter of time until the focus will shift to the graduate and professional schools.

All of these national reports and the politics of the curriculum that has evolved at the national level at most provide the environment within which the college and university citizens make the real decisions on campus. The politics of curriculum at the national level does not generate detailed debate in Congress or the Executive Branch, or even in the halls of many state legislatures. The national political discussion involves the campuses with the occasional interest of politicians. The legislatures, governors, and federal officials are always interested in budgets but only rarely in curriculum; their curricular interest is usually flagged by reports written by campus citizens. Because curricular decisions emerge in a culture that emphasizes campus autonomy, we must consider in greater detail the paradigm of curricular politics as campuses play the game in the 1980s.

THE POLITICS OF CHANGE: MAKING CURRICULUM DECISIONS ON UNIVERSITY STANDARD TIME

Commentators have always correctly viewed campus politics as especially Byzantine. Woodrow Wilson could say that he went to Washington from Princeton University to find a less complicated political system. Many wags have observed that political conflict on campuses is so petty and mean be-

304   Part 3: The Academic Community

cause so little is at stake. Wilson was right; the omnipresent wag is wrong. Since substantive academic decisions are the heart of the university, much is at stake in these decisions: principle, status, resources. The very fact that so much is at stake and that the culture of the university prizes consultation make decisions about curriculum especially laborious and time consuming.

In many areas of university life and across the spectrum of institutions, the faculty no longer has an extensive and meaningful role in decision making. Yet it is in the arena of curriculum that the faculty role is still primary and certainly meets the standard set by the American Association of University Professors (AAUP) in its 1966 Statement on University and College Government.[13] This reality means that even considering incremental decisions about the nature of departmental curriculum takes a long time to talk through. When an institution reviews its whole educational program for assessment and possible reform, one measures the consultative process in years not months. This leads universities to be very conservative institutions.

Clark Kerr has observed that most of the changes in American higher education have come from creating new institutions, not from dramatically changing old ones.[14] And the model of departmental dominance of research institutions has not changed significantly since the Second World War. Changes occur within institutions at the margin, seldom at the core. And they generally evolve over long periods of time. Even revolutions and *coup d'etats* on campuses take a couple of years. This fact that everything in universities takes so long to decide leads to what I call university standard time. The irony of this fact is that the knowledge produced and disseminated in colleges and universities is on the cutting edge. This new understanding becomes immediately available to the research community around the world, as does the latest rumor about the love life of a distant colleague. We may explain this discontinuity in the distinction between research dissemination and agreement for action.

To clarify the reality of curriculum decision making for the whole institution, I will offer a synthetic cause of change drawn from a number of examples. This example uses the case study database of the Carnegie Foundation study that led to Ernest Boyer's lastest work, *College,* and from my own impressions gathered from over two hundred college visits.[15] It is enough to offer only one example, because the paradigm I will describe is unusually typical across institutional types ranging from community colleges through elite private universities.

The example is a review of the undergraduate curriculum with special attention to what is or ought to be common in the required work for all students. The usual initiative for such a review comes from either a dean or a provost/academic vice-president. Once the proposal for such a review emerges, it becomes the enterprise of the faculty or university senate. The campus creates a committee, sometimes appointed by the president or provost, other times selected by the faculty, and often chosen by both. It includes senior faculty carefully balanced by discipline and by educational ideology—particularly designed not to have too many innovators—with a sprinkling of senior administrators and one or two figurehead students. The senior administrator(s) and the faculty charge the committee to review the undergraduate curriculum and the existing requirements or lack thereof and then to report to the faculty senate for first review no later than "next term."

During the first few months of deliberation, the committee will have a debate within itself that will invoke all of the national reports and will generate as many as a dozen opposing plans for dramatic reform of the undergraduate curriculum. Impatience will quickly reduce twelve options to three or four, which will invariably include modest change in an existing "Chinese menu," restoration of Western civilization and a "Great Books" core, abolition of all requirements, and/or a distinctive approach unique to the particular campus usually in the form of courses with "subject and . . ." titles, such as international affairs and physics, or the environment and economics. "Next term" comes much too quickly, so the committee reports it has only begun its deliberation and will report next year.

Some enlightened committees initiate empirical studies of experiences of similarly situated institutions based on telephone surveys and also the actual longitudinal course patterns of students based upon samples of transcripts. These studies are often designed by a physical scientist on the committee and served by a part-time institutional researcher who spends most of his/her time doing budget and enrollment projections.

During the second year of deliberation, the committee spends some time reviewing the empirical studies. Often it finds a *de facto* core usually clustered in the required courses of the physical sciences and one or two spectacular lecturers who have been teaching for forty years. Everyone is suitably shocked by the lack of sequence experienced by most students outside their majors and the parochialism of the *de facto* core. The debates of the first year in the committee are repeated in complete detail, but at the end of the debate, there are two factions about equally balanced: those who wish a dramatic reform and those who wish only to modify the existing Chinese menu. The chairperson of the committee reports the close division to the faculty senate but assures his/her colleagues that the committee will report "next term" with a firm plan.

In the meantime the president has been fund-raising with the theme that the institution is in the midst of a major rethinking of its educational program with careful attention to quality. He assures alumni and foundations that the institution is carefully monitoring quality through a new testing program that will be part of the reform. The provost is busy modeling the alternative curriculum changes for their impact on the budget and quietly directing the budget process to bolster those who support the provost's view of the appropriate curricular changes. The provost and chairperson of the select committee on the curriculum are meeting regularly with senior faculty and deans to build coalitions to support the recommendations that they wish to be the heart of the committee report.

Between one and two years later than originally promised, the select committee reports to the faculty senate a plan, which is heralded as a major change in the requirements for all undergraduates. The reform actually takes the existing Chinese menu and reduces the choices in each column and establishes another committee to evaluate proposed courses for inclusion in the general education program. There are two minority reports—one from a quarter of the committee that wanted a truly major restructuring with lots of required courses and a lone faculty member and the student representatives who wished to do away with requirements altogether.

The first minority report refers to Columbia, Chicago, and William Bennett; the latter invokes that "hot" university, Brown. The second minority report is an odd combination of student rhetoric about free choice and maturity and the faculty member's invocation of specialized accrediting agency requirements that supposedly limit campus flexibility in his discipline, usually either engineering, computer science, chemistry, or management. The majority report is replete with references to Harvard, Derek Bok, and Ernest Boyer, selecting from each the most radical statements that then are used to justify even the most modest change.

When the committee reports to the faculty senate—or to the whole faculty in a small college—the senate first repeats presentations that posit each of the dozen alternatives considered and reconsidered by the committee. This process exhausts the first scheduled meeting. The senate then schedules a special meeting to continue the discussion. At this second meeting the majority report is the sole item on the agenda. The discussion moves item by item through the report. There are dozens of amendments from the floor. At the end of this meeting the original recommendations have been substantially amended to look more like the existing Chinese menu. The one recommendation that emerges with no change is the creation of a committee to oversee the implementation of the final plan.

At yet another meeting the senate completes the amendment process and sends an amended proposal back to the select committee for revision and editing for resubmission for an up-or-down vote at the next meeting. At that meeting the faculty senate approves the revised recommendations on a 55/45 vote. The senate then sends the program to the provost for comment and approval along with an assessment of the budgetary impact. The provost forwards the approved plan with a budgetary analysis to the president, who, with the provost, returns the plan to the senate with a request that its implementation be spread-out over a three-year period for budgetary reasons. The senate complains but finally agrees. The new curriculum will begin in the next academic year, that will usually be at least four years after the senate and president first appointed the select committee. For those four years the institution as a whole will have been reviewing its undergraduate curriculum as a political priority, an activity that seems to occur about every twenty years and that makes, for that short period of history, academic matters the center of campus politics.

Significant variations on this political-process theme are relatively rare. In many community colleges, the academic dean—the equivalent of the provost—may take a much more active role and the faculty a more reactive role. In a historically Black college the campus president and its Title III Coordinator may be the only serious actors. An elite private university will have a council of elders composed of the most visible and senior professors and the dean of the undergraduate college as the main actors on stage with subsequent decision making a *fait accompli*.

There are some extraordinary exceptions. A large private university in the West, facing near bankruptcy and precipitously declining enrollment, saw its newly installed president—himself a long-term faculty member—and the board of trustees pass a core curriculum without substantive faculty consultation and impose it on the faculty whose only leeway was in specifying the implementation. The legacy of this procedure was continuing faculty disaffection with the president and the board and lukewarm implementation. There is now general agreement that the core curriculum was a good idea and the fortunes of the institution seem to have improved significantly.[16]

The new president of a small private college in the East presented a general outline of a curriculum plan combining career preparation and a strong liberal arts program as part of his case for himself in the hiring process. Soon after his selection, he presented a comprehensive plan to the faculty that then massaged it and devised its own implementation strategy in the course of approving the sweeping curricular changes. One must distinguish this latter example from the former in that the administration did not impose the curriculum. The faculty through traditional collegial consultation approved the initiative of the president.[17]

Both of these examples anticipated the national reports; the reports influenced neither. The first case implemented a very traditional core curriculum; the latter case substantively tried to harness the student careerism of the 1970s and 1980s to the traditional values of liberal education. Neither offered a strikingly new approach to the nature of undergraduate education.

The central case and the variations on them document the institutional conservatism of universities and colleges. Even when there is political radicalism on the spectrum of national political views and dynamic discovery of new knowledge, the political process for deciding about the curriculum seems to guarantee an institutional entropy that tolerates little change. The power of departments that is central to the organization of knowledge by disciplines creates a number of decentralized power centers that seem to exercise veto more than contribute to shifting coalitions. Undoubtedly some are more equal than others in the university or college setting. Those who are most equal are the faculty with the most research, the most students, and the most to get out of the status quo.

We have now catalogued some of the complexity of the political process in curricular decisions on campus and the difficulty of substantial reform. None of the examples offer evidence to assess the connection between the political process and the quality of the educational experience. It is important to understand that the quality of the educational venture begins in the classroom but also depends upon the whole campus environment. Ernest Boyer in *College,* following the precedent of *Involvement in Learning,* correctly includes in his review and suggestions a critical assessment of co-curricular life, the role of libraries, and the admissions process. The campus political process seldom gives this complexity its due, because the professionals engaged in the correlative work are second-class citizens in the campus political community. They are middle- and lower-rank academic administrators who lack the power of the purse vested in senior administrators. They do not have the collective authority of the faculty who deal with curriculum issues. They are not as well organized as a vocal student minority.

On campuses with university senates rather than faculty senates, one might expect the other constituencies to have more authority. In fact, few university senates have worked effectively, and most seem to leave all participants feeling impotent. No campus political systems seem to have institutionalized the capacity to make judgments in the interest of the long-term instead of yesterday and today.

STRATEGIES FOR IMPROVING QUALITY AND REFORMING CURRICULUM

This account of the politics of the curriculum in higher education may discourage those interested in improving the quality of teaching and learning. Two caveats are in order: brevity has required an emphasis on one part of the curriculum—the undergraduate experience taken as a whole—not graduate and professional education or the departmental curricula constituting the major as a significant part; second, earlier, Kerr made the point that substantively new opportunities were provided in American higher education by the creation of new institutions, not by the substantial reform of the old. Both of these caveats should moderate the message of most of this chapter: that the politics of the curriculum often precludes dramatic change. In particular programs on every campus, quality is effectively monitored and the substantive nature of the programs often changes surprisingly quickly through the individual actions of faculty at the lead in their disciplines and groups of faculty in departments committed to their students. As new organizational needs have surfaced at the systems level, new institutions have emerged. The creation of a national system of community colleges and the transformation of teachers colleges into comprehensive universities testify to higher education's flexibility.[18]

It is easier to be flexible in a period of expanding rather than steady or contracting resources. The percentage of family income invested in higher education in the 1970s and 1980s has not changed significantly; inflation was about equal to increases in federal aid. Federal budget deficits and sluggish economic growth make it unlikely that significant new resources will be available in the 1990s as we move into the twenty-first century. Therefore, we must think creatively about dealing with the lethargy of existing campuses. We do have a silver lining to the current grey: the retirement of faculty between 1995 and 2010. New blood may—but only might—bring new curricular ideas.

The focus of the spate of reports and the efforts at curricular reform has been revision of requirements and reallocation of current faculty efforts in teaching and learning as well as the elevation of teaching and learning on the priority agenda of campuses. This focus has been eminently reasonable for the 1980s. But the time has now come to begin careful reconsideration of the substance and the procedure of decisions about academic matters. We can expect a fifteen-year window for appointments, an opportunity unprecedented since the 1960s.[19] Decisions in the 1990s as to who will be appointed to faculty positions will set the course of higher education for the first half of the next century.

One lesson of the past few years has been that members of the university community—on particular campuses and nationally—are willing to enter into a serious discussion about the nature of teaching and learning and debate quite vigorously the curriculum in a specific college or university. The problem has been that the deliberative institutions have been creaky in part because of lack of exercise. Many sectors of the campus community have not even been effectively heard. Neither the middle-level administrators who deal with student life nor the alumni as a constituency prepared to take a more active role in the current life of the campus is considered an important factor in the contemporary campus political system. Presidents, provosts, and boards of trustees need to create deliberative bodies for all segments of the college community, delegating authority and power where appropriate, and then resolving conflicts through small, representative cabinets that advise the whole institution and whose word decides most issues.

Faculty in particular have felt quite strongly that the campus has excluded them from university-wide decision making. The work on the curriculum may go some distance to correct this view, but it will not change until faculty believe they are consulted on issues of overall direction and the allocation of resources. This observation leads me to the most important lesson of the politics of curriculum during the 1980s for the 1990s and beyond.

The best American institutions in the eyes of both faculty and students, according to the Carnegie Foundation surveys, are the selective liberal arts colleges.[20] In these institutions all members of the collegium believe they are important contributors to a community where they are respected and where the quality of life is high. The only other component of American higher education that has a similar self-image and probable reality is the handful of elite, private research institutions such as the Ivy League, Chicago, and Stanford.

In so far as a governance structure that seriously considers academic matters can build such a community, it can actually contribute to the quality of American higher education. Such a strategy is far more likely to improve the quality of American higher education than assessment, testing, and management by objectives.

Regardless of what we do self-consciously, significant changes loom on the horizon of learning. In addition to the turnover of personnel with the turn of the century, we are already in the midst of the infiltration of new technologies that students and faculty will bring to the curriculum in a manner that could occasion profound change. Networks of microcomputers make possible patterns of study, interaction, and research that can greatly improve learning. University standard time may become quite compressed in so far as networks of knowledge deliver participants from the need to resolve schedule conflicts and as they make available original data and research on a real time basis.

The social revolution driven by technological forces will not occur by majority vote; it will occur by mass connection. Political action will likely confirm these changes, but they will have already become a reality. The knowledge revolution—and the access of individuals directly to networks of knowledge is the revolution of the inexpensive microcomputer and optical laser media and communications—will change the power relationships of the players of the academic games. Brilliant lecturers will lose to superb seminar leaders and insightful computer conferencing chairs. Research librarians and microcomputer hackers will be teaching traditional faculty. The norm will continue to be "publish or perish," but publication may mean to be stored in a prestigious computer bulletin-board or listed as a central participant in a select computer conference.

No matter how extensively networked we all become, electronic connections will never guarantee either community or quality, though they can contribute to both. All curriculum change depends upon academic politics, which is unlikely to change, unless there is as much campus political action as there is national educational talk. All academic change both begins and ends with writing and talking—what John Austin called "performative utterances," words that actually change things. Our task is to understand the realities of academic politics in an institution that is engaged in technological evolution on a new scale through market forces. Only then will talk and reports be about academics but not academic. This is the leadership challenge as we turn to the twenty-first century.

NOTES

1. The following commentary on the modern history of the college curriculum has been informed by but should not be blamed on Frederick Rudolph, *Curriculum* (San Francisco: Jossey-Bass, 1977) and Clifton Conrad, editor, *ASHE Reader on Academic Programs in Colleges and Universities,* (Lexington, Mass.: Ginn Press, 1985).
2. See Daniel Bell, *Reforming General Education* (New York: Columbia University Press, 1964).
3. (Washington, D.C.: U.S. Government Printing Office, 1983).
4. (Washington: National Endowment for the Humanities, 1984) ERIC document number ED247880.
5. *Study Group on the Conditions of Excellence in American Higher Education* (Washington, D.C.: National Institute of Education, 1984).
6. (Washington, D.C.: Association of American Colleges, 1985).
7. Paper presented to the faculty seminar on "Ideas of the University," Southern Methodist University, Dallas, Texas, March 12, 1986, 19.
8. (Denver: Educational Commission of the States, 1986).
9. (Washington, D.C.: National Governors Association, 1986).
10. (New York: Harper and Row, 1987).
11. (New York: Harper and Row, 1983).
12. For a comparison with other reports, see Janet R. Johnson and Laurence R. Marcus, *Blue Ribbon Commissions and Higher Education: Changing Academe from the Outside* (Washington, D.C.: ASHE-ERIC, 1986).
13. *AAUP Policy Documents* (The Redbook) (Washington, D.C.: AAUP, 1984).
14. Clark Kerr, *The Uses of the University* (New York: Harper and Row, 1980), introduction.
15. As a consultant to the Carnegie Foundation, I reviewed all of the survey data and also all of the 29 case studies prepared as background for the book. These data reinforced each other and proved the power of research that combines quantitative survey data with case studies, in this instance written by journalists who spent at least two weeks on the campuses about which they reported.
My review of these data has persuaded me of the general wisdom of the analysis and recommendations by Ernest Boyer in *College,* but my impression of the case study data suggests that the general quality of undergraduate education for the majority of students in American colleges is worse than one might conclude by Boyer's evenhanded reporting, since about twenty-five of the twenty-nine reports described harassed and/or disinterested faculty teaching passive and unprepared students. Yet the best ranks with the most excellent in the world.
16. The evidence for this report emerged in a consulting mission when I visited the university.
17. The evidence for this report is drawn from conversations with the president and other staff as well as review of documents submitted to me by the college.
18. Kerr, ibid.
19. Howard Bowen and Jack Shuster, *American Professors* (New York: Oxford University Press, 1986).
20. Boyer, ibid. and my review of both case and survey data.

Part 4

Concluding Perspectives

16

The Insulated Americans:
Five Lessons From Abroad

Burton R. Clark

*EDITOR'S NOTE: Although written in 1978, the following chapter is just as
relevant today. The issues dealt with by Burton Clark continue to be on the
agenda for American higher education. His ability to place these key questions in an international perspective and the useful comparisons he draws
makes this chapter as important today as it was a decade ago.*

In thinking about postsecondary education, Americans tend to remain isolated and insular. The reasons are numerous: Ours is the largest national
system; we know this massive complex is the system most widely acclaimed
since the second quarter of this century; we are geographically separated
from the other major national models; we have many unique features; and we
are busy and have more pressing things to do in Montana as well as in New
York than to ask how the Austrians and Swedes do it. But there is a great
deal to learn about ourselves by learning about the experiences of others in
this important sector of society, and it is wise that we learn in advance of the
time when events force us to do so.

To use an analogy: American business could have studied the Japanese
way of business organization, and the German way, and even the Swedish
way a quarter of a century ago instead of waiting until virtually forced to do
so in the 1970s by worsening competitive disadvantage and deepening worker
discontent. Cross-national thinking encourages the long view in which, for
once, we might get in front of our problems. We might even find out what
not to do while there is still time not to do it. The perspectives that I draw
from comparative research indicate that we are now making changes that
not only deny the grounds on which we have been successful to date but will
probably lead to arrangements that will seriously hamper us in the future.

To help develop a broad analytical framework within which legislators,
chief executive officers, educational officials, faculty, and others can make

---

Reprinted with permission from *Change* (November 1978).

wiser decisions in postsecondary education, I will set forth some rudimentary ideas in the form of five lessons from abroad. The basic points are interconnected. The first three of these lessons are largely "do nots" or warnings, and they set the stage for the last two, which are affirmations of what should remain central in our minds as we think about leadership and statesmanship in postsecondary education.

Central bureaucracy cannot effectively coordinate mass higher education. Many nations have struggled for a long time to coordinate higher education by means of national administration, treating postsecondary education as a subgovernment of the national state. The effort has been to achieve order, effectiveness, and equity by having national rules applied across the system by one or more national bureaus. France has struggled with the possibilities and limitations of this approach for a century and a half, since Napoleon created a unitary and unified national system of universities. And Italy has moved in this direction for over a century, since the unification of the nation.

Many of the well-established systems of this kind, in Europe and elsewhere, have not only a nationalized system of finance, but also: (a) much nationalization of the curriculum, with common mandated courses in centrally approved fields of study; (b) a nationalized degree structure, in which degrees are awarded by the national system and not by the individual university or college; (c) a nationalized personnel system, in which all those who work for the university are members of the civil service and are hired and promoted accordingly; and (d) a nationalized system of admissions, in which federal rules determine student access as well as rights and privileges. Such features naturally obtain strongly in Communist-controlled state administrations, such as East Germany and Poland, where the dominant political philosophy affirms strong state control, based on a hierarchy of command. In some countries, such as West Germany, heavy reliance on central bureaucracy takes place at the state or provincial level of government rather than at the federal level, but often the results are no less thorough.

Back in the days of "elite" higher education, when the number of students and teachers was small, this approach worked to some degree—and we now know why. A bargain was struck, splitting the power between the bureaucrats at the central level and the professors at each institution. There were few middlemen—no trustees, since private individuals were not to be trusted with the care of a public interest, and not enough campus administrators to constitute a separate force. Professors developed the personal and collegial forms of control that provided the underpinnings for personal and group freedom in teaching and research. They elected their own deans and rectors and kept them on a short-term basis. Hence the professors were the power on the local scene, with the state officials often remote, even entombed hundreds of miles away in a Kafkaesque administrative monument. State administration sometimes became a bureaucracy for its own sake, a set of pretenses behind which oligarchies of professors were the real rulers, nationally as well as locally. The public was always given to understand that there was single-system account-ability, while inside the structure power was so fractured and scattered that feudal lords ruled sectors of the organizational countryside. In general, this was the traditional European mode of academic organization—power con-centrated at the top (in a central bureaucratic staff) and at the bottom (in the hands of chaired professors), with a weak middle at the levels of the university and its major constituent parts.

But the unitary government pyramid has become increasingly deficient over the last 25 years as expansion has enlarged the composite of academic tasks as well as the scale of operations. As consumer demand grows, student clienteles are not only more numerous but more varied. As labor force de-mands proliferate, the connections to employment grow more intricate. As demands for knowledge multiply, inside and outside the academic occupa-tions, the disciplines and fields of knowledge increase steadily in number and kind. The tasks that modern higher education is now expected to perform differ in kind from those demanded traditionally in other sectors of public administration, and the challenge is to find the structure best suited for these new roles. There is a need to cover knowledge in fields that stretch from archaeology to zoology, with business, law, physics, psychology, you name it, thrown in. Across the gamut of fields, knowledge is supposed to be dis-covered—the research imperative—as well as transmitted and distributed—the teaching and service imperatives. On top of all this has come an accele-rated rate of change which makes it all the more difficult for coordinators, who tend to be generalists, to catch up with and comprehend what the specialists are doing.

Clearly, a transition from elite to mass higher education requires dra-matic changes in structured state and national systems. The success of mass higher education systems will increasingly depend on: (a) plural rather than singular reactions, or the capacity to face simultaneously in different direc-tions with contradictory reactions to contradictory demands; (b) quicker re-actions, at least by some parts of the system, to certain demands; and (c) a command structure that allows for myriad adaptations to special contexts and local conditions. A unified system coordinated by a state bureaucracy is not set up to work in these ways. The unitary system resists differentiated and flexible approaches.

In such countries as Sweden, France, and Italy, many reformers in and out of government are now beginning to realize this, so that the name of their game at this point in history is decentralization—efforts to disperse academic administration to regions, local authorities, and campuses. But this is ex-tremely difficult to do through planned, deliberate effort. Federal officials with firmly fixed power do not normally give it away—abroad any more than in the United States—especially if the public, the legislature, and the chief executive still hold them responsible. But at least things are changing; respon-sible people in many countries have become convinced that the faults of unitary coordination far outweigh the virtues, and they are looking for ways to break up central control. They are almost ready to take seriously that great admirer of American federalism, De Tocqueville, who maintained over a century ago that while countries can be successfully governed centrally, they cannot be successfully administered centrally. There is surely no realm other than higher education where this principle more aptly applies.

Meanwhile, the United States, historically blessed with decentralization and diversity, within states as well as among them, is hankering after the promised virtues: economy, elimination of overlap, less redundancy, better articulation, transferability, accountability, equity, and equality. Our dominant line of reform since World War II has been to impose on the disorder of a market system of higher education new levels of coordination that promise administered order. We continue to do this at an accelerating rate. In fact, if our current momentum toward bureaucratic centralism is maintained, first at the state level and then at the national, we may see the day when we catch up with our friends abroad or even pass them as they travel in the direction of decentralization.

Unless strong counterforces are brought into play, higher education at the state level will increasingly resemble a ministry of education. Administrative staffs will grow, and the powers of central board and staff will shift increasingly from weakly proffered advice toward a primary role in the allocation of resources and in the approval of decisions for the system as a whole. Legislators, governors, and anyone else looking for a source to berate, blame, or whatever will increasingly saddle the central board and staff with the responsibility for economy, efficiency, equity, and all the other goals. And the oldest organizational principle in the world tells us that where there is responsibility, the authority should be commensurate. The trend toward central political and bureaucratic coordination is running strong. Just how strong can be easily seen if we compare state structures of coordination between 1945 and 1975. Robert Berdahl, Lyman Glenny, and other experts on state coordination have noted that in the 1960s alone a remarkably rapid centralization took place, with the states shifting from structures of little or no formal coordination to coordinating boards with regulatory powers.

To see just how fast such an evolutionary trend can change matters at the national level in a democratic nation, we have only to observe Great Britain. Like us, the British were long famous for institutional autonomy. As government money increasingly became the sole source of support, they devised the ingenious University Grants Committee (UGC), which, between 1920 and 1965, became the foremost world model for how to have governmental support without governmental control. But things have changed in the last decade. UGC, which initially received its moneys directly from the treasury and doled out lump sums with few questions asked, now must work with and under the national education department.

The national department has always supervised and sponsored the nonuniversity sector, which operates without a buffer commission. But recently it has become a more aggressive instrument of national educational policy as determined by the party in power and senior administrators in the department. Along with the UGC, it has been swept along toward a stronger regulatory role. Now, in the mid-1970s, central offices in Britain ask all kinds of questions of the institutions, favor one sector at the expense of another, tell some colleges previously out of their purview to close their doors, and suggest to other universities and colleges that they ought not attempt A, B, and C if they hope to maintain the good will of those who must approve the next budget. Britain is still far from having a continental ministry of education, but evolution in that direction has recently been rapid. For the best of short-run reasons, the central administrative machinery is becoming the primary locus of power.

Our own centralization is first taking place at the state level. This allows for diversity and competition among the state systems, some outlet for personnel and students when any one system declines or otherwise becomes particularly unattractive, and the chance for some states to learn from the successes and failures of others. Apparently, it can pay sometimes to be an attentive laggard. But we are certainly heading in the direction of bureaucratic coordination. Most important, our central offices at the national level have adopted a different posture in the mid-1970s from one or two decades earlier. We have already bowed to the quaint notion of taking away federal moneys flowing to an institution when it fails to obey a particular federal rule. Such an approach characterizes the sternest type of relationship between government and higher education in democratic countries with national ministries of education.

Our national policy will ricochet around on such matters for some years to come, while federal officials learn to fit the punishment to the crime. But the new world of national coordination into which we are moving rapidly was made perfectly clear by Secretary of Health, Education, and Welfare Joseph Califano, in a speech at the 1977 meeting of the American Council on Education. In front of an audience of hundreds of university and college presidents, he pointed out that since a recent bit of legislation opposed by academics was now national law, they would have to "comply," and he would have to "enforce." From the market to the minister in a decade! Others in Washington, inside or outside of government, feel free these days to speak of "federal supervision of education" (see Samuel Halperin, "The Federal Future in Education," *Change,* February 1978). Where one stands depends largely upon where one sits, and those who sit in Washington, consumed by national responsibilities and limited to a view from the top, will generally stand on formal coordination, by political and bureaucratic means, of national administration.

In short, we could learn from our friends on the European continent who are now realizing that their national and often unified administrative structures can't cope with mass higher education. Particularly, we could take a lesson from the British, who evolved rapidly in the last decade toward dependence on central bodies as an answer to the immediate demands of economy and equity. But as matters now stand, it appears that we will not do so. Rather we seem determined to learn the hard way, from brute experience.

The greatest single danger in the control of higher education is a monopoly of power, for two good reasons: A monopoly expresses the concerns and perspectives of just one group, shutting out the expression of other interests; and no one group is wise enough to solve all the problems. The history of higher education exhibits monopolies and near monopolies by various groups. Students in some medieval Italian universities, through student guilds, could hire and fire professors and hence obtain favors from them. Senior faculty in some European and English universities during the last two centuries were answerable to no one and hence could sleep for decades. Trustees in some early and not-so-early American colleges could and did fire presidents and professors for not knowing the number of angels dancing on the head of the ecclesiastical pin, or, within our lifetime, for simply smoking cigarettes and drinking martinis. Autocratic presidents in some American institutions, especially teachers colleges, ran campuses as personal possessions; and state bureaucratic staffs and political persons in Europe and America, past and present, democratic and nondemocratic, have often been heavily dominant.

A monopoly of power can be a useful instrument of change: Some states in Western Europe, normally immobilized in higher education, have effected large changes only when a combination of crisis events and a strong ruler produced a temporary monopoly, e.g., France in 1968 under DeGaulle. But the monopoly does not work well for long. It soon becomes a great source of rigidity, resisting change and freezing organization around the rights of just a few.

In the increasingly complex and turbulent organizational environment of the remaining quarter of this century, no small group will be smart enough to know the way. This holds even for the central bureaucratic and planning staffs, who are most likely to evolve into near monopolies of control. State and party officials in East European countries have been finding out that they cannot, from on high and by themselves, effect even so simple an exercise as manpower planning—allotting educational places according to labor force targets. They have been forced by their errors to back off from total dominance and to allow more room for the academic judgments of professors and the choices of students. As mentioned earlier, various countries in Western Europe are attempting to halt and reverse a long trend of centralization in order to move decision making out to the periphery, closer to participants and to the realities of local operating conditions.

All organized systems of any complexity are replete with reciprocal ignorance. The expert in one activity will not know the time of day in another.

The extent of ignorance is uncommonly high in systems of higher education, given the breadth of subjects they cover. The chief state higher education officer may not be able to do long division, let alone high-energy physics, while the professor of physics, until retrained and reoriented, is ignorant in everyday matters of system coordination. Here is a fundamental feature of modern organized life: While higher education has been moving toward the formation of large hierarchies traditionally associated with business firms and government agencies, those organizations have been driven to greater dependence on the judgment of authorities in different parts of the organization as work becomes more rooted in expertise. That authority flows toward expert judgment is evident in such mechanisms as peer review and committee evaluation. The organized anarchy of the university remains a useful model of how to function as those at the nominal top become more ignorant.

Another great danger in the control of higher education is domination by a single form of organization. No single form will suffice in mass higher education. Here again some of our European counterparts have been fundamentally unlucky and we can learn from their misfortune. The European university has been around for eight centuries, predating in most locales the nation states that now encompass it. Over the centuries, the assumption grew that genuine higher education meant university education, and that made it difficult to bring other forms into being or to give them prestige. Thus, some nations were swept into mass education with only the nationally supported public university legitimated as a good place to study. As a result, since 1960, this dominant form has been greatly overloaded, with large numbers of students and faculty making more and more heterogeneous demands. This has weakened the traditional function of the university—basic research. In many European countries it is now problematic whether most basic research will remain within the university as teaching time drives out research time and as governments sponsor and protect the science they think they need by placing it in research institutes outside the university systems. Differentiation of form has to occur, but it will happen the hard way in those countries where one form has enjoyed a traditional monopoly.

In the United States, we are in fairly good shape on this score, despite recent worry about homogenization. We have at least five or six major sectors or types of institutions, and the best efforts to classify our 3,000 institutions reveal no less than a dozen or more categories, taking into account extensive differences among the hundreds of places now called universities, the still greater number called colleges, and the 1,000 community colleges. Here no single form dominates the system. But we may have cause to worry about voluntary and mandated convergence.

Institutional differentiation is the name of the game in the coordination of mass higher education. Lesson four is the flip side of lesson three, but the point is so fundamental that it can stand restatement. It answers the most important, substantive question in high-level system coordination and governmental policy: Will and should our universities and colleges become more or less alike? The pressure of the times in nearly all countries is heavily toward institutional uniformity. Yet cross-national comparison tells us that differentiation is the prime requirement for system viability.

One of the great pressures for institutional uniformity derives from the search for equality and equity. For a long time in this country the notion of what constitutes educational equality has been broadening. At first, equality of access simply meant equal chances of getting into a limited number of openings—selection without regard to race, color, or creed. This changed to a position that there should be no selection, that the door should be open to all. But while this idea was developing, a differentiated arrangement of colleges and universities was also taking shape. Everyone could get into the system, but not into all its parts: We differentiated among the roles of the community college, the state college, and the state university, made differential selection an important part of the process, and allowed private colleges and universities to do business as they pleased. This saved us from some of the deleterious effects of letting everyone in. Now the idea of equality is being carried a step further as observers and practitioners take critical note of our institutional unevenness. The effort will grow to extend the concept of educational equality to mean equal treatment for all. To make this possible, all institutions in a system should be equated.

Europeans have already had considerable experience with this idea. It has been embedded in those systems comprising a set of national universities and not much else. The French, Italians, and others have made a sustained attempt to administer equality by formally proclaiming and often treating the constituent parts of the system as equal in program, staff, and value of degree. Still, back in the days when selection was sharp at the lower levels, only 5 percent or less graduated from the upper secondary level and were thereby guaranteed a university place of their choosing. But mass elementary and now mass secondary education have virtually eliminated the earlier selection in some countries and radically reduced it in others. As a result, much larger numbers have come washing into the old undifferentiated university structure, like a veritable tide, with all entrants expecting governmentally guaranteed equality of treatment. There has been no open way of steering the traffic, or of differentiating, which is surely the grandest irony for a national system founded on rational, deliberate administrative control.

This European version of open-door access has recently generated enormous conflict within almost all the European systems. Unless some way is found to distinguish and differentiate, everyone who wants to go to medical school has the right to attend; everyone who wants to go to the University of Rome will continue to go there—when they last stopped counting, it was well above 150,000; and the French apparently had over 200,000 at the University of Paris before a deep crisis forced them to break that totality into a dozen and one parts. Ideally, more degree levels, with appropriate underpinnings, will also have to develop, since the heterogeneous clientele, with its more uneven background and varied aptitude, needs programs of different length and different stopping places. But to attempt to effect selection, assignment, and barriers now, precisely at the time when the doors have finally swung open, is morally outrageous to the former have-nots and to the political parties, unions, and other groups that articulate their interests. The battle rages on the national stage, with virtually all education-related ideologies and interests brought into play. In America, we have been saved from this by a combination of decentralization and differentiation.

Other strong pressures for institutional uniformity come from within higher education systems themselves. One is a voluntary movement of sectors, now referred to as an academic drift, toward the part that has highest prestige and offers highest rewards. The English have had trouble resisting such convergence, since the towering prestige of Oxford and Cambridge has induced various institutions to drift toward their style. In addition, administered systems tend toward mandated convergence. Within the European unitary systems, this is expressed in the thousand and one details of equating salaries, teaching loads, laboratory spaces, and sabbatical leaves. Have-nots within the system become pressure groups to catch up with the haves (e.g., in America, state college personnel seek equality with university personnel). Then, too, impartial and fair administration demands system-wide classifications of positions and rewards, with salaries for everyone going up or down by the same percentage. From Warsaw to Tokyo there is a strong tendency in public administration generally to expand and contract in this fashion, equalizing and linking the costs, with the result that future costs become more restrictive.

Since the historical development of our institutions has presented America with the necessary differentiation, a central task is to maintain it by legitimating different institutional roles. We have been relatively successful in initiating tripartite structures within our state systems, but cannot manage to fix this division. A classic case is the unstable role of the state college. In one state after another, the state colleges will not stay where they are supposed to, according to plan, but at a blinding rate—that is, within a decade or two—take on some or all of the functions of universities, alerting their printers to the change in title that soon will be lobbied through the legislature. In contrast, the two-year colleges have accepted their distinctive role and—outside of Connecticut and a few backward states—have prospered in it.

This has been in the face of predictions, a quarter century ago, that two-year colleges would renounce their obviously undesirable role and evolve into four-year institutions. That convergence was cut off at the pass, more by the efforts of community college people themselves than by weakly manned state offices. There came into being a community college philosophy and a commitment to it, notably in the form of a "movement." Some leaders even became zealots, true believers, glassy eyes and all. Around the commitment, they developed strong interest groups with political muscle. Today, no one's patsy, they have a turf, the willingness and ability to defend it, and the drive and skill to explore such unoccupied territory as recurrent education and lifelong learning to see how much they can annex. When did we last hear about a state college movement? If the name of the game is institutional differentiation, the name of differentiation is legitimation of institutional roles.

Planning and autonomous action are both needed as mechanisms of differentiation, coordination, and change. The difference between the acceptance of roles and the trend toward covergence, both here and abroad, suggests that we cannot leave everything to the drift of the marketplace. Unless the anchorage is there for different roles, institutions will voluntarily converge. Clearly defined roles stand the best chance of surviving. A strong state college was never far from a weak university in the first place. It took only the addition of a few more Ph.D.s to the faculty and a little more inching into graduate work in order to say: Why not us? Teachers colleges were once quite different from universities, but as the former evolved into comprehensive state colleges, their institutional role became fuzzier and harder to stabilize. In contrast, our two-year units were inherently different from universities. Perhaps the rule is: Organizational species that are markedly different can live side by side in a symbiotic relation; species that are similar, with heavily overlapping functions, are likely to conflict, with accommodation then often taking the form of convergence on a single type.

Distinct bases of support and authority seem to contribute to the stability of differentiated roles. The French have a set of institutions, the *Grandes Ecoles,* that continue to be clearly separated from the universities; many of them are supported by ministries other than the ministry of education. In Britain, teachers colleges until recently were a distinctive class of institutions, operating under the control of local educational authorities. Now that the national department of education has been sitting on them, their separate and distinct character is undergoing erosion. In the United States, the community colleges worked out their separate indentity primarily under local control. They came into higher education from a secondary school background and, straddling that line, have often been able to play both sides of the street. This local base has afforded some protection.

So if we must plan and coordinate at higher levels, as we must to some degree, then we should be deliberately attempting to separate and anchor institutional roles. And as formal coordination takes over, multiple sources of sponsorship and supervision will be the best guarantee of institutional diversity. Multiple agencies protect multiple types and check and balance each other. A power market of competing agencies will replace the market of competing institutions.

But not all developments must be planned. A higher order of statesmanship is to recognize the contribution—past, present, and future—of autonomous action and organic growth. There are numerous reasons for pointing our thinking in this direction. One is the basis for our relative success: The strength and preeminence of American higher education is rooted in an unplanned orderliness that has permitted different parts to perform different tasks, adapt to different needs, and move in different directions of reform. "The benefits of disorder" (see *Change,* October 1976) ought not be inadvertently thrown away as we assemble permanent machinery for state and national coordination.

There is another reason for putting great store in emergent developments. Whether we can effectively plan diversity remains highly problematic. The arguments for planned diversity are strong. State higher education officials surely can point to some successes in the last two decades, as in the case of new campuses in the New York state system that have distinguishing specialties. But we must not congratulate ourselves too soon, since our immature central staffs have not had time yet to settle down as enlarged central bureaucracies loaded with responsibilities, expectations, and interest group demands.

Our central coordinating machinery has not been in place long enough to become the gathering spot for trouble. But the news from abroad on such matters is not promising. The experience of other countries suggests that the balance of forces in and around a central office, especially in a democracy, may not permit planned differentiation to prevail over planned and unplanned uniformity. One of the finest administrators in Europe—Ralf Dahrendorf, now head of the London School of Economics—recently addressed himself to "the problems expansion left behind" in continental and British higher education and saw as central the need to distinguish, to differentiate. He confessed that he had reluctantly come to the conclusion that deliberate differentiation is a contradiction in terms. Why? Because in the modern world the pressures to have equal access to funds, equal status for all teachers, and so on, are too strong.

People who are held responsible for getting things done are, by the nature of their roles, inclined to value and trust deliberate effort over spontaneously generated developments. But it is the better part of reality to recognize what sociologists have long seen as the imposing weight of the unplanned. As put by Dahrendorf in taking the long view in Britain and continental Europe: "The more one looks at government action, the more one understands that most things will not be done anyway, but will happen in one way or another."

Our central procedural concern ought to be the relative contribution of planned and autonomous actions, especially in regard to differentiation. Both are needed and both are operative, so we need to assess different mixtures of the two. With current combinations tilting toward controlled action, we need to add support to the organic side. We shall need to be increasingly clever about planning for unplanned change, about devising the broad frameworks that encourage the system's constituents to generate, on their own, changes that are creative and adaptive to local contexts.

In the changing relation between higher education and government, higher education is becoming more governmental. It moves inside government, becomes a constituent part of government, a bureau within public administration. On this, perspectives from abroad are invaluable, since we are the laggards who can look down the road that others have already traveled. No small point from abroad is transferable, since context is everything, but the larger portraits of relations should catch our attention, principally to stimulate our thinking about options, potentialities, and limits.

Lessons from abroad help us construct longer time frames through which to analyze the character of our institutions. For example, in considering the problem of a new U.S. Department of Education, we need to ask what it will look like a decade, a quarter century, a half century hence, when it is many times larger in personnel, greatly extended in scope, vertically elaborated in echelons, and well established as a bureaucratic arm of the state alongside Agriculture, Labor, and Commerce. Up to this point, the largest advanced democratic country to attempt to order higher education by means of a national department has been France, a country one fourth the size of the United States, where the effort has been crowned with failure and the name of reform is decentralization. We will be the first nation to attempt to "supervise" 3,000 institutions in a country of over 200,000,000 people by means of double pyramids in which a national department is placed over the state structures, with both levels exercising surveillance over private as well as public institutions. Before taking that step, we need to gain more perspective on what we are doing.

Especially under the time constraints of governmental policy making, our canons of judgment nearly always suffer from overconcentration on immediate problems and short-run solutions. Comparative vision helps to correct these defects, thus reducing the probability of unanticipated, unwanted consequences. Anyone who studies other countries intensively will have seen futures that do not work.

17

Conclusion

Robert O. Berdahl and Philip G. Altbach

A SENSE OF PERSPECTIVE

If the preceding chapters have accomplished anything, they ought to have helped create a sense of perspective. Clearly Part One, focusing on the conceptual framework, offered abundant evidence to illustrate that the issues of autonomy, academic freedom, and accountability are not new to academe, but that some of their current and emerging dimensions are. If "financial exigency" acts as a temptation for institutions to use it as a means of ridding themselves of unorthodox faculty members, then eternal vigilance to guard academic freedom will be necessary. If state legislative performance audit committees can demand that universities and colleges define their outputs in measurable terms to allow more precise evaluation, these institutions must consider their strategies carefully. If a court of law can order a professor to jail for his refusal to reveal his vote on a tenure matter, then (irrespective of the merits of the case) we've come a long way from Metzger's "localized institution" governing itself in isolated splendor. Duryea's and Metzger's chapters, then, provided background from which to appreciate the more contemporary perspectives of McConnell and Slaughter.

Kerr and Gade explored the emerging issues that universities and colleges will have to confront in the coming years, and Hanson and Stampen analyzed the economic factors impinging on higher education. While we have largely been preoccupied with *process* issues, it is useful to be reminded of the major substantive concerns that will have to be handled by those processes. Enrollment declines, fiscal problems, faculty reallocation, and other controversial matters will all have to be dealt with in the coming decade.

The emphasis in Part Two shifted from the conceptual concerns of the opening section to a detailed exposition of the major external constituences that act to influence and/or control the actions of universities and colleges. Here the focus was more on the rationales behind the roles of state and federal governments, the courts, and the variety of private and voluntary associations. In a sense, McGuiness, Hobbs, Gladieux and Lewis, and Harcleroad have served as quasi-advocates for the legitimacy of the roles that their respective constituencies play in American higher education. It remains for the reader to decide in each case whether the relations in question are in rough balance or whether they need adjustment either toward more autonomy or more accountability.

Part Three then shifted the focus to the ways in which the various internal constituencies have responded to the increasing external pressures. Trow reported a certain reassertion of lay board authority and stronger presidential leadership in the face of demand for retrenchment and increased accountability. Altbach pointed to a faculty apparently less sure of its professional status in an "industry" under heavy pressure, with some portions hoping to recoup through external collective bargaining what they felt they had lost internally through changes in power relationships.

Levine has shown how the student community has turned to political channels external to the university and college to find more forceful expression for student views. At a time when this volume confirms the increasing role of the state and federal governments, it seems quite logical for the student movement to widen its efforts to include those citadels of power. Finally, Spitzberg analyzed the ways in which campus forces have reacted to recent major reports advocating curricular reform.

WHERE DO WE GO FROM HERE?

Is the academy really in a state of crisis, or are things being exaggerated for dramatic effect?

While the word "crisis" is often used, it is our view that we are in the midst of an unprecedented situation. In addition, we view the combination of enrollment decline, federal and state budget cuts and general fiscal austerity, and much more demanding accountability measures as placing universities and colleges that have grown used to expansion in students and budgets under far greater than normal strain.

Some voices—from greatly respected sources—counsel universities and colleges to take more careful stock of their essential identities and to consider what operating freedoms they must have to achieve those identities. They must then try to arrive at explicit understandings with surrounding public authorities to honor such relationships. Shils, in an essay on "Government and University" addresses this concern as involving

> interdependence and conflict of government and universities, with what each owes the other and what each owes to values which are inherent in its own distinctive nature and which are not necessarily harmonious with the values of the other. I would aim at a "constitution" of university and state according to the idea of each.[1]

Shils's essay is essentially concerned with relations between the major research universities and the U.S. federal government, but his plea for a clearer consensus of values and orientations could be extended to all post-secondary education.

In a vastly different context, Lord Ashby made a similar point. He observed that the African universities that had been founded by the British in their former colonies suffered from a unique dilemma. They inherited a written university charter from the British. But African social and educational conditions made this charter constricting, illogical, and in part inappropriate.[2] Ashby urged that the universities rethink their charters and agree on those essential aspects of governance that they must be prepared to defend. (The smaller the list, he points out, the easier it will be to reach agreement.) Then, at a time *other* than that of a crisis in university-state relations, university personnel would open discussions with state officials about an accommodation concerning university/state relationships. Finally, after such an agreement, the academic community should have the courage and the determination to oppose as forcefully as necessary any violations of the agreement.

While Ashby's proposal was addressed to certain African universities, our earlier chapters have revealed some parallel ambiguities in American universities' current relations with their governments. Thus, the Carnegie Commission in 1973 offered the following recommendation:

> Coordinating agencies at the state level should seek to establish, in cooperation with public and private institutions of higher education, guidelines defining areas of state concern and areas of institutional independence that avoid detailed control.[3]

The commission reasoned that although campuses had "largely occupied" "by default" the "substantial sphere of ambiguity in the past," governmental authority was expanding and moving into those areas. "The ambiguities that once were an asset are now a liability. Greater precision of understanding is now highly desirable."[4]

Not all agree, however. Stephen Bailey, former Vice President of the American Council on Education, argued:

> at heart we are dealing with a dilemma we cannot rationally wish to resolve. The public interest would not . . . be served if the academy were to enjoy an untroubled immunity. Nor could the public interest be served by the academy's being subjected to an intimate surveillance. Whatever our current discomforts because of a sense that the state is crowding us a bit, the underlying tension is benign.[5]

Bailey then dissented from the concordat approach, saying that "the precise border between the state and the academy is, and must be kept, fuzzy. For if a precise delineation is sought, . . . the state has more than the academy of what it takes to draw the line."[6]

But if Bailey cautions not to define limits, in another address he urges that the academy should seek to understand the difference beween the *efficiency* that is owed to Caesar and *effectiveness* that is owed "to God." Furthermore, he warns that sometimes efficiency is the enemy of effectiveness and when this is so, the academy must resolutely defend the greater value.[7]

We have, in this volume, proposed no panaceas. Rather, we have attempted to illustrate how the intersection between higher education and society functions at a time of considerable stress for academic institutions and those who work in them. The relationship is complex and involves external constituencies such as government, the courts, and others and all of the internal communities that make up an academic institution. In addition, the imponderables of enrollment declines, budget cuts, and changing student interests are added to an already complex situation. If this volume has not provided clear solutions, at least it has raised important questions. Even more, it has suggested ways of approaching the relationship between higher education and society.

NOTES

1. *Newsletter on The International Council on the Future of the University,* 3, no. 5 (1976).

2. Eric Ashby, *Universities: British, Indian, African* (Cambridge, Mass.: Harvard University Press, 1966).

3. Carnegie Commission, *Governance of Higher Education* (New York: Mc-Graw-Hill, 1973), 29.

4. Ibid., 28-29.

5. Stephen Bailey, "Education and the State," in *Education and the State,* John Hughes ed., (Washington, D.C.: American Council on Education, 1974).

6. Ibid.

7. Stephen Bailey, "The Limits of Accountability" (remarks at New York Regents Trustees' Conference, New York, N.Y., February 8, 1973).

Bibliography

This selected bibliography is intended to provide a listing of key materials related to the topics considered in this volume. It has been prepared with the assistance of the contributors to this volume, who have provided the references in their areas of expertise. The stress is on a short list of the most important writings, mainly recent materials, concerning these topics. The bibliography is intended to provide a preliminary guide to further reading and research, rather than a comprehensive listing of material.

P. G. Altbach
R. O. Berdahl

GENERAL REFERENCES: HIGHER EDUCATION
IN AMERICAN SOCIETY

Ashby, Eric. *Any Person, Any Study: An Essay on Higher Education in the United States.* New York: McGraw-Hill, 1971.

Ben-David, Joseph. *Trends in American Higher Education.* Chicago: University of Chicago Press, 1972.

Blits, Jan H., ed. *The American University: Problems, Prospects, and Trends.* Buffalo, N.Y.: Prometheus Books, 1985.

Carnegie Commission. *Priorities for Action: Final Report of the Carnegie Commission on Higher Education.* New York: McGraw-Hill, 1973.

Carnegie Council on Policy Studies in Higher Education. *Three Thousand Futures: The Next Twenty Years for Higher Education.* San Francisco: Jossey-Bass, 1980.

Chickering, Arthur W., ed. *The Modern American College.* San Francisco: Jossey-Bass, 1981.

Cohen, Arthur M., and Florence B. Brawer. *The American Community College.* San Francisco: Jossey-Bass, 1982.

Dressel, Paul. *The Autonomy of Public Colleges.* New Directions for Institutional Research, no. 26. San Francisco: Jossey-Bass, 1980.

Finn, Chester E. Jr. *Scholars, Dollars and Bureaucrats.* Washington, D.C.: Brookings Institution, 1978.

Hook, Sidney; Paul Kurtz; and Miro Todorovich. *The University and the State.* Buffalo, N.Y.: Prometheus Books, 1978.

Jencks, Christopher, and David Riesman. *The Academic Revolution.* Chicago: University of Chicago Press, 1977.

Kerr, Clark. *The Uses of the University.* Cambridge, Mass.: Harvard University Press, 1982.

Klitgaard, Robert. *Choosing Elites.* New York: Basic Books, 1985.

Parsons, Talcott, and Gerald M. Platt. *The American University.* Cambridge, Mass.: Harvard University Press, 1973.

Perkins, James, ed. *Higher Education: From Autonomy to Systems.* New York: International Council for Educational Development, 1972.

Riesman, David. *On Higher Learning.* San Francisco: Jossey-Bass, 1980.

Rudolph, Frederick. *Curriculum: A History of the American Undergraduate Course of Study Since 1636.* San Francisco: Jossey-Bass, 1977.

Stadtman, Verne E. *Academic Adaptations: Higher Education Prepares for the 1980s and 1990s.* San Francisco: Jossey-Bass, 1980.

Wolff, Robert Paul. *The Ideal of the University.* Boston: Beacon Press, 1969.

HISTORICAL OVERVIEW

Brody, Alexander. *The American State and Higher Education.* Washington, D.C.: American Council on Education, 1935.

Cobban, A. B. *The Medieval Universities.* London: Methuen, 1975.

Cowley, W. H. *Presidents, Professors and Trustees.* San Francisco: Jossey-Bass, 1980.

Duryea, E. D. *Prologue to the American System of Higher Education: Higher Learning in Western Culture.* Occasional Paper, no. 4. Buffalo, N.Y.: Department of Higher Education, State University of New York at Buffalo, 1979.

Geiger, Roger. *To Advance Knowledge: Growth of American Research Universities, 1900-1940.* New York: Oxford University Press, 1986.

Herbst, Jurgen. *From Crisis to Crisis: American College Government, 1636-1819.* Cambridge, Mass.: Harvard University Press, 1982.

Hofstadter, Richard, and Wilson Smith, eds. *American Higher Education: A Documentary History*. Chicago: University of Chicago Press, 1961.

Jarausch, Konrad. *Transformation of the Higher Learning, 1860-1930*. Chicago: University of Chicago Press, 1985.

Nevins, Allan. *The State Universities and Democracy*. Urbana, Ill.: University of Illinois Press, 1962.

Reeves, Marjorie. "The European University from Medieval Times." In *Higher Education: Demand and Response*. Edited by W. R. Niblett. San Francisco: Jossey-Bass, 1970, 61-84.

Veysey, Laurence. *The Emergence of the American University*. Chicago: University of Chicago Press, 1965.

Whitehead, John S. *The Separation of Church and State: Columbia, Dartmouth, Harvard and Yale, 1776-1876*. New Haven: Yale University Press, 1973.

AUTONOMY AND ACCOUNTABILITY

Conrad, Clifton, and Richard F. Wilson. *Academic Program Reviews: Institutional Approaches, Expectations and Controversies*. Washington, D.C.: Association for the Study of Higher Education, 1985.

Carnegie Foundation for the Advacement of Teaching. *The States and Higher Education: A Proud Past and a Vital Future*. San Francisco: Jossey-Bass, 1976.

Clark, Burton R., and Ted I. K. Youn. *Academic Power in the United States: Comparative Historical and Structural Perspectives,* Washington, D.C.: American Association for Higher Education, 1976.

Dressel, Paul L. *The Autonomy of Public Colleges*. San Francisco: Jossey-Bass, 1980.

Folger, John K., ed. *Increasing the Public Accountability of Higher Education*. San Francisco: Jossey-Bass, 1977.

Kaplin, William A. *The Law of Higher Education*. San Francisco: Jossey-Bass, 1978.

Lenning, Oscar T. *The Outcomes Structure: An Overview and Procedures for Applying It in Postsecondary Education Institutions*. Boulder, Colo.: National Center for Higher Education Management Systems, 1977.

Marcus, Lawrence; Anita O. Leone; and E. D. Goldberg. *The Path to Excellence: Quality Assurance in Higher Education*. Washington, D.C.: Association for the Study of Higher Education, 1983.

Selden, William K. *Accreditation and the Public Interest*. Washington, D.C.: The Council on Postsecondary Education, 1976.

ACADEMIC FREEDOM

Brubacher, John S., and Willis Rudy. *Higher Education in Transition: A History of American Colleges and Universities, 1636-1976*. New York: Harper and Row, 1976.

Furner, Mary O. *Advocacy and Objectivity: The Professionalization of Social Science, 1865-1905*. Lexington, Ky.: University of Kentucky Press, 1975.

Hofstadter, Richard, and Walter P. Metzger. *The Development of Academic Freedom in the United States*. New York: Columbia University Press, 1957.

Joughlin, Louis, ed. *Academic Freedom and Tenure: A Handbook of the AAUP*. Madison, Wis.: University of Wisconsin Press, 1969.

McIver, Robert. *Academic Freedom in Our Time*. New York: Columbia University Press, 1955.

Metzger, Walter P. "Academic Tenure in America: A Historical Essay." In *Academic Tenure: Report of the Commission*. San Francisco: Jossey-Bass, 1973, 93-105.

Pincoffs, Edmund L., ed. *The Concept of Academic Freedom*. Austin, Tex.: University of Texas Press, 1975.

Schrecker, Ellen W. *No Ivory Towers: McCarthyism and the Universities*. New York: Oxford University Press, 1986.

Slaughter, Sheila. "The Danger Zone: Academic Freedom and Civil Liberties." *Annals of the American Academy of Political and Social Science* 448 (March 1980): 46-61.

CURRENT AND EMERGING ISSUES

Carnegie Council on Policy Studies in Higher Education. *Giving Youth a Better Chance: Options for Education, Work, and Service*. San Francisco: Jossey-Bass, 1979.

————. *Three Thousand Futures: The Next Twenty Years for Higher Education*. San Francisco: Jossey-Bass, 1980.

Glenny, Lyman A. "Demographic and Related Issues for Higher Education in the 1980s." *Journal of Higher Education* 51 (1980): 363-380.

Johnson, Janet R., and Lawrence R. Marcus. *Blue Ribbon Commissions and Higher Education: Changing Academe from the Outside*. Washington, D.C.: Association for the Study of Higher Education, 1986.

Mayhew, Lewis B. *Surviving the Eighties: Strategies and Procedures for Solving Fiscal and Enrollment Problem*. San Francisco: Jossey-Bass, 1979.

ECONOMIC ISSUES

Bowen, Howard R. *Investment in Learning*. San Francisco: Jossey-Bass, 1977.

———. *The Costs of Higher Education*. San Francisco: Jossey-Bass, 1980.

Johnstone, D. Bruce. *Sharing the Costs of Higher Education: Student Financial Assistance in the United Kingdom, the Federal Republic of Germany, France, Sweden and the United States*. New York: College Entrance Examination Board, 1986.

Leslie, Larry L., and Richard E. Anderson, eds. *ASHE Reader on Finance in Higher Education*. Lexington, Mass.: Ginn, 1986.

INSTITUTIONAL GOVERNANCE

Cohen, Michael D., and James D. March. *Leadership and Ambiguity*. Boston, Mass.: Harvard Business School Press, 1986.

Keller, George. *Academic Strategy: The Management of Revolution in American Higher Education*. Baltimore, Md.: Johns Hopkins University Press, 1983.

Millett, John D. *New Structures of Campus Power*. San Francisco: Jossey-Bass, 1978.

Perkins, James A., ed. *The University as an Organization*. New York: McGraw-Hill, 1973.

Peterson, Marvin W., ed. *ASHE Reader on Organization and Governance in Higher Education*. Lexington, Mass.: Ginn, 1986.

Scott, Barbara Ann. *Crisis Management in American Higher Education*. New York: Praeger, 1983.

Smith, Bruce L. R., and Joseph J. Karlesky. *The State of Academic Science: The Universities in the Nation's Research Effort*. New York: Change Magazine Press, 1977. Vol. I: Summary of Major Findings; Vol. II: Working Papers.

Stadtman, Verne A. *Academic Adaptations: Higher Education Prepares for the 1980s and 1990s.* San Francisco: Jossey-Bass, 1980.

STATE GOVERNMENTS

Benezet, Louis T. *Private Higher Education and Public Funding.* Washington, D.C.: American Association for Higher Education, 1976.

Berdahl, Robert O. *Statewide Coordination of Higher Education.* Washington, D.C.: American Council on Education, 1971.

Breneman, David W., and Charles E. Finn, Jr., eds. *Public Policy and Private Higher Education.* Washington, D.C.: Brookings Institution, 1978.

Carnegie Commission on Higher Education. *The Capitol and the Campus.* New York: McGraw-Hill, 1971.

————. *Priorities for Action.* New York: McGraw-Hill, 1973.

Carnegie Commission on Policy Studies in Higher Education. *The States and Private Higher Education.* San Francisco: Jossey-Bass, 1977.

————. *Three Thousand Futures.* San Francisco: Jossey-Bass, 1980.

Carnegie Foundation for the Advancement of Teaching. *The States and Higher Education.* San Francisco: Jossey-Bass, 1976.

Committee on Government and Higher Education. *The Efficiency of Freedom.* Baltimore, Md.: Johns Hopkins University Press, 1959.

Cowley, W. H. *Presidents, Professors and Trustees.* Edited by Donald T. Williams, Jr. San Francisco: Jossey-Bass, 1980.

Dressel, Paul L. *The Autonomy of Public Colleges.* New Directions for Institutional Research. San Francisco: Jossey-Bass, 1980.

Education Commission of the States. *Challenge: Coordination and Governance in the '80s.* Denver, Colo.: Education Commission of the States, 1980.

Glenny, Lyman A. *Autonomy of Public Colleges.* New York: McGraw-Hill, 1959.

Harcleroad, Fred F., ed. *Administration of Statewide Systems of Higher Education.* Iowa City: American College Testing Program, 1975.

Koepplin, Leslie, and David A. Wilson, eds. *The Future of State Universities.* New Brunswick, N.J.: Rutgers University Press, 1985.

Lee, Eugene C., and Frank M. Bowen. *Managing Multicampus Systems.* San Francisco: Jossey-Bass, 1975.

McCoy, Marilyn, and D. Kent Halstead. *Higher Education Financing in the Fifty States: Interstate Comparisons Fiscal Year 1976*. Washington, D.C.: U.S. Government Printing Office, 1979.

Millett, John D. *Conflict in Higher Education*. San Francisco: Jossey-Bass, 1984.

Mingle, James. *Challenges to Retrenchment*. San Francisco: Jossey-Bass, 1981.

Moos, Malcolm, and Francis E. Rourke. *The Campus and the State*. Baltimore, Md.: Johns Hopkins University Press, 1959.

National Commission on United Methodist Higher Education. *Endangered Service: Independent Colleges, Public Policy and the First Amendment*. Nashville, Ky.: National Commission, 1976.

Sloan Commission on Government and Higher Education. *A Program for Renewed Partnership*. Cambridge, Mass.: Ballinger, 1980.

Task Force of the National Council of Independent College and Universities. *A National Policy for Private Higher Education*. Washington, D.C.: Association of American Colleges, 1974.

THE FEDERAL GOVERNMENT AND POSTSECONDARY EDUCATION

History of Federal Role

Honey, John C., and Terry W. Hartle. *Federal-State-Institutional Relationships in Postsecondary Education*. Syracuse, N.Y.: Syracuse University Research Corporation, 1975.

Rainsford, George. *Congress and Higher Education in the Nineteenth Century*. Knoxville: University of Tennessee, 1972.

Rivlin, Alice. *The Role of the Federal Government in Financing Higher Education*. Washington, D.C.: Brookings Institution, 1961.

Policy Process

Bloland, Harland. *Associations in Action: The Washington, D.C. Higher Education Community*. Washington, D.C.: ASHE, 1985.

Finn, Chester E. *Education and the Presidency*. Lexington, Mass.: D.C. Heath, 1978.

Gladieux, Lawrence E. "What Has Congress Wrought?" *Change* (October 1980): 25-31.

Wolanin, Thomas R., and Lawrence E. Gladieux. *Congress and the College.* Lexington, Mass.: D. C. Heath, 1977.

Regulation and Higher Education

Bender, Louis W. *Federal Regulations and Higher Education.* Washington, D.C.: American Association for Higher Education, 1977.

Frances, Carol, and Sharon L. Coldren. *The Costs of Implementing Federally Mandated Social Programs at Colleges and Universities.* Washington, D.C.: American Council on Education, 1976.

Sloan Commission on Government and Higher Education. *A Program for Renewed Partnership.* Cambridge, Mass.: Ballinger, 1980.

Other Publications

Breneman, Davis W., and Chester E. Finn, Jr., eds. *Public Policy and Private Higher Education.* Washington, D.C.: Brookings Institution, 1978.

Finn, Chester E., Jr. *Scholars, Dollars and Bureaucrats.* Washington, D.C.: Brookings Institution, 1978.

LEGAL ASPECTS

Edwards, Harry T. *Higher Education and the Unholy Crusade Against Governmental Regulation.* Cambridge, Mass.: Institute for Educational Management, Harvard University, 1980.

Edwards, Harry T., and Virginia Davis Nordin. *Higher Education and the Law.* Cambridge, Mass.: Institute for Educational Management, Harvard University, 1979.

————.*An Introduction to the American Legal System.* Cambridge, Mass.: Institute for Educational Management, Harvard University, 1980.

van Geel, Tyll. *The Courts and American Education Law.* Buffalo, N.Y.: Prometheus Books, 1987.

Hobbs, Walter C., ed. *Government Regulation of Higher Education.* Cambridge, Mass.: Ballinger, 1978.

Hollander, Patricia A. *Legal Handbook for Educators.* Boulder, Colo.: Westview Press, 1978.

Dick, Howard A. E. *State Aid to Private Higher Education.* Charlottesville, Va.: Michie, 1977.

Kaplin, William A. *The Law of Higher Education: Legal Implications of Administrative Decision Making.* San Francisco: Jossey-Bass, 1978.

———. *The Law of Higher Education 1980.* San Francisco: Jossey-Bass, 1980.

Young, Parker D. *The Yearbook of Higher Education Law 1977 . . . 1986.* Topeka, Kans.: National Organization on Legal Problems of Education, 1977-1986.

PRIVATE CONSTITUENCIES

Cheit, Earl F., and Theodore E. Lobman. *Foundations and Higher Education.* Berkeley, Calif.: Carnegie Council on Policy Studies in Higher Education, 1979.

Cosand, Joseph, et. al. *Higher Education's National Institutional Membership Association.* Ann Arbor, Mich.: Center for the Study of Higher Education, University of Michigan, 1980.

Harcleroad, Fred. *Accreditation: History, Process and Problems.* Washington, D.C.: American Association for Higher Education/ERIC Clearinghouse on Higher Education, Washington, 1981.

———. "Effects of Regional Agencies and Voluntary Associations." In *Improving Academic Management: A Handbook of Planning and Institutional Research.* Edited by Paul Jedamus and Marvin Peterson. San Francisco: Jossey-Bass, 1980.

———. *Voluntary Organizations in America and the Development of Educational Accreditation.* Washington, D.C.: Council on Postsecondary Accreditation, 1980.

Moore, Raymond S. *Consortiums in American Higher Education: 1965-66.* Washington, D.C.: U.S. Government Printing Office, 1968.

Orlans, Harold. *Private Accreditation and Public Eligibility.* Lexington, Mass.: D.C. Heath, 1975.

Selden, William K. *Accreditation: A Struggle Over Standards in Higher Education.* New York: Harper, 1960.

Trivett, David. *Accreditation and Institutional Eligibility.* Washington, D.C.: American Association for Higher Education, 1976.

ACADEMIC PROFESSION

Altbach, Philip G., ed. *Comparative Perspectives on the Academic Profession.* New York: Praeger, 1977.

Altbach, Philip G., and Sheila Slaughter, eds. "The Academic Profession." *Annals of the American Academy of Political and Social Science* 448 (March 1980): 1-150.

Anderson, Charles, and John Murray, eds. *The Professors.* Cambridge, Mass.: Schenkman, 1971.

Bowen, Howard R., and Jack H. Schuster. *American Professors: A National Resource Imperiled.* New York: Oxford University Press, 1986.

Finkelstein, Martin. *The American Academic Profession: A Synthesis of Social Scientific Inquiry Since World War II.* Columbus, Ohio: Ohio State University Press, 1984.

Finkelstein, Martin, ed. *ASHE Reader on Faculty and Faculty Issues in Colleges and Universities.* Lexington, Mass.: Ginn, 1985.

Ladd, E. C., Jr., and S. M. Lipset. *The Divided Academy: Professors and Politics.* New York: McGraw-Hill, 1975.

Lewis, Lionel. *Scaling the Ivory Tower: Merit and Its Limits in Academic Careers.* Baltimore, Md.: Johns Hopkins University Press, 1975.

Melendez, W. A., and R. M. deGuzman. *Burnout: The New Academic Disease.* Washington, D.C.: Association for the Study of Higher Education, 1983.

Schulman, Carol Herrnstadt. *Old Expectations, New Realities: The Academic Profession Revisited.* Washington, D.C.: American Association for Higher Education, 1979.

Shils, Edward. "The Academic Ethos Under Strain." *Minerva* 13 (Spring 1975): 1-37.

Trow, Martin, ed. *Teachers and Students.* New York: McGraw-Hill, 1975.

Wilson, Logan. *American Academics: Then and Now.* New York: Oxford University Press, 1979.

THE COLLEGE STUDENTS

Altbach, P. *Student Politics in America: A Historical Analysis.* New York: McGraw-Hill, 1974.

Astin, A. W., et al. *The American Freshman: Norms for Fall 1979.* Los Angeles: Cooperative Institutional Research Program, 1980.

Fuller, B., and J. Samuelson. *Student Votes: Do They Make a Difference?* Washington, D.C.: U.S. Student Association, 1977.

Levine, A. *When Dreams and Heroes Die: A Portrait of Today's College Students.* San Francisco: Jossey-Bass, 1980.

Lipset, S. M. *Rebellion in the University.* Chicago: University of Chicago Press, 1976.

Yankelovich, D. *The New Morality: A Profile of American Youth in the 1970s.* New York: McGraw-Hill, 1974.

———. *The Changing Values on Campus: Political and Personal Attitudes of Today's College Students.* New York: Washington Square Press, 1972.

PRESIDENTS AND GOVERNING BOARDS

Benezet, Louis, et al. *Style and Substance: Leadership and the College Presidency.* Washington, D.C.: American Council on Education, 1981.

Carnegie Commission on Higher Education. *The Governance of Higher Education: Six Priority Problems.* New York: McGraw Hill, 1973.

Cohen, Michael D., and James G. March. *Leadership and Ambiguity: The American College President.* New York: McGraw-Hill, 1974.

Corson, John. *The Governance of College and Universities.* Rev. ed. New York: McGraw-Hill, 1975.

Cowley, W. H. *Presidents, Professors and Trustees.* San Francisco: Jossey-Bass, 1980.

Hodgkinson, Harold L. *College Governance — The Amazing Thing Is That It Works At All.* Washington, D.C.: Report No. 11 of ERIC Clearinghouse on Higher Education.

Ingram, Richard T., ed. *Handbook of College and University Trusteeship.* San Francisco: Jossey-Bass, 1980.

Kauffman, Joseph F. *At the Pleasure of the Board.* Washington, D.C.: American Council on Education, 1980.

Kerr, Clark, and Marian Gade. *The Many Lives of Academic Presidents.* Washington, D.C.: Association of Governing Boards, 1986.

Kerr, Clark, ed. *Presidents Make a Difference.* Washington, D.C.: Association of Governing Boards, 1984.

Nason, John W. *The Future of Trusteeship*. Washington, D.C.: Association of Governing Boards, 1974.

Rauh, Morton A. *The Trusteeship of Colleges and Universities*. New York: McGraw-Hill, 1969.

Zwingle, J. L. *Effective Trusteeship*. Washington, D.C.: Association of Governing Boards, 1975.

SENIOR ADMINISTRATORS

Adams, Hazard. *The Academic Tribes*. New York: Liveright, 1976.

Corson, John J. *The Governance of Colleges and Universities*. New York: McGraw-Hill, 1975.

Gould, John W. *The Academic Deanship*. New York: Institute for Higher Education, Teachers College, Columbia University, 1964.

Griffiths, Daniel E., and Donald J. McCarty, eds. *The Dilemma of the Deanship*. Danville, Ill.: The Interstate Printers and Publishers, 1980.

Jackson, Philip W. "Lonely at the Top: Observations on the Genesis of Administrative Isolation." *School Review* 85 (May 1977): 425-433.

Kapel, David E., and Edward L. Dejnoska. "The Educational Deanship: A Further Analysis." *Research in Higher Education* 10 (April 1979): 99-112.

Meyer, John W., and Brian Rowan. "Institutionalized Organizations: Formal Structure as Myth and Ceremony." *American Journal of Sociology* 83 (September 1977): 340-362.

Salmen, Stanley. *Duties of Administrators in Higher Education*. New York: Macmillan, 1971.

COMPARATIVE PERSPECTIVES

Altbach, Philip G. *Comparative Higher Education*. London: Mansell, 1979.

———. *Comparative University Reform*. Washington, D.C.: American Association for Higher Education, 1981.

Altbach, Philip G., and David H. Kelly. *Higher Education in International Perspective: A Survey and Bibliography*. London: Mansell, 1985.

Ashby, Eric. *Universities: British, Indian, African*. Cambridge, Mass.: Harvard University Press, 1966.

Ben-David, Joseph. *Centers of Learning: Britain, France, Germany, United States.* New York: McGraw-Hill, 1977.

Ben-David, Joseph, and Awarham Zloczower. "Universities and Academic Systems in Modern Societies." *European Journal of Sociology* 3 (1962): 45-84.

Burn, Barbara; P. G. Altbach; Clark Kerr; and James Perkins. *Higher Education in Nine Countries.* New York: McGraw-Hill, 1971.

Clark, Burton R. *The Higher Education System: Academic Organization in Cross National Perspective.* Berkeley, Calif.: University of California Press, 1983.

Daalder, Hans, and Edward Shils, eds. *Universities, Politicians and Bureaucrats.* Cambridge, England: Cambridge University Press, 1982.

Niblett, W. R., and R. F. Butts, eds. *Universities Facing the Future.* San Francisco: Jossey-Bass, 1972.

Ross, Murray. *The University.* New York: McGraw-Hill, 1976.

Stone, Lawrence, ed. *The University in Society.* Princeton, N.J.: Princeton University Press, 1974.

Van de Graaff, John, et al. *Academic Power: Patterns of Authority in Seven National Systems of Higher Education.* New York: Praeger, 1978.

Contributors

PHILIP G. ALTBACH is chairman and professor in the Department of Educational Organization, Administration and Policy and Director of the Comparative Education Center, State University of New York at Buffalo. He is North American Editor of *Higher Education* and author of *Comparative Higher Education, Student Politics in America,* and other books.

ROBERT O. BERDAHL is professor of higher education and Director of the Institute for Higher and Adult Education, College of Education, University of Maryland at College Park. He has been chairman of the Department of Higher Education, State University of New York at Buffalo, and has served as president of the Association for the Study of Higher Education.

BURTON R. CLARK is Allan Cartter Professor of Education and professor of sociology at the University of California at Los Angeles. He is author of *The Higher Education System* and other books.

E. D. DURYEA is Professor Emeritus of Higher Education at the State University of New York at Buffalo. He is author of *Faculty Unions and Collective Bargaining* and other publications.

MARIAN L. GADE is research associate at the Center for Studies in Higher Education, University of California, Berkeley. She is coauthor of *The Many Lives of Academic Presidents.*

LAWRENCE E. GLADIEUX is Executive Director of the Washington Office of the College Board. He has written extensively on the politics of higher education in America.

W. LEE HANSON is professor of economics at the University of Wisconsin at Madison. He is widely published in the area of the economics of higher education and has supervised the AAUP's annual surveys of academic remuneration.

FRED F. HARCLEROAD is Professor Emeritus of Higher Education at the University of Arizona and is founding director of the Center for the Study of Higher Education there.

WALTER C. HOBBS is associate professor in the Department of Educational Organization, Administration and Policy, State University of New York at Buffalo. He is a sociologist and holds a degree in law. He is editor of *Government Regulation of Higher Education*.

CLARK KERR is President Emeritus of the University of California. He served as director and chairman of the Carnegie Commission on Higher Education and of the Carnegie Council on Policy Studies in Higher Education. He is author of the now classic *The Uses of the University* and other books. He has recently been involved in a study of presidential leadership in higher education.

ARTHUR LEVINE is President of Bradford College in Massachusetts. He has been a senior fellow of the Carnegie Foundation for the Advancement of Teaching. He is author of *When Dreams and Heroes Died: A Portrait of Today's College Students* and other books. Dr. Levine received his advanced degree from the State University of New York at Buffalo.

GWENDOLYN L. LEWIS is senior policy analyst in the Washington Office of the College Board.

T. R. McCONNELL is Professor Emeritus of education at the University of California at Berkeley. He has served as chancellor of the University of Buffalo, dean of the Colleges of Arts and Sciences at the University of Minnesota, and in other administrative positions. In 1957 he organized the Center for the Study of Higher Education at the University of California at Berkeley.

WALTER METZGER is professor of history at Columbia University. He is coauthor of *The Develoment of Academic Freedom in the United States* and has written widely on issues of academic freedom and American higher education.

JOHN D. MILLETT is President Emeritus of Miami University (Ohio) and Chancellor Emeritus of the Ohio Board of Regents. He has also served as an officer of the Academy for Educational Development. Author of a number of books on higher education, he is currently acting as professor of educational leadership at Miami University.

ERIC RIEDEL is Dean of Students at Bradford College, Bradford, Massachusetts.

SHEILA SLAUGHTER is professor and chair of the Division of Educational Policy and Administration, University of Arizona. She has been associate professor of higher education at the State University of New York at Buffalo.

IRVING J. SPITZBERG, Jr., is executive director of the Council on Liberal Learning of the Association of American Colleges, Washington, D.C. He has been dean of the colleges and associate professor of higher education at the State University of New York at Buffalo.

JACOB O. STAMPEN is associate professor in the Department of Educational Administration, University of Wisconsin at Madison.

MARTIN TROW is professor of public policy and director of the Center for Studies in Higher Education, University of California at Berkeley.

Index